T0350654

The Analysis of Firms
and Employees

A National Bureau
of Economic Research
Conference Report

The Analysis of Firms and Employees
Quantitative and Qualitative Approaches

Edited by **Stefan Bender, Julia Lane, Kathryn Shaw, Fredrik Andersson, and Till von Wachter**

The University of Chicago Press

Chicago and London

STEFAN BENDER is a senior researcher at the Institute for Employment Research. JULIA LANE is a senior vice president of Economics, Labor, and Population Studies at the National Opinion Research Center at the University of Chicago and a senior research fellow at the U.S. Bureau of the Census. KATHRYN SHAW is the Ernest C. Arbuckle Professor of Economics in the Graduate School of Business, Stanford University, and a research associate of the National Bureau of Economic Research. FREDRIK ANDERSSON is a senior research associate of the Cornell Institute for Social and Economic Research and a research fellow with the Longitudinal Employer-Household Dynamics Program (LEHD), U.S. Bureau of the Census. TILL VON WACHTER is assistant professor of economics at Columbia University and a faculty research fellow of the National Bureau of Economic Research.

The University of Chicago Press, Chicago 60637
The University of Chicago Press, Ltd., London
© 2008 by the National Bureau of Economic Research
All rights reserved. Published 2008
Printed in the United States of America

17 16 15 14 13 12 11 10 09 08   1 2 3 4 5
ISBN-13: 978-0-226-04287-9 (cloth)
ISBN-10: 0-226-04287-1 (cloth)

Library of Congress Cataloging-in-Publication Data

The analysis of firms and employees : quantitative and qualitative
   approaches / edited by Stefan Bender . . . [et al.].
        p. cm. — (A National Bureau of Economic Research conference
        report)
     Includes bibliograpical references and index.
     ISBN-13: 978-0-226-04287-9 (cloth : alk. paper)
     ISBN-10: 0-226-04287-1 (cloth : alk. paper) 1. Employees.
   2. Industrial organization. 3. Industrial sociology. I. Bender, Stefan.
   HD4901.A652 2008
   331.1—dc22

                                                              2008008259

♾ The paper used in this publication meets the minimum requirements of the American National Standard for Information Sciences— Permanence of Paper for Printed Library Materials, ANSI Z39.48-1992.

National Bureau of Economic Research

Officers

Elizabeth E. Bailey, *chairman*
John S. Clarkeson, *vice-chairman*
Martin Feldstein, *president and chief executive officer*
Susan Colligan, *vice president for administration and budget and corporate secretary*

Robert Mednick, *treasurer*
Kelly Horak, *controller and assistant corporate secretary*
Gerardine Johnson, *assistant corporate secretary*

Directors at Large

Peter C. Aldrich
Elizabeth E. Bailey
John H. Biggs
John S. Clarkeson
Don R. Conlan
Kathleen B. Cooper
Charles H. Dallara
George C. Eads

Jessica P. Einhorn
Martin Feldstein
Roger W. Ferguson, Jr.
Jacob A. Frenkel
Judith M. Gueron
Robert S. Hamada
Karen N. Horn
John Lipsky

Laurence H. Meyer
Michael H. Moskow
Alicia H. Munnell
Rudolph A. Oswald
Robert T. Parry
Marina v. N. Whitman
Martin B. Zimmerman

Directors by University Appointment

George Akerlof, *California, Berkeley*
Jagdish Bhagwati, *Columbia*
Ray C. Fair, *Yale*
Michael J. Brennan, *California, Los Angeles*
Glen G. Cain, *Wisconsin*
Franklin Fisher, *Massachusetts Institute of Technology*
Saul H. Hymans, *Michigan*
Marjorie B. McElroy, *Duke*

Joel Mokyr, *Northwestern*
Andrew Postlewaite, *Pennsylvania*
Uwe E. Reinhardt, *Princeton*
Nathan Rosenberg, *Stanford*
Craig Swan, *Minnesota*
David B. Yoffie, *Harvard*
Arnold Zellner (Director Emeritus), *Chicago*

Directors by Appointment of Other Organizations

Richard B. Berner, *National Association for Business Economics*
Gail D. Fosler, *The Conference Board*
Martin Gruber, *American Finance Association*
Arthur B. Kennickell, *American Statistical Association*
Thea Lee, *American Federation of Labor and Congress of Industrial Organizations*
William W. Lewis, *Committee for Economic Development*

Robert Mednick, *American Institute of Certified Public Accountants*
Angelo Melino, *Canadian Economics Association*
Jeffrey M. Perloff, *American Agricultural Economics Association*
John J. Siegfried, *American Economic Association*
Gavin Wright, *Economic History Association*

Directors Emeriti

Andrew Brimmer
Carl F. Christ
George Hatsopoulos
Lawrence R. Klein

Franklin A. Lindsay
Paul W. McCracken
Peter G. Peterson
Richard N. Rosett

Eli Shapiro
Arnold Zellner

Relation of the Directors to the
Work and Publications of the
National Bureau of Economic Research

1. The object of the NBER is to ascertain and present to the economics profession, and to the public more generally, important economic facts and their interpretation in a scientific manner without policy recommendations. The Board of Directors is charged with the responsibility of ensuring that the work of the NBER is carried on in strict conformity with this object.

2. The President shall establish an internal review process to ensure that book manuscripts proposed for publication DO NOT contain policy recommendations. This shall apply both to the proceedings of conferences and to manuscripts by a single author or by one or more co-authors but shall not apply to authors of comments at NBER conferences who are not NBER affiliates.

3. No book manuscript reporting research shall be published by the NBER until the President has sent to each member of the Board a notice that a manuscript is recommended for publication and that in the President's opinion it is suitable for publication in accordance with the above principles of the NBER. Such notification will include a table of contents and an abstract or summary of the manuscript's content, a list of contributors if applicable, and a response form for use by Directors who desire a copy of the manuscript for review. Each manuscript shall contain a summary drawing attention to the nature and treatment of the problem studied and the main conclusions reached.

4. No volume shall be published until forty-five days have elapsed from the above notification of intention to publish it. During this period a copy shall be sent to any Director requesting it, and if any Director objects to publication on the grounds that the manuscript contains policy recommendations, the objection will be presented to the author(s) or editor(s). In case of dispute, all members of the Board shall be notified, and the President shall appoint an ad hoc committee of the Board to decide the matter; thirty days additional shall be granted for this purpose.

5. The President shall present annually to the Board a report describing the internal manuscript review process, any objections made by Directors before publication or by anyone after publication, any disputes about such matters, and how they were handled.

6. Publications of the NBER issued for informational purposes concerning the work of the Bureau, or issued to inform the public of the activities at the Bureau, including but not limited to the NBER Digest and Reporter, shall be consistent with the object stated in paragraph 1. They shall contain a specific disclaimer noting that they have not passed through the review procedures required in this resolution. The Executive Committee of the Board is charged with the review of all such publications from time to time.

7. NBER working papers and manuscripts distributed on the Bureau's web site are not deemed to be publications for the purpose of this resolution, but they shall be consistent with the object stated in paragraph 1. Working papers shall contain a specific disclaimer noting that they have not passed through the review procedures required in this resolution. The NBER's web site shall contain a similar disclaimer. The President shall establish an internal review process to ensure that the working papers and the web site do not contain policy recommendations, and shall report annually to the Board on this process and any concerns raised in connection with it.

8. Unless otherwise determined by the Board or exempted by the terms of paragraphs 6 and 7, a copy of this resolution shall be printed in each NBER publication as described in paragraph 2 above.

Contents

Acknowledgments

We would like to acknowledge the substantial contribution of a number of people whose contribution was critical to the success of this book and of the original Conference on the Analysis of Firms and Employees (CAFE) 2006 in Nuremberg, Germany.

The sponsors of the conference were critical to its success. We thank Gail Pesyna of the Sloan Foundation; the Economics Program, the Decision, Risk and Management Sciences Program, and the Sociology Program of the National Science Foundation (NSF); the Deutsche Forschungsgemeinschaft (German Research Foundation); and Bernd Fitzenberger of the Research Network "Flexibility in Heterogeneous Labour Markets" of the German Research Foundation and the Institute for Employment Research (IAB).

We also thank the Research Data Center staff in Nuremberg who worked so hard to coordinate all the conference logistics, particularly Dagmar Herrlinger and Michael Stops. We also thank John Haltiwanger for his participation in the planning meetings for the conference as well as his assistance in obtaining NSF support for the conference. Helena Fitz-Patrick of the National Bureau of Economic Research (NBER) and Parker Smathers of the University of Chicago Press provided invaluable support in getting the papers finalized and in appropriate publication format.

Finally, we are grateful to all the attendees, discussants, and chairs whose thoughtful participation made the entire conference an extremely rewarding endeavor.

Introduction

Stefan Bender, Julia Lane, Kathryn Shaw, Fredrik
Andersson, and Till von Wachter

Motivation for Book

The analysis of the interactions of firms and employees has followed two
distinct paths. One path has focused on large-scale, often nationally representative, data sets on firms and employees, typically housed at federal statistical agencies. In some cases, this path has intensively used administrative data, alone or integrated with survey data and, in other cases, the use
of surveys designed to collect information about both firms and workers.
The other path has been the development of specialized surveys and gath-
ering of personnel records of a small number of firms (or even one firm) or
intensive observation (essentially collection of qualitative data) from case
studies based on site visits to firms by researchers, data typically housed at
universities or think-tanks.

Each of these two study approaches has uncovered interesting and useful pieces of information. Researchers working with large-scale, national,
firm-level matched employer-employee data sets have begun to address a
variety of organizational topics, such as determinants of wage inequality,
the use of alternative wage policies (such as the use of incentive pay) and
their impact on worker selection, gender differences in promotion, and

Stefan Bender is a senior researcher at the Institute for Employment Research. Julia Lane
is senior vice president of Economics, Labor, and Population Studies at the National Opinion Research Center at the University of Chicago, and a senior research fellow at the U.S. Bureau of the Census. Kathryn Shaw is the Ernest C. Arbuckle Professor of Economics in the
Graduate School of Business, Stanford University, and a research associate of the National
Bureau of Economic Research. Fredrik Andersson is a senior research associate of the Cornell Institute for Social and Economic Research, and a research fellow with the Longitudinal
Employer-Household Dynamics Program (LEHD), U.S. Bureau of the Census. Till von
Wachter is an assistant professor of economics at Columbia University, and a faculty research
fellow of the National Bureau of Economic Research.

differences in alternative career paths within and across firms. They have also been able to examine the impact of job and worker reallocation on worker and firm outcomes. Still, one weakness of existing empirical analysis of firm outcomes from large, national data sets is that the underlying determinants of firm performance are generally unknown.

In contrast, researchers who have been engaged in intensive study of a small number of firms through either case studies or specialized surveys have been able to describe rich contextual variation in organizational decision making. Many of these studies have been conducted within the context of projects affiliated with the Sloan Foundation's Industry Centers and the NBER/Sloan joint projects sponsoring site visits. These studies have highlighted, among other things, the importance of human resource practices such as the use of teams for the successful adoption for the use of new technologies (e.g., information technology) and have as a common theme the link between business success how businesses organize their workers. While such work has demonstrated the tremendous value added of specialized surveys and the insights to be derived from the intensive qualitative data collection associated with site visits, questions are often raised about the ability to generalize results from small, potentially nonrepresentative samples.

The combination of these two empirical approaches means that it is possible to envision the development of a new field of economics, one that is at the nexus of labor economics, industry studies, and industrial organization. The focus of this field is inherently the organizational structure of businesses with a focus on how workers are organized. Matched employer-employee data that include the information from large-scale data sets as well as from specialized surveys and site visits provide a momentous opportunity for a research agenda that is focused on the study and understanding of the interaction of firms and workers.

This book results from a conference that was planned to foster just such a research agenda.[1] An overarching goal of the conference was to bring together both senior and junior researchers from the two study fields—traditional labor economists and industry studies researchers, particularly those who have conducted case studies—to illustrate the different insights to be gained from the two approaches and provide the stimulus for a next

---

1. The Conference on Firm and Employees (CAFE) was held September 29 to 30, 2006, in Nuremberg, Germany, sponsored by the Institute for Employment Research (IAB), the Data Access Center (FDZ-BA/IAB), The Deutsche Forschungsgemeinschaft (German Research Foundation), their Research Network "Flexibility in Heterogeneous Labour Markets," the National Bureau of Economic Research, the Alfred P. Sloan Foundation, and the National Science Foundation. Invited keynote speakers included Dan Hamermesh (University of Texas, Austin), Ed Lazear (Stanford University), Richard Freeman (Harvard University), and Mari Sako (Oxford University), who all have done path-breaking work related to the topics of the conference. Over 160 papers were submitted, of which about 40 were accepted after an extensive refereeing process. Over 100 researchers from around the world participated.

generation of research. The potential for such data to answer key empirical questions in economics has been well described elsewhere.[2] The list includes the effect of firm policies on the job ladders and career paths of workers; the effects of workforce composition on business growth and survival; as well as the micro-level analysis of the demand for labor, including the impact of technological and structural change.

The book features eleven papers selected from that conference. They were selected by referees on the basis of their quality as well as for the new insights that they provided about the interactions between firms and their employees. The next sections of this introduction provide an overview of the major findings that have been made possible as a result of these new data sets. These span several different facets of the relationship between firms and workers, beginning with shedding more light on the relationship between human resource practices and productivity, then examining how firm differences in the organization of production are related to differences in human resource practices, how changing ownership affects the organization of production, and, finally, how the changing trade patterns, particularly globalization, affect firm competitiveness and then works through to their employees. The final section provides an overview that highlights the innovative nature of the data sets themselves.

The Major Findings

Human Resource Practices and Firm Productivity

Personnel economics has long been concerned with the fundamental question whether human resource practices such as incentive contracts or monitoring affect workers' productivity and worker turnover and how they relate to firms' efforts to innovate and gain competitiveness in an evolving marketplace. A recent surge in new data sets and data collection efforts has led to an increasing amount of ambitious empirical work describing and testing some of the key relationships between firms' personnel strategies and worker and firm outcomes. The first three chapters in this volume give an excellent introduction into three of the most prominent and promising directions in this growing research area. Each of the three chapters is based on a unique new data source and addresses a core relationship between human resource practices at a different level of aggregation. The first chapter uses a large matched administrative employer-employee data set from the United States to analyze the relationship between human resource practices, research and development (R&D), and worker productivity in a sample of firms in the electronics industry. The second chapter augments a

---

2. See, for example, Abowd, Haltiwanger, and Lane (2004) and Brown, Haltiwanger, and Lane (2006).

traditional analysis of a large firm's personnel records with innovative survey data on workers' preferences, attitudes, and behaviors in a social context to study the determinants of turnover and worker productivity in the trucking industry. The third chapter tests predictions of a model of subjective evaluation and effort in a moral hazard setting using data from an exceptionally detailed matched worker firm survey from the French manufacturing industry.

Firms constantly face the problem of adjusting their production processes and their workforce to impulses from technological progress and increasing competition. A recurring theme is the question of how firms adjust their human resource (HR) practices to cope with the evolving economic environment, and whether some HR practices are more helpful in successfully implementing or developing new technologies than others. A core difficulty in providing an empirical answer to this question is that most data sets that contain information on investment into new technologies and R&D for a sufficient number of firms typically have little information on firms' HR structures. The first innovation of the first chapter, by Andersson, Brown, Campbell, Chiang, and Park, is to construct measures of HR practices based on longitudinal earnings and turnover information from the universe of workers in a large sample of firms in a particular industry (electronics). The chapter then analyzes the joint of occurrence of indicators such as accession and separation rates or within-job wage growth in HR "clusters" and describes the practices of firms with high and low investment in R&D. In a last step, the authors examine whether the interaction between R&D and HR practices significantly affects worker productivity. The chapter then interprets its tremendous amount of new information in the context of an economic model where firms have to decide whether to produce technology (R&D) in house or acquire it in the market and have to structure their HR practices to train, retain, or hire the appropriate workforce. The chapter's comprehensive descriptive empirical approach based on explicit firm-level HR measures grounded in economic intuition should pave the way to further fruitful analysis of the incidence and effect of HR practices using increasingly available matched administrative employer-employee data.

One of the great benefits of this approach is the potential to analyze the personnel choices and their correlation with worker and firm outcomes for a broad range of firms, workers, and phenomena of interest. The price to pay for this gain in insight is the focus on broader measures of HR practices. While ideal for describing recurring patterns and correlations, sometimes the relationships between firms' internal institutions and workers' incentives and productivity emphasized by the theory are more subtle. This is especially true for more recent modeling approaches emphasizing behavioral aspects of the firm-worker relationship, such as trust or loyalty. The second chapter in this volume, by Burks, Carpenter, Götte, Monaco,

Porter, and Rustichini, describes an ambitious data collection effort and research agenda aimed at uncovering specific and intricate links between HR practices, worker incentives and attitudes, and worker turnover and productivity. To do so, the chapter combines longitudinal personnel records of a large trucking firm in the United States with a panel survey of a cohort of newly hired workers geared to elicit a detailed range of behavioral and preference parameters. Thereby, a key innovation is to obtain information on risk and loss aversion or cooperation through standard survey questions as well as responses to small laboratory experiments such as prisoners' dilemma games. The second chapter describes this tremendous effort in detail and puts it into the context of a statistical analysis of how turnover and effort evolve with tenure at the trucking firm. The results show a large and increasing amount of variance in productivity of truck drivers and a differential effect of selective exit on variance as job tenure increases. While traditional analyses of firms' personnel records typically have to stop at this point, the added survey data will enable the authors to draw more specific conclusions about the determinants of turnover and the role of behavioral factors in future work. The strategy of combining firms' personnel records with innovative and detailed survey information documented in this chapter indicates another potentially highly fruitful area for future work.

While the second chapter exploits detailed information on a single firm to gain insights into particular aspects of the structure and effect of HR practices, sometimes representative surveys also contain information on both workers and firms amenable to a study of certain personnel policies. Such is the case with the French survey of Computerization and Organizational Change that collects information on team production and evaluation strategies for a small sample of workers in a representative sample of French firms. The third chapter, by Diaye, Greenan, and Urdanivia, exploits this source of information to test a model of the effect of subjective evaluation of workers' effort via interviews in the context of team and group work. Although increasingly common in practice, the analysis of evaluation interviews is rendered difficult due to complex interactions of various incentives, a lack of appropriate data, and identification issues due to unobserved heterogeneity. The chapter extends existing theoretical work to derive various predictions of how evaluation interviews should affect workers' effort and pay and uses propensity score methods to test this prediction, controlling for selection. The results indicate that evaluation interviews both attract high-productivity workers and have a direct effect on productivity within worker type. As survey data sets incorporate more detailed measures on work effort, organization, and HR practices, similarly ingenuous combinations of specific theoretical modeling and statistical methodologies aimed at identification in other areas of personnel economics should become more common.

Firm Differences in Human Resource Practices

The chapters in this section provide evidence on differences in human resource practices by firms from a variety of different perspectives: over time (von Wachter and Bender), across firms (Hellerstein, Neumark, and McInerney), and within a firm (Manchester).

How much firms affect wages has been at the core of the literature analyzing the interrelationship between firms and workers. The evidence is clear that such firm-specific factors as firm size, unionization, and industry structure have important impacts. The interesting contribution of the von Wachter and Bender chapter is to show for a broad sample of establishments that some firm-specific effects are a function of the initial entry-level conditions that exist when a cohort of workers is hired. As the authors point out, there are two possible reasons for these entry-level differences. The first of these is that the quality of jobs and career opportunities differ for two cohorts; the second is that the degree of rent sharing between workers and firms depends on the extant market conditions at the time of entry. Their analysis exploits their longitudinal information on individuals, together with the firms that hire them, to show that at least some of the substantial wage differences that are observed across firms are due to transitory rents and disappear over time.

Another strand of the literature has focused on the role of labor market segregation in explaining race and sex wage differentials. A related strand has focused on workplace segregation by skill, as the productivity of more-educated workers has increased relative to less-educated ones. However, much of the work has focused on explaining cross-sectional differences across establishments, with the inevitable resulting concerns about omitted confounding factors. The work by Hellerstein, Neumark, and McInerney provides extremely useful initial evidence about both levels of segregation in the United States in 1990 and 2000 as well as changes. They find that racial and ethnic segregation is pervasive. And, while observed segregation by ethnicity has changed little, segregation by race has increased substantially. Most interestingly, the longitudinal nature of their data make it possible for them to show that the increase in racial segregation has been exacerbated by the entry and exit of establishments and by the changing industrial composition of the United States. Hellerstein, Neumark, and McInerney find that segregation by sex, even after controlling for occupational differences and despite countervailing industrial changes, has declined. Segregation by education is also substantial and has increased slightly over the decade.

The third chapter advances our understanding about a third HR practice in which substantial firm heterogeneity has been observed: training. Becker's seminal work suggests that firms will only provide specific training and that workers will bear the full cost of general training as general training will increase the likelihood that workers will leave the firm. Despite this theoretical prediction, there is not only abundant evidence that many firms offer tuition reimbursement programs, but also evidence that firms do this to reduce turnover. The Manchester chapter uses primarily a case study approach to examine whether there is an empirical basis that supports the notion that turnover is reduced. She finds that the five-year separation probability of workers who get tuition reimbursement is reduced by over 50 percent, but suggests that the reason is that the investment is complementary to firm-specific human capital. Hence, her results reconcile empirical observation with the Becker theoretical prediction.

Effects of Ownership Changes on the Organization of Production

While the previous sections featured chapters that examined differences in the ways in which firms treated workers, this section turns to examining what happens within firms as a result of changes in such fundamental features as ownership structure. The transition experienced by economies of Central and Eastern Europe provides a unique opportunity to examine such effects. The two studies on the effects of ownership in this volume, while quite different in their approach to the subject, both represent work that advance our understanding of one such key aspect of transition, the effects of ownership on wages and HR policies. The chapter by Earle and Telegdy uses a large linked employer-employee database for Hungary to analyze the effects of state and foreign ownership on wages. The chapter by Friebel and Panova is a case study of the HR policies in one insider-privatized Russian firm.

A key advantage of the Earle and Telegdy chapter, relative to previous studies of the effects of ownership that are based on either firm-level or worker-level data, is the use of longitudinal employer-employee data, which allows for identification of ownership effects taking into account differences in worker characteristics as well as nonrandom selection of firms into ownership status. The raw estimates show large wage differences across ownership types, but the authors find that ownership type is highly correlated with the education, experience, gender, and occupation of workers, suggesting ownership type may be systematically selected with respect to such characteristics. Nonetheless, the large unconditional wage gaps in the data are little affected by conditioning on worker characteristics. Ownership type is also correlated with firm size, industry, and productivity; controlling for industry reduces the estimated gaps, and controlling for employment size reduces them further. The chapter also exploits the presence of many switches of ownership type in the data to estimate firm fixed effects and random trend models, accounting for unobserved firm characteristics affecting the average level and trend growth of wages. The results from these specification differ little in their implications for the effect of privatization, but they reduce the estimated effect of foreign ownership. Overall, the results imply that the substantial unconditional wage differentials are mostly, but not entirely, a function of differences in worker and firm characteristics and that linked panel data are necessary to take these correlated factors into account.

Why the operations of firms governed by private owners are quite different from those that are foreign-owned is something that has received a great deal of attention in the literature. While the Hungarian privatization process was not insider-dominated in the same way as other East European economies, most notably Russia, one hypothesis is that insider privatization results in little behavioral change. The fact that insiders benefited much from privatization in Russia raises suspicion about the efficiency of some of the privatization policies, and results suggest that insider-privatized firms do not restructure. However, the study by Friebel and Panova sheds new light on this puzzle in the transition literature by drilling down into the HR practices and the internal labor market of a single insider-privatized Russian firm. The results show career paths prior to transition that are quite similar to the career paths in western firms. In contrast to previous beliefs they find strong micro-evidence for restructuring activities after insider privatization. The employment of blue-collar workers decreased substantially, white-collar workers are recruited from outside the firm, while incumbent white-collar workers are shifted across functions within the firm (but do not leave the firm). As a result, the firm becomes "top loaded," and career paths from lower levels in the hierarchy are effectively blocked, which consistent with the internal labor market literature can have adverse effects on the efficiency of the firm (see Gibbons and Waldman 1999).

In summary, privatization of state-operated enterprises is a key aspect of transition. Both these chapters present evidence that firm governance affects the HR practices and efficiency of firms, but perhaps in more complicated ways than economists thought when first tasked with forming transition policies in Central and Eastern European countries. Indeed, these two chapters highlight the relative unpreparedness of the economics profession to fully understand the impact of transition policies.

Globalization, Trade, and Labor Markets

Economists have long theorized about the impact of globalization and trade on the earning and employment outcomes of workers. Unfortunately, because the impacts of trade are typically measured at the firm level, and the policy interest is on the long-run outcomes of workers, little data have been available to examine the impact. These three chapters provide some of the first empirical evidence on the topic in analytic work only possible because of the existence of linked longitudinal employer-employee

(LEE) data.[3] The chapters also highlight the new availability of LEE data, which were only available in Northern Europe a decade ago. Muendler uses Brazilian data, the Becker and Muendler chapter examines German multinationals, and Van Biesebroeck uses data from three African nations.

The very thought provoking piece by Muendler sets out to examine an issue of concern in every country: the impact of trade liberalization on workers. While economists at the International Monetary Fund (IMF) and the World Bank have long advocated liberalization as a path to economic growth and prosperity, arguing that the resulting reallocation of resources and economic growth would result in the absorption of displaced workers in the growing part of the economy. The rise of socialist leaders throughout South and Central America attest to the lack of popular confidence in such economic theories. Brazil's experience with trade liberalization in 1990 provides a useful opportunity to examine the facts. Muendler uses LEE data to examine the long-run outcomes of individual workers who worked in firms directly subject to foreign competition (i.e., in sectors in which foreign import penetration increased substantially) and compared them to observationally equivalent individuals in observationally equivalent firms. He finds, as expected, substantial displacement of workers; they also find that neither comparative-advantage sectors nor exporters absorb displaced workers for years. In addition, firms in the new-growth sectors have significantly more displacements and significantly fewer accessions than the exiting firms in the import-competing sector. As a result, workers are much more likely to transition to the informal sector and unemployment. Spells of unemployment last longer, and spells in the formal sector are much more likely to fail.

Another hotly debated impact of globalization is the outsourcing of jobs by multinational enterprises (MNEs). Lou Dobbs, a CNN reporter wrote a recent book, *Exporting America,* which has received enormous attention in the United States. He vehemently argues that too many U.S. companies are sending American jobs overseas and choosing to employ cheap overseas labor—going so far as to list "job exporters" on his Web site. A very different picture is painted in the Becker and Muendler chapter that uses German LEE data to examine the facts in some detail. They find that MNEs that increase their foreign direct investment (FDI) exposure become more competitive, and the resulting expansion acts to significantly reduce the rate of job loss. Indeed, the annual separation rate of workers at MNEs is about 14 percent, compared with the 18 percent separation rate of non-MNEs. One important result that is inconsistent with prior expectations

---

3. Although there has been some work on this topic by Lori Kletzer (http://econ.ucsc.edu/Faculty/facLkletz.shtml) or by Chris Ruhm (http://www.nber.org/papers/w5621), the studies are essentially based on worker surveys. Muendler is the first to use LEE data to analyse the long-term effects in a developing country.

about the nature of Germany's comparative advantage is that job savings are greater for more-educated than less-educated workers.

Although the previous two chapters deal with employment outcomes, policymakers and economists are equally interested in the impact of globalization on earnings. This is particularly interesting in the case of Africa, which has been receiving increasing attention in the development literature, but is probably underresearched due to lack of adequate data. The Van Biesebroeck chapter examines patterns in earnings outcomes of workers in manufacturing plants in three countries that differ substantially in levels of economic development: Zimbabwe, Kenya, and Tanzania. He finds that the more developed a country is (and the more exposed to foreign markets), the more wages match the productivity of the individual worker, controlling for other characteristics. Intriguingly, given the importance placed on education as an investment strategy for developing countries, wages substantially exceed productivity for the most-educated workers in the least-developed countries. This research provides some intriguing evidence that suggests that more-developed countries are also likely to have more efficient labor markets—although obviously the direction of causality is difficult to establish.

Data Sources

The data sets used in this book are truly international in flavor—and in a sense provide a world tour of the interrelationships between firms and workers. Four chapters (Andersson, Brown, Campbell, Chiang, and Park; Hellerstein, Neumark, and McInerney; Burks, Carpenter, Götte, Monaco, Porter, and Rustichini; and Manchester) use data on U.S. firms and workers. One of the first analyses of South American data is provided by the Muendler chapter, which studies Brazil. Crossing the ocean to Africa, Van Biesebroeck's chapter provides a study using data from Tanzania, Kenya, and Zimbabwe. The world tour continues with a trip north to the western part of Europe, with chapters from France (Diaye, Greenan, and Urdanivia) and Germany (Becker and Muendler; Bender and von Wachter). It ends in Eastern Europe (Russia, Friebel, and Panova) and Hungary (Earle and Telegdy).

One of the themes of the conference was to see how qualitative data analysis could be used to examine employers and employees. There are three case studies in the book; two are based on administrative records of the firm (Manchester; Friebel and Panova). Burks, Carpenter, Götte, Monaco, Porter, and Rustichini is a statistical case study of a single trucker firm and its employees, which matches proprietary personnel and operational data. They combine traditional survey instruments with behavioral economics experiments.

The other chapters contribute to the second theme of the book, which was quantitative data, primarily LEE data. Although each chapter has the LEE component in common, a major contribution of the book is the description that the authors provide of how they create their LEE data sets by combining different sources with different identification techniques. The basic approach is well illustrated by von Wachter and Bender, who use a single data source for building up their linked employer employee data. And, although most of the chapters use different official data sets and are linked over a unique firm identifier, two chapters (Becker and Muendler; Hellerstein, Neumark, and McInerney) illustrate the use and validity of alphanumerical matching algorithms, such as Automatch, based on the name and addresses of the firms. A different approach is used by Earle and Telegdy who have neither identifiers nor addresses as a basis for linking one data set: they use subsets of common variables to get unique firms per cell for matching.

Other striking features are evident upon examination of the chapters. The first is the imaginative set of methods whereby data can be collected from individual firms; the second is how many more data sets have become available since the seminal review by Abowd and Kramarz in 1999; and the third is the number of innovative approaches taken to enhance the breadth and depth of information derived from linked data.

Several chapters illustrated the potential richness of looking at single firms in detail. One example is the chapter by Manchester, who analyses the impact of tuition reimbursement programs by examining data from a single firm as well as from a cross section of firms. A panel of observations was constructed based on seven point-in-time observations from administrative records for the firm. Individuals are observed on December 15 of each year from 1999 to 2005, and the data include gender, age, and race as well as start date, job characteristics, and annual wage rates. The chapter by Friebel and Panova also uses the raw data from the HR department of the firm they study. There is one personnel file for each individual in the firm. This file contains information about entry into the firm; exit date (that is, separation); dates of movements across job titles; an occupational code; the departmental affiliation; as well as such personal characteristics as age, education, gender, place of birth, place of university education, field of study, party and trade union membership, ethnicity, marital status, and number of children. Finally, the firm provided them with information about the job history of each individual: military service, date of leaving previous job, last employer. In probably the richest case study analysis in the book, the chapter by Burks, Carpenter, Götte, Monaco, Porter, and Rustichini show the enormous potential of a detailed data collection effort. The team matched proprietary personnel and operational data to new data collected by the researchers to create a two-year panel study of a large subset of new hires that included both standard survey instruments and the results of behavioral economics experiments. The team collected information on employees that went beyond the standard demographic information to also capture information on risk and loss aversion, time preference, planning, nonverbal IQ, and the Multidimensional Personality Questionnaire (MPQ) personality profile. The project, which is in its beginning stages, will follow employees over two years of their work lives. Among the major design goals are to discover the extent to which the survey and experimental measures are correlated and whether and how much predictive power, with respect to key on-the-job outcome variables, is added by the behavioral measures.

Table I.1 provides a brief summary of the LEE data sets described in each chapter, together with a reference to the Abowd and Kramarz (1999) paper. As is to be expected, data sets that already existed have been considerably updated and enhanced; in a number of cases, new data sets have appeared.

The basic richness of LEE data is well illustrated by the von Wachter and Bender chapter: the size and universality of the data mean that they can track the outcomes of quite narrowly defined subgroups of workers as well as the firms that employ them. Their data includes information on all employees covered by social security, representing around 80 percent of the German workforce, with detailed histories for each worker's time in covered employment. Their data are unusually rich for LEE data as they not only include basic demographic information, as well as data on occupation, industry, job status, education, and individual-level information on gross daily wages subject to social security contributions and the exact dates when the employee worked in the social security system. The unique establishment identifiers available were used to create a separate data set of establishment characteristics that were aggregated up from the employment register and merged back onto the individual-level data. Characteristics include, among others, establishment size, employment growth, and average wages.

Muendler's chapter features one of the first LEE data sets for a developing country: Brazil. The data set is derived from a nationwide, comprehensive set of administrative records of workers employed in the formal sector. The ministry of labor estimates that well above 90 percent of all formally employed workers in Brazil are covered in Relação Anual de Informatições Sociais (RAIS) throughout the 1990s. As is typical with LEE data derived from administrative records, the sample size is enormous: information on 71.1 million workers (with 556.3 million job spells) at 5.52 million establishments in 3.75 million firms over the sixteen-year period 1986 to 2001. The data also have the rich feature of providing the month of accession and the month of separation in addition to such other relevant worker information includes tenure at the establishment, age, gender, and educational attainment; job information includes occupation and the monthly average wage; establishment information includes sector and municipality classifications. As is also often the case with LEE data derived from administra-

Table I.1   **Summary of linked employer-employee data sets**

Author	Country	Brief description	Abowd & Kramarz comparison
Andersson et al.	United States	a. Longitudinal individual data from the LEHD b. 1997 Economic Censuses c. The 1991–1998 Census/NSF R&D Surveys (firm-level R&D)	New data set
Diaye et al.	France	COI survey	Enhanced data set
Von Wachter & Bender	Germany	Social security records—total population	Referenced in Abowd & Kramarz
Hellerstein et al.	United States	1990 and 2000 DEEDs	Updated and expanded
Earle & Telegdy	Hungary	a. Hungarian Wage Survey b. Tax Authority data	New data set, new country
Muendler	Brazil	RAIS	New data, new country
Becker & Muendler	Germany	a. Social security records of the German Federal Labor Agency b. Midi database (MIcro database Direct Investment, formerly direk), collected by Deutsche Bundesbank c. Commercial corporate structure database markus (from Verband der Vereine Creditreform)	Updated and enhanced (by b and c)
Van Biesebroeck	Tanzania, Kenya, and Zimbabwe	A stratified sample of manufacturing firms in three consecutive years	New data sets, new countries

tive records, the basic data set can be enhanced by matching into other administrative records—in this case, export data.

The Andersson, Brown, Campbell, Chiang, and Park chapter further illustrates the potential for enhancing basic LEE data by using multiple data sources. In order to answer their research question, they use data from three sources: longitudinal and near-universal individual data from the Longitudinal Employer-Household Dynamics Program (LEHD) program to construct and characterize the HR practices of firms; they add firm characteristics from the 1997 Economic Censuses (e.g., measures of revenue, material costs, total hours, capital stock, four-digit industry code) as well as from the 1991 to 1998 Census National Science Foundation (NSF) R&D Surveys (firm-level R&D).

A very similar approach is taken by Becker and Muendler, who construct their LEE set from three confidential micro-data sources, from multiple sources, and complement them with sector-level information on

German foreign trade. This chapter illustrates some of the matching challenges common to LEE data, in that the three data sources do not share common firm identifiers. The authors surmount the problem by using a string-matching procedure to identify clearly identical firms and their establishments. The result of their efforts is to create an impressively large data set that constitutes a cross section of establishments around year 2000, including a total of 39,681 establishments whose German parent firms conduct FDI abroad and 1,133,920 control establishments out of 3.8 million establishments in the full worker sample (1998 to 2002).

Not all LEE data are derived from official administrative records. Indeed, Van Biesebroeck's uses stratified samples of manufacturing firms in three African countries that were collected by three different research teams, coordinated by the Regional Program of Enterprise Development at the World Bank. When working with survey data, one of the most difficult decisions is whether to choose a sample that is representative of firms or one that is representative of workers. In this case, the latter was chosen: firms were sampled to give (the firm of) each manufacturing worker equal probability to be included in the sample—an implicit stratification by employment size. The second choice is how many employees to interview within each firm. The cost constraints that are an integral part of survey work impose a trade-off between firm and worker diversity: the more employees interviewed in a firm (and, hence, the more within firm diversity is captured), the fewer firms can be interviewed (resulting in less across-firm diversity). In the African countries, a maximum of ten employees per firm were interviewed each year, resulting in an unbalanced panel of firms with, on average, 110 to 183 observations per year in each country.

Another example of a survey approach is evident in the Diaye, Greenan, and Urdanivia chapter, which analyzes a French matched employer-employee survey on computerization and organizational change. In contrast to the African case, however, the sampling unit is the firm, and the frame is a representative sample of manufacturing firms with more than fifty employees and a sample of randomly selected employees within these firms. The French sample chose the opposite trade-off from the African, interviewing a small sample of employees (one, two, or three) within each firm and, hence, getting more firm diversity. An interesting feature of the French survey, and one that emphasizes the value added of surveys relative to administrative records, is that the labor force section provides a detailed description about the organization of work, particularly whether that work is structured around group activities. In addition, the survey captures different measures of effort, which would be impossible to capture in administrative records.

The Earle and Telegdy chapter also draws on data from multiple sources. The worker data come from the Hungarian Wage Survey, compiled by the National Employment Office and maintained by the Institute of Economics of the Hungarian Academy of Sciences. The latter organization also links these data to some firm-level information. The authors have further linked this database (using common variables in both databases) to a universal tax database containing detailed information on all Hungarian firms using double-sided accounting. Employers are included in the Wage Survey according to whether their employees are selected by a random procedure: in the first two years of the survey, workers are selected using a fixed interval of selection, while subsequently workers are selected by birthdate. Firms were included only if they have employees born on these dates. Although this approach provides a random sample of workers within firms and includes, on average, about 6.5 percent of production workers and 10 percent of nonproduction workers, the sample of firms is related to size. The authors, therefore, use weights related to size and response probabilities in their analysis, and the final sample consists of a panel of 21,238 firms linked with a within-firm random sample of 1.35 million worker observations.

The final approach that can be used to create LEE data sets is to match existing surveys with existing administrative data. This approach is described in the Hellerstein, Neumark, and McInerney chapter. They draw a sample of workers from the Sample Edited Detail File (SEDF), which contains all individual responses to the Decennial Census of Population one-in-six Long Form. Respondents are asked to provide the name and address of their employer in the previous week. This information is then matched to the name and address information in the Census Bureau's Business Register list (BR), based on administrative records. This procedure yields a very large data set with workers matched to their establishments, along with all of the information on workers from the SEDF. Even more interesting, because the data are constructed for both 1990 and 2000, the authors are able to examine changes in establishments over time.

Summary and Outlook

In summary, the chapters in this volume all represent research that relies on advances in data collection methods in one way or another. These range from combining case study data with personnel records of a single firm, ideally suited to understand issues such as how HR policies affect workers and the performance of firms, to the creation of new multi-source, nationally representative LEE data sets, ideally suited to capture empirical irregularities related to the dynamics of the economy. It is easy to envision further advances along each of these lines, but perhaps even more promising is the crossing of the two paths. The studies in this volume clearly demonstrate the relative advantages of the two approaches and the results often complement each other in a way that adds to our overall understanding.

The benefits of being able to combine data from the two study approaches within a single framework are obvious, as is the increasing potential for cross-national comparisons (see Hamermesh 2007). Today they are more feasible than before thanks to new data collection tools and new integration techniques. Indeed, active research is in progress to match data sets from many different sources to inform research about active labor market policies, price setting, and employment dynamics. Similarly, international comparisons of LEE and firm surveys are beginning to emerge (Lazear and Shaw, forthcoming; Freeman, Kruse, and Blasi, forthcoming).

However, there are clearly important and big challenges in terms of data access issues and disclosure avoidance that need to be addressed. The creation and analysis of high-quality information are core elements of the scientific endeavor. No less fundamental is the ability to replicate scientific analysis. Yet the firm-level data that is described in this book are often not accessible to others for replication and validation. It will be critical to develop widely available access modalities for the qualitative data, often housed at universities and research centers, and administrative data, often housed at statistical agencies. Only recently has the research community begun to address such key issues that will ultimately affect the scientific nature of the research as well as our ability to access and gather new data. Some progress has already been made, including the development of remote access capabilities and new synthetic data methods, but this is likely to remain a key challenge for the research community in the foreseeable future.

References

Abowd, John, John Haltiwanger, and Julia Lane. 2004. Integrated longitudinal employer-employee data for the United States. *American Economic Review* 94:224–29.

Abowd, John, and Francis Kramarz. 1999. The analysis of labor markets using matched employer-employee data. In *Handbook of labor economics.* Vol. 3B, ed. O. Ashenfelter and D. Card, 2629–2710. Amsterdam: North-Holland.

Brown, Clair, John Haltiwanger, and Julia Lane. 2006. *Economic turbulence: Is volatility good for America?* Chicago: University of Chicago Press.

Freeman, Richard B., Douglas Kruse, and Joseph Blasi. Forthcoming. Worker reports on labour practices and outcomes in a single form across countries. *Labour Economics.*

Gibbons, Robert, and Michael Waldman. 1999. A theory of wage and promotion dynamics in inside firms. *Quarterly Journal of Economics* 114 (1999): 132–58.

Hamermesh, Dan. 2007. Fun with matched employer-employee data. *Labour Economics,* forthcoming.

Lazear, Edward P., and Kathryn L. Shaw, eds. Forthcoming. *An international comparison of the structure of wages.* Chicago: University of Chicago Press.

1

Human Resource Practices and Firm Productivity

1

The Effect of HRM Practices and R&D Investment on Worker Productivity

Fredrik Andersson, Clair Brown, Benjamin Campbell, Hyowook Chiang, and Yooki Park

1.1 Introduction

As the pace of technological change has quickened and global competition has shortened product life cycles, firms have had to rethink their technology investment strategies and their human resource management practices in order to remain competitive. The main contribution of this chapter is to examine the relationship between firm-level technological advance-

Fredrik Andersson is a senior research associate of the Cornell Institute for Social and Economic Research, and a research fellow of the Longitudinal Employer-Household Dynamics Program (LEHD) of the U.S. Bureau of the Census. Clair Brown is a professor of economics and director of the Center for Work, Technology, and Society (IIR) at the University of California, Berkeley. Benjamin Campbell is an assistant professor of management and human resources at the Fisher College of Business, Ohio State University. Hyowook Chiang is an economist at Welch Consulting. Yooki Park is an associate at McKinsey & Company.

The data used are confidential data from the U.S. Census Bureau's Longitudinal Employer-Household Dynamics Program (LEHD), which is partially supported by the National Science Foundation Grant SES-9978093 to Cornell University (Cornell Institute for Social and Economic Research), the National Institute on Aging (R01-AG18854-01), and the Alfred P. Sloan Foundation. Support was also provided by the Institute of Industrial Relations at the University of California at Berkeley, and the Institute for Technology, Enterprise, and Competitiveness (ITEC/COE) and Omron Fellowship at Doshisha University. We have benefited from discussions with and comments from Charlie Brown, Peter Cappelli, Erica Groshen, Andrew Hildreth, Julia Lane, Daniel Parent, Linda Sattler, Eric Verhoogen, Till von Wachter, and Edward Wolff, seminar participants at Berkeley and Wharton, participants at the NBER Summer Institute and the Conference on the Analysis of Firms and Employees (CAFE), and the anonymous reviewers. This document has undergone a Census Bureau review more limited in scope than that given to official Census Bureau publications and is released to inform interested parties of ongoing research and to encourage discussion of work in progress. The views expressed herein are attributable only to the author(s) and do not represent the views of the U.S. Census Bureau, its program sponsors, or data providers. The U.S. Census Bureau is preparing to support external researchers' use of these data; please contact U.S. Census Bureau, LEHD Program, FB 2138-3, 4700 Silver Hill Rd., Suitland, MD 20233, USA.

ment (as proxied by research and development investment [R&D]) and firms' human resource management (HRM) practices for high-skill workers in a high-tech industry, and then examine how this relationship is connected to firm performance.

Although the relationship of technological change and labor market outcomes at the individual-worker level has been well-studied,[1] surprisingly little is known about what happens within the firm. Specifically, there is little empirical research on whether firms' technology choices are consistent with their human resource practices and whether there is a statistical relationship between technology, human resources, and performance at the firm level.

At the individual level, there is a long line of research observing the correlation of technical change and compensation for high-skill workers and examining the mechanisms underlying the relationship.[2] However, there is little large-scale work looking at the relationship of technology and worker outcomes within firms. In this project, we examine the worker/technology relationship within firms and focus on one specific industry where we can employ detailed industry controls.

Previous research has demonstrated that technology interacts with human resource practices through several channels. Technology may alter the development of and returns to human capital (Krueger 1993; Handel 1999; DiNardo and Pischke 1997; and Entorf and Kramarz 1998). Additionally, technology can interact with individual outcomes through changes in work design (Hunter and Lafkas 2003; Bresnahan, Brynjolfsson, and Hitt 2002; Zuboff 1988; Autor, Levy, and Murnane 2002; Brown et al. 1997; and Barley and Orr 1997) or changes in work organization (Cappelli 1996; Bresnahan, Brynjolfsson, and Hitt 2002; O'Shaughnessy, Levine, and Cappelli 2001; and Caroli and Van Reenen 2001).

We propose a mechanism connecting technology and HRM practices at the firm level that links the skill bias and the organization change approaches. We propose a make-versus-buy model of workforce skill adjustment. If technology and labor force skills are complements in a firm's production function, and if the HRM system impacts the cost of acquiring, developing, and retaining the portfolio of skills in a firm, then the firm's choice of HRM system affects its ability to adjust worker skill levels to maximize the value of their technological investments. In other words, if firms choose to augment the skill of their workforce to complement an investment in technology, they face the traditional make-versus-buy problem. Firms can structure their HRM practices to develop and retain the

---

1. See Brown and Campbell (2002) for a detailed review of the impact of technological change on the work and wages of individuals.

2. Seminal works in this area include Bound and Johnson (1992), Levy and Murnane (1992), Katz and Murphy (1992), Juhn, Murphy, and Pierce (1993), Berman, Bound, and Griliches (1994), and Allen (1997).

necessary skills in-house, or they can structure their HRM practices to at-tract and recruit workers with the necessary skills on the external market.

For the econometric portion of the chapter, we utilize data from the Lon-gitudinal Employer-Household Dynamics (LEHD) program that covers all establishments and their employees in seven large states over the period 1992 to 2001. Our analysis and interpretation is informed by fieldwork through the Sloan Competitive Semiconductor Manufacturing Program. The fieldwork began in 1992 and involved detailed data collection and in-tensive interviews at over three dozen semiconductor manufacturing firms. The insights and understanding developed through these site visits are the basis of our examination of the HRM-technology-productivity relation-ship in manufacturing firms within the electronics industry.

The analysis capitalizes on the strengths of both detailed industry study and large-scale survey approaches to develop a framework for estimating the relationship between firm productivity, R&D, and HRM practices us-ing near-universal data from the LEHD program. The detailed industry knowledge facilitates interpreting of the results and understanding the context in which the results are embedded. This combined method expands the "insider econometrics" approach to the industry level of analysis.

Industries exhibit wide variation in their market and organizational structures, which affects their rate of technological change, their degree of and response to global competition, and, in general, their reaction to envi-ronmental factors. Because industries differ in dimensions that are hard to measure using traditional large-scale survey responses, industry-specific knowledge gained through fieldwork is critical in understanding how to in-terpret estimated statistical relationships within and across industries (Brown, Haltiwanger, and Lane 2006). Fieldwork research allows us to study the trade-offs that managers make in developing and implementing new technology and HRM practices, and they help us understand the tim-ing of these decisions. Although technology and HRM practices are re-lated through the production process, we observe that technological changes can be implemented much faster and, therefore, more often than HRM practices can be changed. Firms' choice of HRM practices can be made more independently of the external market than the choice of a new technology, which is tied to a choice of customers and markets.

While it is important to understand the underlying structure of a firm to interpret results, detailed firm or industry studies cannot be used for gen-eralizations across firms or industries or for estimating national impact be-cause we do not know whether the specific firm experiences are represen-tative (Sturgeon et al. 2006). In order to generalize from an industry study, we need estimations from a comprehensive survey across firms and work-ers in the industry that show the observed relationship across key variables, such as HRM practices, R&D expenditures, and productivity. Our ap-proach is to combine comprehensive micro-data and detailed industry knowledge in a way that leverages each approach's strengths and increases the quality and usefulness of both types of data. For micro-data to be estimated and interpreted properly, research teams must have both a deep understanding of the industries involved and expertise in the use of micro-data.

Specifically, this study combines both micro-data and detailed industry knowledge to analyze the impact of R&D and HRM systems on firm performance within the electronics industry (Standard Industrial Classification [SIC] 35 and 36).[3] Although firms in the electronics industry have a high level of R&D investment relative to other industries, there is a large variance in investment between firms within the industry. Studying one industry simplifies the analysis of the relationship of R&D and HRM by focusing on firms that are fairly comparable in structure and face similar market trends and measurement issues.

We use workers' outcomes within establishments to construct a variety of measures of establishment-level HRM outcomes for high-education workers and then link these HRM measures to plant and firm characteristics. First, we document the firms' HRM systems. Implementation of HRM systems is more important than implementation of individual components because there are synergies and complementarities in HRM practices (Kandel and Lazear 1992; and Milgrom and Roberts 1995). We perform a cluster analysis of firms and HRM measures to identify and describe the most common HRM systems. Next, we employ principal components analysis to identify groups of correlated HRM measures. We then regress worker productivity on the principal HRM components interacted with R&D.

We find substantial variation in HRM practices for high-education workers across firms in this industry. Human resource management bundles appear to include both spot market and internal labor market outcomes. Consistent with Bauer and Bender's (2004) finding using comparable German data that technological advancement is correlated with worker churning for high-skilled workers, we find that for firms with high levels of R&D, HRM practices that provide multiple ports of entry, low turnover and performance incentives are positively related to worker productivity. For low R&D firms, HRM practices that offer multiple ports of entry and low wage variance for recent hires are positively related to productivity. Additionally, the results indicate strong clustering of HRM practices across firms, with high R&D firms much more likely to implement more market-oriented practices than low R&D firms in this high-tech industry. These findings are consistent with the implications of our make-versus-buy model of workforce skills, where firms with a high rate of technological change that buy

---

3. The LEHD program links universal and longitudinal records on employees' earnings and employment from states' Unemployment Insurance (UI) systems with detailed cross-sectional data from Census Bureau's Economic Censuses and Census/NSF R&D surveys.

new skills on the external market and selectively retain and reward experienced workers will demonstrate higher productivity than comparable firms with fewer ports of entry with similar earnings growth, which indicates more internal skill development. Also, firms with a low rate of technological change implement HRM systems that are consistent with providing training to workers rather than buying required skills, which may be more efficient in these firms with slower technological change.

The next section presents a framework for firms' R&D investment decisions and firms' HRM decisions and how these decisions are related to productivity. Then we describe the data set and our measurements for HRM practices, R&D investment, firm performance, and other firm characteristics. We present statistical results on firm performance, HRM, and R&D and discuss to what extent the results are consistent with our hypotheses. Finally, we conclude with a summary and a discussion of the implications of the research.

1.2   HRM Practices and Workforce Skill Adjustment Costs

Our analysis looks at HRM practices within firms and builds on the Internal Labor Market analysis embedded in the work of Prendergast (1996) and Doeringer and Piore (1971). In the empirical work, there is mixed evidence on measuring internal labor markets within firms. Using data from a single firm, Baker, Gibbs, and Holmstrom (1994) find that some aspects of the employment relationship are consistent with the theory of internal labor markets. Lazear and Oyer (2004) use matched data from the Swedish Employers Confederation from 1970 to 1990. They find that the strict model of internal labor markets does not seem to hold because external forces play a large role in firms' wage setting policies. Topel and Ward (1992) observe high mobility and earnings growth among young male workers that is more consistent with matching models and on-the-job search than internal labor markets. Because of the mixed evidence, we perform a cluster analysis of firms in our sample to examine the distribution of different sets of HRM practices and find a diverse set of HRM outcomes, even within a homogenous industry.

Given the diverse outcomes, we focus on developing an understanding of the underlying process that might explain the diversity. The basic concept of the framework is that HRM practices affect the cost structure of how firms adjust the skills of their workforce. If technology and worker skills are complementary, then the firm's HRM decisions and R&D decisions will be related.

Even in the high-tech electronics sector, the speed of technological change varies across firms in different product markets. For example, consider the semiconductor industry, which is one of the industries included in our sample. Within the semiconductor industry, graphic chips for video games typically have a generation life of approximately eighteen months and analogue chips typically have a generation life of five years. Memory chips and microprocessors typically have a generation life between two and three years. Generation life is critical in defining a firm's constraints in making technological investment, as product prices are above marginal costs early in the cycle before supply brings the prices down. Across the electronics industry more broadly, product life and speed of technological change have an even longer time horizon. For example, our sample also includes manufactures of "current-carrying wiring devices." In contrast to the semiconductor industry, the wire industry is marked by very long product life spans and low levels of innovation.

The firm's HRM system structures how labor inputs are bought and created over time. We assume the cost of labor inputs are determined by the following HRM practices:

- Screening and hiring
- Skill development (both learning by doing and formal training)
- Retention of experienced workers
- Adjustments in headcount by skill (quits and layoffs)

At any given point in time, these HRM practices determine the cost and skills of the firm's workforce. Here we focus only on high-education workers because they are the workers who develop and implement new technology.

If firms adopt a technological change that alters the optimal composition of their workforce, firms may choose to adjust the skills embedded in their workforce. Given the decision to adjust workforce skills, firms must make two major decisions in creating the optimal skill-experience composition in the workforce:

1. Decide whether to provide formal training in the new technology to their existing workers or to purchase these skills through new hires (we call this the make-buy decision)

2. Decide which experienced engineers (and other workers) they will retain (we call this the retention decision)

The firm will make the first decision based upon the relative costs, including both the payroll costs and the time-to-market costs, of making or buying the required skills for the new technology. Under the assumption that the cost of "making" the required skills is the worker adjustment cost of acquiring skills (training cost) and is proportional to the size of technological jumps over a given time, and that the cost of "buying" the required skills is the firm's adjustment costs in hiring new workers, which is invariant to the size of the technological jump, then for sufficiently large technological jumps, "buying" will be relatively less costly than "making" new skills.

The second decision will depend upon the costs of retention as well as the production function. Specifically, firms will structure incentive systems to retain the workers who are most valuable to the firm. For a new technology that requires new skills and restructures skill demand in the firm, the firm must decide which workers to retain. This decision depends on the portfolio of skills supplied in the firm compared to the portfolio of skills necessary for the new technology and the costs of obtaining the new portfolio, which include a comparison of the make decisions (primarily retraining costs) compared to buy decision (cost of new hires, layoffs, and worker morale). The costs to workers of retraining depend on their opportunity wage and the required effort associated with retraining, which depends on how much retraining is required. Workers with skill sets far behind the latest technology will face higher retraining costs but require lower incentives by the firm for retention, while workers who are better matches to the new technology will face lower retraining costs and the incentives required by the firm for retention are higher.

How does the firm's product life, and thus rate of R&D spending, affect how the HRM system operates? We assume that a new technology requires a mix of experience on the previous generation of technology and new skills that require formal education (or training). Firms in short product-life markets, and thus with high R&D spending, must have a mix of engineers with the new skills required for the new technology and engineers with experience on the last generation of technology, and we assume that experience and new skills are complements. Firms in long product-life markets, and thus with low R&D spending, rely more on engineers with experience because the engineers will focus on cutting costs, improving quality, and improving throughput over the life of the product.

If worker costs of retraining increases proportionally with size of technological change (as proxied by R&D), and firm hiring transaction costs are invariant to size of technological change, then R&D and flexible hiring practices will be positively related to worker productivity. In a competitive labor market, implementation of new technologies in an industry will impact the external market opportunities for engineers. To counteract turnover of key workers, who are the workers with skills more compatible with the new technology, firms will structure their HRM system to provide incentives (both in compensation and in job assignment) in order to retain workers who match well to the new technology and who face lower personal retraining costs. How long it is beneficial for the high R&D firm to retain and use their technical workers' skills will determine the incentive structure implicit in their pay system compared to opportunity market wages as well as their average tenure (and turnover rate).

HYPOTHESIS 1: *Firms with high R&D that choose an HRM system that allows hiring of workers with required skills and fosters retention of selected experienced workers will have higher worker productivity than those that create the required new skills strictly through retraining of workers or strictly through new hires.*

Firms with low R&D improve performance not through product market innovation, but through incremental improvement in the product and production process. Experience is valuable in making these improvements, and firms that provide incentives to retain workers will have higher productivity. Performance-based pay that is tied to improvements may also motivate workers to higher productivity, although this pay may be awarded to a team rather than an individual technical worker in order to encourage group activity and because evaluating individual contributions may be difficult.

HYPOTHESIS 2: *Firms with low R&D that choose an HRM system that fosters retention of experienced workers and allows some performance-based pay will have higher worker productivity than those that do not have a compensation structure that reduces quits and rewards improvements.*

In the next section, we discuss the data and measures we will use to examine the previous hypotheses linking HRM practices to worker productivity for firms on different technology paths.

1.3   Data Set and Measures

We use data from three sources in our analysis. We use longitudinal and near-universal individual data from the LEHD program to construct and characterize the human resource practices of firms; we add firm characteristics from the 1997 Economic Censuses (e.g., measures of revenue, material costs, total hours, capital stock, four-digit industry code) as well as from the 1991 to 1998 Census/National Science Foundation (NSF) R&D Surveys (firm-level R&D).

The LEHD data have been extensively described elsewhere (see Haltiwanger, Lane, and Spletzer 2000; Abowd, Haltiwanger, and Lane 2004),[4] but it is worth noting that these data have several advantages over household-based survey data. In particular, the earnings are quite accurately reported as there are financial penalties for misreporting. The data are current, and the data set is extremely large.

1.3.1   HRM Variables

In characterizing the human resource practices of a firm, we utilize the measures of earnings, earnings growth, accession rate, and separation rate for selected cohorts within each firm to create the following components of

---

4. The LEHD database consists of quarterly records of the employment and earnings of almost all individuals from the unemployment insurance systems of a number of U.S. states in the 1990s. The UI records have also been matched to internal administrative records at the Census Bureau that contain information on date of birth, place of birth, race, and sex for all workers.

firms' HRM systems for high-education (or professional) workers, who we know from our fieldwork are primarily technical workers:

- Accession rate: Ratio of the total number of new hires to the total number of workers in 1997.
- Ratio of mean initial wage to market initial wage: Average wage of new hires of an individual establishment divided by average wage of new hires of all establishments in electronics industry (SIC 35 and 36) in 1997.
- Standard deviation of initial earnings: Standard deviation of earnings of new hires in 1997.
- Separation rate for workers with two years experience: Proportion of workers who are no longer working for a certain establishment in 1997 among all workers who are hired in 1995 at the same establishment.
- Within-job wage growth for workers with two years experience: Wage growth between 1995 and 1997 of workers hired in 1995.
- Standard deviation of within-job wage growth for workers with two years experience: Standard deviation of wage growth between 1995 and 1997 of workers hired in 1995.
- Separation rate of workers with five years experience: Proportion of workers who are no longer working for a certain establishment in 1997 among all workers who are hired in 1992 at the same establishment.
- Within-job wage growth for workers with five years experience: Wage growth between 1992 and 1997 of workers hired in 1992.
- Standard deviation of within-job wage growth for workers with five years experience: Standard deviation of wage growth between 1992 and 1997 of workers hired in 1992.

One limitation of the data is that the current observed HRM practices in a firm reflect outcomes for workers who are both new to the firm and have been at the firm for any number of years. To capture the entire profile of workers and their wage growth, it is necessary to use the longitudinal variation in the data in order to construct the HRM measures. Currently the limited data on R&D expenditures allows us to examine only one cross section of the data, while the HRM measures capture longitudinal variation.

Another limitation for this study is that we lack direct measures of some important worker and job characteristics, especially education and occupation. We use imputed education values developed by the LEHD staff to distinguish high-education workers from other types of workers.[5]

___

5. While data on education for the individuals in our sample are not directly observed, LEHD staff has imputed education for every individual based on probabilistic links to external data. The statistical model takes advantage of the common observable characteristics in LEHD and Decennial data—most important earnings, industry, geography, gender, and

1.3.2   R&D Measure

The following variable represents firm-level technology practices: *R&D spending rate* is measured as the average total R&D costs per payroll over 1991–1998.

Because Census/NSF R&D surveys are conducted at the firm level, we assume that all establishments of the same firm equally benefit from their firm level R&D.

Research and development is just one component of firms' technology investment decisions, and as a result it is an imperfect proxy for investment in technology. However, R&D may be a good proxy for picking up firm's ability to learn and develop new knowledge (Cohen and Levinthal 1989). Also, because the relationship between R&D and new technology depends on the success of the investments and the length of period until implementation takes place, there may be an issue with the timing of investments and HRM choices. We partition the firms in our sample into two sets: firms with above-mean R&D investment and firms with below-mean investment.

1.3.3   Firm Performance Measure

To represent firm performance, we use following productivity measurement: *Labor productivity* is the log of real value added per total hours worked where the value added is the establishment-level revenue adjusted for inventory change net of materials input, and total hours worked include both production worker hours and nonproduction worker hours.

In the next section, we identify common HRM systems, the underlying HRM components that differentiate firms' HRM systems, and the relationship of these components to worker productivity.

1.4   Empirical Analysis

First, we perform a cluster analysis of firm HRM practices to identify the most common HRM systems for high-education workers. Next, we employ principal components analysis to identify groups of correlated HRM measures. We then implement a principal components regression to examine the statistical relationship of worker productivity with HRM practices for different technology paths.

1.4.1   HRM Cluster Descriptions

Firms implement HRM practices in bundles, and so we expect a high-level of correlation of adopted bundles across firms. We perform cluster

---

age—to impute education based on draws from the conditional distribution of educational categories in the 1990 Decennial Census. Details of the statistical model can be obtained from the authors.

analysis to identify the most common bundles of HRM practices implemented by firms and to group firms with similar practices. In order to maximize the degree of separations between the groups of firms, clusters of firms are based on canonical variables of HRM variables using Ward's minimum variance method.[6]

In table 1.1, we present the cluster results for the HRM variables for high-education workers (summary statistics of the first four clusters of HRM practices are reported, and the last group of firms represents the aggregation of multiple small clusters that are not disclosable according to Census Bureau confidentiality requirements).

Each cluster represents a prototype HRM system, which we indicate by name. We then discuss how we think the HRM system is operating within the firm based upon the components and our fieldwork observations.

- **Cluster 1 = Performance-Based Internal Labor Market (ILM):** Firms in Cluster 1 offer lower than average initial earnings and slow, but steady earnings growth, lower than average turnover and low earnings dispersion. These characteristics are consistent with hiring less-experienced workers and advancing them along well-defined pay scales. Entry of workers and their initial earnings reflect skill requirements, so average initial earnings of new hires are higher and have higher variance than in a bureaucratic ILM. After approximately two years, workers are selected (based upon performance) for faster career development, and members of a cohort compete for entry into these favored positions, which have higher earnings growth and lower separation rates. Those who do not receive skill development have lower earnings growth and higher separation rates.
- **Cluster 2 = Spot Market with Rewards:** Firms in Cluster 2 exhibit pay tied to the external labor market (both at entry and with experience) and above-average turnover. Firms can identify workers' talents and skills and hire and pay accordingly (matching is good). Firms can monitor worker performance and pay workers according to contribution. Initial earnings and earnings growth reflect market rates for skill

6. In Ward's minimum-variance method, the distance between two clusters is the analysis of variance (ANOVA) sum of squares between the two clusters added up over all the variables. At each generation, the within-cluster sum of squares is minimized over all partitions obtainable by merging two clusters from the previous generation (Ward 1963). The assumptions under which Ward's method joins clusters to maximize the likelihood at each level of the hierarchy are multivariate normal mixture, equal spherical covariance matrices, and equal sampling probabilities. Therefore, we first obtain approximate estimates of the pooled within-cluster covariance matrix of the HRM variables when the clusters are assumed to be multivariate normal with spherical covariance using the approximate covariance estimation for clustering developed by Art, Gnanadesikan, and Kettenring (1982). The Approximate Covariance Estimation for CLUStering (ACECLUS) procedure provides us with canonical versions of earnings (or person and firm effect), earnings growth, and worker churning that we use in the cluster analysis.

Table 1.1   HRM practice clusters for high-education workers

Variable	Cluster 1: Performance-based ILM	Cluster 2: Spot market with rewards	Cluster 3: Bureaucratic ILM	Cluster 4: Spot market	Residual firms	Sample
Accession rate	0.141	0.141	0.131	0.135	0.169	0.140
	(0.116)	(0.096)	(0.103)	(0.079)	(0.102)	(0.095)
Ratio of mean initial wage to market initial wage	0.807	1.027	0.539	1.153	1.437	0.830
	(0.382)	(0.214)	(0.265)	(0.180)	(0.222)	(0.350)
SD of initial earnings	6,108	10,024	2,754	13,672	21,430	7,419
	(10,210)	(1,029)	(987)	(1,188)	(594)	(5,939)
Separation rate at 2 years tenure	0.414	0.462	0.406	0.486	0.435	0.430
	(0.194)	(0.185)	(0.197)	(0.205)	(0.174)	(0.195)
Within job wage growth at 2 years tenure	0.052	0.066	0.071	0.056	0.067	0.060
	(0.071)	(0.061)	(0.061)	(0.076)	(0.067)	(0.068)
SD of within job wage growth at 2 years tenure	0.121	0.129	0.116	0.156	0.127	0.120
	(0.060)	(0.076)	(0.074)	(0.073)	(0.093)	(0.076)
Separation rate at 5 years tenure	0.425	0.452	0.403	0.446	0.531	0.430
	(0.176)	(0.172)	(0.197)	(0.163)	(0.171)	(0.177)
Within job wage growth at 5 years tenure	0.030	0.030	0.026	0.028	0.033	0.030
	(0.029)	(0.027)	(0.029)	(0.025)	(0.031)	(0.027)
SD of within job wage growth at 5 years tenure	0.054	0.060	0.053	0.055	0.062	0.060
	(0.030)	(0.019)	(0.030)	(0.022)	(0.025)	(0.024)
N	273	120	235	57	56	741

Notes: Table shows within-cluster means. Numbers in parentheses are standard deviations. HRM = human resource management. ILM = internal labor market. SD = standard deviation.

and talent, with large initial variance, and variance does not increase over tenure. Separation rate is higher than in ILMs.
- **Cluster 3 = Bureaucratic ILM:** Firms in Cluster 3 have very low initial earnings (with low variance), below-average earnings growth the first two years, and low turnover. Initial earnings of new hires are similar as most workers enter at the same level and have similar (and reliable) earnings growth. Firms experience low separation rates.
- **Cluster 4 = Spot Market:** Firms in cluster 4 offer high initial wages with large variance, below-average earnings growth (with large variance), and high turnover. Firms hire and pay workers as in spot market, but identification of worker's talents and effort at hire is imperfect and monitoring of worker performance is imperfect. Variance of initial earnings is higher than in spot markets with rewards. Early separation rate is higher than in spot market because the bad matches (both at hire and in rewards) end.

We find that firms are concentrated in clusters 1 and 3: 37 percent of all firms are in Cluster 1, 32 percent are in Cluster 3, 16 percent are in Cluster 2, and 8 percent are in Cluster 4; apparently the primary variables in differentiating systems are wage variation and initial earnings.

We classify firms as high or low R&D firms based on whether their R&D investment is above or below the mean and present their HRM cluster distributions in table 1.2. For low R&D firms, 82 percent are in Clusters 1 and 3 (ILMs), and 14 percent are in Clusters 2 and 4 (spot markets); for high R&D firms, 60 percent are in Clusters 1 and 3, and 31 percent in Cluster 2 and 4. This indicates that high R&D firms are more likely to implement spot-market-oriented HRM practices than low R&D firms although there are still many high R&D firms in the performance-based ILM cluster. Further, low R&D firms are more likely than high R&D firms to implement Bureaucratic ILMs, although there are many low R&D firms that implement performance-based ILM.

Table 1.2   **High-education HRM cluster sizes by firm R&D level**

	Low R&D firms		High R&D firms	
Cluster 1: Performance-based ILM	120	(16.2)	153	(20.6)
Cluster 2: Spot market with rewards	34	(4.6)	86	(11.6)
Cluster 3: Bureaucratic ILM	125	(16.9)	110	(14.8)
Cluster 4: Spot market	8	(1.1)	49	(6.6)
Residual firms	13	(1.8)	43	(5.8)

Notes: Numbers in parentheses are percentages. HRM = human resource management. ILM = internal labor market.

Table 1.3   Explained variance by HRM components

Component	Fraction of variance explained	Cumulative explained variance
1	0.255	0.255
2	0.172	0.428
3	0.135	0.562
4	0.108	0.671
5	0.091	0.761
6	0.077	0.838
7	0.061	0.900
8	0.056	0.956
9	0.044	1.000

Notes: Variance explained by relative weights of each factor's eigenvalues from a principal. HRM = human resource management.

1.4.2 HRM Principal Components Analysis

Because firms adopt discrete bundles of HRM variables, we anticipate a high degree of multicollinearity across the nine underlying HRM variables. In order to avoid overfitting our regression models, we implement a principal components regression framework.

First, we construct the principal components of the underlying HRM variables using eigenvectors of the correlation matrix as coefficients.[7] Each component is a linear combination of the underlying variables, and we retain the combinations that capture the most variance in the underlying data and then rotate the axes to facilitate interpretation of the components. In table 1.3, we present a summary of the variance explained by the nine HRM components. The values in the table represent a proportion of the eigenvalue from each principal component. We find that there is a lead HRM component with several secondary components of lesser importance. For the subsequent analysis, we focus on the first six components, which explain 84 percent of the variance for the set of HRM variables.

Table 1.4 reports the HRM component patterns for high-education workers.[8] The first component, which we label "ports of entry," corresponds to a high level of initial earnings relative to market and a high standard deviation in initial earnings. This is the lead component and indicates

7. These principal components are then ordered by variance, and the largest components are retained and then rotated to ease interpretation. Detailed descriptions of the technique are given in, for example, Sen and Srivastava (1990, 253–55) or Draper and Smith (1981, 327–32). While this technique has found use in some of the applied statistics literature, the technique has been shown to produce poor results in certain data sets (e.g., refer to Hadi and Ling [1998] for illustrations.)

8. The first six components from the principal components analysis were orthogonally transformed through a varimax rotation. Subject to a threshold test of .50 for significance, each human resources (HR) variable has a significant loading in exactly one component.

Table 1.4   **HRM component patterns for high-education workers**

Variable	Component 1: Ports of entry	Component 2: Turnover rate	Component 3: Wage growth	Component 4: Hiring rate	Component 5: Performance incentives	Component 6: Early matching
Accession rate	0.05	0.20	0.05	**0.94**	0.01	0.01
Ratio of mean initial wage to market initial wage	**0.89**	0.13	0.02	0.02	−0.01	0.05
SD of initial earnings	**0.82**	0.05	0.04	0.07	0.23	−0.02
Separation rate at 2 years tenure	0.01	**0.90**	−0.01	0.00	0.11	−0.08
Within-job wage growth at 2 years tenure	−0.07	0.02	**0.93**	−0.09	0.02	0.01
SD of within-job wage growth at 2 years tenure	0.03	−0.07	0.01	0.01	0.06	**0.99**
Separation rate at 5 years tenure	0.22	**0.77**	−0.01	0.31	−0.08	0.00
Within-job wage growth at 5 years tenure	0.23	−0.06	**0.66**	0.35	0.28	0.00
SD of within-job wage growth at 5 years tenure	0.16	0.05	0.14	0.01	**0.95**	0.06

Notes: Component pattern matrix from the top six components of a principle components analysis with varimax rotation. Weights ≥ .50 are in boldface. SD = standard deviation. HRM = human resource management.

how many ports of entry are used by the firm, as opposed to hiring at an entry level and promoting from within. A high value on this component describes firms that hire workers at many different levels of experience and skill, which increases the level and variance in initial earnings. The second component, labeled "turnover rate," reflects a high separation rate after two and after five years of tenure. The third component, labeled "wage growth" reflects high levels of within-job wage growth after both two and five years of tenure. The fourth component, "hiring rate," reflects the overall hiring rate in 1997. The fifth component, "performance incentives," reflects a large variance in within-job earnings growth after five years tenure, which indicates that by this point the firm has selected certain workers for career development and advancement. The sixth component, "early matching," reflects a large variance in within-job earnings growth after two years tenure, which indicates that new hires are already selected for specific job tracks and career development.

In table 1.5, to check the correspondence between the components and the underlying variables, we present the means of each component for the HRM clusters from the previous section. The ILM systems (Clusters 1 and 3) have negative averages for ports of entry (with bureaucratic much lower than performance-based). Spot-market systems (Cluster 2 and 4) have positive means for turnover and for early matching. Overall, the component scores are consistent with our labeling of the clusters.

We further summarize the components by presenting component means by R&D level. Table 1.6 demonstrates that relative to low R&D firms, high R&D firms exhibit higher values for ports of entry, turnover, wage growth, hiring rate, early matching, and a lower rate for performance incentives. These differences are consistent with the suggestion that high R&D firms are more likely to implement more market-oriented HRM systems, and low R&D firms are more likely to implement HRM systems with more long-term performance incentives.

1.4.3   Worker Productivity Regressions

Next, we map the HRM variables for each firm to continuous variables corresponding to the components identified in the preceding and consider the impact of these HRM components on firm performance. Specifically, we regress productivity on the principal HRM components both with and without interaction with R&D spending. We measure firm performance as log worker productivity and control for log of physical capital (in order to capture capital intensity) and product market at the four-digit SIC (in order to capture product lifespan differences). We estimate two specifications: one specification with no R&D interactions and a second specification where R&D categories (high, low) are interacted with the HRM components. We employ principal components as regressors instead of the underlying HRM variables because of multicollinearity concerns and to

Table 1.5   Component means for high education HRM clusters

	Cluster 1: Performance-based ILM	Cluster 2: Spot market with rewards	Cluster 3: Bureaucratic ILM	Cluster 4: Spot market	Residual firms
Component 1: Ports of entry	-0.088	0.288	-0.606	0.570	1.206
Component 2: Turnover rate	-0.084	0.178	-0.103	0.249	0.216
Component 3: Wage growth	-0.081	0.036	0.059	-0.069	0.062
Component 4: Hiring rate	0.031	-0.143	-0.061	-0.265	0.056
Component 5: Performance incentives	-0.070	-0.016	0.014	-0.212	-0.261
Component 6: Early matching	-0.071	0.052	-0.131	0.381	0.058
N	273	120	235	57	56

Notes: See text for definition of clusters and factors. HRM = human resource management. ILM = internal labor market.

Table 1.6   **High-education HRM component means by firm R&D level**

	Low R&D firms	High R&D firms
Component 1: Ports of entry	−0.283	0.121
Component 2: Turnover rate	−0.023	0.016
Component 3: Wage growth	−0.100	0.058
Component 4: Hiring rate	−0.143	0.017
Component 5: Performance incentives	0.058	−0.141
Component 6: Early matching	−0.058	−0.004
N	300	441

Notes: See text for definition of components. HRM = human resource management.

address latent variable issues. As a robustness check, we also present results using a continuous measure of R&D in place of the dichotomous R&D measure.

We observe that several HRM components are related to worker productivity (see table 1.7). Specifically, firms with high levels of R&D investment are likely to benefit from HRM systems with multiple ports of entry, performance incentives, and lower turnover, while firms with low R&D are likely to benefit from HRM systems without early matching.

Firms with multiple ports of entry, which facilitate the hiring of workers with required skills, have higher labor productivity. This effect is more important (and significant) in the high R&D firms, which supports Hypothesis 1. Performance-based pay appears to be more important in high R&D firms than in low R&D firms. Firms with higher separation (turnover) rates appear to have lower firm performance, although this is significant only for high R&D firms. The effect of turnover rate on worker productivity appears to be significant only for high R&D firms, which does not support Hypothesis 2. Because these statistical relationships do not control for firms growing or shrinking, separation rates and hiring rates may reflect poor performing firms losing workers and high performing firms adding workers. Firms with early matching or sorting of workers appear to have lower worker productivity, although this is significant only for low R&D firms.

In tables 1.8 and 1.9, we examine the robustness of our results to changes in the construction of the R&D measure. Instead of the dichotomous measure used in the previous analysis, we examine if the results are robust to use of a continuous measure of R&D intensity. In table 1.8 we reestimate the model in table 1.7 where firm performance is a function of capital-labor ratio, continuous R&D, and HRM components. In the first specification, we have no R&D-HRM interactions; in the second specification, we interact HRM practices with the continuous R&D measure. In specification 1, we find very similar results to the model estimated with dichotomous

Table 1.7 High-education HRM components on firm performance

	Col. (1)	Col. (2)
Intercept	2.3187***	2.2247***
	(0.2491)	(0.2532)
ln(K/L)	0.3004***	0.3022***
	(0.0306)	(0.0306)
C1: Ports of entry	0.0837***	
	(0.0272)	
C1 × low R&D		0.0577*
		(0.0323)
C1 × high R&D		0.1397**
		(0.0500)
C2: Turnover rate	−0.0564**	
	(0.0264)	
C2 × low R&D		−0.0132
		(0.0413)
C2 × high R&D		−0.0829**
		(0.0346)
C3: Wage growth	0.0137	
	(0.0251)	
C3 × low R&D		0.0014
		(0.0352)
C3 × high R&D		0.0307
		(0.0359)
C4: Hiring rate	0.0389	
	(0.0262)	
C4 × low R&D		0.0842
		(0.0540)
C4 × high R&D		0.0326
		(0.0297)
C5: Performance incentives	0.0284	
	(0.0252)	
C5 × low R&D		0.0124
		(0.0406)
C5 × high R&D		0.0614*
		(0.0339)
C6: Early matching	−0.0146	
	(0.0246)	
C6 × low R&D		−0.0709**
		(0.0355)
C6 × high R&D		0.0450
		(0.0351)
R^2	0.66	0.66
N	760	760

Notes: Dependent variable is log worker productivity. Both specifications include controls for four-digit SIC. Standard errors in parentheses. HRM = human resource management.

*Denotes significance at the 10 percent level.

**Denotes significance at the 5 percent level.

***Denotes significance at the 1 percent level.

Table 1.8   High-education HRM components and continuous R&D on firm performance

	Col. (1)	Col. (2)
Intercept	2.3631***	2.2492***
	(0.2506)	(0.2580)
ln(K/L)	0.2979***	0.2966***
	(0.0306)	(0.0308)
R&D (continuous)	0.0332	0.0297
	(0.0219)	(0.0225)
C1	0.0794***	0.1664***
	(0.0273)	(0.076)
C1 × R&D		0.0291
		(0.0246)
C2	−0.0558***	−0.0543
	(0.0264)	(0.076)
C2 × R&D		−0.0004
		(0.0208)
C3	0.0111	0.0541
	(0.0252)	(0.057)
C3 × R&D		0.0193
		(0.0210)
C4	0.0358	0.0176
	(0.0262)	(0.044)
C4 × R&D		−0.0108
		(0.0199)
C5	0.0337	0.1021**
	(0.0254)	(0.052)
C5 × R&D		0.0277
		(0.0193)
C6	−0.0149	0.0478
	(0.0246)	(0.048)
C6 × R&D		0.0236
		(0.0141)
R^2	0.66	0.66
N	760	760

Note: See table 1.7 notes.
*Denotes significance at the 10 percent level.
**Denotes significance at the 5 percent level.
***Denotes significance at the 1 percent level.

R&D. However, when we examine the interactions in specification 2, we find differences between the continuous and dichotomous models. In the continuous R&D model, the turnover HRM practice (Component 2) is no longer significant, but the performance incentive practice (Component 5) is significant.

The differences in the interaction terms in the continuous and dichotomous models suggest that the relationship between R&D intensity and

Table 1.9   **High-education HRM components and R&D interactions on firm performance**

	Col. (1)
Intercept	2.2936***
	(0.2643)
ln(K/L)	0.3003***
	(0.0306)
R&D (continuous) × low	0.0357
	(0.0247)
R&D (continuous) × high	0.0448
	(0.0467)
C1 × low R&D	0.0552*
	(0.0324)
C1 × high R&D	0.1247**
	(0.0524)
C2 × low R&D	−0.0125
	(0.0413)
C2 × high R&D	−0.0823***
	(0.0346)
C3 × low R&D	−0.0025
	(0.0353)
C3 × high R&D	0.0293
	(0.0360)
C4 × low R&D	0.0882
	(0.0541)
C4 × high R&D	0.0254
	(0.0303)
C5 × low R&D	0.0206
	(0.0411)
C5 × high R&D	0.0611*
	(0.0343)
C6 × low R&D	−0.0716***
	(0.0356)
C6 × high R&D	0.0459
	(0.0351)
R^2	0.66
N	760

Note: See table 1.7 notes.
*Denotes significance at the 10 percent level.
**Denotes significance at the 5 percent level.
***Denotes significance at the 1 percent level.

HRM practices are not linear. In table 1.9, we estimate a model where we control for continuous R&D, but interact the HRM components with the dichotomous R&D indicator. We find highly similar results to the dichotomous interactions presented in table 1.7. Taken together, the two models suggest that the largest effect attributable to the interactions between R&D and HRM components occurs at the high-end of the R&D scale.

Overall, the regression results provide some preliminary evidence for Hypothesis 1 and mixed support for Hypothesis 2. The analysis suggests that high R&D firms benefit from HRM systems that offer multiple ports of entry, low turnover, and performance incentives, while low R&D firms benefit from HRM systems that offer multiple ports of entry and low wage variance for recent hires. The empirical results for high R&D firms are consistent with Hypothesis 1 because firms have higher productivity if they implement systems that allow hiring at many ports of entry and have tools to retain and retrain key workers. The empirical results on low R&D firms provide mixed support for Hypothesis 2. We do find that low turnover is correlated with firm performance; however, we did not hypothesize that ports of entry would play a substantial role in determining firm performance, and we do not find performance-based pay to have as large an impact as hypothesized. Although the flexibility in hiring at multiple ports of entry does not go with our strict rendition of ILM systems, this result is consistent with other empirical analyses that have found multiple ports of entry in ILMs (Baker, Gibbs, and Holmstrom 1994; Lazear and Oyer 2004).

1.5   Discussion

This chapter presents evidence of the relationship between firms' technology investment decisions, HRM practices, and productivity. We find that in the high-tech electronics industry, there is a positive correlation between performance and buying new skills (i.e., hiring at many ports of entry) for both high and low R&D firms, but the relationship is considerably stronger for high R&D firms. Interestingly, high R&D firms benefit from lower turnover and from having earnings that reward performance over a five-year period, which indicates that firms need to keep their technical workers, and the skills they have, for one project generation and into the next generation. Low R&D firms benefit from treating their workers comparably once they are hired, which indicates a positive correlation between performance and making new skills over time. In other words, high R&D firms appear to be more productive if they implement performance-based ILM systems, while low R&D firms appear to be more productive if they implement a modified bureaucratic ILM system that allows hiring at multiple ports of entry with comparable treatment once hired.

A key underlying assumption of our research method is that we can infer HRM practices statistically from administrative data. Although it would be interesting to compare our inferred HRM practices to company descriptions or employee perceptions of HRM systems in place, the data do not allow this. Fieldwork observations indicate that actual practices and company-described HRM policies are often divergent (Pfeffer and Sutton 1999). Our inferred practices are consistent with our previous research on the semiconductor industry, where we directly observed HRM practices through field work. Using extensive data collected from in-depth site visits, Brown and Campbell (2001) demonstrate that more-advanced semiconductor fabrication plants pay higher initial wages and have shorter career paths than less-advanced plants. These results from the field work data are similar to the results in this administrative data-based project. The similarity provides evidence that inferring HRM practices from administrative data is a sound practice.

A strength of this research is the richness of the data set utilized combined with interpretation through the lens of detailed industry knowledge. There is very little research that ties observed firm-level HRM systems to performance outcomes: the LEHD data allows us to analyze HRM systems and outcomes within firms for a large sample of firms, and the detailed industry knowledge allows us to understand the important issues and the context of the results. While the LEHD data provide ample sample sizes and longitudinal variation, the lack of direct measures of workers' skills or occupation and of technological change constrains the statistical estimation and limits our interpretation of the results.

Although these results must be interpreted with care, they have potential implications for understanding the mechanisms that tie together technological change and workers' outcomes. Because technological change impacts workers at the plant level, knowledge of how HRM systems interact with technological investment to drive productivity at the plant level will inform our understanding of how labor markets work in technologically dynamic industries.

References

Abowd, John, John Haltiwanger, and Julia Lane. 2004. Integrated Longitudinal Employer-Employee Data for the United States. LEHD Program Technical Paper no. TP-2004-02. Washington, DC: Longitudinal Employer-Household Dynamics Program, U.S. Census Bureau.

Allen, Steven G. Technology and the wage structure. 1997. NBER Working Paper no. 5534. Cambridge, MA: National Bureau of Economic Research.

Art, D., Ramanathan Gnanadesikan, and Jon Kettenring. 1982. Data-based metrics for cluster analysis. *Utilitas Mathematica* 21A: 75–99.

Autor, David, Frank Levy, and Richard Murnane. 2002. Upstairs, downstairs: Computers and skills on two floors of a large bank. *Industrial and Labor Relations Review* 55 (3): 432–47.

Baker, George, Michael Gibbs, and Bengt Holmstrom. 1994. The internal economics of the firm: Evidence from personnel data. *Quarterly Journal of Economics* 109 (4): 881–919.

Barley, Stephen R., and Julian E. Orr, eds. 1997. *Between craft and science: Technical work in U.S. settings.* Ithaca, NY: Cornell University Press.

Berman, Eli, John Bound, and Zvi Griliches. 1994. Changes in the demand for skilled labor within U.S. manufacturing industries: Evidence from the Annual Survey of Manufacturing. *Quarterly Journal of Economics* 109 (2): 367–97.

Bound, John, and George Johnson. 1992. Changes in the structure of wages in the 1980's: An evaluation of alternative explanations. *American Economic Review* 82:371–92.

Bresnahan, Timothy, Erik Brynjolfsson, and Lorin Hitt. Information technology, workplace organization and the demand for skilled labor: Firm-level evidence. *Quarterly Journal of Economics* 117:339–76.

Brown, Clair, and Benjamin Campbell. 2001. Technical change, wages, and employment in semiconductor manufacturing. *Industrial and Labor Relations Review* 54 (2A): 450–65.

———. 2002. The impact of technological change on work and wages. *Industrial Relations* 41 (1): 1–33.

Brown, Clair, John Haltiwanger, and Julia Lane. 2006. *Economic Turbulence: Is a Volatile Economy Good for America?* Chicago: University of Chicago Press.

Brown, Clair, Yoshifumi Nakata, Michael Reich, and Lloyd Ulman. 1997. *Work and pay in the United States and Japan.* New York: Oxford University Press.

Cappelli, Peter. 1996. Technology and skill requirements: Implications for establishment wage structures. *New England Economic Review* (May–June):139–53.

Caroli, Eve, and John Van Reenen. 2001. Skill-biased organizational change? Evidence from a panel of British and French establishments. *Quarterly Journal of Economics* 116 (4): 1449–92.

Cohen, Wesley, and Daniel A. Levinthal. 1989. Innovation and learning: The two faces of R&D. *Economic Journal* 99 (397): 569–96.

DiNardo, John, and Jorn-Steffen Pischke. 1997. The returns to computer use revisited: Have pencils changed the wage structure too? *Quarterly Journal of Economics* 112:291–303.

Doeringer, Peter, and Michael Piore. 1971. *Internal labor markets and manpower analysis.* Lexington, MA: Heath.

Draper, Norman Richard, and Harry Smith. 1981. *Applied regression analysis.* 2nd ed. New York: Wiley.

Entorf, Horst, and Francis Kramarz. 1998. The impact of new technologies on wages and skills: Lessons from matching data on employees and on their firms. *Economics of Innovation and New Technology* 5 (2–4): 165–97.

Hadi, Ali S., and Robert F. Ling. 1998. Some cautionary notes on the use of principal components regression. *The American Statistician* 52 (1): 15–19.

Haltiwanger, John, Julia Lane, and James Spletzer. 2000. Wages, productivity, and the dynamic interaction of businesses and workers. NBER Working Paper no. 7994. Cambridge, MA: National Bureau of Economic Research.

Handel, Michael J. 1999. Computers and the wage structure. Working Paper no. 285. Annadale-on-Hudson, NY: Levy Economics Institute.

Hunter, Larry W., and John J. Lafkas. 2003. Opening the box. Information technology, work practices, and wages. *Industrial and Labor Relations Review* 56 (2): 224–42.

Juhn, Chinhui, Kevin M. Murphy, and Brooks Pierce. 1993. Wage inequality and the rise in returns to skill. *Journal of Political Economy* 101:410–42.

Kandel, E., and Edward Lazear. 1992. Peer pressure and partnerships. *Journal of Political Economy* 100 (4): 801–17.

Katz, Lawrence F., and Kevin Murphy. 1992. Changes in relative wages, 1963–1987: Supply and demand factors. *Quarterly Journal of Economics* 107:36–78.

Krueger, Alan. 1993. How computers have changed the wage structure: Evidence from microdata 1984–1989. *Quarterly Journal of Economics* 108:33–60.

Lazear, Edward P., and Paul Oyer. 2004. Internal and external labor markets: A personnel economics approach. *Labour Economics* 11:527–54.

Levy, Frank, and Richard Murnane. 1992. U.S. earnings levels and earnings inequality: A review of recent trends and proposed explanations. *Journal of Economic Literature* 30:1333–81.

Milgrom, Paul, and John Roberts. 1995. Complementarities and fit: Strategy, structure and organizational change in manufacturing. *Journal of Accounting and Economics* 19:179–208.

O'Shaughnessy, Kevin, David I. Levine, and Peter Cappelli. 2001. Changes in managerial pay structure 1986–1992. *Oxford Economic Papers* 3:482–507.

Pfeffer, Jeffrey, and Robert I. Sutton. 1999. Knowing "what" to do is not enough. *California Management Review* 42:83–108.

Prendergast, Canice. 1996. What happens within firms? A survey of empirical evidence on compensation policies. NBER Working Paper no. 5802. Cambridge, MA: National Bureau of Economic Research.

Sen, Ashish, and Muni Srivastava. 1990. *Regression analysis: Theory, methods, and applications.* New York: Springer-Verlag.

Sturgeon, Timothy J., Frank Levy, Clair Brown, J. Bradford Jensen, and David Weil. 2006. *Services Offshoring Working Group final report.* Cambridge, MA: MIT Industrial Performance Center, September.

Topel, Robert H., and Michael P. Ward. 1992. Job mobility and the careers of young men. *Quarterly Journal of Economics* 107 (2): 439–79.

Ward, J. H. Jr. 1963. Hierarchical grouping to optimize and objective function. *Journal of the American Statistical Association* 58:236–44.

Zuboff, Shoshana. 1988. *In the age of the smart machine: The future of work and power.* New York: Basic Books.

Using Behavioral Economic Field Experiments at a Firm
The Context and Design of the Truckers and Turnover Project

Stephen V. Burks, Jeffrey Carpenter, Lorenz Götte,
Kristen Monaco, Kay Porter, and Aldo Rustichini

2.1 Introduction

The Truckers and Turnover Project is a statistical case study of a single large trucking firm and its driver employees. The cooperating firm operates in the largest segment of the for-hire trucking industry in the United States, the "full truckload" (TL) segment, in which approximately 800,000 people

Stephen V. Burks is an associate professor of economics and management at the University of Minnesota, Morris. Jeffrey Carpenter is an associate professor of economics at Middlebury College. Lorenz Götte is a senior economist in the Research Center for Behavioral Economics and Decisionmaking at the Federal Reserve Bank of Boston. Kristen Monaco is a professor of economics at California State University, Long Beach. Kay Porter is a business research manager at the cooperating firm. Aldo Rustichini is a professor of economics at the University of Minnesota.

Earlier versions of this paper have been issued as NBER Working Paper no. 12976 (March 2007), IZA Discussion Paper no. 2789 (May 2007), and, also, under a different title—"Adding Behavioral Economics Field Experiments to the Industry Studies Toolkit: Predicting Truck Driver Job Exits in a High Turnover Setting"—as a Sloan Industry Studies Working Paper (2007). This paper was presented at the Sloan Industry Studies Annual Research Conference, held in Boston, MA, April 25 to 27, 2007, and the authors gratefully acknowledge the support of the Alfred P. Sloan Foundation for the conference. It was also presented at the Conference on the Analysis of Firms and Employees (CAFE), held September 29 to 30, 2006, in Nuremberg, Germany, and the authors gratefully acknowledge the financial support provided to the Conference by the Institute for Employment Research (IAB), the Data Access Center (FDZ-BA/IAB), the Deutsche Forschungsgemeinschaft (German Research Foundation), their research network "Flexibility in Heterogeneous Labour Markets," the Alfred P. Sloan Foundation, and the National Science Foundation. The authors gratefully acknowledge generous financial support for the Truckers and Turnover Project research from the John D. and Catherine T. MacArthur Foundation's Research Network on the Nature and Origin of Preferences; the Alfred P. Sloan Foundation; the Trucking Industry Program at the Georgia Institute of Technology (one of the industry studies programs initiated by the Sloan Foundation); the University of Minnesota, Morris; the Federal Reserve Bank of Boston; and from the cooperating motor carrier. We also especially thank the managers and employees of the cooperating carrier, whose involvement and active support made the project possible. The de-are employed, according to the 2002 Economic Census. The TL segment has a high turnover labor market for its main employee group, tractor-trailer drivers, and the project is designed to address a number of academic and business questions that arise in this setting.

One major part of the project matches proprietary personnel and operational data to new data collected by the researchers to create a two-year panel study of a large subset of new hires. The most distinctive innovation of this project component is the data collection process, which combines traditional survey instruments with behavioral economics experiments. The survey data include information on demographics, risk and loss aversion, time preference, planning, nonverbal IQ, and the MPQ personality profile. The data collected by behavioral economics experiments include risk and loss aversion, time preferences (discount rates), backward induction, patience, and the preference for cooperation in a social dilemma setting. Subjects will be followed over two years of their work lives. Among the major design goals are to discover the extent to which the survey and experimental measures are correlated, and whether and how much predictive power, with respect to key on-the-job outcome variables, is added by the behavioral measures.

The panel study of new hires is being carried out against the backdrop of a second research component, the development of a more conventional in-depth statistical case study of the cooperating firm and its employees. This component involves constructing large historical data sets from fragmented legacy IT sources and using them to create multivariate models of turnover and productivity. Two main emphases are on the use of survival analysis to model the flow of new employees into and out of employment, and on the correct estimation of the tenure-productivity curve for new hires, accounting for the selection effects of the high turnover.

The project is designed to last three and a half years, with the first half-year for set up, and then a year for the initial intensive data collection in the panel study of new hires, in parallel with the construction of the data sets for the statistical case study and the initial generation of modeling from these data. Then there will be two years of lower-intensity work while follow-up data is collected from the participants in the panel study of new hires.

The balance of the chapter is structured as follows. Section 2.2 sets the context by describing the U.S. trucking industry and the role of the TL seg-

signers of the field experiments used in the project thank Catherine Eckel and Kate Johnson for sharing protocol and design details from field experimental work in Mexico and for offering helpful advice on our design issues. We also thank Urs Fischbacher, the developer of the z-Tree software used in the economic experiments, for rushing development of a new version with features we needed. The views expressed herein are those of the authors, and not of the Federal Reserve System, nor the Federal Reserve Bank of Boston, nor of any of the employers of any of the authors, nor of the project sponsors.

ment within it. Section 2.3 discusses the nature of the labor market for TL drivers and why it has had a high turnover equilibrium for about twenty-five years. Section 2.4 discusses the nature of the research relationship with the cooperating firm and how it was constructed. Section 2.5 discusses the statistical analysis of historical operational and human resource data from the firm. It has two main subparts: Section 2.5.1 exhibits preliminary findings on turnover, and section 2.5.2 does the same for productivity. Section 2.6 describes the design of the panel study of new hires and has four main subparts. Section 2.6.1 describes the context of the project's use of behavioral economic field experiments. Section 2.6.2 covers the process by which new students are trained as tractor-trailer drivers, and section 2.6.3 discusses the schedule for the data collection effort at the training school. Section 2.6.4 lists and describes the five data collection activities (three experiments and two survey-type instruments) that take place during the first two-hour session of each data collection event, while section 2.6.5 does the same for the six activities (three experiments and three survey-type instruments) during the second two-hour section of each data collection event. Section 2.7 reflects on the implications of the project for the relevant research communities and public policy. Appendix A lists the project team during the first two project years, and appendix B provides a list and time line for the main data elements being collected by the project.

2.2   The U.S. Trucking Industry

2.2.1   Segments within the Industry

To a casual observer, one truck looks much like another, but in fact, the operations that provide trucking services in the United States are meaningfully differentiated from each other on several dimensions. At the broadest level, trucking operations are broken into private carriage versus for-hire carriage, based on a legal relationship: whether the carrier also owns the freight (private carriage) or is hauling it for another party (for-hire carriage).[1] In recent years, for-hire carriers, one of which is the focus of the present study, have typically operated about one-third of the heavy trucks in the overall U.S. fleet, but about three-fifths of the total miles run by such vehicles (Burks, Monaco, and Myers-Kuykindall 2004a).[2]

For-hire trucking is itself further broken into a number of distinct seg-

1. Private carriers are firms primarily in nontrucking lines of business who provide trucking services internally as support functions to their primary business operations. Examples might be deliveries of food by a retail grocery chain to its stores in trucks it also owns or pickups of parts for assembly at an auto plant by the auto manufacturer's freight vehicles.
2. Heavy freight vehicles are defined here as having a gross vehicle weight (GVW) of more than 26,000 pounds, the level at which weight alone is sufficient to require the driver to hold a commercial driver's license (CDL).

ments, separated along three cross-cutting dimensions. Within each segment, interfirm competition is significant, but across segments it may be muted, or in some cases even absent. The 2002 quinquennial Economic Census, because of its use of the relatively new North American Industrial Classification System (NAICS), which is based on production process characteristics, gives a good overview of the structure of the for-hire trucking industry at this level of segmentation. For-hire truck transportation as a whole, NAICS category 484, generated $165.56 billion in revenue in 2002, or about 1.56 percent of that year's gross domestic product (GDP).[3]

The first broad scale distinction within for-hire trucking is between firms that use general purpose equipment (i.e., standard enclosed van trailers) to handle general commodities and those that use specialized equipment to handle special commodities (examples of the latter would be refrigerated vans, flatbeds, tank trailers, and various other types of specialized equipment). According to the Economic Census, in 2002, general freight operations generated $111.60 billion annual revenue (67.4 percent of the total), and specialized freight had $54.01 billion annual revenue (32.6 percent of the total). A second cross-cutting broad scale distinction is between firms that make long distance intercity hauls and those that specialize in operations in and around a particular metropolitan area. In 2002, the Economic Census reports $120.21 billion in annual revenue for long-distance trucking (72.6 percent of the total) and $45.35 billion for local hauls (27.4 percent).

A third cross-cutting broad scale distinction is based on the size of the typical shipment hauled, and this dimension on which firms differ is of particular relevance to the present study. It is easiest to understand this distinction by considering full-truckload service in contrast to the other two, less-than-truckload (LTL) and parcel service. At one end of the spectrum are firms like the one providing data for the current study. The archetypal TL carrier sends a driver with a tractor-trailer to a shipper's dock to fill up the trailer with a load, typically weighing from 10,000 to 48,000 pounds.[4] The driver takes the loaded trailer wherever in the United States the shipment is destined and unloads at the consignee's dock. The driver is then dispatched empty, possibly after waiting for a while, to the next location where a full load is available for pick up. Full-truckload carriers may use specialized equipment for special commodities, but if they haul general commodities, they use general purpose equipment to maximize the chance of backhauls.[5]

By contrast, both parcel and LTL firms aggregate large numbers of in-

---

3. Calculation is by the authors; total GDP is from the U.S. Department of Commerce, Bureau of Economic Analysis: http://www.bea.gov/.

4. The variation is because some less-dense freight exhausts a trailer's volume at low weight levels, while higher-density freight hits the weight limit before the volume limit.

5. That is, this is to maximize the chance of picking up a return load from near the point at which a first one is delivered.

dividual shipments collected at local terminals by local drivers into full trailer loads and move them between terminals on fixed route systems. Parcel carriers handle very small shipments (each piece typically being no larger than 150 pounds, with the average nearer to 50 pounds), and LTL carriers aggregate medium-sized shipments (widely varying, but with average size around 1,000 pounds). The Economic Census does not group parcel service firms with the for-hire trucking industry, but with air freight carriers. However, it does capture LTL and TL firms within trucking. In 2002, the TL segment dominated the general freight portion of (nonparcel) for-hire trucking, with 67.9 percent of the total employment and 83.8 percent of the total revenue. If the segments of specialized freight that are primarily TL by shipment size are added to the mix,[6] then TL's share of the total employment of 1.137 million jumps to 72.8 percent, and its share of the total revenue of $124.50 billion rises to 77.1 percent.

2.2.2   Differences in the Type of Competition within Segments

The differences across the segments in the operational routines needed affect the form and intensity of competition within each segment. Specifically, in the parcel and LTL segments, the need for a fixed network of freight rehandling terminals creates an entry barrier.[7] While competition among parcel and LTL carriers is frequently strong, it generally takes place among incumbents. This is evidenced by the numbers of firms in the long-distance parcel and LTL segments. In parcel, there are really only four firms with full national coverage (UPS, FedEx, DHL, and the USPS).[8] There are more LTL firms, but the number is still small. The 2002 Economic Census identifies eighty-nine long-distance general freight LTL firms with five or more establishments, which is the minimum number of terminals needed to give significant geographic scope; there are only fifty-seven firms with ten or more.

But in TL there are essentially no entry barriers. Because TL carriers do not normally rehandle freight once it is loaded, they do not typically require terminals, nor regular route patterns, for cost-competitive operations. So a one-truck carrier can cover the entire nation, and in doing so is competitive, on a load-by-load basis, with most of the services offered by

6. Essentially, this means adding all specialized freight except household goods moving.

7. A brand new LTL carrier that wants to serve more than a single metropolitan area must create and operate a network that is of minimum size necessary to attract sufficient traffic from shippers with differing destination demands, relative to the total shipment flow densities in the geographic area it wishes to serve. But such networks exhibit strong economies of density (a combination of both scale and scope economies)—at low volumes, the average costs are high, but they fall rapidly as volume increases. The expenses of running such a network until a large enough market share is obtained to make the new network cost competitive with those of incumbent carriers are nonrecoverable (or "sunk") if the firm exits. And the existence of a sunk cost of entry is the classic definition of an entry barrier.

8. Local parcel service is easier to enter, and there are many firms of small geographic scope.

one of the TL-segment's giants. When more complex service coordination is the key factor in market penetration, small firms can subcontract to third-party logistics providers.[9] And in fact, there is a continual flow into, and out of, the TL segment, mostly by firms operating at small to medium scales. In TL, the 2002 Economic Census identified 25,831 long-distance general freight firms.[10] The market concentration levels in these two segments also show the differing nature of competition. In LTL, the 2002 Economic Census puts the revenue share of the top four long-distance general freight LTL firms at 36.3 percent, while it calculates the share of the top four long-distance general freight TL firms to be only 14.7 percent.

The implication of these facts is that most of TL service is what business analysts call a "commodity business" and what economists call "perfectly competitive." As a result, the firms "at the margin," whose choices set prices for the whole market, in TL are often not the big players, exploiting economics of scale, but may instead be the small firms in the competitive fringe of the industry segment. Their pricing is, in turn, driven significantly by the wages drivers in such firms are willing to accept. Small firms generally face more modest wage expectations from their employees than do large ones, and they also have the benefit of more personal relationships between owners, managers, and drivers. And owner-operators, who make up a significant subset of the small firms, can always choose to pay themselves less in order to get started in the business. Large firms can choose to pay a modest premium above the level set by such firms because they may have cost efficiencies in other areas, and they may be able to maintain a small price premium due to offering customers a number of different services in an integrated fashion, but if they raise their wages too high, they will make their costs uncompetitive. This industry structure sets the context for the derived demand for truck drivers in TL freight and the consequent nature of the labor market for TL drivers.

2.3 The Labor Market for TL Drivers

2.3.1 Segmented Labor Markets Emerge

The American Trucking Associations' (ATA) quarterly turnover report typically shows the average turnover rate at large TL motor carriers to be in excess of 100 percent per year (ATA Economic and Statistics Group 2005).[11] Driver turnover among these carriers is an economically signifi-

---

9. Because a TL carrier can subcontract actual movements in a spot market to owner-operators, it is possible for a firm to enter TL for-hire carriage initially with zero trucks.

10. Unlike the case of LTL, because TL firms don't have freight terminal networks, single establishment firms can be of national geographic scope, but, in fact, 997 of these had more than one establishment, which is still more firms than in the LTL segment.

11. The ATA is a federation of several separate trucking associations.

cant phenomenon—truckload carriers make up the largest segment of for-hire motor carriage by employment, with approximately 600,000 drivers working at any given time (U.S. Census Bureau 2004).[12] This segment of the universe of for-hire trucking firms emerged into its present form after the economic deregulation of 1980, which transformed the structure of the trucking industry. Before deregulation, the nature of the entry barriers created by government policies resulted in lots of TL output by firms using the LTL-type organization of production, with a fixed network of freight handling terminals (Belzer 1995; Burks 1999). But in the postderegulation period, carriers specialized quite strongly in one or another specific shipment size, from the smallest (parcel), through middle-sized shipments (LTL), to the largest ones (TL) (Corsi and Stowers 1991; Belzer 1995; Burks, Monaco, and Myers-Kuykindall 2004b).

As the TL industry segment emerged, so did a parallel segmentation of the labor market for truck drivers (Belzer 1995; Burks 1999).[13] Drivers wanting to enter employment at parcel and LTL carriers generally found job queues,[14] while the labor market for TL driving jobs began exhibiting high rates of turnover. In fact, the labor market in the TL segment has essentially been in a high turnover equilibrium since soon after the end of the recessions of 1981–1982.[15]

2.3.2   The TL Driver's Job

To understand this situation, we start with a short description of the human capital investment needed to become a driver and then discuss the working conditions encountered by the typical driver. Driving a tractor-trailer requires training for, and passing, the state-administered written and driving tests for a commercial driver's license (CDL). Typically a high school equivalent level of literacy is required, and training begins with at least two weeks mixed between classroom work and in-truck practice. This is usually followed by a few days to as much as a few weeks of initial driving experience, which is often obtained with an experienced driver riding in the cab as a coach, while the trainee is still driving on a "learner's permit," before he or she has taken the final test for the CDL. While the CDL test is administered separately by each state, as of 1991 they do so under

12. The calculation is this: in the 2002 Economic Census, TL firms have 72.8 percent of the total employment of 1.137 million workers in (nonparcel) trucking, and the usual rule of thumb is that about 75 percent of the labor force employed by a TL firm is made up of drivers, the balance being made up of sales, customer service, administrative, and managerial employees.

13. In fact, the argument of the second cited work is that the labor market segmentation was itself a significant driver of the parallel industry segmentation.

14. This was especially true at unionized carriers, but was also true to some degree at nonunion ones.

15. It is an indication of the institutionalization of the high turnover secondary labor market equilibrium in TL trucking that the ATA has published its turnover report continuously since 1996.

Federal standards for what must be included. It comprises both written and driving portions, and the minimum legal age at which it may be taken is twenty-one. Trucking firms generally considered a driver to be satisfactorily experienced after a year of work, so the level of human capital required places the job somewhere between unskilled and skilled, and it is best labeled as "semiskilled."

Once a driver is licensed, the key problem in retention is generally perceived to be the working conditions faced by a tractor-trailer operator in the archetypal long-haul, randomly dispatched, forty-eight-state service provided by most TL firms. In addition to the stresses of handling a big rig among swarms of cars, many drivers have very long weekly work hours on an irregular schedule. In one published survey of long-haul drivers, 21.9 percent reported working seventy plus hours each week, and two out of three drivers reported working sixty plus hour weeks (Stephenson and Fox 1996). Other surveys report similar findings (Belman and Monaco 2001). A survey of long-haul drivers in the Midwest found the median driver worked sixty-five hours, with 25 percent reporting eighty or more hours. In a twenty-four-hour period, the median hours worked was 11, median hours driving was 8.5, and median hours in nondriving work was 2 (Belman, Monaco, and Brooks 2005). These hours contrast to those in two industries in which there are occupations with similar human capital requirements, manufacturing and construction, which had average work weeks of 40.8 and 38.3 hours in 2004, respectively (Bureau of Labor Statistics 2002).

A related issue is that long-haul drivers are often away from home for multiple weeks at a time, with little predictability about the date of return. In the same survey previously mentioned, only 20.7 percent of TL drivers reported that they were home almost every day, while 28.7 percent of drivers in the same study reported being home less often than once every two weeks (Stephenson and Fox 1996). In the survey of drivers from the Midwest, the median long-haul driver had last been home four days prior to the interview, though one-quarter had been away from home ten days or longer (Belman, Monaco, and Brooks 2005). A less tangible issue is that both drivers and firms like to think of CDL holders as professionals, in command of a big rig and responsible for its safe operation. But trucking is a service business, and a primary job function of the driver is to make shippers and receivers happy. The implications vary by customer shipping or receiving location, but this can place drivers somewhat lower than they might expect on the supply chain status hierarchy.

Of course, not every driver in TL operations faces the same conditions. The foregoing description applies to those "running the system," or being randomly dispatched across the forty-eight U.S. states. Some TL operations are dedicated to the service of particular large customers, and drivers in these operations have a more restricted set of pickup and delivery locations; more regular schedules, on average; and generally enjoy more time at home, as well. And some TL operations move freight between cities via trailer-on-flat-car (TOFC) or container-on-flat-car (COFC) intermodal methods. Drivers in these operations usually have regional or local runs to and from intermodal facilities and are often home nightly, or nearly so.

Given these facts, a labor economist would expect to observe a "compensating differential" built into the wages of TL drivers that have the worst conditions. In other words, other things equal, TL firms should offer long-haul randomly dispatched drivers a higher earnings level than stay-at-home jobs requiring similar human capital to compensate for their poorer working conditions. But dissatisfaction over wage compensation levels is frequently cited as a leading reason for TL driver turnover (Cox 2004).

2.3.3   Buying "Effective Labor"

Perhaps a better way to think of the firm's decision problem, which captures the nature of the driver labor market and the TL driver's job, is to consider the nature of "effective labor" in this context. For a TL firm, this is the application of labor services to move trucks to and from geographically specific customer locations on the particular time schedule desired by the firm. There are three main factors that go into the cost of effective labor in this setting. One is the cost of recruiting and training new drivers to replace those who leave, to account for the lower productivity of inexperienced drivers, and also to account for any growth in business. A second is the cost of paying compensating differentials to drivers with the worst conditions to slow driver exits. The third is the operational cost of making driver working conditions better. In response to stochastic customer demands, the most efficient allocation of equipment frequently calls for irregular schedules and little time at the driver's home terminal. When this is the case, making schedules more regular and increasing the driver's time at home is costly.

The key point is that these three cost factors can, to a significant degree, be traded off against each other, with higher expenditure in one area lowering the expenditure in another. The firm's goal can then be construed in the standard manner: it is to find the cost-minimizing mix of these factors. Historically, the best thinking among many competing TL firms appears to be that spending more on recruiting and training is a cheaper way to get the needed units of effective labor than paying more to raise compensating wage differentials or improve schedules.[16]

A stable equilibrium characterized by high turnover rates defines what labor economists call a "secondary labor market" (Cain 1976; Dickens and

---

16. There is actually another cost factor in "effective labor" that is nonnegligible, the costs of accidents, which inexperienced drivers have at a higher rate than do experienced ones. We do not address that cost in this paper.

Lang 1993).[17] The persistence of the secondary labor market for drivers in TL trucking since sometime in the early 1980s has occasioned much discussion in the trucking industry trade press over the years, as well as a number of academic studies (examples include Casey 1987; Griffin, Rodriguez, and Lantz 1992; Stephenson and Fox 1996; Griffin and Kalnbach 2002; Beadle 2004). Through the ATA, the industry has commissioned significant analytic efforts to understand the management issues raised by a high turnover business model and the long-term demographic trends affecting the viability of the model (Gallup Organization 1997; ATA Economic and Statistics Group 2005). The major findings suggest that firms are aware of the trade-offs among the components of effective labor and that within this framework firms adjust to changes in the conditions of the demand for, and supply of, effective labor. It appears that as a result, the labor market as a whole also adjusts, perhaps with some lags, to such changes.

A major study done by consultants at Global Insight for the ATA links the supply of truck drivers to the supply of labor for semiskilled jobs in construction because this type of work often represents the next best opportunity for likely truckers. The labor demands in these two industries are driven by significantly different macroeconomic factors. During the 1990s, when the derived demand for drivers was high, there was a modest premium—truckers' earnings were an average of 6 to 7 percent above a position demanding similar levels of human capital in construction. The downturn of the economy in 2000 to 2001 created slack in the trucking labor market, but the arrival of low interest rates kept the derived demand in construction relatively stronger. As a result, for a few years, the average long-haul driver could expect to make less than if employed in the construction industry. By 2004, the gap had narrowed, with long haul drivers' earnings 1.5 percent below that of construction workers (Global Insight, Inc. 2005). These facts suggest that wage levels do adjust over time to changes in the balance of labor supply and labor demand, but the persistence of the high turnover numbers shows that the levels of compensating differential being offered are not sufficient to lower turnover to the levels typical in other blue-collar jobs.[18]

It is well documented that the flows into and out of industry (as well as related movements of dissatisfied drivers between firms) represent a substantial cost to firms. A study by the Upper Great Plains Transportation Institute found in 1998 that replacing one dry van TL driver conservatively costs $8,234, and the industrywide cost total was estimated at nearly $2.8 billion in 1998 dollars (Rodriguez et al. 2000). The study's authors sug-

---

17. Correspondingly, the ATA typically reports turnover rates at LTL firms to be in the 10 percent to 20 percent range, which makes them roughly equivalent in turnover to nontrucking jobs requiring similar amounts of human capital.

18. The Global Insight study used government data that does not distinguish TL from LTL among drivers for firms in long-distance trucking, but TL drivers make up the predominant share of the categories they analyze.

gested that this estimate is conservative, but it gives an idea of the magnitude of the turnover costs that TL firms must balance against the alternative costs of raising wages or adjusting operational and dispatching decisions in order to lower turnover.

One might well ask whether firms have fully explored the possibilities for trade-offs among the three factors behind the cost of effective TL labor. Most firms are operating with high turnover costs and relatively lower costs for compensating differentials and operational adjustments that improve driver lifestyles. Is it possible that some large discrete shift along the frontier could move a firm out of a "local cost minimum" in this region to a different local minimum that might be lower in total costs?

In fact, J.B. Hunt, then the second largest firm in the industry, engaged in a highly publicized experiment with switching from a business model with high turnover and modest wage costs to one with higher wage costs but lower turnover in 1996. It took the portion of its workforce facing the worst conditions (long and irregular dispatches) and raised wages by 35 percent, while at the same time closing down its driver training schools (Cullen 1996; Isidore 1997). The net result was a cut in both turnover and accident rates by approximately one-half (Belzer, Rodriguez, and Sedo 2002). However, the long-run net financial benefits were not as clear (Waxler 1997); most of the other large firms in the industry, including the one providing data for the present study, continue to train many of their new drivers from scratch, and nearly all TL firms use the high turnover–modest-pay-premium model.

The long-run dynamics of driver labor supply and demand are made more complex by the growth of the long-haul TL industry. Between 2004 and 2014, Global Insight projects it will grow at a rate of 2.2 percent, which translates into an additional 320,000 heavy-duty long-haul new jobs. This statistic does not include the number of drivers needed to replace those who will retire during this time; the industry will need to find an estimated 219,000 additional drivers to replace the one in five drivers who are fifty-five years old or older and are approaching retirement. Concurrently with an increase in demand for drivers, the growth rate of the overall U.S. labor force will slow from 1.4 percent to .5 percent between 2005 and 2014 (Global Insight, Inc. 2005). Another challenging trend for the industry is that to date, Hispanics, who comprise the fastest growing segment in the workforce, represent a lower percentage of drivers than they do of the overall labor supply. It is possible that the conjunction of these factors means that a secular trend toward higher prices for trucking labor has begun. This, in turn, could shift the nature of the trade-offs that firms face among the components of effective TL labor, and—along with fuel price trends and the limitations on the growth of labor productivity in trucking (Boyer and Burks 2007)—it could also dampen the long-run growth prospects of the industry (Reiskin 2006).

2.4   Working with the Cooperating Firm

The cooperating trucking firm is a large company of national geographic scope, with divisions that operate in several of the segments of TL trucking, including long-haul random dispatch service, dedicated carriage for large customers, and intermodal services. By revenue and employment it is among the top one hundred firms in TL. The firm began as a family-owned enterprise in the regulatory era, although it has grown through multiple acquisitions as well as internal expansions, and the original family has not been centrally involved in top management for some time.

Under family control, the management culture was stable and effective, but was also, by design, relatively inward looking. It was based on long-term employment relationships with managerial and administrative ranks filled with "trucking people," whose careers tended to be built within this single firm. A significant portion of the management started as front-line driver supervisors or, in some cases, as drivers and then worked their way up. Managers at the firm tended to learn their skills on the job and did not see much need to look elsewhere, except to service vendors who could provide expertise relevant to particular practical business problems, such as targeted marketing surveys.

During the period between deregulation and the end of the twentieth century, the firm made many major and critical strategic moves, some of which were quite daring. But the decisions leading to these moves were primarily based on the vision and judgment calls of the trucking people in top managerial positions. There was little thought of broad strategic planning in the formal sense. Early in the new millennium, a new CEO, who had significant formal training in management-related areas, directed the first exercise in formal strategic planning in the firm's history, following a process recipe provided by a major consultancy. This exercise began to increase the interest within the firm in planning as a useful activity and also increased interest in establishing the analytic foundations for planning work.

The University of Minnesota, Morris, faculty began to work with the firm starting in the fall of 2002, initially on a single pilot project in the form of faculty-guided analysis by an advanced undergraduate student. The project was successful and laid the foundation for an expanding series of faculty-guided research projects over the next two years on a variety of topics. These projects operated on a gift-exchange basis: the faculty and students contributed their time as teaching and learning functions and the firm paid out-of-pocket expenses and provided access (under appropriate confidentiality restrictions) to proprietary business data. The core of the process involved selecting topics of both business and academic interest and for which advanced undergraduates could provide analyses of business use, as well as generating course-level academic output. By the third year of such projects, about twenty students supervised by six different faculty members had done small projects on several continuing topics, from the analysis of exit interviews, to some initial turnover and productivity analyses, to work on the recruitment and retention of Hispanic employees.

Within the firm, the linchpin of the process was a senior executive who had joined the firm from the outside and who had significant prior experience working fruitfully with academics. He was promoted to responsibility for a number of the aspects of human resources and driver training and moved into his new role just as the firm as a whole was opening up internally to the importance of strategic analysis. From this initial contact, UMM came to work with several other executives, at similar or higher levels of authority and responsibility, on specific projects.

On the UMM side, the linchpin was an industry studies connection: the initial supervising faculty member (Burks) worked with the Sloan-funded Trucking Industry Program as a doctoral student and as a postdoctoral fellow.[19] This added academic depth and polish to trucking industry institutional knowledge he had originally begun acquiring in his youth, when he worked as a tractor-trailer driver during the era of deregulation, between two bouts in graduate school. Burks's background, along with a passion for all things trucking-related, gave him credibility with executives and allowed him to guide the UMM side of the relationship so that useful business deliverables always accompanied the academic results of interest to faculty and students.

On the basis of the relationship constructed through the student projects, Burks and a second UMM researcher, biostatistician Jon Anderson, developed a small project contractually sponsored by the firm for the summer of 2004. This project began exploring the historical data retained by the firm for strategic purposes, including the analysis of the determinants of driver productivity and turnover. The larger scale design of the Truckers and Turnover Project was developed from the starting point provided by the results of this project. Burks, who devoted a sabbatical year to the project, is the principal organizer, and he has been joined in creating and developing the substantive content of the project by the coauthors of the present chapter, as well as by a number of other colleagues, who are based at several other institutions.[20]

2.5   Research Component One: Statistical Case Study of Historical Data

Research Component One is a statistical case study of some of the historical personnel and operations data of the cooperating trucking firm. There are three interrelated parts to this component. The first is building

19. Burks was a doctoral student at the University of Massachusetts at Amherst; the Trucking Industry Program (TIP) was then located at the University of Michigan and is now hosted by the Georgia Institute of Technology.
20. A complete list of coinvestigators appears in appendix A.

the data sets needed for analysis, the second is analyzing turnover, and the third is analyzing driver productivity. The goal of the first part is to take the many different data and report outputs produced by the fragmented legacy information technology (IT) resources at the firm and construct from them data sets that permit useful strategic and tactical analyses. Because the firm's IT investments began in the early mainframe era, and those investments were focused primarily on solving succeeding generations of practical business problems, the data storage and reporting functions at the firm do not lend themselves easily to strategic use. Data set assembly, documentation, and validation are consuming, and will continue to consume, a very large part of the project's resources.

The goal of the second part is to use survival analysis to map the differences in turnover by driver group, to use hazard functions to explore the different time paths of exits by driver group, and to use Cox proportional hazard multivariate regression to analyze the interaction between the various factors that can affect exits. The goal of the third part is to use panel data multivariate regression models to map the tenure-productivity curve of new drivers as they gain experience, using a fixed effects variant to make a first-order adjustment for the impact of selection on the tenure-productivity relationship. Once the panel data model is sufficiently robust, the estimated fixed effects will then be further dissected statistically.

A key (proprietary) business deliverable from this part of the project will be the assembly of the results of the turnover and productivity models to create an "expected net value of human capital" model for the investment in recruiting and training various types of drivers, who are utilized in various types of operational settings at the firm. Central academic results are expected to be generated from both the turnover and productivity models. Additionally, the analysis of Research Component Two, the panel study of new hires, will be integrated with the results of the analyses from the statistical case study. We next briefly describe the challenges and sketch a few pilot findings from the turnover and productivity analyses.

2.5.1   Initial Work on Turnover

The proprietary human resource data set used for initial turnover analysis was constructed from three distinct initial data files, which share the feature that each record provides information on one driver during one calendar week. The constituent files covered different calendar periods, so we utilize the calendar window during which all three overlap, September 1, 2001, through March 31, 2005. The first file, Weekly Hires, consists of some of the data elements recorded about a driver during the week he or she is hired. Drivers who are rehired during the calendar window have more than one line in this file. The second file, Weekly Separations, contains information recorded about a driver during the week that he or she separates from the firm. Drivers who are rehired and who, as a result, also separate more than once during our calendar window have more than one line in this file. The third file, Weekly Employment, consists of one observation in each week for each driver employed during that week. Combining all three data sets gives a complete picture, week by week, of flows in, flows out, and who is currently working for the firm.

However, there are some important limitations in these data and a resulting major problem with analyzing them. The Weekly Hire and Weekly Separations data files contain a number of useful variables, including several key breakout variables, such as the driver's division (e.g., dedicated, intermodal, system) and what kind of prior training or experience the driver had when they joined the firm.[21] Unfortunately, the Weekly Employment data file is missing these key variables. This means that at the present initial stage of the analysis we don't have this information on the drivers who do not experience either a hire or a separation event during our calendar window. And our information is incomplete for drivers who experience only a hire or only a separation event. In particular, the division to which the driver is assigned is known prospectively at the time of the hire event. But it changes later for many drivers, and we only have the updated information in the separation event record for that subset that does depart.

To partially compensate for these problems, we take the following steps. Breakout variables that are of interest in the present study are carried forward to all observations on a given driver, from that driver's hiring observation. This gives us reasonably accurate information on the previous trucking industry training or experience of each driver (because this is not information that changes with tenure). It also tells us which division of the firm's operations a new driver is expected to be assigned to at the time of hire. Because the data on the type of work assignment is so noisy after this process, and because we would only be able to update it for those who exit, we do not pursue specific findings about the impact of the type of work on retention in the present analysis.[22]

A further implication of the data limitations is that we restrict ourselves in this initial work to the subset of drivers for which we observe a hiring event during our calendar window because we do not have either hire or separation observations for long-time incumbent employees and so are missing their key breakout variable values. Given an industry context in

---

21. Not included, on the other hand, are items such as age, gender, level of formal education, or ethnic category.

22. We experimented with the following procedure. We flowed the values from the separation observation backward, to all prior observations of that particular driver, for the variable recording division to which the driver is assigned—for those drivers who have an observed separation only. (This overwrote the forward-flowed divisional assignment data from the time of hire for those separated drivers for whom we observe the hire event.) This gives us improved information on those who separated, but at the cost that noise is differentially left in the observations on those who do not separate. The results were not credible, so we abandoned this part of the analysis until further information can be added to the data set.

which there are large inflows all the time, however, this subgroup is of significant independent interest, irrespective of what might be found if a more inclusive group could be analyzed. Also, because we are not confident that we can correctly identify all the characteristics of second or later spells of employment, we here only examine the first spell of employment during our calendar window, for those drivers who have more than one observed hiring event.[23] These restrictions still leave us with a lot of data: we analyze a set of more than 500,000 observations covering more than 5,000 distinct individual drivers, observed during the period from September 1, 2001, through March 31, 2005.[24]

Our procedure will be to first examine the survival curve for the entire set of drivers we consider here, along with the associated hazard function, which exhibits the time path of exit risk that gives rise to the survival curve. Then we will separate out the survival curves for discrete subgroups of interest and test for differences between them, and we will also examine the hazard functions for each subgroup for useful insights. It should be noted that our analysis does not distinguish between the possible different reasons for separation. In particular, of the separation events that we observe, 76.4 percent are voluntary quits, while 23.6 percent are discharges for cause, but our survival curves and hazard functions include both.[25]

Descriptive Results for All First-Hire-Event Employment Spells

We begin by examining the survival pattern for the first observed employment spell of all drivers having a hire-event during our calendar window. Figure 2.1 displays the central results. The vertical axis indicates the percentage of the population initially entering employment that remains after each amount of time on the job, shown on the horizontal axis in weeks from the start of employment.

Some key qualitative facts emerge from this picture. First, turnover rates do look extremely high. At 10.1 weeks, 25 percent of the population is gone, 50 percent have left by 29.1 weeks (the median survival time), and 75 percent have departed by 75 weeks. Second, there is a leveling off of departures in the second six months on the job, followed by an acceleration at the end of the first year. This is consistent with the fact that most of the trainees observed here who undergo the firm's full training program sign a

23. This does not prevent us from examining rehires, as a significant number of the first spells we observe are of rehired drivers.

24. The precise number of drivers and observations is suppressed for confidentiality reasons.

25. The primary statistical methodology is survival analysis. Standard descriptive and analytical methods are problematic when the key dependent variable (here, the length of job tenure) is a time period, as ongoing spells observed at any given point in time are censored: they continue for an unknown further period. Instead, a conditional probability approach is needed to correctly take into account the statistical information contained in censored observations (Kiefer 1988; Cleves, Gould, and Gutierrez 2004)

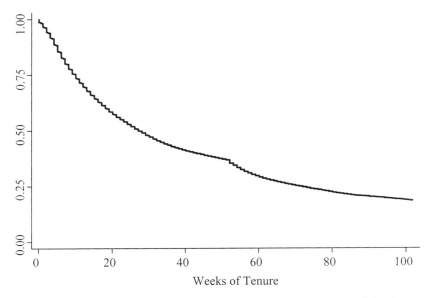

Fig. 2.1   Kaplan-Meier survival curve: Estimates the percentage remaining from this set of drivers at each week of tenure

contract to pay back about half the cost of training (several thousand dollars) if they do not complete a year of service after training. Plus, the job options within trucking are more plentiful for drivers with a year of experience. The surprise, in fact, is that so many new drivers leave before the first year is up. Clearly, these departures cause both the firm and the drivers to incur real costs.

Further insights may be obtained by examining the hazard function for this group of drivers. (See figure 2.2.) The vertical axis indicates the probability of leaving during any particular week shown on the horizontal axis, given that the driver made it to the beginning of the week.[26] Here the differences in risk of departure are shown more clearly. Exit risk is highest at about six to eight weeks, which is approximately when new trainees first pull a load by themselves, without the assistance of an instructor-driver in the cab. Once drivers make it past this stage, exit risk declines sharply until the one-year mark is reached, when separation risk spikes to almost the

26. Or, to be slightly more careful, the vertical axis shows a "departure rate" because it is the conditional probability just described, divided by the number of analysis-time units contained in each unit on the horizontal axis. In our case the denominator is 1, so the rate is also a simple conditional probability. Formally, the hazard function is defined to be the ratio of the density of employment duration to the employment duration survival function, or $h(x) = f(x)/S(x)$.

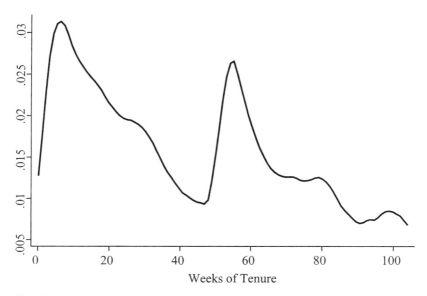

Fig. 2.2   Smoothed hazard function: Estimates the rate of departure from this set of drivers at each week of tenure, conditional on survival to the beginning of the week

same level as at the beginning. Drivers who make it to the end of two years are essentially self-selected to have a high likelihood of turning out to be longer-term employees.

Descriptive Results by Level of Previous Experience or Training

Drivers who are hired by the cooperating firm arrive with different levels of prior training and prior experience. In figures 2.3 and 2.4 and table 2.1, the differing performance of these subgroups with respect to retention gives rise to separate survival curves and hazard functions. The best retention is exhibited by the small group (4 percent of the total) of rehires. This can be observed from the fact that their survival curve is well above the curves of the other subgroups and is quantified in table 2.1. We can see in the table that rehires have the longest time period of any group at which 75 percent still remain (almost four months), and at which 50 percent still remain (over five years). Rehires also have a retention period for 25 percent of the starting population that is so long that it cannot be meaningfully calculated in our data. This is not surprising—rehires are the self-selected subset of drivers who are not only experienced drivers, but who have worked at least once already at the cooperating firm. Having explored other opportunities, they now choose to return to this firm as their best current option.

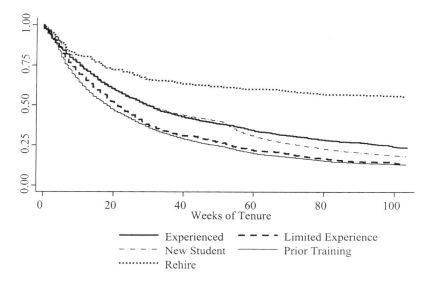

Fig. 2.3   Kaplan-Meier survival curves by type of student: Estimates the percentage remaining from each subset at each week of tenure

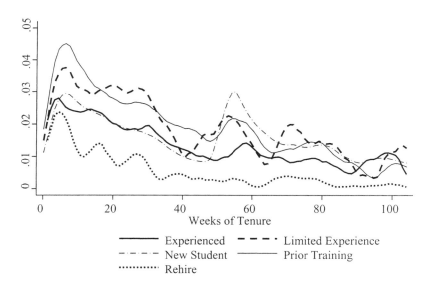

Fig. 2.4   Smoothed hazard functions by type of student: Estimates the rate of departure from each subset of drivers, conditional on survival to the beginning of the week

Table 2.1   Weeks of job tenure by type of student

Drivers for whom a "hire event" is observed (N > 5,000)	Percent of drivers	75% of drivers remaining	50% of drivers remaining	25% of drivers remaining
		Estimated job tenure (weeks)		
All drivers	100	10.1	27.4	72.1
Rehire	4	16.6	284.7	n.a.[a]
Experienced	8	10.4	29.4	98.3
New students	73	11.1	30.1	73.1
Limited experience	3	8.1	21.1	53.1
Prior training	14	6.7	18.1	49.1

[a]Rehires have a retention period for 25% of the starting population that is so long that it cannot be meaningfully calculated in the data.

The hazard function for these drivers is distinctive as well. It shows a modest spike in exit probability early, with falling exit risk thereafter, and also a very distinct periodicity during the first year, which likely reflects the incentive effects of the firm's quarterly bonus system. Rehires are eligible for the firm's quarterly bonus immediately upon starting work and also have experience with the incentive provided by the particular bonus system offered by the firm. The periodicity in the rehire hazard function suggests drivers in this group who may consider leaving during the first year are likely to wait until they have completed a quarter and have qualified for the bonus before separating. Also noteworthy, and sensible, is that there is no "first-year-effect" spike in the rehire hazard rate—this effect in the aggregate hazard function is entirely due to the behavior of other subgroups.

Next consider experienced drivers. These are students who have significant levels of over-the-road tractor-trailer experience with other employers before coming to the cooperating firm. Like rehires, they only have to take a refresher training course that takes a few days, instead of the multiple-week basic training course all other drivers new to the firm are required to pass. Their retention performance is not as good as that of the rehires, but it is still well above that of the lowest groups, with 75th, 50th, and 25th percentile retention periods of 10.4, 29.4, and 98.3 weeks, respectively. Their hazard function shows the usual pattern of an early peak, with later declines, and appears to have a muted version of the periodicity seen in rehires. This would make sense, as experienced drivers are eligible for the bonus system immediately, but don't have as much experience with its incentives as rehires.

The next item to note is akin to Sherlock Holmes's famous observation about the mysterious behavior of the dog in the night. The dog didn't bark when it should have, and correspondingly one would expect new students with no prior background of any kind in trucking to have different (and in particular, poorer) retention performance than experienced drivers.[27] But in these data, both new students who are learning the industry from scratch and experienced drivers who are new to the cooperating firm have closely similar retention behavior for nearly the first entire year of employment. New students actually do slightly better than experienced drivers near the end of the first year. At that point, their hazard function spikes very sharply, and their performance drops below that of experienced drivers. This is likely associated with the facts that their training contracts are completed and they then have enough experience to easily switch trucking firms if they desire. Because new students are by far the largest group (73 percent) of drivers for whom we observe a hire event, their behavior is very important in determining that of the entire aggregate driver population. Thus, the size of their initial aggregate spike in exit risk, as well as that after a year of service, both strongly shape the aggregate survival curve and hazard function.

As it turns out, a Chi-square statistical test of the significance of the difference in overall survival performance between new drivers and those with experience at firms other than the one providing the data shows that experienced drivers do better overall, at the 5 percent significance level ($p = .018$). But, as table 2.1 shows, the effect is all driven by the one-year exits of new drivers, and the magnitude of the effect is much smaller than the difference between either of these groups and rehires.[28] For instance, 50 percent of the rehire group is estimated to still be at work for the cooperating firm 5.48 years after the hire event we observe, while for drivers with experience at other firms, it is only 6.8 months, and for new students it is essentially the same, at 6.9 months.[29] At longer durations of employment, we see a modest difference: 25 percent of the drivers with experience at other firms still remain at 22.6 months, while it is only 16.9 months for the same proportion of new drivers.

Last, consider the retention performance of the two final groups: drivers with some prior experience and those with some prior training. Both these groups are identified by the driver recruiting staff at the cooperating firm as having some background in trucking, but not enough to qualify the student to take only the short training course for fully experienced drivers. To extend the previous allusion, here is a dog barking loudly—these two groups do quite badly, by comparison to students wholly new to trucking. The job tenure lengths for the retention of the 75th, 50th, and 25th percentiles of

27. The mysterious behavior (in "The Silver Blaze") was that the dog did not bark when someone removed a valuable race horse from the barn, which was a clue to the thief's identity.
28. The pairwise differences between rehires and new drivers, and between rehires and experienced drivers, are both significant—the Chi-square p-values for Type 1 error are zero to four decimal places.
29. The base time unit for the statistical analysis is weeks, so months are everywhere calculated as weeks divided by 4.33.

students with limited driving experience is 1.87, 4.94, and 12.25 months, respectively. This tells us that only 25 percent make it to the completion of their one-year-service-after-training employment contract; the other 75 percent are incurring a multithousand dollar debt in order to leave early.[30] Students with only some prior training, but no prior experience, do even worse, with retention periods for the 75th, 50th, and 25th percentiles of only 1.58, 4.18, and 11.33 months, respectively. So less than one-quarter of these students complete their training contracts. (The difference between these two groups is significant by the Chi-square test, at the 5 percent level [p-value of .045.])[31]

Why should these students be at the bottom of the performance ranking when normally prior training or experience would be expected to improve retention? A reasonable hypothesis is that it has to do with the distinctive characteristics of a high-turnover, secondary labor market. In this type of market, there is always demand for drivers at some job or other. So someone with prior experience of any kind, as well as the graduates of any of the many commercial driver training schools, can get some job, as long as they have a CDL. It may not be a very desirable job, but it is possible to accumulate experience if one is willing to put up with some of the poorer working conditions available in an industry segment known for having poor conditions on average. In this context, coming to the cooperating firm and being willing to assume the debt contract that accompanies the full training program is a bad signal. There may be many specific reasons outside a prospective driver's control that lead to such a decision. For example, the student could have experienced some kind of family event that stopped his or her prior training before the CDL exam or caused him or her to quit a prior job quickly. But, on average, students with some prior training or some prior experience are likely either to be job switchers who just couldn't do better for the time being, but who will be looking to leave as soon as possible, or to be job candidates who were unsuccessful at someone else's training course, or were otherwise judged inadequate by other firms. Either of these reasons means the student is more likely to depart.

2.5.2   Pilot Work on Productivity

The pilot work on productivity utilized a different set of data files from the cooperating firm than did the turnover work described in the preceding section. We began with two data files, one containing basic information (especially hire date and separation date, if any) on all the drivers who had separated during the period of one year (for example, in some of the pilot

---

30. Except for those who are hired by a rival firm that is willing to pay off their indebtedness—something which is known to occur in this labor market.

31. The pairwise differences between either of these groups and any of those with better retention performance is highly significant—the Chi-square p-values for Type 1 error are zero to four decimal places.

work we used 2003), and the second, extracted at the end of that year, containing similar information on all currently employed drivers. Then two separate additional files containing demographic information, and racial and ethnic identity from voluntary Equal Employment Opportunity Commission (EEOC) employee disclosure forms, were added.

Merging these using the internal employee number (driver number) as an identifier immediately caused problems. It turned out that driver numbers are not unique, but are recycled on a regular basis, so we had to delete some duplicate cases that really represented different drivers.[32] "Hire date," a key variable for survival analysis also turned out to be problematic. As one might expect in a high turnover setting, a small but significant number of drivers become reemployed, some having as many as four or five successive employment spells. The problem was that drivers gone for less time than some threshold (six months at one point, but varied over time) kept their original hire date, while those gone longer were assigned a new one. The latter fact made it impossible to distinguish rehires from new drivers with recycled driver numbers.

To do a productivity analysis, the key addition to the records already described was information from the firm's payroll records, which provide a week-by-week compilation of the items added to (or deducted from) each employee's pay, with each such transaction constituting a line of data. The taxes and fringe benefit co-pays were in a separate data source to which we did not have access, but even so the initial files had as many as forty-four transactions per driver per pay period, with more than one million lines of data per file. We proceeded to document the different variables that contained coded information about the driver's work assignment and pay structure, consulting subject-matter experts at the firm regularly. Each variable could take on multiple values, the meanings of which to some degree changed over time as operational needs changed. In addition, we began to document all the meanings of the values of the key variable specifying what type of transaction each line of the payroll file contained. There were several hundred distinct values of this variable, including values denoting several different types of mileage pay, dozens of types of lump sum pay for specific tasks, dozens of types of pay advances and pay deductions, and so on.

After documentation, we next "rolled up" the payroll file. We sorted the file by driver and pay-week and then accumulated all the transaction-level information we were interested in having on a weekly basis into new variables so that the last transaction in each driver-pay-week record contained cumulative information for the week. The kinds of information in the re-

32. For the pilot work, we did not want the responsibility of making use of social security numbers, although a secure method for making use of the relevant identification information has been developed for later work.

sulting records included such key items as the total (paid) miles, and the amount paid for them, and the total number of dispatches. Also included was information on various kinds of ancillary activities when they generated a pay transaction, such as paid customer stops, pay supplements for very short runs, paid maintenance delays, and so on. The payroll data thus provides a very rich set of information about what each driver does during each week.

However, the payroll file records what drivers are actually paid for, which is in general a subset of what they actually do. So, for instance, the first pickup stop and first delivery stop on each loaded dispatch are not separately compensated. Extra pickup or delivery stops are paid when they occur on long-distance random dispatch loads, but only some of the time when they are on a scheduled run dedicated to a particular customer that is engineered to have multiple stops. Most drivers are primarily compensated by the mile, and these drivers are paid miles for all their dispatches, which normally includes loaded miles, plus miles pulling an empty trailer, repositioning for a new load, and also any bobtail miles (i.e., without a trailer). However, drivers generally run more miles than those for which they are paid. Paid miles are based on a least-distance routing algorithm, which is historically standard in the industry but which undercounts the actual miles by several percent (recent guesstimates by managers at our firm for the average undercount range from 4 percent to 6 percent).[33] Despite these limitations, the payroll data provide a very useful starting point for the productivity analysis.[34]

Descriptive Productivity Results for Inexperienced Long-Haul Random Dispatch Drivers

We began our pilot work with a subset of drivers for the years 2002 and 2003. The subset is those drivers who were inexperienced at hire (i.e., those who had to take the full training course offered by the firm), who were assigned to drive solo (as opposed to in a team) on long-haul random dispatch runs, and who were in their 5th week to 156th week of tenure with the firm.[35] This gave us more than 100,000 pay-week observations on more than

33. This is, in part, because the standard algorithms are to and from standard reference points, and given the circuity of the road network, this undercounts actual miles on average. It is also because drivers are responsible for selecting a practical route for a large loaded tractor-trailer, which is often more circuitous than the least-distance version. In addition, drivers may choose to deviate for other reasons (for example, to run on a turnpike where the salt trucks will be out at night in the Pennsylvania mountains in winter, as opposed to a non-toll highway on which such services are more uncertain), as long as they don't exceed certain percentage standards for excess miles and meet delivery schedules.

34. For later work, it is expected supplemental information will be added from a separate operational events data set also maintained by the firm. It is not the place to start because it has its own limitations and also because it is about an order of magnitude larger than the payroll data set.

35. Drivers begin receiving mileage pay when they first pull a load on their own, without a trainer in the truck with them, and the earliest this occurs is about the fifth week.

2,000 drivers. Examining the key dependent variable, miles per week, we observed very high variance (see figure 2.5). In particular, there were negative values and also very high positive values. The former turned out to be due to mistaken pay being charged back against a driver's earnings and the latter to a small number of drivers from the firm's early days who were permitted to accumulate vacation earnings over several years and were being paid upon retirement. We decided to trim the extremes and had to choose whether to leave in zero-miles weeks or use only positive-miles ones and what upper bound to use.

The actual maximum number of miles that a solo driver could legally run during this period, given state speed limits and Federal Hours of Service Regulations for operators of commercial vehicles, was about 4,000 per week. But during at least part of this period, until the practice was ended, some drivers at the firm were paid for their runs only after they submitted completed paperwork for each dispatch. This meant that if they held their paperwork they could have one (or even two) weeks in a row with zero paid miles and then a week with very high miles. We decided to trim only the negative values, leaving zero-miles weeks in, and also trimmed values over 6,500 after looking at the distribution of the upper tail.

Further examination showed that almost 20 percent of our observations were of zero-miles pay weeks. So we first trimmed out all the pay-week ob-

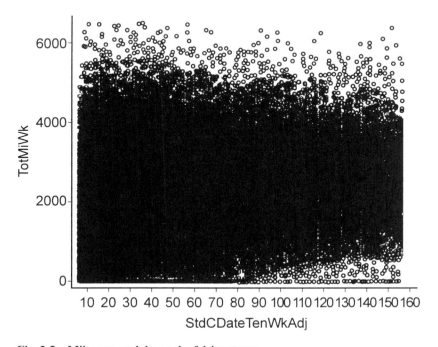

Fig. 2.5   **Miles per week by week of driver tenure**

servations that were associated with any payroll transaction that could exogenously cause the driver to either miss work or be paid on a nonmileage basis. This included pay weeks with disability pay, vacation or holiday pay, salary (sometimes paid to driver-trainers), lump-sum training pay, and the like. Then we discovered that the payroll system was generating dummy paychecks for drivers who had separated from the firm, for several weeks after separation when the driver left owing money, for example, for things like cash pay advances or purchases at a store at a company terminal. When all of these cases were trimmed out, we reduced the number of weeks with zero miles substantially, but 6 percent of our observations remained with zero miles per week.

Figure 2.6 exhibits a simple descriptive version of the tenure-productivity curve for this subset of drivers. Even after all the trimming, the remaining weeks with zero miles affect the mean values quite significantly. Without zero-miles weeks, the initial increase to full productivity is achieved at about nine months, whereas with zero-miles weeks it is nearer to a year. There is a sharp drop in the curve at one year of tenure with zero miles included. This is undoubtedly related in some way to the fact that drivers with one year of experience can more easily switch firms and also

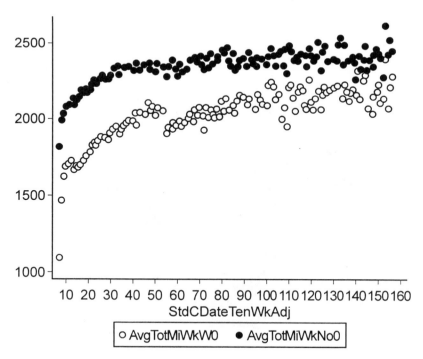

Fig. 2.6   Average miles per week, by week of tenure, with and without zero-miles weeks

to the fact that most of the drivers in this subset, all of whom have taken the firm's training, assume a debt of several thousand dollars for its cost, which is forgiven at the end of a year of service after training is completed.[36] The balance of the pilot analysis keeps all the zero-miles weeks in the data set, but a goal of the full statistical case study is to dig deeper into this phenomenon and develop better evidence on whether they all should be included when analyzing productivity.

The Impact of Selection on the Tenure-Productivity Curve

A major goal of the statistical investigation of productivity is to analyze the true causal effect of increasing tenure on expected miles per week (the treatment effect), while accounting for any impact the high turnover rate might have (the selection effect). A priori, a reasonable hypothesis would be that drivers with lower productive capacity would be more likely to leave at any given level of tenure. In order to test this hypothesis, we start by running a fixed effects panel data ordinary least squares (OLS) regression model, with total miles per week as the dependent variable. We use all the independent variables from the payroll data set that plausibly measure exogenous factors that affect productivity. These include driver tenure (a linear term and as many higher-order terms as prove significant) and the number of dispatches (linear term plus those higher-order terms that prove significant). We also include variables such as the number of short-haul pay supplements, the number of paid maintenance delays, as well as dummy variables for each week of the calendar year (to capture any time-period effects or time trends), and a dummy variable for each terminal at which drivers are based (to capture any geographic effects of the home base). We use robust standard errors. The pilot version of this model has an adjusted R^2 of .66.

The fixed effects model constrains the coefficients on all the independent variables to be the same across all drivers, but permits each driver to have his or her own regression plane intercept, or constant. This constant, or fixed effect, which is estimated by the regression, may be thought of as a measure, specific to the model and the data, of the degree of "job match" between the driver and his employment at the firm. In the context of the model, it is the number of miles which the driver "brings to the job each week" (which can be positive or negative), according to the model estimate. Allowing this specific flexibility in the regression model provides a statistical adjustment for the relative speed with which drivers of high and low job match turn over, in predicting the miles each driver will operate per week. So we take the predicted values from the model and compute the average of these values over each week of tenure on the job. These averages, when

---

36. New drivers also earn their first week of paid vacation at this point, but that cannot be the reason for the drop in the averages, as those weeks have been removed from the data.

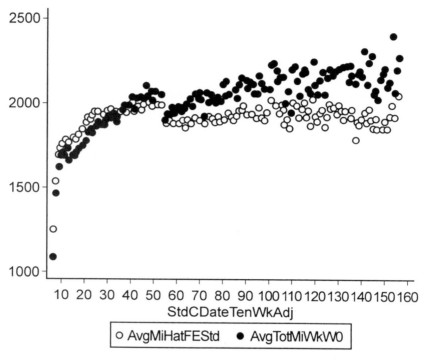

Fig. 2.7 The tenure-productivity curve with (AvgMiHatFEStd) and without (AvgTotMiWkW0) the fixed effects correction for selection

graphed, produce a "selection-corrected" tenure-productivity curve. In figure 2.7, we compare this new tenure-productivity curve with the simple descriptive version of the same curve we exhibited in figure 2.6.[37]

When both curves are level and the selection-corrected tenure-productivity curve is below the old curve, the graph suggests that the true effect of tenure on productivity is smaller than it appears in the simple descriptive case. This implies that drivers with poor job matches are leaving differentially faster than those with good ones, which is in accord with our hypothesis. By contrast, when the selection-corrected tenure-productivity curve is either rising more rapidly than the old curve, or is above it when they are level, it says that the true effect of tenure on productivity may be larger than it appears in the simple descriptive case. This could imply that drivers with good job matches are leaving differentially faster than those with bad ones. The pilot results shown in figure 2.7 clearly show that our initial hypothesis is true from about the ninth or tenth month on. But fig-

37. Both curves are for the case in which zero-miles weeks that cannot be specifically explained away are retained in the data set.

ure 2.7 is ambiguous about whether this is also true early in the tenure of new drivers, when the firm has its highest rates of separations. A major goal of the full statistical case study is to clarify these pilot results.

2.6 Research Component Two: Panel Study of New Hires

Research Component Two is a study of 1,069 new driver-trainees who were among those recruited by the firm to start their education at a specific training school operated by the firm. The basic design of the panel study is quite straightforward in conception, although it is quite labor intensive and costly to carry out. A large amount of data is being collected on each driver trainee, starting with an initial contact while each was in the first phase of training, and then continuing with follow-up data collections over two years of the trainee's work life at the firm, or until the trainee exits the firm, whichever comes first.

The follow-up data collections include these elements: (1) a follow-up paper survey for the driver mailed to his or her home every six months, for two years, as long as they stay employed by the firm; (2) an exit survey for the driver mailed to the driver's home soon after their separation, if it occurs during the first two years; (3) a weekly survey with two questions sent over the satellite unit to the driver's truck;[38] (4) an initial survey (and consent form) for the driver's spouse or significant other, asking about family/work-life issues, and mailed to the driver's family soon after the driver entered the study; (5) a follow-up survey to the driver's family mailed every six months up to two years; and (6) an exit survey for the driver's family mailed upon driver separation, if it occurs during the first two years. As subjects are informed as they enter the study, a cash gift of $5 is included in each survey mailing, with the goal of increasing the response rate. Finally, the drivers' on-the-job performance data will be collected as part of future updating of the master data files for the turnover and productivity studies of Research Component Two.

2.6.1   The Use of Behavioral Economic Experiments

A central project design goal is to perform a multivariate statistical analysis of the relationship between all the factors that are being measured and the success on the job of the trainees, where employee success is measured first by the length of time they are retained by the firm and, second, by their productivity on the job.[39] While the researchers (and the firm's managers) start with a number of hypotheses about what might matter in predicting each of these outcome variables, this research component is essentially a

---

38. The two questions are: "How happy are you with your job right now?" (Likert scale response), and "How many miles do you expect to run next week?"

39. The analysis has the potential to be extended to include safety performance, but that is not part of the present project.

large-scale empirical investigation, designed to let the data tell us which factors matter statistically and which do not. In this regard, it is particularly exciting that we have the opportunity to employ both traditional measurement instruments and a selected set of behavioral economic experiments.

There are many reasons one might have for doing behavioral economic experiments in the field. But one cross-cutting categorization is whether the investigation is primarily about treatment effects or about differences in individual characteristics. A treatment effect is exactly what it sounds like: analogous to studying the aggregate differences in the symptoms of ill patients who randomly received a specific medical treatment, as compared to those who randomly did not, an economic treatment effect is the difference in aggregate behavior across two variants of the experimental setting.[40] An example is the difference in average transaction prices between traders in a pit market and those in a double-auction market for the same commodity and with the same valuations and costs.

However, simple behavioral economic experiments can also be thought of as measurement tools for the characteristics, including the preferences, of individual subjects, as argued in Camerer and Fehr (2004). This is the approach that fits the specifics of the institutional setting of the Project. We anticipate that the results we accumulate will provide significant evidence on the relative utility of conventional and experimental measures of individual characteristics in predicting on-the-job outcomes and in complementing or substituting for each other.

One methodological point should be noted. We plan to look at the relationships among the various measures we are collecting on each subject, as there is little evidence in the literature on this topic for many of our measures, let alone evidence using the subject population from which we are drawing our participants. If this were our only goal, it would be important to vary the order in which the different measures are implemented during the initial data collection, as it is quite possible that order effects could be important for some of these relationships. Order variations are a standard feature of many experimental economic designs when individual subjects take part in more than one experiment.

However, because the central design goal of our project is to examine the predictive power of the various measures with respect to individual on-the-job outcomes, a countervailing methodological need is to present—as nearly as possible—exactly the same set of stimuli to each subject so that the relationship to the outcome variables is always the same. In addition, the complexity of administering the data collection process at the field site made it essentially impossible to vary the order, once we found a sequence

---

40. Of course, one of the key features which makes experimental evidence the scientific gold standard is that random assignment to treatment and nontreatment groups means that any causal factors not directly controlled for in an effective experimental design wash out of the results because they equally affect both groups.

of data collection events that fit the schedule. For these reasons, the sequence of measurements in the initial data collection was not varied.

The initial data collection process took place on a Saturday in the middle of the first two weeks of the training process for new driver trainees. We next describe the training process to provide context for understanding where the initial data collection fits in the new driver's work life.

2.6.2   The Driver Training Process

The first two weeks of training for every inexperienced driver take place at one of the driver training schools maintained by the firm. The initial training includes a large dose of classroom work in which students are introduced to the firm and learn essential facts about the equipment they'll be operating, the regulations governing commercial vehicle operators and operations, map reading and course-plotting, and the safety rules and procedures specific to the firm. It also alternates hands-on training time between truck simulators and an actual Class 8 tractor-trailer.[41] Trainees first drive bobtail (tractor with no trailer), and then with an empty and a loaded trailer, on the school's property. Once the trainee has qualified for a CDL learning permit and is judged ready by the instructors, he or she quickly begins driving on the actual roads and highways surrounding the school, with a driver-trainer in the right seat of the tractor.

The simulators have two purposes. One is to speed familiarization with the basic features and operational characteristics of the Class 8 tractor-trailer. An example is learning how to correctly shift a ten-speed transmission, which requires frequent double-clutching, coordinated at first by conscious attention to engine RPMs in comparison to road speed, especially for downshifts. Another basic feature drivers are first exposed to in the simulator is how to maneuver around corners on city streets with a rig that is about 65 feet (just under 20 meters) long, and that includes a trailer that is 53-feet (16.2 meters) long. A second main function of the simulators is to give drivers practice at responding to dangerous settings that could never be practiced in real life, such as how to avoid going off the road in response to a blow-out on a steering axle tire, first on dry pavement, and then on glare ice on a freeway in the middle of car traffic.

Trainees who complete the initial two-week training process are officially hired by the firm on their date of completion, after passing a basic skills qualification test. Once hired, the driver goes back to his or her home base at one of the firm's terminal locations. While the content of the CDL

---

41. By definition, Class 8 vehicles that can operate on the National Highway System (NHS) have a maximum GVW of between 33,000 pounds and 80,000 pounds. The units utilized by most truckload carriers, including the cooperating firm, are at the top of this range, and have a maximum GVW of 80,000 pounds. (The NHS is a large subset of all U.S. highways designated by the U.S. Department of Transportation (USDOT), on which federal size and weight standards prevail.)

exam is federally regulated, the exact rules governing driver training vary from state to state.[42] So depending on their proficiency level and on the state in which they will be based, trainees may also take the CDL exam at the training school, or they may do so later, at a location nearer their home base. Whether they have the CDL yet or are still using a learner's permit, all new drivers have a second training phase, during which the trainee works for between one and three more weeks, actually hauling freight from their home base, but with a certified driver trainer in the right seat of the tractor. When the trainer judges the trainee ready (and he or she has acquired a CDL), the new driver is assigned a tractor of his or her own and goes to work on his or her own.

As is mentioned in previous sections, it is typical for the TL carriers that train all or most of their new drivers to offer the training on a credit contract. The contract specifies that the trainees assume a debt of several thousand dollars, which is approximately the market value of the training. According to the contract, the firm provides both phases of the training, including access to the classroom, instructors, and trucks, plus needed classroom supplies. For the first phase of training, transportation to and from the training school, a hotel room while at training, and lunches during the training day are also covered. The trainee owes no payments on the credit extended as long as they stay employed by the firm, and the debt is fully discharged if the trainee completes a specific period of service after the point they begin working on their own (either one year, at many firms, including this one, or eighteen months at some others). Trainees who do not complete the period of service, however, become legally liable for repayment of the amount of credit extended.

2.6.3   The Initial Data Collection Process

The initial data collection process was piloted in October through December, 2005, and went to full operation on twenty-two Saturdays during January through August, 2006. The school starts a class into the initial two-week training process (described in the preceding section) every week on Sunday (thus, two classes are in residence at any given time). So trainees in target classes received a one-page flier advertising the study as part of their orientation on their first day at school. The flier explained the opportunity to take part in the University of Minnesota study the next weekend and that trainees who volunteered could expect to earn cash by participating. At the beginning of the class day on the Saturday of data collection, Burks conducted an informed consent process in which he introduced himself as a former driver turned university researcher and explained the goals and

---

42. The CDL comes in three categories, "Class C" through "Class A," and for freight vehicles are differentiated primarily by the ascending maximum GVW of the trucks the bearer can operate. The Class A CDL is required to operate Class 8 vehicles on public roads.

procedures of the study to the potential subjects. The study is governed by the standards of the Human Subjects Protection Committee of the University of Minnesota's Institutional Review Board (IRB), so a formal consent document was used which spelled out the risks and benefits of taking part in the study.[43]

The data collection at the training school was set up as two, two-hour-long blocks, spent doing tasks with the researchers, either on computers or with paper and pencil, with a short break in between. Training classes range from thirty-five to seventy students, and the largest group that could be accommodated at one time for data collection was thirty-two subjects, so each class was broken into two groups. The first group worked with the researchers from early to late morning, and the second group from late morning to midafternoon. On data collection days, the class day was structured so that those potential subjects who chose not to take part did not have extra training available, but instead could spend the extra time in the break room. The buses that transport students to and from the hotel bring everyone at one time in the early morning and take everyone back at one time in the afternoon. Given the monetary compensation being offered, the relatively low opportunity cost of taking part, and the credible guarantee of confidentiality from the University, 91 percent of the trainees offered the opportunity chose to join the study. Initial data was collected from 1,069 participants, with clean information on 1,036 of these.[44]

Except for one instrument (the Educational Testing Service's test of Quantitative Literacy, labeled "Numeracy" in our schedule), all the instruments were administered on a wireless network provided by the cooperating firm of refurbished Dell notebook computers, with a newer Dell notebook as the master controlling computer. The software used was z-Tree (Fischbacher 2007), the toolbox for constructing computer-administered economic experiments and surveys developed at the Institute for Empirical Economics at the University of Zürich.[45] The data collection took place in a temporary computerized experimental economics laboratory that the

---

43. This document included the following key facts: (1) the kind of data collection activities involved, both initially and later, (2) that subjects would receive $20 in initial cash "thank you gifts" for taking part, and have the opportunity to earn substantially more, (3) that the money paid to them was coming not from the firm but from two nonprofit foundations, (4) that under university rules for protecting research participants, the new data collected about them would be kept confidential from everyone except academic investigators approved by the Institutional Review Board (IRB), including specifically that it would never be available to their managers at the trucking firm, and (5) that participation was completely voluntary.

44. Due to a programming glitch, one item, Hit 15 Points, has valid information for only 893 subjects.

45. Because we are running a licensed adaptation of a nonverbal IQ instrument that requires the display of a large number of graphics files, each of which is a scanned image of a page with a pattern-matching task, we ran a beta version of z-Tree that was extended to handle graphics files. Our special thanks to developer Urs Fischbacher for providing this new version in time for our project.

research team set up in one of the classrooms at the training school on the Friday before the data collection dates on Saturdays, and which was then removed at the end of the Saturday event. The team hand-built a set of cloth dividers hung from frames adapted from portable garment racks, which were installed between all the computer stations in order to separate subjects during the data collection. Because the data collection sessions exceeded the endurance of notebook PC batteries, extra power outlets were installed in the walls and a set of portable extension cords were deployed as part of the laboratory set up. The wireless network was part of a virtual local area network (VLAN) set up by the firm's IT support personnel under a data security agreement approved by the University of Minnesota Human Subjects Committee. The VLAN separated the computers on which the confidential data was being collected from the rest of the firm's network and provided secure data storage until the initial data collection was complete, and the project moved back to the UMM campus.

Table 2.2 shows the time sequence and schedule for the actual data collection event of February 25, 2006. This class of trainees was relatively large, at fifty-nine students. Fifty-one out of fifty-six, or 91 percent, chose to take part.

While it was theoretically possible for a subject to end up with only the initial $20 "thank you gifts," we always paid at least a dollar or two more. The actual payouts depended in part on the use of stochastic devices (plastic bowls filled with colored or numbered poker chips), as described in the following account of each data collection activity. The average total earnings for the four-hour period of the initial data collection were $53, with a minimum of $21, and a maximum of $168. By design, we wanted most subjects to be pleased about their initial interaction with the researchers, given the follow-up contacts with them which are called for by the design.

The latter fact—that we needed to gain not only the immediate but also the longer-term cooperation of our subjects—also affected the protocol for subject behavior during the four-and-one-half-hour sequence of data events. With undergraduate students in a university experimental economics laboratory and with a protocol that takes significantly less time than the project's, it is not hard to ask subjects to be quiet, to not speak to their neighbors, to not do other tasks on the computers, and not to read, write, or use cell phones or PDAs. In order to provide a neutral setting, this is the behavior requested—and normally received from—typical student subjects in economic experiments, unless the treatment being investigated is one involving changing some aspect of this, such as allowing specific types of communication. We established expectations of our driver-trainee participants that were similar to this, but found that to receive willing compliance we had to allow for participants who finished ahead of others on tasks that took a long time to get up and leave the lab setting temporarily. We did this explicitly during the Numeracy instrument and during the MPQ in-

Table 2.2   Data collection activity time allocations: February 25, 2006

Actual time	Scheduled time	Total time	Informed consent process
7:13	7:10		Start informed consent process
59			How many people in the room?
7:29	7:30	0:16	Finish informed consent process

			Session 1a
7:30	7:30	0:09	Check-in
7:39	7:40	0:04	Information
7:43	7:42	0:19	*Activity 1: Prisoner's Dilemma*
			Computer generated: Pay on beliefs for what percentage of people will send $5 as person 1, how much person 2 sends if person 1 sends $0, and how much person 2 sends if person 1 sends $5, $1 each
8:02	8:09	0:39	*Activity 2: Multidimensional Personality Questionnaire*
			No payment
8:41	8:47	0:12	*Activity 3: Risk/Loss Aversion*
			1 question, #23; *green* by drawing out of a bowl; everyone paid for their selection
8:53	8:58	0:27	*Activity 4: Demographics*
			No payment
	9:16		*Activity 5: Big Red Button*
			Computer generated
			Release participants
9:09			First person left at this time
9:20	9:26		Last person left at this time

			Session 2a
9:37	9:40	0:08	Check-in
9:45	9:45	0:02	Information
9:47	9:47	0:09	*Activity 1: Time Preferences*
			2 subjects, #12 and #19; 1 question, #18
9:56	9:57	0:47	*Activity 2: Nonverbal IQ*
			Start time of test *10:02*
			2 subjects, #8 and #21; pay $1 for each correct answer; pay on "pre" and "post" beliefs, $2 each
10:43	10:30	0:25	*Activity 3: Numeracy (Quantitative Literacy)*
			Start time of test *10:44*
			2 subjects, #8 and #18; pay $2 for each correct answer; pay on "pre" and "post" beliefs, $2 each
11:08	10:55	0:08	*Activity 4: Ambiguity Aversion*
			1 question, #7; *blue* by drawing out of a bowl; everyone paid for their selection
11:16	11:05	0:12	*Activity 5: Hit 15 Points*
			Computer generated
11:28	11:28	0:12	*Activity 6: Risk, Impatience, and Cooperation Survey*
			No payment
			Release Participants
11:35			First person left at this time
11:40	11:40		Last person left at this time

(continued)

Table 2.2   (continued)

Actual time	Scheduled time	Total time	Informed consent process
			Session 1b
12:15	12:30	0:10	Check-in
12:25	12:40	0:03	Information
12:28	12:42	0:23	*Activity 1: Prisoner's Dilemma*
			Computer generated; pay on beliefs for what percentage of people will send $5 as person 1, how much person 2 sends if person 1 sends $0, and how much person 2 sends if person 1 sends $5, $1 each
12:51	1:09	0:35	*Activity 2: Multidimensional Personality Questionnaire*
			No payment
1:34	1:47	0:13	*Activity 3: Risk/Loss Aversion*
			1 question, *#21; blue* by drawing out of a bowl; everyone paid for their selection
1:47	1:58	0:32	*Activity 4: Demographics*
			No payment
	2:16		*Activity 5: Big Red Button*
			Computer generated
			Release participants
2:04			First person left at this time
2:19	2:26		Last person left at this time
			Session 2b
2:25	2:40	0:09	Check-in
2:34	2:45	0:02	Information
2:36	2:47	0:11	*Activity 1: Time Preferences*
			2 subjects, *#17* and *#16;* 1 question, *#7*
2:47	2:57	0:39	*Activity 2: Nonverbal IQ*
			Start time of test *2:53*
			2 subjects, *#17* and *#22;* pay $1 for each correct answer; pay on "pre" and "post" beliefs, $2 each
3:26	3:30	0:28	*Activity 3: Numeracy (Quantitative Literacy)*
			Start time of test *3:30*
			2 subjects, *#17* and *#16;* pay $2 for each correct answer; pay on "pre" and "post" beliefs, $2 each
3:54	3:55	0:11	*Activity 4: Ambiguity Aversion*
			1 question, *#22; blue* by drawing out of a bowl; everyone paid for their selection
4:05	4:05	0:16	*Activity 5: Hit 15 Points*
			Computer generated
4:21	4:28	0:16	*Activity 6: Risk, Impatience, and Cooperation Survey*
			No payment
			Release participants
4:29			First person left at this time
4:37	4:40		Last person left at this time

strument, when differences in reading speed made the differences in completion time especially large, and we also allowed participants to read after completion if they were done early during the MPQ.

We next turn to a brief description of each item in the sequence of data collection events.

2.6.4   Session One Data Collection Events

The first two-hour block of data collection activities consists of three behavioral economic experiments and two more conventional measures.

Prisoner's Dilemma

Our version of this experiment is a sequential and strategic one. Person 1 (the first mover) and Person 2 (the second mover) each are allocated $5. Person 1 can send either $0 or $5 to Person 2, and Person 2 can respond by sending $0, $1, $2, $3, $4, or $5 back. All funds sent are doubled by the researchers. Each subject provides their complete strategy in the game: they make both an unconditional decision for the first-mover role and a conditional one for the second-mover role (first, how to respond to being sent $0 and, second, how to respond to being sent $5, doubled to $10.) Subjects are randomly matched and their role selected by the computer after their decisions. This is a variant of the task used in Burks, Carpenter, and Götte (2006).

Before each decision screen, subjects are also asked how they think other participants in the room will act in this experiment. The first question is "What percent of the participants do you think will send their $5 as Person 1?" and pays $1 if the subject is correct within plus or minus 5 percent. The second and third questions are "If Person 1 does not send/does send, what is the average that participants in this room will send back?" and pays $1 for each question if the subject is within plus or minus $0.25 of the actual average.

There will be four main data items of potential interest from this experiment: first-mover choices, the estimate of first-mover behavior of others, second-mover conditional choices, and the estimate of the second-mover choices of others. We intend to analyze what other factors about the participants predict their choices in this experiment, as well as use some aspects of their choices as predictors of other experimental responses, and also of some kinds of on-the-job behavior. A potential workplace application is in predicting on-the-job cooperation. The TL driver's job is relatively individualized, but there are two instances in which the data store from Research Component One may in the future be augmented to permit the construction of an on-the-job measure of cooperation.[46]

One of the benefits of the strategic form of this experiment is that the

---

46. See appendix B, items 4.1 and 4.2.

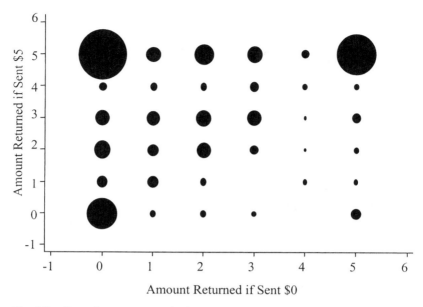

Fig. 2.8   Second-mover strategies in the sequential prisoner's dilemma

second-mover choices provide a fairly clear typing of the respondents, in terms of who is an egoist (never sends anything to the first mover), who is a conditional cooperator (sends back exactly what the first mover sent), and who is an altruist (always sends everything), with some gradations possible for intermediate dollar responses. As figure 2.8 shows, participant behavior is varied in this experiment, but "pure" versions of these three strategies predominate among second movers (shown by the large circles, which are sized proportionally to the number of respondent choices they capture). The three pure strategies make up 61 percent of the total responses, and most of the rest are intermediate responses. Those responses below and to the right of the 45-degree line fall in the "wingnut" category; these participants may have misunderstood the instructions, a hypothesis we can test by correlating these responses with some of our measures of cognitive performance.

Multidimensional Personality Questionnaire (MPQ)

The Multidimensional Personality Questionnaire (Patrick, Curtin, and Tellegan 2002), otherwise known as the MPQ, is the second measurement instrument. This is a standard personality profile that consists of eleven different scales that represent primary trait dimensions: well-being, social potency, achievement, social closeness, stress reaction, alienation, aggression, control, harm avoidance, traditionalism, and absorption. The short version used in the study has 154 multiple-choice questions. Almost all of the 154 questions have the same four possible answers: "Always True," "Mostly True," "Mostly False," and "Always False." There is no separate payment for this survey.

A principal use of this scale will be to generate a set of control variables in regression modeling of on-the-job outcomes. We also expect to look at how the traits defined by the MPQ relate to answers to the other survey instruments and to behavior in the experiments. As figure 2.9 shows, the trainee drivers are similar overall to the benchmark population presented in Patrick, Curtin, and Tellegan (2002), which is promising given that our primary goal is to use the variation across individuals in the components of the MPQ. Some initial hypotheses, for instance, are that high "achievement" orientation should be correlated with job success as a TL driver, especially given the incentive-pay method faced by these drivers. One noteworthy point is the apparent difference from the population in the factor "unlikely virtues." The questions in this factor are set up so that only someone who is "too good to be true" will have a high score, and the authors of the instrument intend it as a check on the truthfulness of the subject's re-

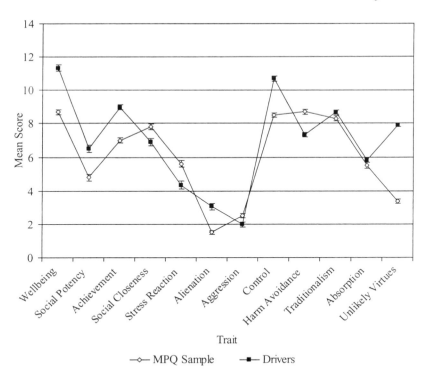

Fig. 2.9   Multidimensional Personality Questionnaire profile of subjects compared to MPQ reference population profile

sponses. This MPQ factor offers the prospect that we may be able to control for this effect to some degree in multivariate analysis by using the unlikely virtues score as a regressor.

Risk/Loss Aversion

In the risk/loss aversion experiment, there are twenty-four questions that are divided into four blocks of six questions each (see table 2.3). There are two possible choices for each question, an amount of money received with certainty, and a 50/50 gamble that pays a higher dollar amount if "your color" is chosen and a lower dollar amount if the "other color" is chosen. To avoid any hint of experimenter control over the outcome, subjects choose which color (blue or green) is theirs for the random outcomes as their last response.

Each of the four blocks of six questions follows the same format. In each block, the amount for "your color" and the "other color" do not change, and the amount of the "for sure" option increases by $0.50 per question. The design is intended to identify where the subject crosses over from the "for sure" option to the "gamble" option, relative to where a risk-neutral person would do so. After all subjects have made their decisions, one poker

Table 2.3	Risk/loss aversion		
Question no.	For sure	Your color	Other color
1	Win $2.00	Win $10.00	Win $2.00
2	Win $3.00	Win $10.00	Win $2.00
3	Win $4.00	Win $10.00	Win $2.00
4	Win $5.00	Win $10.00	Win $2.00
5	Win $6.00	Win $10.00	Win $2.00
6	Win $7.00	Win $10.00	Win $2.00
7	Win $0.00	Win $5.00	Lose $1.00
8	Win $0.50	Win $5.00	Lose $1.00
9	Win $1.00	Win $5.00	Lose $1.00
10	Win $1.50	Win $5.00	Lose $1.00
11	Win $2.00	Win $5.00	Lose $1.00
12	Win $2.50	Win $5.00	Lose $1.00
13	Lose $2.50	Win $1.00	Lose $5.00
14	Lose $2.00	Win $1.00	Lose $5.00
15	Lose $1.50	Win $1.00	Lose $5.00
16	Lose $1.00	Win $1.00	Lose $5.00
17	Lose $0.50	Win $1.00	Lose $5.00
18	Lose $0.00	Win $1.00	Lose $5.00
19	Win $1.00	Win $5.00	Win $1.00
20	Win $1.50	Win $5.00	Win $1.00
21	Win $2.00	Win $5.00	Win $1.00
22	Win $2.50	Win $5.00	Win $1.00
23	Win $3.00	Win $5.00	Win $1.00
24	Win $3.50	Win $5.00	Win $1.00

chip is drawn by a participant that identifies which question (one through twenty-four) everyone will be paid on, and then a second participant draws a colored chip to determine whether the winning color, for subjects who chose the gamble on the selected question, is green or blue.

The choice blocks overlap the zero-dollar point in order to allow inference about the likelihood that the implied utility function has different slopes in the positive and negative domains. But there is no set of choices only in the negative domain because the project is relying on the long-term responsiveness of participants, and pilot work showed that a choice block fully in the negative domain was perceived as too unfriendly a task.

Figure 2.10 shows the distribution of the total number of risky choices for our subject pool and shows that there is significant variation across participants, which is desirable for the purpose of using the variations across individuals to predict other behavior. Risk aversion and/or loss aversion are potentially key explanatory factors in TL firm turnover because nearly all of each driver's pay is based on piece rates (cents per mile for a fixed number of miles for each dispatch). Paychecks can vary quite substantially from one week to the next, and, thus, there is a certain level of short-run financial risk that goes with the job. The question for the study is to what extent this form of experimental measurement of financial risk is predictive of the impact of pay fluctuations on driver turnover, as compared to things such as survey responses and credit score.

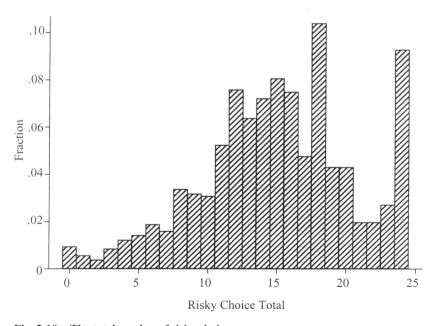

Fig. 2.10   The total number of risky choices

Demographics

This instrument is a compilation of thirty-seven demographic questions. The types of questions vary, but the areas that are covered include education level, languages, marital status, previous job experience, family lifestyle, racial or ethnic identity, country of birth, how many people are in the household, household income, and networking done while at training. These questions are mostly multiple choice, with a few numerical answer questions as well. There is no separate payment for completing this demographic questionnaire.

Figure 2.11 shows the distribution of ages of the trainee drivers, as compared to the distribution among blue-collar workers, as computed from the March 2005 Current Population Survey. The minimum age to acquire the CDL is twenty-one, so there are no new trainees that are less than this minimum age. However, in general the trainee pool is similar in distribution to the entire population of blue-collar workers in the United States, albeit with a modest shift toward the age range of twenty-one to thirty.

Figure 2.12 shows the distribution of the highest education level completed among the trainee drivers, with the distribution among blue-collar

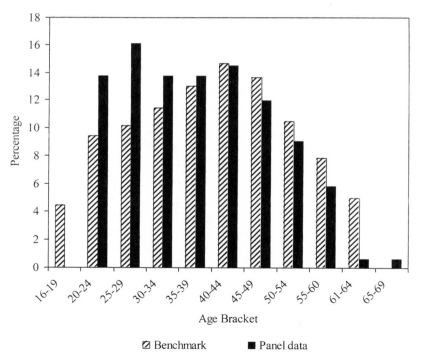

Age Bracket

☑ Benchmark   ■ Panel data

Fig. 2.11   Distribution of participant age with benchmark

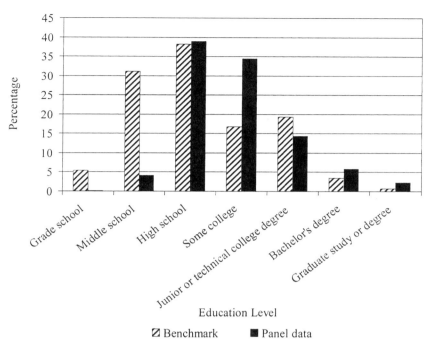

☑ Benchmark   ■ Panel data

Fig. 2.12   Participant education levels with benchmark

workers in the United States as a comparison. The minimum literacy requirements for the TL driver job are undoubtedly the reason there are very
few trainees with very low educational attainment, compared to the blue-
collar workforce in the United States. It is interesting that the trainee group
has a much higher proportion of individuals with some college, but possibly a lower proportion with a junior college or technical degree, as compared to the population of blue-collar workers. Given that someone who
has acquired some level of useful education in college is overqualified for
this job, this pattern is consistent with the view that completing a two-year
degree is indeed correlated with job market success as fewer of these individuals are in our subject pool. A speculation about the apparently slightly
higher proportion of four-year-degree holders in the trainee group, as
compared to the benchmark, is that these are folks with other options who
are attracted (at least initially) by the TL-driver lifestyle.

The Red Button

This experiment is designed to measure short-term impatience. It is the
last data collection event in the first of the two, two-hour sessions, and it is
followed by ten to twenty minutes of break time, during which participants
can use the restroom and stretch their legs and get something from the

vending machines if they wish. It is directly preceded by the demographic questionnaire, to which it is linked. This means that, unlike most of the other instruments, subjects do not have to wait until everyone else completes the prior activity, but instead each participant can start the red button task as soon as he or she has individually completed the demographic questionnaire. This setup is designed to minimize peer effects in the red button task as each subject will start the task at a different time.

The red button activity takes exactly ten minutes, and the task is to wait quietly until a timer on the task screen counts down from 600 seconds to zero. As described in section 2.6.3, during each session subjects are requested in general to either work on the task at hand or wait quietly. We ask that they do not to talk to their neighbors, nor engage in any other activity, such as pulling out something to read. During the red button task, these rules are quite strictly enforced. Participants are paid $5 if they complete the task by waiting the full ten minutes. However, subjects may choose to end this experiment earlier if they wish. Each click of a button below the countdown clock on the computer screen, which is labeled "Reduce Waiting Time," will cut the individual's waiting time—but each click also costs them $1. The first click reduces the waiting time by five minutes; the second click reduces the waiting time by three more minutes, and the third click reduces the waiting time by an additional two minutes. Once the timer says zero, no matter how long the subject has waited, then he or she is free to get up and leave the room for break time. As figure 2.13 shows, 29 percent of the participants clicked at least once. This is actually lower than we aimed for; our initial calibration runs may have led us to set the opportunity cost of the first click too high.

Patience is relevant to quit decisions, and being impatient can lead to poor job performance when a significant part of the job involves being able to wait on customer docks and then hurry up when customers are ready. Being patient in traffic is also a relevant job skill. We expect to investigate the extent to which red button choices will predict impatience on the job, as measured by quit decisions, controlling for prior earnings and prior waiting time during the earlier data collection activities.

2.6.5   Session Two Data Collection Events

The second two-hour block of data collection activities contains three behavioral economic experiments and three more conventional measures.

Time Preferences

In this experiment, there are twenty-eight questions that are divided into four blocks of seven questions each. There are two possible choices for each question: a smaller amount of money paid sooner, and a larger amount of money paid later. Each of the four blocks of seven questions follows the same format. The amount for the higher payoff at a later date is al-

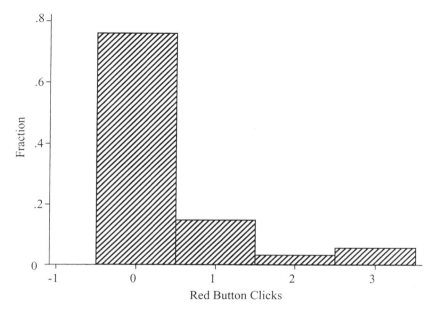

Fig. 2.13   Clicks to reduce waiting time at a cost

ways $80, and the amount for the lower payoff at an earlier time begins at $75 and decreases by $5 intervals to $45. The point at which a subject switches from the later payoff to the earlier one (if a switch is made) provides an implicit point estimate of the subject's discount rate over that time horizon.

The time frames are (1) today (Saturday) versus Monday; (2) today versus next Thursday; (3) Monday versus Monday plus one week, and (4) Monday versus Monday plus four weeks. The two matched pairs of time frames are designed to allow subjects that have different discount rates for choices with and without a front-end delay, that is, with and without an initial delay for both payments.[47] After all subjects have made their decisions, a participant draws one poker chip to select which of the twenty-eight questions will be activated, and then two poker chips are chosen the same way which identify two of the subjects in the session who will be paid for their choices on that question. Payments are, of course, made on the dates requested, either in person, or with an official bank check mailed in a University of Minnesota envelope.

As figure 2.14 shows, the three modes of the distribution of future

47. The contrast between choices in which one option is an immediate payment versus those in which both payments involve a delay will permit us to observe "impatience for immediate results," often described in the literature as quasi-hyperbolic discounting, if it should appear.

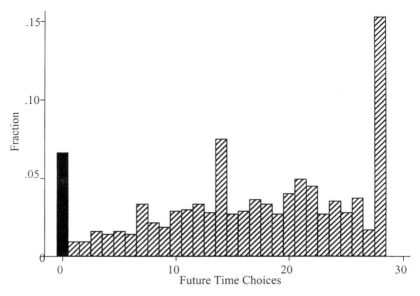

Fig. 2.14   Total future choices

choices are at zero, fourteen, and all, with a median of seventeen future choices out of a possible twenty-eight. There is a wide dispersion in individual responses. We expect to examine the relationship between this measure and such other measures as nonverbal IQ, risk/loss aversion, and impatience. And we will investigate the extent to which it adds predictive power to our statistical models of quits.

Nonverbal IQ

The IQ instrument used is a computerized adaptation of the Standard Progressive Matrices by J.C. Raven (Raven, Raven, and Court 2000); the authors created the adaptation under license from The Psychological Corporation.[48] Each question is presented as a graphic image. On top is a large rectangular box containing some kind of a pattern with a piece missing out of the lower right hand corner. On the bottom are six (or eight) possible pieces that could be used to complete the image on top. Each section starts with easy images and gets progressively more difficult.

The original instrument consists of five sections, each containing twelve questions. Our version is not fully comparable to the standard results for the instrument because we are actively administering only the last four sec-

48. Pilot work was done with two other instruments, but one had irresolvable licensing issues, and the other proved unsuitable for our setting. The first several administrations of the Raven's instrument were done with paper and pencil, while we arranged the license for the computerized adaptation (used by permission of Harcourt Assessment).

tions, due to time constraints. The original is primarily benchmarked in an untimed format, and we cut our subjects off after thirty-one minutes, having given a warning three minutes earlier.[49] The simplest way to match our data with the untimed reference benchmarks is to note that everyone in our subject pool finished the fourth section before the announcement of a time limit. Our correction is then simply to multiply our subjects' scores on sections two, three, and four by 5/3 to scale them up to the same range as the score for untimed subjects doing all five sections.[50]

After both verbal and written instructions and two practice questions, subjects fill out a "confidence question" that asks them how they think they will do as compared to other subjects in the room, by placing themselves in the correct quintile of the distribution of scores. When the Raven's task has been completed, the same confidence question is asked again. Subjects are paid an additional $2 for placing themselves in the correct quintile. In addition, two subjects are randomly chosen to be paid $1 per correct answer, for total possible earnings of $48 each for their question answers. Starting at about subject 200, we also began asking whether subjects want to find out their own score and the group average when they receive their payout.[51]

Figure 2.15 shows approximately how our panel compares to a standard benchmark population (citizens of Iowa City, IA, in the late 1990s.) On a scale of 0 to 60, our subject pool has a higher density between 36 and 44, and a lower one from 54 on up. The median for our subjects is about two points lower than that for the benchmark population. The distribution looks reasonable compared to groups of workers in other countries against which the regular version of the instrument has been benchmarked. The primary use of this measure in the project analysis will be as a control variable in predicting on-the-job outcomes. But we also expect to look at the relationships between this indicator of nonverbal IQ and the other participant characteristics that we measure. We will also examine how IQ, confidence about one's performance both before and after the task, and the desire for full information about one's performance are related.

Numeracy (Quantitative Literacy)

This instrument is part of the test of adult quantitative literacy from the Educational Testing Service. The full instrument consists of two sections, of which only the first section was used here, due to time constraints. The section is made up of twelve questions and subjects are given exactly twenty

---

49. There is one published benchmark from a French subject pool using a thirty-minute time limit, but including all five sections.

50. This approach produces unbiased estimates at the cost of greater variance.

51. The two selected to be paid for correct answers will learn their score from their payoff, so they will just get the average as new information, but these two subjects are selected after this question is asked.

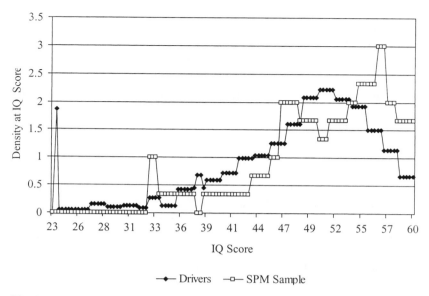

Fig. 2.15   **Density of (adapted) nonverbal IQ instrument scores for drivers compared to density of benchmark population scores**

minutes to complete the test. The test requires subjects to be able to add, subtract, compare numbers, compute a percentage, fill out a form, and to be able to read and understand a short problem, among other things.

As with the nonverbal IQ, after instructions and a brief practice question, subjects fill out a "confidence question" that asks them how they think they will do as compared to other subjects in the room, by quintiles. When the numeracy task has been completed, the same confidence question is asked again. Subjects are paid an additional $2 for placing themselves in the correct quintile. Two subjects are randomly chosen to be paid $2 per correct answer, for total possible earnings of $24 each for their question answers. In addition, at about subject 200 we began asking whether subjects want to find out their own score and the group average when they receive their payment.[52]

The distribution is not directly comparable to the distribution for the full instrument (i.e., when both sections are administered), but we appear to be getting good dispersion in performance (see figure 2.16). The mean score is 71 percent. The primary use of this in the project analysis will be as a control variable in predicting on-the-job outcomes. The job of TL driver re-

---

52. As with the nonverbal IQ indicator, the two selected to be paid for correct answers will learn their score from their payoff, so they will just get the average as new information, but these two subjects are selected after this question is asked.

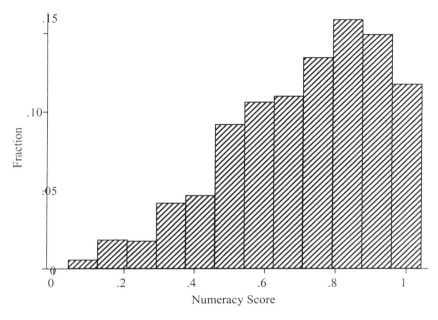

Fig. 2.16   Distribution of numeracy scores

quires continual application of numeracy skills, for example, in map reading and route planning, or in calculating hours remaining and hours coming available at specific future times, under the hours of service regulations for commercial motor vehicle operators. But we also expect to look at the relationships between this indicator of numeracy and the other participant characteristics that we measure. We will also examine how numeracy, confidence about one's performance both before and after the task, and the desire for full information about one's performance are related.

Ambiguity Aversion

Our ambiguity aversion experiment is identical to the risk/loss aversion experiment described in section 2.6.4, except for one detail: it is no longer known to be a 50/50 gamble if the subject chooses the uncertain option. Two blue poker chips and two green poker chips are placed in the bowl from which the winning color is drawn, and then out of sight of the subjects, six more chips are added that can be all green, all blue, or any mixture thereof. As a result, subjects only know that there is at least a 20 percent chance that green will be drawn and at least a 20 percent chance that blue will be drawn. All other features of the experiment are unchanged: there are four panels of six choices each, with the dollar values for certain and lottery outcomes as before. All subjects choose the certain payoff or the lottery in each question in each panel and then which color is theirs for the lottery outcomes.

Figure 2.17 shows results for the first panel, when the choice is between a fixed amount ranging from $2.00 to $7.00 or a lottery with outcomes of $2 or $10. The horizontal axis shows the total number of lotteries chosen in the initial risk/loss aversion task, while the vertical axis shows the same total for the ambiguous version. Participants who made the same choices in both cases would be on the 45-degree line. The size of the circles shows the number of participants at each node of the grid, and it is apparent that many subjects did change the number of lotteries they selected in widely varying ways. We will be looking to see which subjects choose more or fewer risky options and whether their shift, if any, is related to other experimental or survey measures and to on-the-job success.

Hit 15 Points

This is a backward induction, or planning, task in the form of a small game between subject and computer. The computer and the subject take turns adding points to the "points basket," and during each turn, the subject or the computer must add either one, two, or three points to the points basket. The goal is to be the player to add exactly the fifteenth point. The number of points in the points basket at the beginning of the round varies, and the computer and participant take turns going first. The first round is

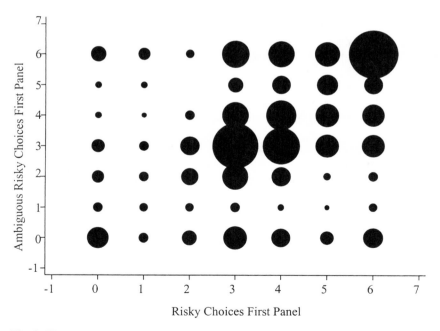

Fig. 2.17   Ambiguity and lottery choice

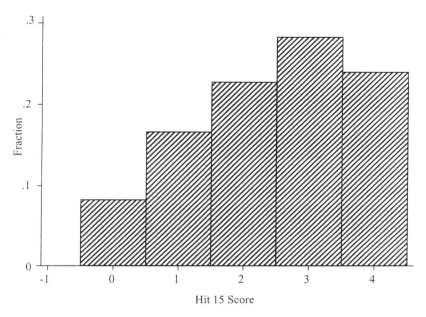

Fig. 2.18   Success in the Hit 15 Points game

set so as to give the subjects an example of how the first stage of backward induction works. Before each decision is made by the subject as to what number of points they want to add to the points basket, the subject is asked whether he or she will win or if the computer will win. The subjects are paid $1 for each round that they win.

Figure 2.18 shows the distribution of scores on this task. The median falls between two and three correct rounds of the game.[53] Together with numeracy, we anticipate that this measure will be predictive of on-the-job success, and especially of high versus low productivity. The TL truck drivers have to do numerical backward induction every day, to calculate back from routing and delivery goals that are from a few hours to a few days ahead, in order to decide on the optimal course of action in the present. One regularly used application is in figuring out how many hours they need to get to their destination and how many hours they have available to drive under the regulations governing the hours of service for commercial vehicle operators.

Risk, Impatience, and Cooperation Survey

The last instrument used during the Saturday initial data collection events with the panel study participants is a list of attitude questions about

---

53. As mentioned earlier, the N is 893 for this task, as we discovered a programming error in the z-Tree code for the game after 176 subjects had already taken part.

risk preferences, patience and impatience, and cooperation. It was assembled from a selection of papers in the literature that propose various survey-response measures for these characteristics of subjects. We intend these to also be tried out as control variables in order to see if they are useful and, if so, whether they are substitutes or complements to the experimental measures in predicting behavior on other measures and on-the-job success.

2.6.6   Other Measures of Interest

The applicant information collected by the cooperating firm on trainees provides a few other data items of interest. There is an indicator of whether the participant is a smoker (whether the trainee requested a hotel room in which smoking is permitted during initial training). This may turn out to be related to risk attitudes. In addition, because the trainees apply for credit for the training contract, the firm is able to supply us with a credit score. We want to examine the relationships among our measures of risk/loss aversion, ambiguity aversion, time preference, and impatience, on the one hand, and the credit score, on the other. We also are interested in determining whether the credit score useful in predicting on-the-job success, and, if so, whether it is a complement or substitute for our other measures.

2.7   Some Implications of the Truckers and Turnover Project

The present chapter has presented the context and design of the Truckers and Turnover Project at a stage when much of the initial data collection has taken place, but while follow-up data is still being collected and before results have become available. The proof of this pudding will, of course, be in the eating, when data collection is complete and results are available. But there are three points that can be made about the project at this stage. The first two are about research methodology, and the third is about the policy significance of the subjects of the project.

2.7.1   For the Industry Studies Community

First, for the industry studies research community, the project stands as a kind of "proof of concept" for adding behavioral economic experiments to the already rich mix of data collection techniques it utilizes. The Sloan Foundation's Web site states that the Foundation's goal in supporting industry studies is "to build a strong community of industry studies scholars who contribute to academia, to industries, and to government." Along with an interdisciplinary approach, the defining feature of this work according to the Foundation is that "industry studies scholars develop a deep understanding of particular industries by grounding their research in direct observation" (2007). The conventional tools for direct observation range from in-depth participant observation, to shorter structured site visits and interviews, to the collection of proprietary internal data for statistical analysis. To this list, the Truckers and Turnover Project prospectively adds behavioral economic field experiments. The key, in addition to having an existing cooperative research relationship between academics and firm(s), is to design the behavioral experiments to fit the specific institutional and business context. The new data-collection techniques must both complement more traditional approaches and also must credibly add value, from both an academic and a business standpoint. In this regard, the essentially individualized production process of TL motor freight is especially suited for an initial exploration of the uses of experiments that measure individual characteristics of employees. But one can easily imagine more complex social dilemma experiments being applied in teamwork employment settings, for instance.[54]

2.7.2   For the Experimental and Behavioral Economics Communities

Second, for the behavioral and experimental economics communities, the project also stands as a kind of "proof of concept" for the specific manner of applying behavioral experiments to the workplace used. As mentioned in section 2.6.1, there are a wide variety of scientific motives for conducting specific types of economic experiments, but one large cross-cutting categorization is whether the primary interest is in treatment effects or in measuring the characteristics of individual subjects. The latter is the purpose here, in keeping with the goal mentioned in the preceding paragraph about targeting the design to the specific institutional context.

The laboratory and the field are both relevant sources of empirical data to be used in the generation and evaluation of economic theory. But it is often difficult to translate the import of findings from studies in the fully controlled, abstract, and simplified setting of the lab directly to the uncontrolled and complex world of real employment relations and production processes. The approach here is close to what Harrison and List (2004) call a "framed field experiment," in which the experiments are similar to those that might be done in a lab with student subjects, but are instead conducted in the field setting of the driver training school, with new driver-trainees as subjects so that the framing for the (relatively abstract) experimental tasks is provided by these contextual factors. We anticipate finding some new empirical regularities when we examine the ability of our experiments to predict on-the-job outcomes, and, if so, we will have provided significant evidence for their "external validity," that is, for the ability of the lab measurements we use to capture individual characteristics that are important in practice in a specific real workplace setting.

2.7.3   The Larger Significance of Our Subject Pool

The last point we want to make is about the economic and human importance of the subjects of our study, driver-trainees in the truckload seg-

---

54. For some promising work along these lines, see the series of papers on fruit pickers in England by Bandiera, Barankay, and Rasul (2005, 2006).

ment of the motor freight industry. Much has been made in the last decade of the growth of the knowledge economy and of the role of workers who have the specific education and skills to prosper in it. But what about those who do not fit this description? In 2005, fully 40 percent of the U.S. workforce had a high school degree or less, and only 29 percent had a four-year college degree or more (Mishel, Bernstein, and Allegretto 2006, 153). As the United States continues its transition from a manufacturing economy to one in which service occupations and service industries dominate total employment, nonknowledge service workers will become an increasingly important part of the overall picture. The job of TL tractor-trailer driver is an archetypal example of nonknowledge work that is important in the knowledge economy.

The United States is a geographically large economy, so transportation and distribution have always been a key complement to U.S.-based production. And as the international trade in goods looms larger and larger in U.S. production and consumption, the more essential become the tasks associated with physically transporting traded goods and their ingredients here in the United States. Unlike some other types of services, the tasks involved in physically moving freight here are not subject to direct competition from abroad. According to the 2002 quinquennial Economic Census, trucking is the largest single industry in transportation services by employment, and the truckload segment of trucking had a headcount of approximately 800,000. This means that about 600,000 persons are TL tractor-trailer drivers at any one time.[55] Yet the ATA's survey results say that the typical turnover rate at TL firms is at least 50 percent per year.[56] If these figures are taken at face value, it means that several hundred thousand people train for and try out this job each year, only to leave it within a few months, probably having incurred a significant debt for training that most have little hope of repaying. Our pilot findings on turnover at the cooperating firm do not contradict this interpretation of the industry facts.

In this context a primary goal of the Truckers and Turnover Project is to use the best available means to measure the individual characteristics that make for success in this job. We will then ask whether the findings have actionable implications for business strategy and for public policy with respect to the labor market and education. Clearly, improving the match between job and employee by even a small amount would be a real improvement in economic circumstances for both firms and employees. It may even be that our findings will help in understanding how and to what extent the nature of these jobs can be improved, by quantifying more clearly the costs and benefits of lowering turnover.

55. This is by the rule of thumb that drivers make up about 75 percent of employment at a typical TL firm

56. The rate for large carriers typically averages over 100 percent, but most firms are small, and the rates for this group are usually between 50 percent and 100 percent per year.

Appendix A
The Truckers and Turnover Project Team

Project Organizer:

1. Stephen Burks, Division of Social Science, University of Minnesota, Morris; IZA; and Trucking Industry Program (Georgia Institute of Technology)

Project Coinvestigators (each colleague is collaborating on at least one component of the project, some on multiple components):

1. Jon Anderson, Division of Science and Math, University of Minnesota, Morris
2. Jeffrey Carpenter, Department of Economics, Middlebury College; IZA; and Norms and Preferences Research Network
3. Andrew Clark, Centre National de la Recherche Scientifique, PSE (France), and IZA
4. Lorenz Götte, Research Center for Behavioral Economics and Decisionmaking, Federal Reserve Bank of Boston, and IZA
5. Aldo Rustichini, Department of Economics, University of Minnesota, Twin Cities
6. Kristen Monaco, Department of Economics, California State University at Long Beach; and Trucking Industry Program (Georgia Institute of Technology)

On-site Research Team Members 2005 to 2006:

1. Kay Porter, Business Research Manager, Cooperating Firm
2. Adam Durand, Research Intern (fall 2005), University of Minnesota, Morris
3. William Leuthner, Research Intern (spring 2006), University of Minnesota, Morris
4. Erin Christenson, Research Intern (summer 2006), University of Minnesota, Morris

Appendix B

Summary List and Time Line for Data Items Collected

1.   Project Component One: Statistical Case Study

Data items here come in separate data report files, each of which has different data definitions and data errors. These are joined into a master data file by the project team, in a labor-intensive data validation, cleaning, documentation, and merging process. Initial data set covers January 1, 2002, through December 31, 2005, by construction from the individual years. Updates are planned on semiannual or quarterly basis.

1.1. Payroll-based data. Rolled-up totals of activities for which drivers are paid, by driver and week. Some pay deductions, but not all that would be of economic interest, are included. Typical items of interest include paid miles, the number of units of mileage pay (approximately the number of dispatches), and the number of times supplementary pay was received for particular work event (examples: hand unloading, weighing the rig on a scale). Includes operations-related driver characteristics (e.g., the terminal at which the driver is based). Not included in the initial version: the identity of the direct supervisor. Created by project team from pay transaction files.

1.2. Demographic data. Marital status, gender, and (for those drivers choosing to self-identify to the firm) racial category. Not included, as not captured electronically by firm: educational attainment. Birthdates are automatically included only in 2006 updates and later (see item 3.4).

1.3. Weekly list of drivers employed, with a limited set of driver characteristics. (Used as a check on payroll-based data because payment is not always made in the week activities took place.)

1.4. Weekly list of drivers hired in that week, with a limited set of driver characteristics.

1.5. Weekly list of drivers who separated in that week, with a limited set of driver characteristics.

1.6. Application records. Variables from the application process for those for whom a hire event is observed; has significant number of missing values. Typical items of interest: did applicant request a smoking hotel room when attending the training school, and how did applicant learn about the training opportunity?

2.   Project Component Two: Panel Study of New Hires

2.1. Initial Intake Data on Driver Trainees. Collected from December 12, 2006, through August 8, 2007, on twenty-three Saturdays. 1,069 trainees entered the study, and there is good data on 1,036 of them, except that a bug in the initial version of Hit 15 Points (item 2.1.2.5) limits good data that includes this item to a subset of 893 persons.

2.1.1. First Data Collection Block.

> 2.1.1.1. Sequential strategic form Prisoner's Dilemma experiment. Choices as first and second mover, plus estimates of others' choices are collected.

> 2.1.1.2. Multidimensional Personality Questionnaire. Standard (short form of) instrument identifying eleven personality factors.

> 2.1.1.3. Risk/Loss Aversion experiment. Four panels of seven choices, each between a small monetary gamble and a small fixed sum.

> 2.1.1.4. Demographic profile. List of more than fifty questions compiled by project team, including information on educational attainment, labor market history, next best employment opportunity, and so on.

> 2.1.1.5. Red Button experiment. Subjects offered opportunity to leave for break early at a payoff cost.

2.1.2. Second Data Collection Block.

> 2.1.2.1. Time Preferences experiment. Four panels of six choices, each between a smaller amount at an earlier time and a larger amount at a later time. Two panels include "today" as the earlier time, and two panels have a front-end delay, with "Monday" (two days after the Saturday data collection) as the earlier time.

> 2.1.2.2. Nonverbal IQ: Sections two, three, and four of the original five sections of the Raven's Progressive Matrices. Participants are asked to rate their relative performance before and after the instrument, as well as whether they want to know their score and the group average upon receiving their final payout.

> 2.1.2.3. Quantitative Literacy: Section one of Form A of the Quantitative Literacy portion of the Educational Testing Service's (ETS) Tests of Applied Literacy Skills. (ETS provides standardized scoring only for subjects that do both sections of this test.) Participants are asked to rate their relative performance before and after the instrument, as well as whether they want to know their score and the group average upon receiving their final payout.

> 2.1.2.4. Ambiguity Aversion experiment. Repetition of Risk/Loss Aversion, except that we provide less information about the probability distribution in the gamble choices.

> 2.1.2.5. Hit 15 Points backward induction experiment.

> 2.1.2.6. Miscellaneous questions from the psychology and behavioral economics literature about impatience, risk, cooperation, and so on.

2.2. Follow-up Data from Trainees and their Families. The follow-up data collection period runs through August of 2008.

    2.2.1. Human Resources Data from Firm.

        2.2.1.1. Subset of Applicant Flow data, including whether trainee requested a smoking room at training.

        2.2.1.2. Credit score of the trainee (available because trainees sign a credit contract for training costs).

        2.2.1.3. If and when a driver exits, the exit date and a code for up to three reasons for the separation.

    2.2.2. Mail Surveys to New-Hire Panel Drivers.

        2.2.2.1. Continuing driver surveys. Forty-five questions about current opinions and recent work events, including some open-ended ones, sent to currently employed drivers between two and four weeks after the following tenure milestones: six months, twelve months, eighteen months, and twenty-four months.

        2.2.2.2. Exited driver surveys. Forty-four questions about current opinions, recent work events, and the driver's exit event, sent between two and four weeks after exit.

    2.2.3. Mail Surveys to Families of Trainees.

        2.2.3.1. Initial survey to families of new-hire panel drivers, to approximately match in timing the initial intake information from drivers. Not actually started until the beginning of April of 2006, at which time the families of all panel participants who had entered since December 2005, were surveyed. Thirty-five questions developed by project team, including some open-ended ones.

        2.2.3.2. Surveys to families of continuing drivers. Thirty-five questions about current opinions and recent family-work-life events, including some open-ended ones, sent to families of currently employed drivers between two and four weeks after the following tenure milestones: six months, twelve months, eighteen months, and twenty-four months.

        2.2.3.3. Surveys to families of exited drivers. Twenty-nine questions about current opinions, recent family-work-life events, and the driver's exit event, sent between two and four weeks after exit.

    2.2.4. Weekly two-question survey to currently employed drivers, in their trucks, via satellite link, on Wednesdays. Question 1: How satisfied are you with your job right now (1–5 Likert response scale)? Question 2: How many pay miles do you expect to run next week? These data will be documented, cleaned, and merged with the main panel study data set, at some point in the future.

    2.2.5. Time-at-home records. The firm's recording of when drivers request to be at home, and how well the firm does at fulfilling those requests, is accumulating in a data file that starts in early 2006, and is expected to be updated through August 2008. These data will be documented, cleaned, and merged with the main panel study data set at some point in the future.

3.   Control Groups for New Hire Panel Study

3.1. The initial intake data collected on driver trainees (all the items in 2.1) was also collected from 100 undergraduate students recruited at the University of Minnesota, Morris, in a campus computer lab, during the spring semester of 2007. The same protocol was used throughout, with the exception that the demographic profile questions were modified to be appropriate for student subjects.

3.2. The initial intake data collected on driver trainees (all the items in 2.1) is also planned to be collected from 100 adult subjects who are residents of Stevens County, MN, the rural county in which the University of Minnesota, Morris, campus is situated. The plan is to recruit subjects from the county who are not students, nor faculty, nor professional staff, during the summer and fall semesters of 2007. The same protocol will be used throughout, with the exception that the demographic profile questions will be modified to be appropriate for these subjects.

4.   Miscellaneous Supplementary Data

4.1. Records of use of the satellite link in each tractor to report trailers needing maintenance. Available on all drivers by week from mid-2006; to be updated periodically. May be usable to generate an index of on-the-job cooperation with other drivers.[57]

4.2. Records of the use of the satellite link in each tractor to respond to a particular message from the firm's central dispatch office. Available on all drivers by week from mid-2006, to be updated periodically. May be usable to generate an index of on-the-job cooperation with the firm.[58]

4.3. Identification of direct supervisors by driver and work week. This

---

57. When a driver is directed to hook onto a trailer spotted at a customer location but the trailer turns out to be mechanically faulty and can't be used, it is a negative job event. This happens when the driver who previously had the trailer did not report it as bad, either because he did not realize it was or because he refused to take the time to do so. So when a driver does take the time to report as mechanically faulty a trailer he is dropping and will not immediately use further, thereby delaying the start of his next assignment, he can be said to incur a personal cost to provide a public good for drivers. The main issue in constructing an index is limiting confounds with unobservable factors, such as whether the driver is reporting the trailer as bad because he needs it repaired for his own immediate use.

58. Responding to the macro from the central office is a formal, but not a substantive, job requirement. Responding primarily helps anonymous staff members at the firm's central office, so if a driver delays proceeding with his current assignment to respond, it can be con-

data is potentially available in a supplementary file that may permit the historical data set used for the statistical case study to be updated. Updates from 2006 and later will include this information in data files already being amalgamated to make the statistical case study data set.

4.4. Birthdates. These are in the standard demographic data files on all drivers starting in 2006. Birthdates for drivers observed in earlier years reside in a supplementary file that must be documented and cleaned and merged with the 2002 to 2005 statistical case study data set.

5.   Merging New Hire Panel and Statistical Case Study Data.

Beginning in the second half of 2008, when the statistical case study data files have been updated to include all of 2007 and at least some of 2008, it is intended to merge the two data sets together for those drivers who are in both data files. This will permit the regression models developed for the statistical case study to be run on the panel study drivers, with the ability to test what additional predictive power is added to those models by the new data items collected in the new hire panel portion of the study.

References

Alfred P. Sloan Foundation. 2007. Industry studies. *Programs: Standard of living and economic performance.* http://www.sloan.org/programs/pg_standard.shtml.

ATA Economic and Statistics Group. 2005. Employee turnover and workforce changes: Q4:2004. *Trucking Activity Report* 13:7.

Bandiera, O., I. Barankay, and I. Rasul. 2005. Social preferences and the response to incentives: Evidence from personnel data. *Quarterly Journal of Economics* 120 (3): 917–62.

———. 2006. The evolution of cooperative norms: Evidence from a natural field experiment. *B.E. Journals in Economic Analysis and Policy: Advances in Economic Analysis and Policy* 6 (2): 1–26.

Beadle, A. D. 2004. Building driver shortage. *Traffic World* 268 (42): 26–27.

Belman, D. L. and K. Monaco. 2001. The effects of deregulation, de-unionization, technology, and human capital on the work and work lives of truck drivers. *Industrial and Labor Relations Review* 54 (2A): 502–24.

Belman, D. L., K. Monaco, and T. Brooks. 2005. *Sailors of the concrete sea: A portrait of truck drivers' work and lives.* Lansing, MI: Michigan State University Press.

Belzer, M. H. 1995. Collective bargaining after deregulation: Do the teamsters still count? *Industrial and Labor Relations Review* 48 (4): 636–55.

Belzer, M. H., D. Rodriguez, and S. Sedo. 2002. Paying for safety: An economic

sidered a personally costly form of cooperation with management. The main issue in constructing an index is limiting confounds with unobservable factors, such as with variations in the level of exposure to such macro requests.

analysis of the effect of compensation on truck driver safety. FMCSA Report. Washington, DC: Federal Motor Carrier Safety Administration.

Boyer, K., and S. V. Burks. 2007. Stuck in the slow lane: Traffic composition and the measurement of labor productivity in the U.S. trucking industry. IZA Discussion Paper no. 2576. Bonn, Germany: Institute for the Study of Labor.

Bureau of Labor Statistics. 2002. Historical hours and earnings—Average hours and earnings of production or non-supervisory workers on private non-farm payrolls by major industry sector, 1964 to date. U.S. Department of Labor. ftp://146.142.4.23/pub/suppl/empsit.ceseeb2.txt.

Burks, S. V. 1999. The origins of parallel segmented labor and product markets: A reciprocity-based agency model with an application to motor freight. PhD diss., University of Massachusetts, Amherst.

Burks, S. V., J. Carpenter, and L. Götte. 2006. Performance pay and the erosion of worker cooperation: Field experimental evidence. IZA Discussion Paper no. 2013. Bonn, Germany: Institute for the Study of Labor.

Burks, S. V., K. Monaco, and J. Myers-Kuykindall. 2004a. The balance between private and for-hire carriage and trends in the use of large trucks (1977 to 1997). *Journal of the Transportation Research Forum* 43 (2): 159–71.

———. 2004b. Trends in the use of large trucks by truckload and less-than-truckload motor carriers in the 1990s. *Journal of the Transportation Research Forum* 43 (2): 173–87.

Cain, G. G. 1976. The challenge of segmented labor market theories to orthodox theory: A survey. *Journal of Economic Literature* 11 (4): 1215–57.

Camerer, C., and E. Fehr. 2004. Measuring social norms and preferences using experimental games: A guide for social scientists. In *Foundations of human sociality: Economic experiments and ethnographic evidence from fifteen small-scale societies,* ed. J. Henrich, R. Boyd, S. Bowles, C. Camerer, E. Fehr, and H. Grintis, 55–95. Oxford: Oxford University Press.

Casey, J. F. 1987. An assessment of the truck driver shortage. *Transportation Executive Update* 1 (1): 20–23.

Cleves, M. A., W. A. Gould, and R. G. Gutierrez. 2004. *An introduction to survival analysis using Stata, revised edition.* College Station, TX: Stata Press.

Corsi, T., and J. R. Stowers. 1991. Effects of a deregulated environment on motor carriers: A systematic multi-segment analysis. *Transportation Journal* 30 (3): 4–28.

Cox, K. 2004. TL driver turnover rate reaches new record high. *Transport Topics* (January 5):5, 35.

Cullen, D. 1996. You get what you pay for: J. B. Hunt Transport Services Inc.'s driver compensation package. *Fleet Owner* 91 (11): 82–83.

Dickens, W. T., and K. Lang. 1993. Labor market segmentation theory: Reconsidering the evidence. In *Labor economics: Problems in analyzing labor markets,* ed. W. Darity, Jr., 141–80. Norwell, MA: Kluwer Academic.

Fischbacher, U. 2007. z-Tree: Zurich Toolbox for Ready-made Economic Experiments. *Experimental Economics,* forthcoming.

Gallup Organization. 1997. Empty seats and musical chairs: Critical success factors in truck driver retention. Arlington, VA: ATA Foundation.

Global Insight, Inc. 2005. *The U.S. truck driver shortage: Analysis and forecasts.* Arlington, VA: American Trucking Associations.

Griffin, G., and L. Kalnbach. 2002. Predicting and classifying voluntary turnover decisions for truckload drivers. Report no. MPC-02-135. Fargo, ND: Upper Great Plains Transportation Institute, North Dakota State University.

Griffin, G. C., J. M. Rodriguez, and B. M. Lantz. 1992. Job satisfaction in U.S.

commercial drivers. Report no. DP-90. Fargo, ND: The Upper Great Plains Transportation Institute, North Dakota State University.

Harrison, G. W., and J. A. List. 2004. Field experiments. *Journal of Economic Literature* 42 (4): 1009–55.

Isidore, C. 1997. Hunt gambles on pay raise to keep drivers. *Journal of Commerce* 411 (28917): 1A.

Kiefer, N. M. 1988. Economic duration data and hazard functions. *Journal of Economic Literature* 26:646–79.

Mishel, L., J. Bernstein, and S. Allegretto. 2006. *The state of working America, 2006–2007.* Ithaca, NY: ILR Press.

Patrick, C. J., J. J. Curtin, and A. Tellegan. 2002. Development and validation of a brief form of the Multidimensional Personality Questionnaire. *Psychological Assessment* 14 (2): 150–63.

Raven, J., J. C. Raven, and J. H. Court. 2000. Section 3: The Standard Progressive Matrices. In *Manual for Raven's Progressive Matrices and Vocabulary Scales.* San Antonio, TX: Psychological Corporation.

Reiskin, J. 2006. Shipper changes cut distances that truckload freight travels. *Transport Topics* (March 13):1, 49.

Rodriguez, J., M. Kosir, B. Lantz, G. Griffin, and J. Glatt. 2000. The costs of truckload driver turnover. Report no. SP-146. Fargo, ND: Upper Great Plains Transportation Institute, North Dakota State University. 1–18.

Stephenson, F. J., and R. J. Fox. 1996. Driver retention solutions: Strategies for for-hire truckload (TL) employee drivers. *Transportation Journal* 35 (4): 12–26.

U.S. Census Bureau. 2004. *Truck transportation: 2002.* Washington, DC: Economics and Statistics Administration, U.S. Department of Commerce.

Waxler, C. 1997. J. B. Hunt Transport shares may drop further. *Forbes* 159 (8): 382–83.

3

Subjective Evaluation of Performance and Evaluation Interview
Empirical Evidence from France

Marc-Arthur Diaye, Nathalie Greenan, and Michal W. Urdanivia

"If the economic organization meters poorly, with rewards and production only loosely correlated, then productivity will be smaller; but if the economic organization meters well productivity will be greater."   —Alchian and Demsetz (1972, 779)

3.1 Introduction

A main contribution of linked longitudinal employer-employee data is to provide a decomposition of wage rates into components due to individual heterogeneity and to firm heterogeneity. In France, Abowd, Creecy, and Kramarz (2002) show that the person effect and firm effect account, respectively, for 70 percent and 20 percent of the variation of wages. The person-effect component is bigger in France than in the United States where it represents half of the wage variation.

This indicates that the devices used by firms to attract or select workers with specific characteristics play a central role in determining the firm's wage structure. However, these devices have not been investigated thoroughly by economic analysis. In this paper, we are going to assess individual evaluation

Marc-Arthur Diaye is an associate professor at the Center for the Study Political Economics at the University of Evry, and a research fellow at the Center for Labor Studies. Nathalie Greenan is a researcher at the National Centre for Scientific Research and a research director at the Center for Labor Studies. Michal W. Urdanivia is a PhD student in the Department of Applied Mathematics at the University Panthéon-Sorbonne, and a research assistant with the Center for Labor Studies.

This paper was presented at the Conference on Analysis of Firms and Employees (CAFE 2006) held September 29 to 30, 2006, in Nuremberg, Germany. We gratefully acknowledge the financial support provided by the Institute for Employment Research (IAB), the Data Access Center (FDZ-BA/IAB), The Deutsche Forschungsgemeinschaft (German Research Foundation), their Research Network "Flexibility in Heterogeneous Labour Markets," the Alfred P. Sloan Foundation, and the National Science Foundation. We are deeply indebted to Emmanuel Duguet, Lynn Zucker, and the two referees who helped us to improve this paper. We thank the participants at the CAFE 2006, the BETA-Cereq (University Louis Pasteur) seminar on labor markets, the PSE-Jourdan seminar on labor markets and inequalities (especially Andrew Clark), and the TEAM Seminar of the Centre d'Economie de la Sorbonne for their comments.

interview, a human resource management (HRM) practice that could contribute to the two goals of selecting workers and stimulating their effort. In France, 52 percent of employees with more than one year of seniority in manufacturing had been evaluated at least once in 1997. At that time, evaluation interviews were not regulated at the national or at the industry level.

As an HRM practice, the function of evaluation interviews is not clearcut. Sometimes viewed as formal performance appraisal systems, evaluation interviews often use complex evaluation grids referring to loosely defined behavioral characteristics as well as to precisely defined goals and measured criteria.

To assess evaluation interviews, it is useful to analyze them theoretically and to investigate empirically how they are implemented within firms. The theoretical framework we are going to use in this paper is the one (hereafter the DGU model) proposed by Diaye, Greenan, and Urdanivia (2007).

Intuitively, individual evaluation interviews are used to assess performance once the employee has undertaken her or his task. We will use here the term of ex post evaluation interviews. But, if we refer to a classic wage-setting mechanism, there is no need for evaluation. The incentive wages drives the employee toward the level of effort that is optimal for the employer. In the DGU model, ex post evaluation interviews insure risk adverse agent against technological or market uncertainty.

In the French context, Crifo, Diaye, and Greenan (2004) observe that evaluation interviews are significantly more frequent when the employee is involved in collective work. The model of ex post evaluation interviews is limited to give account of the function of evaluation interviews when employees work in teams because individual performance appraisal become difficult when the output cannot be separated between the members of a team (Alchian and Demsetz 1972). Diaye, Greenan, and Urdanivia (2007) propose a model of ex ante individual evaluation interviews specific to the teamwork context, where evaluation comes first, before the constitution of teams and aims at fostering a team spirit. They conclude their theoretical approach by establishing some predictions about drivers and outcomes of individual evaluation interviews.

In this paper, we want to assess empirically part of these predictions. Our empirical investigation rests on a matched employer-employee survey (section 3.2) on organizational change and information and communication technology (ICT) use (computerization and organizational change [COI]). In the labor force section of the survey, employees are asked whether they have been interviewed individually at least once in 1997. They also give information on work organization, on personal characteristics, and on outcomes. The business section of the survey gives a detailed set of firm-level characteristics reflecting technological and organizational choices implemented in French manufacturing at the end of the 1990s. We use a propensity score methodology (section 3.3) to evaluate (section 3.4) the causal effect of individual evaluation interviews on effort, work overload, and wage setting. In section 3.5, we conclude.

3.2   The Data

We are going to use a matched employer-employee survey, the survey on computerization and organizational change (COI), to assess the DGU model of evaluation interviews. The information we have in the survey will not allow us to test all the predictions from their model. However, from the employee section of the survey, we have some information on the characteristics of work (whether individual or collective), on evaluation interviews, on effort, and on wages. This will allow us to cover the main features underlined by the DGU model. More precisely, we will be able to test whether evaluation interviews lead to higher levels of effort than classical incentive schemes (prediction 1). Our estimation strategy will also allow us to assess the existence of a selection effect associated with the implementation of evaluation interviews in individual and collective work organizations (prediction 2). Furthermore, using measures of work overload, we will check whether evaluation interviews drive workers toward an excessive work intensity leading to inefficiencies (prediction 3). Indeed, according to the DGU model, evaluation interviews in a context of supermodular technology (i.e., the conditional probability of success of the task is a strictly increasing convex function of the employees' level of effort) lead to an overintensification of work in the sense that the employees' level of effort will be higher than the one "required" by the firm. The reason is the selection effect regarding disutility of effort. Prediction 3 is a possible consequence of this result on overintensification. It is important to test this implication because work overload is a major factor of stress and has long-term implications on the health of the workforce, especially in a context of aging. Finally, we will be able to test our predictions on wage differentials and on the employees' knowledge of the rules driving wage setting between the scheme with evaluation interviews and the classical incentive scheme (prediction 4).

The COI survey was conducted at the end of 1997 by the French public statistical system.[1] We are going to work on a representative sample of

---

1. The conception and coordination of the COI survey has been directed by the Center for Labor Studies. The survey has been carried out in a consortium involving the Ministry of Labor (DARES), the Ministry of Industry (SESSI), the Ministry of Agriculture (SCEES), and the National Institute of Statistics and Economic Studies (INSEE). It benefited from very high response rates: 82 percent for employers and 75 percent for the employees. For a detailed description of the survey, see Greenan and Hamon-Cholet (2001) or http://www .enquetecoi.net.

manufacturing firms with more than fifty employees and on a sample of randomly selected employees within these firms. In matched employer-employee surveys, the budget constraint implies a trade-off between trying to capture the diversity of firms and trying to capture the diversity of the workforce within firms. By choosing to interview small sample of employees (one, two, or three) within each firm, COI chooses to favor the diversity of firms. As interviewed employees have at least one year of seniority within the firm, they belong to its core workforce.

In the full sample of the labor force section of the survey, there are 4,295 employees. However, in our analysis, we do not take into account employees with supervision activities (1,214 individuals) or employees working part time (177 individuals). Indeed, the former combine a position of Principal and of Agent that we have not investigated theoretically, while part time leads to badly measured effort and wages. We obtain a subsample of 2,904 employees.

The available information on the practice of individual evaluation interviews stems from the following question: Do you have at least one evaluation interview per year (yes / no)? Because of their seniority in the firm, we know that all interviewed employees had the opportunity of being evaluated at least once.

The labor force section of the COI survey describes in detail work organization. It includes a whole set of questions capturing whether work is structured around group activities. From these questions, we build up five different measures of interaction between employees in the course of the work process: being part of a team, time spent in teamwork, intensity of communication with other workers, level of support from other workers, participation in meetings (see appendix A for detailed questions). These five measure are positively correlated, with correlations ranging between 0.04 (intensity of communication with time spent in team work) and 0.18 (being part of a team and level of support from other workers). Thus, they measure different dimensions of collective work. We derive from these five measures a synthetic binary indicator of collective work. When it takes the value 1, the employee is considered as being a "collective" worker, when it takes the value 0, he or she is considered as being an individual worker. According to this variable, our sample of employees breaks down into 1,537 individual workers and 1,367 collective workers.

Table 3.1 gives the distribution of individual evaluation interviews according to our synthetic binary indicator of collective work. In 1997, 37.2% of the employees have been interviewed at least once. Evaluation interviews are positively correlated with collective work: 47 percent of collective workers have been evaluated against 29 percent of individual employees.

The COI survey also measures different effort indicators. Productive effort is measured through two questions indicating if the employee works

Table 3.1   Evaluation among individual workers and collective workers

Evaluation	Individual workers	Collective workers
Yes	445 (29%)	637 (47%)
No	1,092 (71%)[a]	730 (53%)
Total	1,537 (53%)	1,367 (47%)

[a]Percentage with respect to the analyzed subsample of 2,904 employees.

longer than the usual hours some days or some weeks. Productive effort is considered as *very high* if the employee sometimes increases hours worked for personal reasons, as *high* if he or she sometimes increases hours worked in response to the firm's demand, and as *low* if longer hours never happen. According to these three situations, the productive effort indicator, respectively, takes a value of 2, 1, or 0. The cognitive effort indicator is a binary variable indicating if the employee makes propositions to improve his or her workstations, the production process, or the machines. It measures an involvement in collective knowledge building about the productive activity, allowing continuous improvement of the production process.

Two additional measures are included in the analysis to identify if effort is going beyond reasonable levels, creating an overload that could be detrimental for work efficiency and for the employee's health. A first variable indicates how often an employee has to hurry in the course of his or her work. Four states are taken into account: hurrying almost all the time, hurrying for one quarter of the time or more, hurrying for less than a quarter of the time, and never. The hurry variable, respectively, takes the value 4, 3, 2, and 1 according to the intensity of the pressure. Work overload is also measured through a binary indicator telling whether the employee often has to interrupt one task to carry out another urgent and nonanticipated one.

Finally, we measure the employee's annualized net wage in euros. As it comes from an administrative data file used to compute social contributions, it is precisely measured and includes all bonuses, taxed allowances, and compensations in kind. We also build up an indicator of the employees' ability to predict their wages. It rests on a question about the elements that have a big influence on the employee's wage or promotion, followed by a list of eight items. We compute the ratio of the number of yes responses to the list of items, on the number of yes and no, which gives an indicator taking its value between 0 and 1. Zero means that the employee has no idea of how to increase his or her wage or chance of promotion, 1 means that the employee knows that he or she can improve his or her situation and is aware of what to do to obtain this outcome.

3.3   Estimation Strategy

We want to measure the impact of evaluation interviews on effort, work overload, and wages, but we know from the DGU model that evaluation interviews induce a selection process. Employees with a low disutility of effort and, in the case on teamwork, with a team spirit are going to be attracted by jobs where evaluation interviews are conducted periodically. A possible way to measure outcomes related to evaluation interviews, taking into account the selection effect, is to consider evaluation interviews as treatments and to apply a propensity score method to match each treated individual with a nontreated individual with the same characteristics in order to turn our nonexperimental data into a quasi experiment.

A simple way to test the predictions of the DGU model is to consider evaluation interviews as treatments and to evaluate the effect of this treatment on the chosen variables for measuring effort, wages, and beliefs about wages. More precisely, let t be a dummy variable equal to 1 if the employee declares being evaluated and 0 otherwise. Three quantities are of interest to us. The first is the average treatment effect over the whole population, written C; the second is the average treatment effect over the treated individuals, written C_1; and the third is the average treatment effect over the nontreated individuals, written C_0. More precisely, let Y be the chosen variables for measuring effort, wages, and beliefs about wages. Then C measures the variation of Y that would be observed if the whole population was treated; C_1 is an evaluation of the effect of the treatment in the usual sense because it concerns the treated population; and C_0 is a prospective evaluation in the sense that it measures what would happen if the nontreated population was treated. We have:

$$C = E(Y_1 - Y_0)$$
$$C_1 = E(Y_1 - Y_0 \mid t = 1)$$
$$C_0 = E(Y_1 - Y_0 \mid t = 0),$$

where Y_1 is the observed value of Y that results when receiving treatment (that is, when being evaluated), Y_0 is the observed value of Y that results when not receiving treatment (that is, when not being evaluated), and $E(.)$ denotes expectation in the population. Intuitively, an estimate of an average treatment effect could be the difference between the average of Y over the population of treated individuals and its average over the population of nontreated individuals, that is,

$$\overline{Y}_1 - \overline{Y}_0,$$

where $\overline{Y}_1$ and $\overline{Y}_0$ are, respectively, the average of Y for treated (evaluated employees) and the nontreated (nonevaluated employees).

However, broadly speaking, the main problem when evaluating the effect of a treatment is that for each individual we only observe

$$Y = t \times Y_1 + (1 - t) \times Y_0 = \begin{cases} Y_1 & \text{if } t = 1 \\ Y_0 & \text{if } t = 0 \end{cases}.$$

Then it can be shown that the average difference between treated and non-treated individuals can be the cause of a selection bias because the data does not result from a randomized experiment. And when testing evaluation effects (on effort, overload, and wages), there is a need to control for naturally occurring systematic differences in background characteristics between the treated population and the nontreated population, which would not occur in the context of a randomized experiment. Moreover, according to prediction 2, individual evaluation interviews affect employees' efforts through a selection effect associated to disutility or to team spirit, an incentive effect that in our case is estimated by the average treatment (evaluation) effect. Therefore, in order to estimate the average treatment (evaluation) effect, it is also necessary to control for the selection bias due to disutility. Although it seems difficult to control "directly" for this selection effect because disutility or team spirit are not observable characteristics, we can assume that they are grounded on observable background characteristics of the employee and of the employer, and, hence, controlling for them allows to control for the selection.

We will discuss in the next section the background characteristics we will take into account to estimate the effect of individual evaluation interviews. We choose to use the propensity score methodology introduced by Rosenbaum and Rubin (1983). This method reduces the entire collection of background characteristics to a single composite characteristic that appropriately summarizes the collection. Propensity score technology allows to correct the selection bias by matching individuals according to their propensity score, which is the estimated probability of receiving the treatment (of being evaluated) given background characteristics. We are going to use a nonparametric kernel matching estimator proposed by Heckman, Ichimura, and Todd (1997, 1998), which under some regularity assumptions is convergent and asymptotically normal.

3.4   The Results

3.4.1   Determinants of Individual Evaluation Interviews

The first step of the propensity score method is to analyze the determinants of evaluation interviews, taking into account background characteristics that influence the employee's probability of receiving a periodical evaluation interview and the three categories of outcomes we consider: effort, work overload, and wages.

In this step, it is very important to take into account individual effects as well as contextual effects. As we have pointed out, personal characteristics of the employee like team spirit or disutility of effort are going to play a crucial role in influencing both the chances of being evaluated and the outcomes we consider. These characteristics are not directly observable, but we are going to take into account observables that are possibly correlated with them: gender, age, seniority, education level, and occupation. It is clear that these personal characteristics have impacts on effort levels, work overload, and wages.

The fact that our employee sample is matched with a survey describing the characteristics of firms is an important advantage in our estimation strategy. The DGU model has stressed that the production technology plays a role in the diffusion of evaluation interviews. A supermodular technology is more favorable than a submodular technology. In order to control for the technology, we are going to include the regression size and sector dummies. Stemming from an employer database, information on size and sector is much more precise than the information usually included in labor force surveys. We also include a measure of the firm's computerization intensity. We choose to build up a variable describing the intensity of numerical data transfers within and outside the firm. Moreover, evaluation interviews could be complementary to other organizational practices, and these practices could also have an influence on outcomes. Eight new organizational practices are considered in the logistic regression: quality certification, total quality management, methods to analyze products and processes (value analysis; functional analysis; Failure Mode, Effects, and Criticality Analysis [FMECA]), total productive maintenance (TPM), organization in profit center, formal in-house customer/supplier contracts, system of just-in-time delivery, and system of just-in-time production. We also detail different teamwork practices: self-managed teams, problem solving groups, and project teams. Finally, we take into account the evolution of the number of hierarchical layers in the firm and variables indicating difficulties connected with the implementation of organizational changes.

Appendix C presents the parameters estimated of the logistic models explaining individual evaluation interviews for individual workers and for collective workers. In the case of individual workers, we find that employee characteristics have higher explanatory power than employer characteristics. More precisely, male workers in executive or middle management positions with either low seniority (one or two years) or intermediate seniority (seven to ten years) have a higher probability of being evaluated. We have to keep in mind that even though some of the interviewed workers have management positions, they have no formal hierarchical authority as they declare no subordinates. Among the employer characteristics, the only variables with significant influence are size, with a positive impact of the highest size cluster; sector, with a positive impact of five sectors (pharmaceutical, perfumes, and cleaning products; chemicals, rubber, and plastic products; electrical and electronic equipment; electrical and electronic components; and shipbuilding, aircraft, and railway); and quality certification (ISO 9001, ISO 9002, and EAQF).

In contrast, in the case of collective workers, employer characteristics tend to explain more than employee characteristics. Indeed, for team workers the only personal characteristic that influences the probability of being evaluated is the level of education: a second or third level of education is associated with a coefficient that is positive and significant. On the employer side, size, sector, computer intensity, use of new organizational devices, and use of teamwork have a significant impact on the probability of being evaluated. Employers with medium size (between 100 and 999 employees) and belonging to pharmaceutical, perfumes, and cleaning products or to chemicals, rubber, and plastic products use evaluation interviews more frequently. Employers from printing, press, and publishing and shipbuilding, aircraft, and railways have a lower probability of being interviewed. The intensity of computerization favors evaluation interviews of collective workers as well as quality certification and total productive maintenance. Conversely, employers using just-in-time delivery are less oriented toward evaluation interviews for collective workers. Having a nonmarginal fraction of production workers in problem solving groups favors evaluation interviews, while having a small fraction of nonproduction workers participating in self-managed teams and having management involved in project teams has a negative impact on evaluation interviews. In total, evaluation interviews for collective workers seem complementary with information technologies and new organizational practices. These managerial tools could support a supermodular production technology, where the employer has a preference for higher levels of effort.

3.4.2   Observing the Outcomes of Individual Evaluation

We are now going to discuss the matching evaluation of the effect of individual evaluation interviews on individual and collective workers on effort (table 3.2), work overload (table 3.3), and wages (table 3.4). In each table, we first compute as a benchmark the average outcome for individual and collective workers. Second, we compute the average difference in outcome between workers that have been individually evaluated and workers that have not been evaluated. This estimator is often designated as the naive estimator of the treatment effect. Then we compute the three causal effects: the effect on the treated (C1), the effect on the nontreated (C0), and the global effect (C). The first effect is the matching evaluation strictly speaking, the second one represents the effect that evaluation interviews would have if they were implemented on the nonevaluated population of workers, and the last one is the effect that would be obtained if evaluation interviews were extended to the entire population.

Effort

We observe higher levels of productive and cognitive efforts when work is collective rather than individual (table 3.2). This was not entirely expected because our model underlined that one of the advantage of collective work was to share the burden of higher levels of effort between workers. However, other effects might play a role here. The DGU model (as well as the analysis of determinants of evaluation interviews) suggests that collective work is positively correlated with supermodular production technologies. Another explanation could lie in synergy and peer pressure effects connected with collective work.

As predicted by the DGU model, we observe that the level of effort, whether productive or cognitive, is higher when workers are individually evaluated than in the classical incentive scheme (prediction 1).

The causal treatment effect on productive effort is stronger for individual workers than for collective workers. And the selection effect has an opposite sign. Individual workers displaying higher level of effort are selected in the population of evaluated workers, when they are selected out in the

Table 3.2	Individual evaluation interviews and effort	
	Individual workers[a]	Collective workers[b]
Productive effort[c]		
Average productive effort	0.564	0.720
Average difference E/NE	0.127***	0.092***
Effect on the treated (C1)	0.084**	0.120**
Effect on the nontreated (Co)	0.093**	0.100**
Global effect (C)	0.091**	0.110**
Cognitive effort[c]		
Average cognitive effort	0.507	0.722
Average difference E/NE	0.143***	0.140***
Effect on the treated (C1)	0.099**	0.110**
Effect on the nontreated (Co)	0.120**	0.110**
Global effect (C)	0.114**	0.110**

[a]The standard deviation of the treatment effect is computed using bootstrap with 300 simulations. The characteristics of the support over 300 simulations are min = 1,352; max = 1,501; mean = 1,426.48.

[b]The standard deviation of the treatment effect is computed using bootstrap with 300 simulations. The characteristics of the support over 300 simulations are min = 1,124; max = 1,304; mean = 1,229.03

[c]See section B of appendix A for a description of these variables.

***p-value < 0.01.

**$0.01 \geq p$-value < 0.05.

*$0.05 \geq p$-value < 0.1.

case of collective work. This result corroborates prediction 2 although the DGU model gives no specific clue to understand our surprising result on collective workers. The extension of evaluation interviews to the whole population of collective workers would consequently increase productive effort although it is already high in this case.

The observed effects on cognitive effort are more straightforward. Evaluation interviews similarly affect cognitive effort for individual and collective workers: they increase by 14 percent the propensity to make propositions for improving the production process. In the case of cognitive effort, the selection effect has an identic sign among individual and collective workers, but it is stronger in the first case.

Work Overload

Individual and collective workers work with a similar time pressure: the average need to hurry is 2.67 in the first case, 2.64 in the second (table 3.3), indicating that workers have to hurry a little more than a quarter of their time. Our second indicator of work overload is higher for collective workers: 65 percent of collective workers experience task interruptions in the course of their work, whereas 53 percent of individual workers face interruptions.

However, it is in the case of individual workers that evaluation interviews have a significant impact as it appears to mitigate work overload. Individual workers that are periodically evaluated work under lower time pressure

Table 3.3   **Individual evaluation interviews and work overload**

	Individual workers[a]	Collective workers[b]
Hurry[c]		
Average overload	2.666	2.640
Average difference E/NE	−0.143**	−0.110*
Effect on the treated (C1)	−0.142 (ns)	−0.108 (ns)
Effect on the nontreated (Co)	−0.189**	−0.073 (ns)
Global effect (C)	−0.176**	−0.089 (ns)
Interrupt[c]		
Average overload	0.526	0.650
Average difference E/NE	−0.053*	0.009 (ns)
Effect on the treated (C1)	−0.065**	0.002 (ns)
Effect on the nontreated (Co)	−0.066**	−0.003 (ns)
Global effect (C)	−0.066**	−0.000 (ns)

[a]See table 3.2 footnote.
[b]See table 3.2 footnote.
[c]See section C of appendix A for a description of these variables.
***p-value < 0.01.
**$0.01 \geq p$-value < 0.05.
*$0.05 \geq p$-value < 0.1.

and are less exposed to task interruptions. In the case of time pressure, the selection effect seems to play an important role as the causal effect on the treated is not significant. But evaluation interviews also seem to have a protective effect on their own because the effect on the nontreated is negative, significant, and stronger than the naive estimator. Individual workers who have been selected out from evaluation interviews would benefit from their implementation. As far as task interruptions are concerned, the protective effect of evaluation interviews is not explained by a selection effect; it is a pure outcome of this managerial device.

Evaluation interviews do not protect collective workers from work overload, but they do not increase their risk of exposition either. It is also an interesting result, knowing that collective workers produce higher levels of productive and cognitive efforts.

These results could be evidence of prediction 3. Evaluation interviews in a context of supermodular technology lead to an overintensification of work, but not to work overload. On the contrary, they seem to mitigate work overload, either through a selection effect as described in the DGU model, or through a pure effect.

Wage Setting

Collective workers earn more, on average, than individual workers (table 3.4). We also observe that, on average, evaluated employees earn more

Table 3.4   **Individual evaluation interviews and wage setting**

	Individual workers[a]	Collective workers[b]
Annualized net wage (in euros)[c]		
Average net wage	15,003	16,586
Average difference E/NE	1,654***	1,925***
Effect on the treated (C1)	198 (ns)	1,310**
Effect on the nontreated (Co)	275 (ns)	1,062**
Global effect (C)	253 (ns)	1,174**
Employee's ability to predict his or her wage[c]		
Average ability to predict	0.491	0.597
Average difference E/NE	0.164***	0.136***
Effect on the treated (C1)	0.145***	0.110***
Effect on the nontreated (Co)	0.147***	0.100***
Global effect (C)	0.146***	0.100***

[a]See table 3.2 footnote.
[b]See table 3.2 footnote.
[c]See sections D and E of appendix A for a description of these variables.
***p-value < 0.01.
**$0.01 \geq p$-value < 0.05.
*$0.05 \geq p$-value < 0.1.

than employees in a classical incentive scheme, confirming prediction 4. These monetary gains are higher for collective than for individual workers: 1,925 euros per year, on average, against 1,654 euros per year. For individual workers, this difference is entirely explained by the selection effect: the causal effects on the treated is not significantly different from zero, and the causal effect on the nontreated is also nonsignificant. Contrary to individual workers, the monetary gain of collective workers is only slightly lower when selection is taken into account: the gain falls from 1,925 euros to 1,310 euros if we consider the causal effect on the treated, to 1,062 if we consider the causal effect on the nontreated, and to 1,174 if we consider the global effect.

Concerning the employee's ability to predict his or her wage, we first note that this ability is greater, on average, for collective workers than for individual workers, and in both cases the average difference between evaluated and nonevaluated workers is significantly different from zero. Moreover, this effect of evaluation interview still remains significant when one corrects for the selection effect. As stated by prediction 4, evaluated workers have a better knowledge of the rules driving wage setting.

3.5   Conclusion

Diaye, Greenan, and Urdanivia (2007) have proposed a theoretical framework based on a Principal-Agent model to analyze the underlying mechanisms of individual evaluation interviews in the case of individual production and of team production (DGU model). They distinguish an ex post evaluation interview that builds a subjective evaluation of employees' effort and an ex ante evaluation interview which, in the case of team production, works as a coordination device through the fostering of a team spirit. Their theoretical analysis allows deriving testable predictions regarding the effect of individual evaluation interviews on productive and cognitive effort, on work overload, and on wage setting.

Using a matched employer-employee survey on computerization and organizational change (COI), we are able to test part of these predictions and to corroborate them. First, evaluation interviews have a positive impact on productive and cognitive effort. Second, evaluation interviews increase effort through two effects: the classical incentive effect and also a selection effect. Third, the selection effect is stronger in the case of individual production compared with the case of team production. Fourth, evaluated employees earn more than employees in a classical incentive scheme, and fifth, evaluated workers have a better knowledge of the rules driving wage setting.

The DGU model also suggests a higher propensity to evaluate workers in firms when the production technology is of a supermodular type and an overintensification of work in such a technological context. Our empirical results tend to indicate that collective work is positively correlated with supermodular technologies as collective workers are more frequently evaluated and provide a higher level of effort than individual workers. However, evaluation interviews are not associated with work overload. On the contrary, individual workers seem to be protected from work overload when they are evaluated, and collective workers do not register a higher exposure to work overload even though they provide higher levels of effort. This could be an indirect evidence of the selection effect already stressed. Evaluated workers produce higher levels of effort, but their personal characteristics or the characteristics of their employers allow them to better cope with it.

Appendix A

Variables Constructed from the Labor Force Section of the COI Survey

A. Measures of Collective Work

In the COI survey, a sample of randomly selected employees within interviewed firms (one, two, or three per firm) are asked to describe in detail the way they work at the time when they are being surveyed.

Measure 1: Teamwork

This measure is associated to the following question: "Do you sometimes do your work in group or collectively?"
Response is either "yes" or "no."

Measure 2: Time Spent in Teamwork

This measure is constructed from the following question asked to employees who declared working in group or collectively: "How much of your working time do you work in group or collectively?"
Responses are "Almost all the time," "More than a quarter of your time," "Less than a quarter of your time."

Measure 3: Communication in the Firm

This measure is constructed from the following four questions:

"Apart from your superiors, are there other persons who give you indications on what you have to do?" (Responses are either "yes" or "no," or "it does not apply.")

1. "Colleagues you usually work with?"
2. "Other persons or departments in the firm?"

"Apart from your subordinates, do you give indications to other persons on what they have to do?" (Responses are either "yes" or "no" or "it does not apply.")

3. "Colleagues you usually work with?"
4. "Other persons or departments in the firm?"

Then a *low* intensity of communication corresponds to 0 or 1 positive answer among these four questions, and a *high* intensity of communication to at least two positive answers among the four questions.

Measure 4: Support from Other Workers

The measure is constructed from the following three questions:

"If you have a temporary excess workload or if you are uneasy with a difficult task, are you helped by . . ." (Responses are either "yes" or "no" or "it does not apply.")

1. "your superiors?"
2. "colleagues you usually work with?"
3. "other persons or departments in the firm?"

Then a *low* level of support from other workers corresponds to 0 or 1 positive answer, and a *high* level of support corresponds to at least two positive answers among the three questions.

Measure 5: Participation in Meetings

The measure is constructed from the following question: "How many times a year do you participate in meetings in the context of your work?" Then a *low* participation in meetings corresponds to 0 or only one meeting a year, and a *high* participation in meetings corresponds to at least two meetings a year. (See tables 3A.1 and 3A.2.)

B. Measures of Effort

Two dimensions of effort are captured in the COI survey.

The first one describes the **level of productive effort.** It is built from the answers to the two following questions: (1) "Do you work more than ordinarily?" (Response is either "yes" or "no"); (2) If yes, "Do you work more than ordinarily for personals reasons?" (Response is either "yes" or "no.")

Employee's effort is a variable with three levels: 0 when the answer to question (1) is "no," 1 when the answer to question (1) is "yes" and the answer to question (2) is "no," 2 when both the answers to questions (1) and (2) are "yes."

The second one describes the **level of cognitive effort** or, more precisely, the degree of implication into collective knowledge building about the pro-

Table 3A.1   **Five measures of interaction between employees in the work process**

	Frequency	Percent
Measure 1: Teamwork		
No (0)	1,422	48.97
Yes (1)	1,482	51.03
Measure 2: Teamwork intensity		
Less than 1/4 of time (0)	2,045	70.42
1/4 of time or more (1)	859	29.58
Measure 3: Communication intensity		
Low (0)	1,019	35.09
High (1)	1,885	64.91
Measure 4: Level of support		
Low (0)	1,537	52.93
High (1)	1,367	47.07
Measure 5: Participation in meetings		
Low (0)	1,557	53.62
High (1)	1,347	46.38

Table 3A.2   **Correlation coefficients between the five measures of interaction between employees**

	Measure 1	Measure 2	Measure 3	Measure 4	Measure 5
Measure 1	1.00000				
Measure 2	0.63486	1.00000			
Measure 3	0.15159	0.04493	1.00000		
Measure 4	0.17993	0.11736	0.14987	1.00000	
Measure 5	0.13480	0.04775	0.17168	0.08567	1.00000

duction process. It is built from the answers to the following questions: (1) "In the context of your work, do you make propositions to improve your workstation, the production process, the machines . . . ?" (Response is either "yes" or "no.")

C. Measures of Work Overload

Two indicators measure work overload:

- *Hurry* is a discrete variable. It is equal to 1 if the employee states that he or she never has to hurry to do his work. It is equal to 2 if he or she states that it is the case for less than one quarter of the time. It is equal to 3 if he or she states that it is the case for one quarter of the time or more. And it is equal to 4 if he or she states that he or she has to hurry almost all the time.
- *Interrupt* is a dummy variable equal to 1 when the employee states that

he or she often has interrupt one task to carry out another urgent and nonanticipated one. It is equal to 0 otherwise.

D. Measure of Monetary Incentives

Monetary incentives are captured through annualized **net wage** (in euros). It comes from the annual declarations of social data (DADS), which is an administrative file used to compute the tax on wages. It groups all earnings paid in cash or kind between the 1st of January and the 31st of December 1996, less social contributions (social security, pensions, and unemployment benefit).

This compensation includes base wage, all bonuses, taxed allowances, and compensations in kind. Bonuses associated with the two French profit sharing regimes (participation and *intéressement*) are not included when they are not taxed. However, bonuses connected to participation schemes are generally not taxed when the reverse is true for bonuses connected to intéressement schemes. It is the length of the period during which bonuses remain unavailable that determines taxation. In the case of participation, when this unavailability period is shortened to three years, the bonuses become partly eligible to taxation. In the case of intéressement, bonuses are partly exonerated from taxes when they are blocked for a while in a company saving scheme.

If we except bonuses connected with participation, compulsory in firms with more than fifty employees, most of the earnings that contribute to an individualization of compensations are taken into account in our variable. Thus, we may interpret it as an output of the wage policy of the firm.

Last, compensations correspond to employment periods that vary from one employee to the other. We have annualized the information we had, taking into account the number of days worked. This does not correct for part time, but only 6 percent of the employees in our sample declare working part time.

E. Employee's Ability to Predict His or Her Wage

This variable is built from the answers to the eight following questions: "Which of the following elements have a big influence on your wage or on your promotion" (for each element, response is either "yes" or "no" or "it does not apply"): (1) "To do a high-quality work?"; (2) "To carry assignments to the letter?"; (3) "To be on good terms with the boss (bosses)?"; (4) "To be on good terms with the colleague(s)?"; (5) "To take up training courses?"; (6) "To learn how to use new technologies?"; (7) "The firm's performances?"; (8) "Other reasons?"

The employee's ability to predict his or her wage is then the ratio of number of "yes" answers to the number of "yes" or "no."

Appendix B

Variables Constructed from the Firm Section of the COI Survey

A. Firms' Computerization Intensity

This variable in constructed from the following question:

"Did/Does your firm realize data transfers by means of a computer interface . . ." (Response is either "yes" or "no"):

1. "within the management service?"
2. "between management and production service?"
3. "between management and suppliers, subcontractors?"
4. "between management and client firms?"
5. "between management and social organisms public power?"
6. "between conception services and production?"
7. "between conception and suppliers, subcontractors?"
8. "within the production services or between manufacturer unities?"
9. "between production and suppliers, subcontractors?"
10. "between production and client firms?"

Computerization intensity is equal to 1 if there is 0 or 1 "yes"; intensity 2 corresponds to two or three "yes"; intensity 3 corresponds to four or five "yes"; and intensity 4 corresponds to five and more "yes."

B. Average Number of Tasks That Each Type of Worker Is Responsible for (NMT)

This variable is constructed from the question (responses are "Management"/"Production Worker"/"Specialist": more than one answer is possible for each subquestion). "In general, who is/was authorized in 1997 to . . .":

1. adjust installations?
2. perform first level maintenance?
3. allocate tasks to production workers?
4. inspect quality of supplies?
5. inspect quality of production?
6. participate in performance improvements?
7. participate in project teams?
8. stop production in case of an incident?
9. troubleshoot in case of an incident?
10. start production again in case of an incident?

The qualitative variable NMT with four items is constructed as follows:

NMT ≥ 1.7 (High responsibility sharing between the three types of workers: Management, Production Worker, and Specialist)
1.4 ≤ NMT < 1.7 (Medium responsibility sharing)
1 < NMT ≤ 1.4 (Low responsibility sharing)
NTM ≤ 1 (No responsibility sharing)

Appendix C
Logistic Regression Results for the Binary Outcome
"Evaluated/Not Evaluated"

Table 3C.1   The case of individual production

Parameter	Estimate	Standard error	Wald χ^2	Pr > χ^2
Intercept	−2.0329	0.3485	34.0305	<.0001
Sociodemographic characteristics of employee				
Gender[a]	−0.2524	0.1519	2.7595	0.0967
Age[b]				
15–24	−0.1760	0.4762	0.1366	0.7116
25–39	−0.0446	0.1963	0.0515	0.8205
40–49	0.2130	0.1865	1.3044	0.2534
Years in the firm[c]				
1–2	0.6301	0.2374	7.0452	0.0079
3–6	0.2496	0.1952	1.6355	0.2010
7–10	0.3229	0.1756	3.3827	0.0659
Level of education[d]				
Vocational training (CAP and BEP)	−0.0175	0.1503	0.0135	0.9074
Second-level education (BAC)	−0.0885	0.2581	0.1177	0.7316
Third-level education	−0.0496	0.2607	0.0363	0.8489
Professional type[e]				
Executives	0.6554	0.3603	3.3089	0.0689
Middle management	0.7697	0.2356	10.6728	0.0011
Clerk	0.3463	0.2461	1.9801	0.1594
Skilled blue collar	−0.0568	0.1670	0.1156	0.7339
General characteristics of the firm				
Firm size[f]				
100–499	−0.0328	0.1744	0.0355	0.8506
500–999	0.0294	0.2264	0.0168	0.8968
1000 and more	0.6202	0.2525	6.0334	0.0140
Industry sector[g]				
Mineral products	0.4561	0.3481	1.7165	0.1901
Textile	0.4668	0.3269	2.0391	0.1533
Clothing and leather	−0.2872	0.4127	0.4845	0.4864
Wood and paper	0.1410	0.3348	0.1773	0.6737
Printing, press, publishing	0.2648	0.3902	0.4605	0.4974

(*continued*)

Table 3C.1　　　　(continued)

Parameter	Estimate	Standard error	Wald χ^2	$Pr > \chi^2$
Production of propellants and fuels	1.0360	1.4831	0.4880	0.4848
Chemicals, rubber, and plastic products	0.6593	0.2753	5.7342	0.0166
Pharmaceutical, perfumes, and cleaning products	1.7797	0.3673	23.4742	<.0001
Foundry and metal work products	−0.0104	0.2843	0.0013	0.9709
Mechanical engineering	0.1636	0.2718	0.3625	0.5471
Household equipment	0.0894	0.3122	0.0821	0.7745
Electrical and electronic equipment	0.9187	0.4546	4.0840	0.0433
Electrical and electronic components	0.6605	0.2988	4.8870	0.0271
Automobile	0.3523	0.3630	0.9420	0.3318
Shipbuilding, aircraft, and railway	0.6672	0.3829	3.0367	0.0814
Firms' computerization intensity[h]				
Intensity 2	0.0295	0.1914	0.0238	0.8773
Intensity 3	0.1274	0.2034	0.3923	0.5311
Intensity 4	0.0664	0.2266	0.0860	0.7694
Obstacles to the organizational changes[i]				
Tensions between the services	−0.2390	0.1760	1.8428	0.1746
Tensions with the shareholders	0.0501	0.2123	0.0558	0.8133
Difficulties in the relations with the other firms	0.0393	0.1899	0.0429	0.8359
Difficulties to school or to reclassify the staff	−0.0221	0.1621	0.0186	0.8915
Nonexecutive staff adaptations and establishment problems	−0.0908	0.1751	0.2688	0.6041
Executive staff adaptations and establishment problems	0.2754	0.1679	2.6886	0.1011
Clashes with the staff (petitions, strikes, etc.)	−0.0970	0.2035	0.2271	0.6337
Use of new organizational devices[j]				
ISO 9001, ISO 9002, EAQF certification	0.4734	0.1616	8.5854	0.0034
Other certification or total quality management	0.0457	0.1394	0.1073	0.7432
Value analysis, functional analysis, or FMECA method	0.00832	0.1633	0.0026	0.9593
5S method or Total Productive Maintenance (TPM) method	0.2457	0.1768	1.9307	0.1647
Organization in profit centers	0.1212	0.1398	0.7517	0.3859
Formal in-house customer/supplier contracts	0.0257	0.1402	0.0335	0.8547
System of "Just-in-time" delivery	0.1323	0.1786	0.5483	0.4590
System of "Just-in-time" production	−0.0757	0.1793	0.1785	0.6727
Evolution in hierarchical layers between 1994 and 1997[k]				
1 and more	−0.0725	0.2648	0.0750	0.7842
−1	−0.1617	0.1748	0.8556	0.3550
−2 and less	0.1750	0.2874	0.3707	0.5426
Teamwork				
Share of production workers participating in self-managed teams[l]				
10% to less than 50%	−0.1373	0.1965	0.4879	0.4849
50% and more	0.1451	0.2585	0.3149	0.5747
Share of production workers participating in problem solving groups[l]				
10% to less than 50%	0.3005	0.1927	2.4314	0.1189
50% and more	0.5594	0.3928	2.0281	0.1544

Table 3C.1   (continued)

Parameter	Estimate	Standard error	Wald χ^2	Pr $> \chi^2$
Share of production workers participating in project teams[l]				
10% to less than 50%	0.1398	0.1958	0.5101	0.4751
50% and more	−0.9496	0.5843	2.6415	0.1041
Share of other workers participating in self-managed teams[l]				
10% to less than 50%	0.1439	0.2051	0.4921	0.4830
50% and more	−0.1158	0.3478	0.1108	0.7392
Share of other workers participating in problem solving groups[l]				
10% to less than 50%	−0.1922	0.2010	0.9143	0.3390
50% and more	−0.0789	0.3770	0.0438	0.8343
Share of other workers participating in project teams[l]				
10% to less than 50%	−0.2005	0.1941	1.0673	0.3016
50% and more	0.3645	0.3384	1.1598	0.2815
Who is/was authorized in 1997 to participate in project teams?[m]				
Management	−0.2209	0.1608	1.8877	0.1695
Production worker	0.0596	0.1448	0.1694	0.6806
Specialist	−0.2073	0.1627	1.6232	0.2027
Average number of tasks that each type of worker is responsible for[n]				
1.1–1.4	−0.0469	0.1864	0.0635	0.8011
1.5–1.7	0.1619	0.2226	0.5292	0.4669
1.8 and more	0.3439	0.2386	2.0764	0.1496

[a]Reference is "men."

[b]Reference is "50 and more."

[c]Reference is "11 and more."

[d]Reference is "with no degree except CEP or BEPC."

[e]Reference is "unskilled blue collar."

[f]Reference is "99 and less."

[g]Reference is "food industries."

[h]Reference is "intensity 1." See section A of appendix B for the construction of this variable.

[i]The variable is equal to 1 when the firms states that such an obstacle has been either "quite important," "important," or "very important," and 0 when she states that it has been "unimportant."

[j]Response is either "yes" or "no."

[k]Reference is "0."

[l]Reference is "less than 10%."

[m]Response is either "yes" or "no."

[n]Reference is "≤ 1." See section B of appendix B for the construction of the variable.

Table 3C.2   **The case of team production**

Parameter	Estimate	Standard error	Wald χ^2	Pr > χ^2
Intercept	–1.7432	0.3745	21.6633	<.0001
Sociodemographic characteristics of the employee				
Gender[a]	–0.1403	0.1523	0.8481	0.3571
Age[b]				
15–24	0.5015	0.4257	1.3880	0.2387
25–39	0.2781	0.2295	1.4691	0.2255
40–49	0.2781	0.2295	1.4691	0.2255
Years in the firm[c]				
1–2	–0.2096	0.2443	0.7363	0.3908
3–6	0.1818	0.1820	0.9972	0.3180
7–10	0.0170	0.1730	0.0097	0.9217
Level of education[d]				
Vocational training (CAP and BEP)	0.1829	0.1567	1.3621	0.2432
Second-level education (BAC)	0.4481	0.2421	3.4263	0.0642
Third-level education	0.5279	0.2645	3.9823	0.0460
Professional type[e]				
Executives	0.5416	0.3485	2.4147	0.1202
Middle management	0.1200	0.2284	0.2761	0.5993
Clerk	–0.0121	0.2972	0.0017	0.9675
Skilled blue collar	–0.1469	0.1743	0.7101	0.3994
General characteristics of the firm				
Firm size[f]				
100–499	0.3510	0.1765	3.9524	0.0468
500–999	0.7059	0.2080	11.5179	0.0007
1000 and more	0.1941	0.2422	0.6426	0.4228
Industry sector[g]				
Mineral products	–0.2853	0.3202	0.7942	0.3728
Textile	0.3355	0.4096	0.6708	0.4128
Clothing and leather	–0.1220	0.3734	0.1068	0.7439
Wood and paper	–0.4769	0.3661	1.6974	0.1926
Printing, press, publishing	–0.8333	0.4390	3.6032	0.0577
Production of propellants and fuels	1.2745	0.9040	1.9877	0.1586
Chemicals, rubber, and plastic products	0.6759	0.2593	6.7962	0.0091
Pharmaceutical, perfumes, and cleaning products	1.2302	0.3578	11.8237	0.0006
Foundry and metal work products	–0.2956	0.2752	1.1535	0.2828
Mechanical engineering	–0.0338	0.2637	0.0164	0.8980
Household equipment	0.1161	0.3083	0.1418	0.7065
Electrical and electronic equipment	0.3344	0.3679	0.8263	0.3633
Electrical and electronic components	0.1719	0.2950	0.3396	0.5601
Automobile	–0.2314	0.3329	0.4832	0.4870
Shipbuilding, aircraft, and railway	–0.6255	0.3706	2.8479	0.0915
Firms' computerization intensity[h]				
Intensity 2	0.3321	0.1888	3.0940	0.0786
Intensity 3	0.4203	0.1960	4.5997	0.0320
Intensity 4	0.3323	0.2140	2.4118	0.1204

Table 3C.2   (continued)

Parameter	Estimate	Standard error	Wald χ^2	Pr > χ^2
Obstacles to the organizational changes [i]				
Tensions between the services	−0.0540	0.1773	0.0927	0.7608
Tensions with the shareholders	−0.2445	0.2312	1.1179	0.2904
Difficulties in the relations with the other firms	−0.0976	0.1999	0.2382	0.6255
Difficulties to school or to reclassify the staff	0.0598	0.1538	0.1513	0.6973
Nonexecutive staff adaptations and establishment problems	0.0411	0.1639	0.0629	0.8020
Executive staff adaptations and establishment problems	0.1569	0.1589	0.9750	0.3234
Clashes with the staff (petitions, strikes, etc.)	−0.1195	0.1930	0.3833	0.5358
Use of new organizational devices [j]				
ISO 9001, ISO 9002, EAQF Certification	0.4089	0.1604	6.4964	0.0108
Other certification or total quality management	0.1545	0.1389	1.2379	0.2659
Value analysis, functional analysis, or FMECA method	−0.0932	0.1582	0.3470	0.5558
5S method or Total Productive Maintenance (TPM) method	0.4285	0.1631	6.8979	0.0086
Organization in profit centers	0.1763	0.1351	1.7015	0.1921
Formal in-house customer/supplier contracts	0.1045	0.1380	0.5728	0.4492
System of "Just-in-time" delivery	−0.3277	0.1778	3.3980	0.0653
System of "Just-in-time" production	0.1577	0.1781	0.7846	0.3757
Evolution in hierarchical layers between 1994 and 1997 [k]				
1 and more	−0.0279	0.2610	0.0114	0.9150
1	−0.0204	0.1629	0.0156	0.9005
2 and less	−0.3818	0.2959	1.6652	0.1969
Teamwork				
Share of production workers participating in self-managed teams [l]				
10% to less than 50%	0.0247	0.1780	0.0193	0.8895
50% and more	0.0651	0.2613	0.0620	0.8033
Share of production workers participating in problem solving groups [l]				
10% to less than 50%	0.4672	0.1863	6.2869	0.0122
50% and more	0.8599	0.3590	5.7362	0.0166
Share of production workers participating in project teams [l]				
10% to less than 50%	−0.0944	0.1838	0.2640	0.6074
50% and more	−0.0239	0.4492	0.0028	0.9575
Share of other workers participating in self-managed teams [l]				
10% to less than 50%	−0.3616	0.1983	3.3244	0.0683
50% and more	−0.2979	0.3314	0.8082	0.3687
Share of other workers participating in problem solving groups [l]				
10% to less than 50%	0.1016	0.2065	0.2419	0.6229
50% and more	0.2644	0.3815	0.4801	0.4884

(continued)

Table 3C.2   (continued)

Parameter	Estimate	Standard error	Wald χ^2	Pr > χ^2
Share of other workers participating in project teams[l]				
10% to less than 50%	0.1084	0.1851	0.3428	0.5582
50% and more	0.0786	0.3393	0.0537	0.8168
Who is/was authorized in 1997 to participate in project teams?[m]				
Management	−0.3374	0.1701	3.9368	0.0472
Production worker	−0.1134	0.1475	0.5912	0.4420
Specialist	0.1610	0.1591	1.0239	0.3116
Average number of tasks that each type of worker is responsible for[n]				
1.1–1.4	0.0988	0.1917	0.2656	0.6063
1.5–1.7	0.1538	0.2221	0.4796	0.4886
1.8 and more	−0.1319	0.2414	0.2984	0.5849

[a]Reference is "men."
[b]Reference is "50 and more."
[c]Reference is "11 and more."
[d]Reference is "with no degree except CEP or BEPC."
[e]Reference is "unskilled blue collar."
[f]Reference is "99 and less."
[g]Reference is "food industries."
[h]Reference is "intensity 1." See section A of appendix B for the construction of this variable.
[i]The variable is equal to 1 when the firms states that such an obstacle has been either "quite important," "important," or "very important," and 0 when he or she states that it has been "unimportant."
[j]Response is either "yes" or "no."
[k]Reference is "0."
[l]Reference is "less than 10%."
[m]Response is either "yes" or "no."
[n]Reference is " ≤ 1." See section B of appendix B for the construction of the variable.

References

Abowd J. M., R. H. Creecy, and F. Kramarz. 2002. Computing person and firm effects using linked longitudinal employer-employee data. LEHD Technical Paper no. 2002–06.

Alchian A., and H. Demsetz. 1972. Production, information costs, and economic organization. *American Economic Review* 62:777–95.

Crifo P., M.-A. Diaye, and N. Greenan. 2004. *Pourquoi les entreprises évaluent-elles individuellement leurs salariés?* (Why do firms evaluate individually their employees?). *Economie et Prévision* 164–165 (3–4): 27–55.

Diaye M.-A., N. Greenan, and M. W. Urdanivia. 2007. Subjective evaluation of performance through individual evaluation interview: Theory and empirical evidence. NBER Working Paper no. 12979. Cambridge, MA: National Bureau of Economic Research.

Greenan N., and S. Hamon-Cholet. 2001. *Un dispositif d'enquêtes couplées employeurs/employés sur les changements organisationnels et l'informatisation* (A linked employer-employee survey device on organizational changes and ICT uses). Center for Labor Studies. Mimeograph.

Heckman J. J., H. Ichimura, and P. Todd. 1997. Matching as an econometric evaluation estimator: Evidence from evaluating a job training programme. *Review of Economics Studies* 64:605–54.

———. 1998. Matching as an econometric evaluation estimator. *Review of Economics Studies* 65:261–94.

Rosenbaum P. R., and D. B. Rubin. 1983. The central role of the propensity score in observational studies for causal effects. *Biometrica* 70:41–55.

2

Firm Differences in Human Resource Practices

4

Do Initial Conditions Persist between Firms?
An Analysis of Firm-Entry Cohort Effects and Job Losers Using Matched Employer-Employee Data

Till von Wachter and Stefan Bender

4.1   Introduction

Economists have long been interested in how persistent the effects of short-term unexpected shocks in the labor market are on workers' careers (e.g., Okun 1973). Using newly available longitudinal data, an increasing number of papers suggest that the starting conditions in the first year of a worker's job or labor market entry can indeed have long-term effects on earnings and career development (e.g., Oreopoulos, von Wachter, Heisz 2006; Oyer 2006; Kahn 2006). For example, Oreopoulos, von Wachter, and Heisz (2006) find that the effect of graduating college in a recession fades after ten years for the typical worker and has permanent negative effects for less-able graduates. While clearly a concern for policymakers and the public, such lasting effects of entry conditions are also difficult to explain in the context of standard models of wage setting and career development. In particular, they raise the question of whether wages persistently deviate from workers' skills because of market frictions or wage contracts.

This question has received particular attention in the context of cohort

Till von Wachter is an assistant professor of economics at Columbia University, and a faculty research fellow of the National Bureau of Economic Research. Stefan Bender is a senior researcher at the Institute for Employment Research.

We would like to thank David Card, Bob Gibbons, Larry Katz, and conference participants at the Comparative Analysis of Enterprise Data conference (CAED) 2006 in Chicago and the Conference on Analysis of Firms and Employees (CAFE) 2006 in Nuremberg for helpful suggestions. Ana Rute-Cardoso provided helpful comments. This chapter was written as part of the research project "Discrepancies between Market and Firm Wages: An Analysis of Earnings and Worker Mobility" within the German Research Foundation's (DFG) research program "Flexibility in Heterogenous Labor Markets" (SSP 1169). This material is based upon work supported by the National Science Foundation under grant number 0453017. All errors are our own.

effects within firms. A small but influential number of papers have argued that similar workers entering firms in different years receive permanently different wage profiles (Baker, Gibbs, and Holmstrom 1994; Beaudry and DiNardo 1991). Several approaches have been proposed to rationalize such persistent shifts in firms' wage structures. The first maintains that the degree of rent sharing between workers and firms varies with outside market conditions at the time of entry (Beaudry and DiNardo 1991). The second maintains that cohort effects arise from variation in the quality of jobs and career opportunities available within the firm (Okun 1973). If different jobs provide different general experience or training provided by the firm, cohort effects can also arise from permanent changes in workers' skills (Gibbons and Waldman 2004).

Although these explanations have very different underlying views of wage determination, they have similar predictions for the degree of persistence of entry-level conditions. Thus, it is difficult to distinguish among them based on cohort effects in earnings alone. However, these explanations have alternative implications for the persistence of entry-level conditions as workers switch employers. While effects due to rent sharing or job quality should fade for those workers losing their jobs, changes in skills should affect workers' wages even at new employers. Despite offering clear predictions, these hypotheses have not been tested, in part because data used in existing work had little information on workers' job mobility and their employers.

More generally, because existing studies focused on single firms (Baker, Gibbs, and Holmstrom 1994) or particular time periods (Beaudry and Di-Nardo 1991), at present little is known about whether firm-entry cohort effects are a pervasive phenomenon in the wider labor market. Given the degree of heterogeneity in other aspects of firms' wage structures (Abowd and Kramarz 1999) and given the amount of heterogeneity in firm growth rates (Davis and Haltiwanger 1992), it is conceivable that firm-entry cohort effects are a widespread phenomenon that affects firms to different degrees. However, until now little information is available on how pervasive such cohort effects are.

In this chapter, we provide three contributions to the present literature. First, we use data on the complete career histories of all workers in a large German manufacturing sector to describe the prevalence and heterogeneity of firm-entry cohort effects for a large sample of firms over more than twenty years. To ensure the cohort differences in wages we find are not due to selective entry of workers into firms, the nature of our data allows us to control for observable firm and worker characteristics as well as worker fixed effects. In addition, the long time horizon allows us to examine whether entry conditions fade within firms and whether firms' wages tend to converge to a common market wage over time.

Second, we exploit the predictions of the alternative models for the impact of job loss on wages to learn more about the sources of firm-entry cohort effects. To do so, we complement the descriptive analysis with a study of the effects of job displacement on wage changes for workers with high, medium, or low starting wages at the lost job. Thereby, we are particularly interested in whether wage premiums fade upon job loss and whether workers recover some of their past advantages with time since job loss.

Third, we analyze the effect of past wage premiums on the *level* of wages after job loss. Because controlling for observable characteristics past wages are partly a function of unobserved ability, we would expect a positive correlation. However, if the ability of job losers is not observed perfectly by the market, temporary wage premiums may also serve as a temporary signal that fades over time. If, on the other hand, wage premiums are driven by permanent skill differences, we would expect their effect to be stable or increasing.

We find that in the manufacturing sector we study, firm-entry cohort effects are a significant phenomenon. Similar firms pay different wages to similar workers starting their jobs at different points in time. However, we also find that this is not simply a homogeneous market-wide phenomenon—there is considerable heterogeneity between firms and between cohorts in the incidence and strength of cohort effects. A further key result is that in our sample, entry-level differences in wages fade within firms, and there appears convergence to a market wage, but reversion is very slow. Thus, wage differences between cohorts of similar workers are highly persistent but not permanent.

We also find that workers with high starting wages have higher and persistent wage losses at job loss; workers with relatively low starting wages, on the other hand, seem to gain from losing their job. Thus, part of initial wage differences appears to be temporary firm-specific rents. Moreover, there appears to be mean reversion at job loss. However, markets do not seem to be able to fully tell apart ability from rents in the short run, and past wage advantages carry a premium for the level of wage after job loss that fades over time.

These results suggest that firm-entry cohort effects at least in part consist of time varying differences in rent sharing or job quality. Clearly, part of the effects we find may also arise due to the presence of other individual specific rents, for example, from job search. Future research based on a larger sample of firms and workers able to explicitly analyze the persistence of cohort effects at job loss will help to shed light on this question. The results also suggest that characteristics of the previous job, such as job tenure or past wages, are not just a fixed measure of worker quality, as suggested in the prior literature (e.g., Kletzer 1989) but also appear to influence temporary wage components. Among others, this could arise if previous job characteristics affect workers' reservation wages. The effect of these initial conditions fades, consistent with the notion of continued on-the-job search. In addition, previous job characteristics may function as temporary signals of workers' skills.[1]

The outline of the chapter is as follows. First, we give a brief overview of the conceptual background, the empirical approach, and the data we use. Second, we describe the prevalence of cohort effects in a sample of large and stable manufacturing firms. Third, we analyze the effect of past starting wages on the extent of wage changes at job displacement. Fourth, we study the effect of the starting wage on the lost job on the level of ensuing wages. The last section concludes and offers suggestions for future research.

4.2   Conceptual Approach

There are two basic explanations for the persistence of differences in starting wages of workers entering the same firm at different moments in time. The first view suggests that wages contain firm-specific components that can differ across entry cohorts but that are lost as workers move between firms. This may arise due to differences in the degree of rent sharing among workers and firms, for example, due to the degree of pressure in the outside labor market. Or it may arise to the presence of long-term implicit insurance contracts (Beaudry and DiNardo 1991). Alternatively, this may be due to variation in the quality of jobs offered within firms over time (Okun 1973). For example, in periods of high growth, firms may offer more jobs that pay more, either because of higher productivity or due to higher incentive wages. Persistent differences may also arise if some jobs provide higher accumulation of firm-specific skills.

These alternative sources of wage differentials have the similar implication that the wage advantages they may imply for certain cohorts are lost if workers leave the firm. Because voluntary movers may not leave their job if compensated for giving up of these wage premiums, the loss is likely to be visible only for workers who move their job involuntarily. Thus, we would expect wage losses for those job losers to be largest that had the highest wage premiums. For these displaced workers, we would expect to see mean reversion; that is, those workers with below-average cohort wages experience wage gains relative to those workers with above-average cohort wages as absent any skill differentials, both groups draw again wages from the same market wage distribution.

Because the workers with below-average cohort wages could have obtained higher wages on the outside market, some mobility friction must prevent them from moving jobs. Because cohort effects are likely to be more typically in large firms with longer job attachment, this is likely to arise due to the presence of average wage premiums large firms pay (Oi and

---

1. However, in that case the effect of the initial signal should not fade over time (Farber and Gibbons 1996; Altonji and Pierret 2001).

Idson 1999). Nevertheless, we would expect that on average workers with below-average cohort wages are more like to switch employers. Similarly, firms may face an incentive to fire workers with above-average wages if these are due to a higher amount of rents.

The second broad view suggests firm-entry cohort effects arise from changes in workers' general skill level. This may occur if in some periods firms offer a larger amount of jobs with a high degree of experience accumulation or general training (Gibbons and Waldman 2004). In this case, differential entry-level conditions reflect actual differences in workers' skill levels and can arise even in an environment where each worker is paid his marginal product. This is in contrast with the first set of explanations, that each suggested that workers with similar skills would be paid different wages, either because of rent sharing or differences in job quality.

Clearly, the second view suggests that even workers losing their job involuntarily will maintain their wage advantage on their new job at least in the medium run. While in the years immediately following the job loss some of the advantage may be lost as workers have to find a new job match or as the market may be uncertain about workers' ability, in the medium run, workers should again obtain a wage that reflects their higher (or lower) marginal product. This stands in contrast to the implications of the first view, in which all cohort-wage differences should be lost at job loss. In particular, even if past wages may serve as a positive signal for ability in the years immediately after job loss, the effect of past cohort conditions should fade with time since job loss—the opposite implication as from the second view.

The existing empirical literature does not address the question of persistence of conditions on the past job for workers switching employers. One strand of literature aims at characterizing the presence of firm-entry cohort effects, but pays little attention as to what happens when workers leave firms. In this vein, Baker, Gibbs, and Holmstrom (1994) analyze the role of cohort effects within a single firm. Beaudry and DiNardo (1991) use data from the Current Population Survey (CPS) and Panel Study of Income Dynamics (PSID) to analyze the effect of labor market conditions on workers' wages as they stay within the firm. Neither paper analyzes the persistence of the wage effect it finds as workers move between firms, mostly due to a lack of data.

Another strand of literature examines the extent and determinants of wage changes at job loss in detail, but typically pays less attention to the role of past job characteristics.[2] The only important exception is the role of past job tenure. Because there is no market for firm worker-specific skills or match rents, the wage gradient with job tenure can be seen as a form of

---

2. Past industry, occupation, and firm size are an exception. See, for example, Ruhm (1991). Jacobson, LaLonde, and Sullivan (1993), Gibbons and Katz (1991), or Farber (1997, 2003). For a survey of this literature, see Farber (1999).

rent sharing between workers and firms. A worker losing his job should then lose these firm-specific rents. This is what the literature has found, and the effect appears to be particularly strong for a loss in industry tenure (Neal 1995; Parent 2000).

In this context, Kletzer (1989) has found that workers with higher past job tenure have higher wages on the job after job loss. This may signify that workers with high job tenure are also of high ability, that is, positive wage tenure profiles in part reflect ability differences between high- and low-tenured workers.[3] A similar argument holds for the effect of the initial wage on the lost job. Even conditional on observable characteristics—such as age and education—past starting wages will be a function of unobserved worker ability and will thus positively correlate with wages on the current job.

However, past tenure and earnings may also influence workers' reservation wages. In this case, high past wages may lead workers to search for jobs more intensely. If this is the case, there is again an initial correlation of past job characteristics and initial earnings after layoffs. Over time, these workers' wages are again determined by market conditions (workers' skill levels and the overall wage distribution); thus, the effect of the reservation wage would be expected to fade.

In addition, if the market observes workers' ability only imperfectly, it may use past job tenure or past wages as signals to infer about their productivity (Farber and Gibbons 1996; Altonji and Pierret 2001). In this case, part of the positive effect of past job tenure may be due to an initial signaling effect. However, this effect should not fade over time, even if markets learn about workers' ability.

If, on the other hand, firm-entry cohort effects are due to differential skill accumulation, we should observe the opposite phenomenon. Initially, some of the higher skills embodied in the cohort-effect may be discounted if displaced workers receive a wage based on average skills. Over time, as markets learn about workers' true ability, we would expect the effect of past wages to remain stable, or least not to decline further.

4.3 Empirical Approach

The analysis of the chapter consists of two parts, each based on a different sample of firms. The first, descriptive part of the paper studies the importance of firm-entry cohort effects for a sample of large stable firms in the car manufacturing sector in Germany. The second part analyzes wage changes and wage levels of job losers using the complete available career histories of all workers who ever worked in German car manufacturing.

---

3. This idea is also exploited in Abraham and Farber (1987), who use completed job tenure as an indicator for the quality of a job match to correct for selection bias in estimates of the return to job tenure.

The data is drawn from the German employee registry that records complete career information as well as basic demographics for the universe of German workers covered by social security and their employers from 1975 to 2003 and is further described in the following.

The goal of the first part of the paper is to describe the incidence, heterogeneity, and persistence of firm-entry cohort effects within a large but specific sector of the economy. The focus on a single sector allows us to exclude wage differences arising from differential industry trends or business cycles. To study the magnitude and evolution of average cohort wages, we concentrated our analysis on stable establishments with a large enough rate of inflow of new workers in every period. For each of the fifty-five firms that survive our selection criteria further described in the following, we estimate cohort effects following the approach in Baker, Gibbs, and Holmstrom (1994). To do so, we proceed in three steps. First, we collapse our data to the level of firm-tenure entry year cells. Second, we use the cell-level averages to run the following wage regression at the firm level.

(1) $$\overline{\log w}_{fct} = \alpha_f + g_f(\text{ten}) + \lambda_{ft} + \phi_{cf} + \beta_f \overline{X}_{fct} + u_{fct}$$

This modeling approach allows for a firm-specific quartic tenure profile $[g_f(t)]$, a constant and year effects, as well as for firm-specific effects of average entry cohort characteristics. Third, we regress the estimated firm-entry cohort effects (ϕ_{cf}) on a firm-specific trend and treat the residual from that regression as cohort effects for the remainder of our study. As explained in Baker, Gibbs, and Holmstrom (1994) in the presence of year and tenure effects, one cannot identify the linear component of the cohort effect. Because we are mainly interested in examining the presence and significance of cohort effects, the chosen approach suffices for our purposes.

In addition to including average observable characteristics at the cohort level, we also ran the model in equation (1) at the individual level and included worker fixed effects. Unlike in the case of Baker, Gibbs, and Holmstrom (1994), who only had access to data on all workers at a single firm, this is possible in our case because we have the entire career information of workers who ever worked at each of our firms. This further alleviates the concern that the cohort effects identified in equation (1) may still be due to selective entry of workers of different skill levels.

An important aspect of firm-entry cohort effects is their persistence—do differences in entry-level wages last unfettered forever, as found in the firm analyzed by Baker, Gibbs, and Holmstrom (1994), or does convergence take place? Convergence may be of two kinds. First, high-wage cohorts may converge to the average-wage level within the firm. In this case, the relevant benchmark and speed of convergence is determined by the firm-level average. Second, high-wage cohorts may converge to a market-level wage. That is, reversion of high initial starting wages may be faster if they are high relative to the overall market wage.

To examine the extent and speed of reversion of initial wage differences, we modify the preceding model and estimate the following regression for each firm in our sample of large stable firms.

$$(2) \quad \overline{\log w}_{fct} = \alpha_f + g_f(\text{ten}) + \lambda_{ft} + \beta_f \overline{X}_{fct} + \phi_{cf0} + h_f(\text{ten})\phi_{cf1} + u_{fct}$$

Thereby, ϕ_{cf0} measures the difference in initial starting wages for entry cohort c, and ϕ_{cf1} measures the firm-specific rate of decay of the initial effect. We experimented with linear, quartic, and unrestricted specifications for the decay function $h_f(t)$, and found a linear specification works astonishingly well for the most relevant time horizon of about ten years of job tenure.

The second part of the paper studies the effect of starting wages on the effect of job displacements. Once we have identified displacement events and an appropriate estimation methodology, the analysis is relatively straightforward. In particular, we are interested in whether wage losses at job displacement differ by the level of the starting wage at the previous job. Ideally, we would have analyzed the effect of firm-entry cohort effects themselves on the extent of wage loss for workers losing their jobs from our sample of large and stable firms. However, for the sector in question, the sample of such workers was too small for a meaningful analysis.

Thus, in the second part of the paper, we analyze the effect of a job displacement on wage changes and post-job loss wage levels for all workers who worked in German car manufacturing at some point between 1975 and 2003. We define a displaced worker to be a worker who had at least three (or five) years of tenure at a given firm and who had at least thirty days of unemployment following the job move. We experimented with alternative definitions based on mass layoffs at the establishment level, but again found that we had too few workers affected by such events in our sample.[4]

We then study the wage change of displaced workers relative to the wage held prior to job loss for up to fifteen years after the job change. Specifically, the basic model we estimate at the individual level is

$$(3) \quad \log w_{it} = \alpha_i + \sum_{k \geq -3}^{15} D_{it}^k \delta_k + g(\exp_{it}) + \lambda_t + u_{it},$$

where the dummies D_{ik} indicate whether a year is k periods before or after a job loss, and y stands for calendar year. This estimates the effect of wage changes at job loss controlling for a quartic polynomial in potential labor market experience, unrestricted year effects, and worker fixed effects. This model essentially extends Farber's estimates based on the Displaced

---

4. In a separate work using the German Socio-Economic Panel, Görlitz and von Wachter (2006) find that while imposing unemployment does tend to raise the estimated impact of job losses relative to self-reported layoff status, the difference is reduced significantly when worker fixed effects are included.

Worker Survey (DWS) Supplement to the CPS into an analysis covering several periods after the job loss. In particular, this approach does not keep a control group of workers who did not lose their job, and thus differs from the estimation method implemented by Bender et al. (2002) for Germany, based on Jacobson, LaLonde, and Sullivan (1993). Instead, the year effects in this sample are identified from the baseline period of workers later experiencing displacement.[5]

The main estimates we are interested in are estimates of the earnings loss by groups of workers with low, medium, and high starting wages relative to their average wage. Thus, we reestimate the model in equation (3) interacting the time effect as well as the displacement-time effects with dummies for whether a worker's starting wage at the lost job was in the bottom, middle, or top of the wage distribution (we choose the interquartile range as cutoff points). This results in the following model for estimation:

$$(4) \quad \log w_{it} = \alpha_i + \sum_{k \geq -3}^{15} D_{it}^{k,\text{Low}} \delta_k^{\text{Low}} + \sum_{k \geq -3}^{15} D_{it}^{k,\text{Med}} \delta_k^{\text{Med}} + \sum_{k \geq -3}^{15} D_{it}^{k,\text{High}} \delta_k^{\text{High}}$$
$$+ \lambda_t^{\text{Low}} + \lambda_t^{\text{Medium}} + \lambda_t^{\text{High}} + g(\exp_{it}) + u_{it}$$

The estimates of this model show the wage changes by groups of workers with different starting wages relative to their *own* group-specific wage at the time of job loss.

In future work, we plan to include *stayers*—workers who did not lose their job—in the model as a control group to replicate the classic event study design introduced by Jacobson, LaLonde, and Sullivan (1993). We will also analyze wage losses by other worker characteristics such as education, age, or past job tenure. Similarly, we can exploit further prediction regarding the effect of past job characteristics on the wage changes of voluntary movers.

The last set of models we estimate focus on the *level* of log wages after job loss. To do so, we begin by implementing the models estimated by Kletzer (1989), who concentrates on the effect of past job tenure. We first augment Kletzer's model with the effect of past starting wages. Then we extend her approach and interact past job tenure and past starting wages with time since job loss. Thus, we are interested in the coefficients on the interactions with time since job loss in the following model:

$$(5) \quad \log w_{it} = \alpha + \beta_0 \log w_{i0}^{\text{LostJob}} + \beta_1 \tau \log w_{i0}^{\text{LostJob}} + \gamma X_i$$
$$+ g(\exp_{it}) + \lambda_t + \varepsilon_{it},$$

5. To identify the worker fixed effects, we have to exclude one pre-period dummy. To identify the year effects, we have to exclude one additional dummy. Thus, we keep observations on workers up to five years prior to displacement and include dummies for up to three years prior to displacement.

where τ stands for the years since job loss. This model is only estimated based on observations after a job loss. The important extension of Kletzer's model is made possible by the availability of longer time series in our data and allows us to study to what extent the immediate effect of past job and worker characteristics on wages post job loss fades over time. Alternatively, we will be able to see whether past wages are driven by components of actual or predicted worker skill whose effect stays stable.

4.4   Administrative Longitudinal Matched Data

The data used in this chapter are drawn from the German employment register containing information on all employees covered by social security, representing around 80 percent of the German workforce.[6] The employment register takes stock of existing employees at each establishment twice a year. Because the notification procedure for social security also requires employers to record any permanent or temporary change of employment relationships, the employment register contains detailed histories for each worker's time in covered employment. The main information contained in the register for administrative purposes (and, therefore, the most reliable) are gross daily wages subject to social security contributions and the exact periods during which the employee worked in the social security system. In addition, the data contain basic demographic information as well as information on occupation, industry, job status, and education.[7] Most important for the present purpose, the data also contain unique establishment identifiers. These were used to create a separate data set of establishment characteristics that were aggregated up from the employment register and merged back onto the individual-level data. Characteristics include, among others, establishment size, employment growth, and average wages. The relevant entity throughout the empirical analysis is the establishment. Despite the inaccuracy it entails in some cases, we will keep using the terms *establishment* and *firm* interchangeably for the rest of the analysis.[8]

The sample used for this chapter consists of information on the universe of workers and establishments from the West German car-manufacturing

6. An overview of the data is given in Bender, Haas, and Klose (2000); a more detailed description can be found in Bender et al. (1996). For further information and citations as well as accessibility, see http://www.research-data-center.de. Coverage includes full- and part-time employees of private enterprises, apprentices, and other trainees, as well as temporarily suspended employment relationships. The self-employed, civil servants, and students are excluded.

7. The entity reporting is the establishment for which an employee works and can thus change over time. This can lead to mistakes in the coding of some demographic variables (e.g., nationality or marital status) and in particular education (which tends to reflect required rather than actual qualification).

8. Unfortunately, it is currently not possible to link establishments that belong to a common parent firm.

sector. In a first step, we selected all employees who worked at least one day between 1975 and 2003 in an establishment of this sector (a total of 162,332 establishments). To ensure that the sample is consistent in time, we chose only those notifications where the employees worked part or full time. We dropped apprentices from the main analysis to avoid confounding job changes at end of apprenticeship with regular job displacement and to be consistent with the concept of firm-entry cohort effect typically analyzed in the literature. We also dropped workers with missing education and who are younger than twenty-one and older than sixty-four.

Using this sample, we aggregated up the individual-level information into a cell-level data set at the establishment, year, and entry cohort level that contains the size of each entering cohort in each year at the firm, as well as average earnings and basic average demographic characteristics (such as average age, average education, or fraction female). To obtain a meaningful basis for the descriptive analysis of firm-entry cohort effects, from this cell-level data set we extracted a subset of firms that had a sufficiently large inflow of workers each year for an extended period of time. In particular, we required firms to have at least ten entering cohorts with at least ten employees, at least 100 employees over ten years, and at least twenty-one entering cohorts. This leaves us with a total number of fifty-five firms. This restriction ensures both a reasonable sample of firms as well as a meaningful base for calculation of a large number of firm-entry cohort effects. We have experimented with the cutoff points, without a noticeable difference in results. In addition, to ensure we observe each cohort for an extended amount of time, we only consider cohorts entering before 1997.

For the displacement analysis, we selected from our sample of car manufacturing all workers with at least three years of tenure who changed employers and who spend at least thirty days in unemployment after moving. For this sample, we only kept observations that were at least five years before and at most fifteen years after the job loss. Characteristics of various samples of displaced workers are shown in table 4.1.

4.5   Empirical Results

4.5.1   Firm-Entry Cohort Effects in German Car Manufacturing

To illustrate our main descriptive results, we begin by showing the pattern of firm-entry cohort effects for a single large and stable establishment in the car manufacturing sector.[9] Figure 4.1 shows the development of average log real daily wages for biannual entry cohorts ranging from 1976 to 1996. One can clearly see a rising trend and significant fluctuations in en-

---

9. For data protection reasons, we have added random constant with zero mean to the individual wage levels.

Table 4.1   Sample characteristics of stable firms and displaced workers in West-
German car manufacturing, 1975–2003

A. Basic characteristics of 55 stable and large firms in car manufacturing[a]

	Average	SD	Median
Number of cohorts	19.6	4.4	22.0
Employment size	6376.7	9560.8	2161.0
Size of entry cohort	482.3	1678.8	88.0
Average cohort age	39.8	6.3	40.5
Average cohort fraction female	0.11	0.05	0.10
Average cohort years of education	10.50	0.63	10.25
Average cohort starting wage	4.33	0.10	4.31
Average cohort log real daily wage	4.49	0.17	4.49

B. Average characteristics of various samples of displaced workers[b]

Years of Job Tenure Prior to Job Loss	Three	Five	Three, From 55 Large Stable Firms
Fraction female	0.14	0.14	0.14
Fraction non-German	0.17	0.18	0.21
Years of education	10.45	10.39	10.21
Average age	35.30	37.23	34.40
Average potential experience	18.85	20.84	18.19
Average tenure on lost job	5.57	7.70	3.31
Fraction part-time on lost job	0.03	0.03	0.08
Fraction low-skill blue collar on lost job	0.37	0.38	0.50
Fraction high-skill blue collar on lost job	0.43	0.42	0.49
Fraction low-skill white collar on lost job	0.18	0.18	0.29
Average log real daily starting wage	4.25	4.26	4.25
Average log real daily wage	4.13	4.15	4.28

[a]Statistics based on firm-year-cohort observations or averages. Average cohort characteristics are weighted by cohort size.
[b]Sample only includes observations for workers who moved jobs followed by a spell of thirty days of unemployment or more at least once. Averages are taken over workers and worker-years ranging from five years before to fifteen years after job loss.

try wages over time. More important, the difference in entry wages clearly leads to persistent average-wage differences across cohorts. However, the figure also clearly shows a pattern of reversion. Differences in initial wages appear to fade over time.

These patterns are documented explicitly in figure 4.2, which shows the annual entry-cohort effects obtained by estimating equation (1) and detrending the resulting cohort effects. One can clearly see permanent differences in average wages of different firm-entry cohorts. Controlling for observable characteristics reduces the cohort effects only somewhat. This suggests that when the firm pays higher wages, it attracts more able workers. However, if we instead control for worker fixed effects, the cohort wage

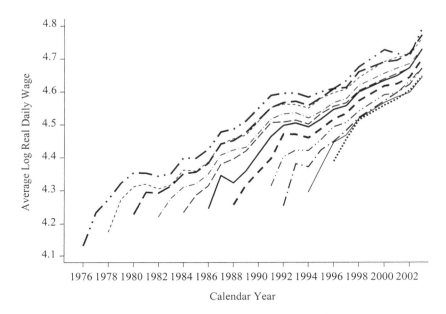

Fig. 4.1 Average wages by biannual entry cohorts for a single firm

Note: For data protection reasons, we have added random constant with zero mean to the individual wage levels.

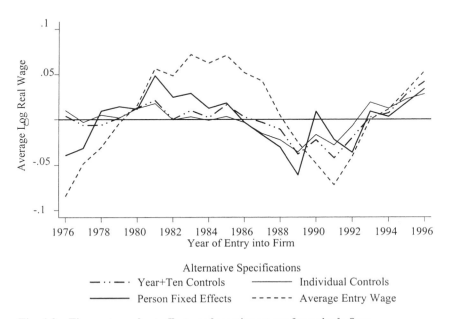

Fig. 4.2 Firm-entry cohort effects and starting wages for a single firm

differences seem to rise, leaving us with no clear conclusion regarding selective entry between cohorts. In either case, we find there are robust differences in average cohort wages over time in this large manufacturing firm, as suggested by Baker, Gibbs, and Holmstrom (1994) for a large financial service firm.

However, contrary to the finding in Baker, Gibbs, and Holmstrom (1994), the pattern in the figure also shows that average cohort differences in wages are smaller than differences in average *starting* wages between firm-entry cohorts. Figure 4.3 shows the time pattern of reversion of initial wage differences explicitly for different specifications of the decay function. Unlike Baker, Gibbs, and Holmstrom (1994), we find a significant albeit slow decay of initial wage differences that lasts up to twenty years. Perhaps not surprisingly, we find a concave tenure wage profile (the profile in Baker, Gibbs, and Holmstrom's [1994] firm was linear). The pattern of decay we find is approximately linear.

The key question then is to what extent the result of statistically and numerically significant firm-entry cohort effects hold for a wider sample of firms as well. The answer to this question is affirmative. We ran the model in equation (1) separately for each firm in our sample of fifty-five large and stable car manufacturing firms and detrended each set of cohort effects as described in section 4.3. The distribution of estimated cohort effects for all firms is shown in figures 4.4 and 4.6 and table 4.2. Figures 4.5 and 4.7 show the distribution and the reversion of initial wage differences.

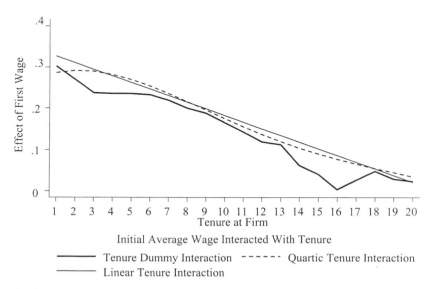

Fig. 4.3   Decline in effect of entry wages with tenure at firm

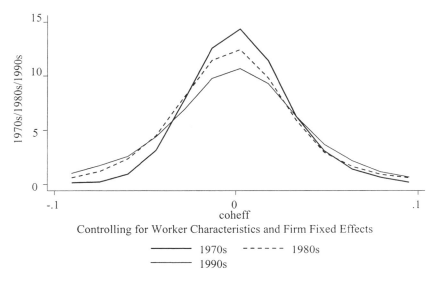

Fig. 4.4   Distribution of firm-entry cohort effects in different years

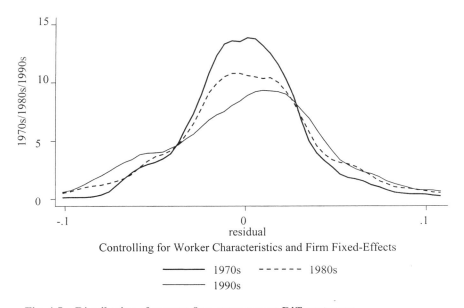

Fig. 4.5   Distribution of average firm-entry wages: Different years

Table 4.2   **Firm-entry cohort effects and average starting wages in German car manufacturing, 1975–2003**

Percentile	Without worker characteristics (year-group)			Controlling for worker characteristics (year-group)		
	1970s	1980s	1990s	1970s	1980s	1990s
A. Distribution of firm-entry cohort effects by decade						
10	−0.041	−0.062	−0.059	−0.041	−0.062	−0.059
25	−0.014	−0.030	−0.027	−0.014	−0.030	−0.027
50	0.003	−0.004	−0.003	0.003	−0.004	−0.003
75	0.020	0.022	0.029	0.020	0.022	0.029
90	0.052	0.052	0.067	0.052	0.052	0.067
B. Distribution of average starting wages of firm-entry cohorts						
10	−0.046	−0.115	−0.112	−0.043	−0.094	−0.098
25	−0.019	−0.058	−0.060	−0.017	−0.048	−0.047
50	0.009	−0.014	−0.009	0.005	−0.011	−0.006
75	0.035	0.021	0.035	0.028	0.018	0.029
90	0.079	0.064	0.092	0.062	0.051	0.068

Notes: Distribution of average cohort wages by year-group. All models estimating cohort effects shown in panel A also include a firm-specific quartic tenure profile, firm-specific year effects, and a firm effects. The resulting firm-entry cohort effects are detrended. Average starting wages are net of year effects and firm effects. The observable characteristics in the right-hand panels are fraction female, fraction non-German, fraction without degree, fraction with apprentice degree, fraction with college degree, fraction low-skilled or high-skilled blue collar, and fraction low-skilled white collar. All models are weighted by the cohort size.

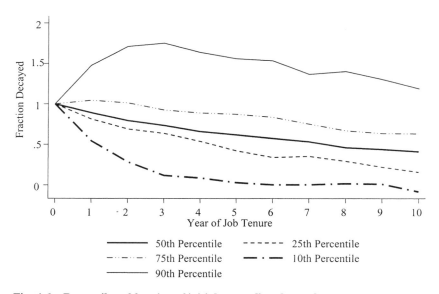

Fig. 4.6   Percentiles of fraction of initial wage effect decayed

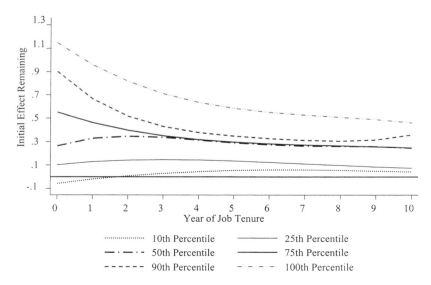

Fig. 4.7   **Decay of initial effect by percentile of average starting wage**

Overall, we obtain five core results:

1. There are significant cohort effects for each firm in the industry we study that are robust to controls for worker and firm characteristics. Similar workers entering firms at different times earn different wages.

2. There is considerable heterogeneity of cohort effects between firms. The entry cohort effects cannot be simply driven by overall labor market conditions in the industry.

3. Heterogeneity in cohort effects (both within and between firms) is increasing over time. The spreading of the German wage distribution occurs in part through cohort effects.

4. Cohort wage differences are largest for entry-level wages and converge over time *within* firms. However, convergence *within* firms is slow, such that persistent differences in average wages remain.

5. Reversion of wages is faster the farther average cohort wages are from the overall market. Outliers tend to convergence *between* firms as well.

The distribution of cohort effects with and without worker characteristics is shown in table 4.2 for the full sample and each of the three decades of our sample. The distribution of F-statistics or p-values is omitted because all cohort effects are significant at the 1 percent confidence level. The table also shows the distribution of average entry-level wages with and without worker controls. The results suggest that there are important and significant differences in average wages of firm-entry cohorts that are robust to controls for average worker characteristics.

The typical detrended cohort effect lies within plus and minus 5 percent of average firm wages. Taken at face value, they suggest that some cohorts in some firms carry premiums or discounts on the order of 5 percent, which corresponds to the wage effect of about one year of labor market experience or a year of education in Germany. Given we cannot identify the linear component of cohort effects, care should be taken with interpreting the specific magnitudes.

The average differences in cohort effects mask even bigger differences in average starting wages between cohorts. Comparing figures 4.4 and 4.5, one can see that the distribution of deviations of cohorts' starting wages from firm-specific averages has fatter tails. Again, although most of the differences are limited in magnitude, some cohorts experience large differences in average wages.

The distribution of cohort effect arises from differences between cohorts within firms. However, a large part of the variation arises from variation between firms for any given cohort. This is apparent from the fact that it holds within decades and can be shown to hold within single years as well. In fact, the annual distribution of cohort effects is similar to the decade-wide distribution, suggesting that an important part of the variation is coming from between firms. Thus, firm-entry cohort effects cannot be simply explained by business-cycle pressures affecting the entire industry. It may be that within the industry, firms producing different products (say trucks or passenger cars) or goods of different qualities face differential demand conditions.

In addition, there may be truly firm-specific differences in the evolution of productivity, employment, and output that affect the fortunes of workers entering firms at different points in time. That similar firms within sectors can experience vastly heterogeneous patterns of employment growth has been suggested in the literature before (e.g., Davis and Haltiwanger 1992). Our findings suggest that such differences can lead to differences in entry-wage levels and average wages between entry cohorts *and* between firms.

Interestingly, the numbers in the tables and figures suggest that the distribution of entry wage differences and cohort effects has been widening over time. The increasing spread is consistent with a widening in the German wage distribution in the 1990s after a period of relative stability. Our results suggest that part of the recent widening is due to an increasing spread in entry-wage differences. However, our results also suggest that this pattern had already started in the 1980s, something typically not found in analyses of the overall wage distribution.

Figure 4.6 shows the distribution of the fraction of the initial difference in average starting wages decayed at each tenure year. The figure suggests first, that the median rate of decay is very slow, leading to a half-life at about eight to nine years. Second, the figure shows that the speed of decay varies widely between firms. For the bottom decile, the entry-wage difference fades within three to four years; for the top 10 percent, the effect actually increases over time. Convergence does not only occur within firms. Figure 4.7 shows that cohorts that have high average wages relative to the overall market have faster speed of convergence. Thus, convergence also occurs between firms toward the average wage in the market.

Overall, these results suggest that firm-entry cohort effects are a significant phenomenon in a broad sample of large and stable manufacturing firms even when controlling for worker characteristics. There is substantial heterogeneity in cohort effects between firms. Convergence within and between firms occurs but is slow. These preliminary estimates suggest that firms' wage structures have a component that systematically varies over time and differs between firms. Our documentation of this *dynamic* component complements and extends existing characterizations of *static* differences in average wages, tenure-wage profiles, and the variance of wages (e.g., Abowd and Kramarz 1999; Abowd, Corbel, and Kramarz 1999; Margolis 1995).

These results also underline the importance of efforts to understand the empirical sources of firm-entry cohort effects and their theoretical underpinnings. The descriptive results in the previous section allow no clear interpretation with respect to the source of cohort effects. On the one hand, the fact that initial wage differences fade suggests that they must have at least in part been driven by temporary differences in cohort-specific rents or job quality. However, the high degree of persistence does not exclude that some of the effect is driven by lasting differences in workers' skill levels. This underscores the need of an explicit test of potential explanations that goes beyond purely descriptive study of wage differences themselves.

4.5.2   Job Losses and Differences in Starting Wages

As discussed at the outset, if differences in cohort wages arise due to differences in temporary rent or job quality, they should fade if workers lose their job. Alternatively, if cohorts obtain a different degree of training or experience, they should carry their higher skills over to their new job. As discussed at the outset, we study this question by comparing the wage losses of job losers with high or low starting wages at the lost job. The analysis of losses in cohort effects per se is left for future work with a larger sample of firms and workers.

As a first step, table 4.3 shows the overall effects of job displacements on wage changes. The time pattern before and after job loss is shown with standard error bands in figure 4.8. The results indicate significant and large wage losses of about 10 percent in the first year that fade in about six to seven years. These results are quite similar to estimates of the effect of job loss in the United States based on the DWS (e.g., Farber 1997, 2003), and similar to estimates in Couch (2001) using a similar methodology and the

Table 4.3   **Wage losses at job loss fifteen years post-job loss, different samples and by starting wage at lost job**

Year to job loss	Three years of pre-job loss tenure	Five Years of pre-job loss tenure	Exits from large and stable firms	Wage loss by interquartile range of starting wage of lost job, Three years pre-tenure		
				Low	Medium	High
−3	0.0043	−0.0002	0.0049	−0.0161	0.0071	0.0188
	(0.0037)	(0.0039)	(0.0157)	(0.0048)	(0.0039)	(0.0046)
−2	0.0053	−0.0087	0.0049	−0.0294	0.0114	0.0366
	(0.0058)	(0.0061)	(0.0244)	(0.0063)	(0.0058)	(0.0062)
−1	0.0031	−0.0221	0.0011	−0.0118	0.0039	0.0221
	(0.0080)	(0.0083)	(0.0336)	(0.0082)	(0.0078)	(0.0082)
0	−0.0331	−0.0624	−0.0313	−0.0378	−0.0372	−0.0192
	(0.0103)	(0.0106)	(0.0430)	(0.0103)	(0.0100)	(0.0102)
1	−0.1048	−0.1745	−0.3397	0.0794	−0.1513	−0.2139
	(0.0126)	(0.0131)	(0.0533)	(0.0126)	(0.0123)	(0.0128)
2	−0.0999	−0.1869	−0.3419	0.0998	−0.1483	−0.2205
	(0.0148)	(0.0153)	(0.0620)	(0.0146)	(0.0144)	(0.0146)
3	−0.0938	−0.1919	−0.3468	0.1193	−0.1436	−0.2251
	(0.0171)	(0.0176)	(0.0713)	(0.0167)	(0.0165)	(0.0167)
4	−0.0791	−0.1873	−0.3244	0.1352	−0.1301	−0.2145
	(0.0193)	(0.0199)	(0.0807)	(0.0188)	(0.0186)	(0.0188)
5	−0.0689	−0.1902	−0.3256	0.1517	−0.1218	−0.2112
	(0.0216)	(0.0223)	(0.0901)	(0.0210)	(0.0208)	(0.0210)
6	−0.0596	−0.1890	−0.3048	0.1571	−0.1132	−0.2028
	(0.0239)	(0.0246)	(0.0995)	(0.0231)	(0.0230)	(0.0231)
7	−0.0515	−0.1909	−0.2867	0.1644	−0.1066	−0.1949
	(0.0261)	(0.0270)	(0.1089)	(0.0253)	(0.0252)	(0.0253)
8	−0.0441	−0.1909	−0.2910	0.1722	−0.1005	−0.1929
	(0.0284)	(0.0293)	(0.1183)	(0.0275)	(0.0273)	(0.0275)
9	−0.0346	−0.1868	−0.2650	0.1728	−0.0929	−0.1820
	(0.0307)	(0.0316)	(0.1278)	(0.0297)	(0.0295)	(0.0297)
10	−0.0212	−0.1843	−0.2602	0.1877	−0.0855	−0.1747
	(0.0330)	(0.0340)	(0.1373)	(0.0318)	(0.0317)	(0.0319)
11	−0.0019	−0.1670	−0.2580	0.2002	−0.0748	−0.1530
	(0.0353)	(0.0363)	(0.1467)	(0.0340)	(0.0339)	(0.0341)
12	0.0164	−0.1562	−0.2317	0.2087	−0.0607	−0.1356
	(0.0375)	(0.0387)	(0.1563)	(0.0362)	(0.0361)	(0.0363)
13	0.0265	−0.1523	−0.2274	0.2163	−0.0566	−0.1266
	(0.0398)	(0.0410)	(0.1657)	(0.0384)	(0.0383)	(0.0385)
14	0.0360	−0.1504	−0.1953	0.2209	−0.0525	−0.1203
	(0.0421)	(0.0434)	(0.1753)	(0.0406)	(0.0405)	(0.0407)
15	0.0449	−0.1495	−0.2034	0.2282	−0.0482	−0.1192
	(0.0444)	(0.0458)	(0.1847)	(0.0428)	(0.0427)	(0.0429)
Constant	3.558	3.595	3.670	3.582		
	(0.0185)	(0.0239)	(0.0980)	(0.0178)		
No. of observations	501,103	284,297	25,059	501,103		
R^2	0.61	0.62	0.63	0.64		

Notes: The entries in the tables are coefficient estimates of regressions of log daily real wages on displacement indicators interacted with dummies for years before and after job displacement. The omitted category are years four and five before job loss. All models also include individual fixed effects, year fixed effects, and a fourth order polynomial in potential labor market experience. The sample excludes apprentices. Standard errors clustered at the individual level are in parentheses.

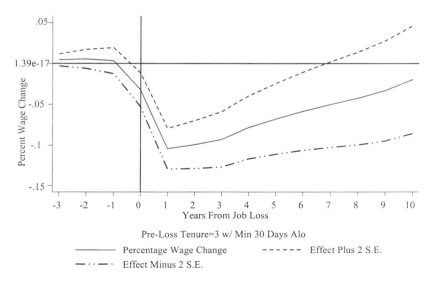

Fig. 4.8   **Wage loss for workers losing jobs in car manufacturing**

German Socio Economic Panel (GSOEP). Burda and Mertens (2001) confirm that high-wage job losers in Germany can experience very large and persistent earnings losses. They also find that job losers in the bottom quartile of the wage distribution tend to exhibit significant gains from job loss.[10]

Our estimates are a larger and more persistent than a recent study of plant closings in Germany using the same administrative data source (Bender et al. 2002). These differences may arise partly due to differences in the definition of job loss, the estimation methodology, the sample used, and the time period covered. In particular, because we impose thirty days in unemployment to identify displaced workers, our approach may lead us to partially overstate the effect of job displacement. Part of the differences may also be due to our focus on workers losing their job in car manufacturing. Because the car-manufacturing sector is typically a high-wage sector, part of the losses we observe are due to losses in the industry wage premium.

Table 4.3 also shows corresponding estimates for workers that had five years of predisplacement tenure and for workers exiting the large and stable firms analyzed in the first part of the chapter. As expected, higher-tenure workers experience larger and more persistent wage losses. However, the wage losses of workers leaving large firms are much larger. As found in von Wachter and Bender (2006), workers leaving large firms per-

10. Burda and Mertens' (2001) estimates imply lower increases at the bottom and higher losses at the top. They do not focus on past starting wages, however, and have a somewhat different definition of layoff. For the top, they demonstrate that including recalls, as we do here, may underestimate the effect of job loss.

manently lose rents associated with jobs at large employers and never fully recover from the initial wage loss.[11]

The remainder of the section analyzes job displacement effects by previous starting wages on wage loss and post-loss wage levels. We obtain four key results:

1. There appears to be mean reversion. In particular, we find large differences in the degree of wage loss by previous starting wages, with the bottom gaining and the top losing.

2. There are permanent winners and losers from job loss. Those workers with high past starting wages experience permanent losses, whereas those with low starting wages experience long-term gains.

3. Pre-job loss starting wage and job tenure have a significant positive impact on wage levels after job loss. As expected, there is positive selection into high tenure and high past starting wages.

4. The effect of pre-job loss tenure and starting wage partly fades with time since job loss. These variables appear to serve as initial signal to the market of worker quality after a job loss.

Table 4.3 and figure 4.9 show the estimates of percent wages lost at job loss for workers with high, medium, and low starting wages (based on the interquartile range of log real starting wages at the previous job). Clearly, workers in the high and medium starting wage groups suffer large and persistent losses and seem to drive the overall effect shown in figure 4.8. Thereby, the medium group tends to recover after ten years, whereas workers in the high group suffer permanent earnings losses of more than 10 percent. The group of workers with the smallest starting wages, on the other hand, has substantial benefits from the job loss that increase over time.

These results suggest that starting wages contain firm-specific rents that fade upon job loss. The results also suggest that there is mean reversion in the labor market. This is consistent with a model of job search in which at job loss workers come from a different part of the wage distribution, but after job loss they are again reset to the mean of the wage distribution irrespective of their previous position. Note that we would not expect to see the effect of previous wages fade fully, as they are likely to contain some information on workers' ability even beyond a person-fixed effect.

4.5.3   The Determinants of Post-Job Loss Wage Levels

To explore this aspect further, table 4.4 analyzes the effect of pre-job loss characteristics on the level of log real wages after job loss. Thereby, the fo-

11. Large firms appear to provide an exceptional career environment that is permanently lost upon job displacement because, on average, workers will transit to a smaller firm. Von Wachter and Bender (2006) show that only apprentices who get displaced from large training firms suffer permanent losses in earnings relative to workers staying at the firm at the end of training. Once they control for the change in firm size at job loss, this excess loss disappears.

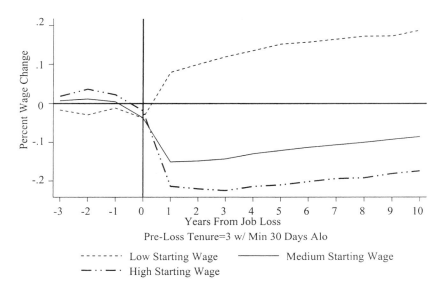

Fig. 4.9   Wage loss at job loss by starting wage at previous job

cus is particularly on the change in the effect of these characteristics over time, as this may further help discern the sources of persistence in the effect of initial conditions.

We first replicate Kletzer's (1989) basic model that includes previous job tenure as basic additional control in a standard human capital model of log wages. We confirm Kletzer's result that past job tenure has a positive effect on current wage levels; in fact, despite the different definition of job loss, our point estimates are quite similar to hers. As in her case, this suggests that the positive correlation of tenure and wages not only arises from specific skills, but also from the fact that high-tenured workers are likely to be more able workers. The next column in table 4.4 also adds the log of previous starting wages to the Kletzer's regression model. Again, we would expect past wages to have a positive effect on current wages as they are a function of components of workers' skills not captured by observable characteristics. This is what we find—a 15 percent difference in starting wages raises wages past layoff by about 1 percent.

In addition to being correlated with actual worker skills, part of the initial effect of past job tenure or past wages may be only temporary. To address this question, the last two columns of table 4.4 show estimates from regression models that interact characteristics of the past job with time since job displacement. Column (3) shows the estimates for past job tenure. When the interaction with past job loss is included, the initial effect doubles, and there is a clear pattern of decay. Thus, the estimates in column (1) capture the average effect of past job tenure all the years prior to job loss

Table 4.4   Effect of characteristics of lost job on wage levels after job displacement, three years pre-job loss tenure

	(1)	(2)	(3)	(4)
Log starting wage at lost job (STWAGE)		0.066		0.119
		(0.0068)		(0.0091)
Years since displacement (YRSINCE)	0.031	0.032	0.063	0.100
	(0.0012)	(0.0012)	(0.0025)	(0.0056)
YRSINCE²	−0.0010	−0.0010	−0.0009	−0.0009
	(0.0001)	(0.0001)	(0.0001)	(0.0001)
Tenure on past job (TEN)	0.0119	0.0121	0.0217	0.0223
	(0.0019)	(0.0019)	(0.0021)	(0.0021)
TEN²	−0.00059	−0.00057	−0.00074	−0.00074
	(0.0001)	(0.0001)	(0.0001)	(0.0001)
Years of education (ED)	0.043	0.041	0.052	0.048
	(0.0010)	(0.0010)	(0.0013)	(0.0014)
Potential labor market experience (EXP)	0.084	0.080	0.082	0.074
	(0.0087)	(0.0088)	(0.0089)	(0.0090)
EXP²	−0.00622	−0.00603	−0.00626	−0.00582
	(0.00063)	(0.00063)	(0.00064)	(0.00065)
EXP³	0.000184	0.000179	0.000189	0.000179
	(0.000019)	(0.000019)	(0.000019)	(0.000019)
EXP⁴	−0.000002	−0.000002	−0.000002	−0.000002
	(0.00000)	(0.00000)	(0.00000)	(0.00000)
TEN * YRSINCE			−0.00127	−0.00129
			(0.0001)	(0.0001)
ED * YRSINCE			−0.00186	−0.00148
			(0.0002)	(0.0002)
STWAGE * YRSINCE				−0.00959
				(0.0013)
No. of observations	231,185	231,185	231,185	231,185
R^2	0.36	0.36	0.36	0.36

Notes: The entries in the table are coefficient estimates of regressions of log real daily wages after a job loss on characteristics of the lost job, year fixed effects, as well as individual characteristics. The specifications mirror closely that of Kletzer (1989). Regressors not listed in the table are a dummy for female and non-German, as well as nine dummies for industry, five dummies for occupation, a dummy for part-time status, and three dummies for blue- and white-collar status, all pertaining to the lost job. The regressions only include the first ten years after a job loss. Apprentices are excluded from the sample. Standard errors clustered at the individual level are in parentheses.

and obscure the fact that the effect fades over time. However, the effect does not fade completely even after ten years after job loss, suggesting, perhaps not surprisingly, that there is still an important correlation between past job tenure and unobserved worker skill.

A similar pattern holds when past starting wages and their interaction with time since job loss are included in the model. The effect of past wages is initially larger and shows a linear pattern of decay (the estimates were not improved by including interactions with higher order polynomials of time since displacement). Again, the effect does not completely fade, suggesting that conditional on observable characteristics past wages do contain information on workers' productivity. However, after ten years, over 80 percent of the initial effect is gone.

These results appear to be consistent with the hypothesis that the initial effect of past tenure and past starting wages captures temporary increases in reservation wages. Over time, reservation wages are determined by current market conditions, and the effect of past rents fades. In addition, as workers continue searching for jobs, their wage is again determined by their skills and overall wage distribution.

Overall, we find that past starting wages contain firm-specific components of earnings that are partly lost when workers are displaced. These components may contain both group-level effects, such as firm-entry cohort effects or average firm-wage premiums, as well as individual-specific rents, for example, from job search. In future work, we plan to use displaced workers from a larger sample to distinguish between these different components. We also find that not all of the effect of past earnings is lost immediately. Some of the past wage may affect reservation wages and search efforts and fades only slowly over time as workers continue to search for jobs. Concluding, the benefit of getting a high paying job is mostly relegated to that job, but has positive spillover effects to future jobs that persist for up to ten years past a job loss.

4.6   Summary and Conclusion

Persistence of entry conditions within firms has intrigued economists for a long time, but few studies were able to provide comprehensive empirical evidence on the incidence and causes of such cohort effects. In this chapter, we have used administrative information on wages and career patterns for all workers who ever worked in the German car industry matched to information on their establishments to make two contributions to the literature. First, we describe the incidence and size of firm-entry cohort effects for a large sample of firms. This allows us to study both the heterogeneity of cohort effects across our industry as well as their persistence both within and between firms.

Second, we have begun to analyze the sources of persistent wage differences between different entry cohorts within firms. In particular, we have analyzed whether initial wage advantages are lost when workers lose their job and spend some time in unemployment. If initial wage differences are driven by differences in general human capital, they should persist when workers are forced to move to new jobs. If they are driven by firm-specific wage components, initial advantages should be lost at a job loss. To probe the degree of persistence of characteristics on the previous job further, we also analyzed the effect of past job tenure and previous starting wages on the level of wages after the job loss.

We find that firm-entry cohort effects are a common phenomenon among larger and stable firms in the German car manufacturing industry. Similar firms hiring similar workers at different points in time pay them different wages. We also find that these differences are quite heterogeneous among firms, such as they cannot be solely explained by marketwide business conditions. Initial wage differences between cohorts do tend to fade over time within firms. Similarly, firms' wages tend to converge to a market wage. However, reversion of initial wage differences occurs slowly.

In the second part, we find that initial wage differences are partly lost at job loss—high-wage workers have much larger and highly persistent wage losses. This suggests that wage differences prior to a job loss are in part driven by temporary firm-specific rents. Part of these rents is likely to consist of firm-entry cohort differences, but they may also contain worker-specific components such as search rents. We also observe mean reversion, that is, low-wage workers seem to permanently benefit from job loss. Consistent with the presence of temporary firm-specific wage components, past starting wages have an initial positive effect on wage levels after a job loss that fades over time. Pre-job loss characteristics appear to affect displaced workers' reservation wages until their wage is again determined by their skills and the overall wage distribution.

The results in this chapter highlight several important questions and areas for future research. First, it will be important to confirm our results with a wider sample of firms covering the entire German economy. An additional important question for future research is to establish to what extent worker mobility contributes to the reversion of initial differences in wages between entry cohorts. Third, using a larger sample we will be able to study the effect of exogenous events such as a mass layoff at the establishment level. Similarly, we will be able to distinguish the loss of group-specific rents, such as average firm wage effects or cohort effects, from the loss of individual specific wage components arising among others from job search.

References

Abowd, John, Patrick Corbel, and Francis Kramarz. 1999. The entry and exit of workers and the growth of employment: An analysis of French establishments. *Review of Economics and Statistics* 81(2): 170–87.

Abowd, John M., and Francis Kramarz. 1999. The analysis of labor markets using matched employer-employee data. In *Handbook of labor economics*. Vol. 3B ed. O. Ashenfelter and D. Card, 2629–2710.

Abraham, Katharine, and Henry Farber. 1987. Job duration, seniority, and earnings. *American Economic Review* 77 (3): 278–97.

Altonji, Joseph G., and Charles Pierret. 2001. Employer learning and statistical discrimination. *Quarterly Journal of Economics* 116 (1): 313–50.

Baker, George, and Michael Gibbs, and Bengt Holmstrom. 1994. The wage policy of a firm. *Quarterly Journal of Economics* 109 (4): 881–919.

Beaudry, Paul, and John DiNardo. 1991. The effect of implicit contracts and the movement of wages over the business cycle. *Journal of Political Economy* 99 (4): 665–88.

Bender, Stefan, Christian Dustmann, David Margolis, and Costas Meghir. 2002. Worker displacement in France and Germany. In *Losing work: International perspectives on job displacement,* ed. Peter Kuhn, 375–470. Kalamazoo, MI: Upjohn Institute.

Bender, Stefan, Annette Haas, and Christoph Klose. 2000. The IAB Employment Subsample 1975–1995. *Journal of Applied Social Science Studies* 120 (4): 649–62.

Bender, Stefan, and Juergen Hilzendegen, Gotz Rohwer, and Helmut Rudolph. 1996. *Die IAB-Beschaftigtenstichprobe 1975–1990: Eine praktische einführung* (The IAB Employees Sample 1975–1990: A practical introduction). Beitraege zur Arbeitsmarkt- und Berufsforschung 197.

Burda, Michael, and Antje A. Mertens. 2001. Estimating Wage Losses of Displaced Workers in Germany. *Labor Economics* 8 (1): 15–41.

Couch, Kenneth A. 2001. Earnings losses and unemployment of displaced workers in Germany. *Industrial and Labor Relations Review* 54 (3): 559–72.

Davis, Steven J., and John Haltiwanger. 1992. Gross job creation, gross job destruction, and employment reallocation. *Quarterly Journal of Economics* 107 (3): 819–63.

Farber, Henry. 1997. The changing face of job loss in the United States, 1981–1995. *Brookings Papers on Economic Activity, Microeconomics:* 55–128.

———. 1999. Mobility and stability: The dynamics of job change in labor markets. In *Handbook of labor economics.* Vol. 3A, ed. O. Ashenfelter and D. Card, 2439–83. Amsterdam: North Holland.

———. 2003. Job loss in the United States, 1981–2001. NBER Working Paper no. 9707. Cambridge, MA: National Bureau of Economic Research.

Farber, Henry, and Robert Gibbons. 1996. Learning and wage dynamics. *Quarterly Journal of Economics* 111 (4): 1007–47.

Gibbons, Robert, and Lawrence Katz. 1991. Layoffs and lemons. *Journal of Labor Economics* 9 (4): 351–80.

Gibbons, Robert, and Michael Waldman. 2004. Task-specific human capital. *AEA Papers and Proceedings* 94:203–7.

Görlitz, Katja, and Till von Wachter. 2006. The impact of job mobility on wage development: What role plays intermediate unemployment? RWI Essen. Mimeograph.

Jacobson, Louis, Robert LaLonde, and Daniel Sullivan. 1993. Earnings losses of displaced workers. *American Economic Review* 83 (4): 685–709.

Kahn, Lisa. 2006. The long-term labor market consequences of graduating college in a bad economy. Harvard University. Mimeograph.

Kletzer, Lori G. 1989. Returns to seniority after permanent job loss. *American Economic Review* 79 (3): 536–43.

Margolis, David. 1995. Firm heterogeneity and worker self-selection bias estimated returns to seniority. CIRANO Working Paper no. 95s-4. Montreal: Center for Interuniversity Research and Analysis on Organizations.

Neal, Derek. 1995. Industry-specific human capital: Evidence from displaced workers. *Journal of Labor Economics* 13 (4): 653–77.

Oi, Walter Y., and Todd L. Idson. 1999. Firm size and wages. In *Handbook of labor economics.* Vol. 3B, ed. O. Ashenfelter and D. Card, 2165–2214. Amsterdam, North Holland.

Okun, Arthur M. 1973. Upward mobility in a high-pressure economy. *Brookings Papers of Economic Activity,* issue no. 1:207–52. Washington, DC: Brookings Institution.

Oreopoulos, Philip, Till von Wachter, and Andrew Heisz. 2006. Short- and long-term career effects of graduating in a recession: Hysteresis and heterogeneity in the market for college graduates. NBER Working Paper no. 12159. Cambridge, MA: National Bureau of Economic Research.

Oyer, Paul. 2006. The macro-foundations of microeconomics: Initial labor market conditions and long-term outcomes for economists. NBER Working Paper no. 12157. Cambridge, MA: National Bureau of Economic Research.

Parent, Daniel. 2000. Industry-specific capital and the wage profile: Evidence from the NLSY and the PSID. *Journal of Labor Economics* 18 (2): 306–23.

Ruhm, Christopher. 1991. Are workers permanently scarred by job displacements? *American Economic Review* 81 (1): 319–24.

Von Wachter, Till, and Stefan Bender. 2006. In the right place at the wrong time: The role of firms and luck in young workers' careers. *The American Economic Review* 96 (5): 1679–1705.

5

Changes in Workplace Segregation in the United States between 1990 and 2000
Evidence from Matched Employer-Employee Data

Judith Hellerstein, David Neumark, and Melissa McInerney

5.1 Introduction

In recent work, we have constructed and described the 1990 Decennial Employer-Employee Dataset (DEED) based on matching records in the 1990 Decennial Census of Population to a Census Bureau list of most business establishments in the United States. We have used the 1990 DEED to estimate earnings and productivity differentials in manufacturing by demographic and skill group (Hellerstein and Neumark 2007), to study the influence of language skills on workplace segregation and wages (Hellerstein and Neumark 2003), to document the extent of workplace segregation by race and ethnicity, and to assess the contribution of residential segregation as well as skill to this segregation (Hellerstein and Neumark, forthcoming).

We just recently completed the construction of the 2000 Beta-DEED

Judith Hellerstein is an associate professor of economics at the University of Maryland, and a research associate of the National Bureau of Economic Research. David Neumark is a professor of economics at the University of California, Irvine, a research fellow of the Institute for the Study of Labor, and a research associate of the National Bureau of Economic Research. Melissa McInerney is a statisician at the U.S. Bureau of the Census, Center for Economic Studies, and a PhD candidate at the University of Maryland, Department of Economics.

This research was funded by National Institute of Child Health & Human Development (NICHD) grant R01HD042806. We also thank the Alfred P. Sloan Foundation for its generous support. We are grateful to Ron Jarmin, Julia Lane, and an anonymous reviewer for helpful comments. The analysis and results presented in this paper are attributable to the authors and do not necessarily reflect concurrence by the Center for Economics Studies, the U.S. Bureau of the Census, or the Sloan Foundation. This paper has undergone a more limited review by the Census Bureau than its official publications. It has been screened to ensure that no confidential data are revealed.

(based on the 2000 Census of Population).[1] In this paper, we use the 1990 and 2000 DEEDs to measure changes in establishment-level workplace segregation over the intervening decade, an analysis for which the DEEDs are uniquely well-suited. We study segregation by education, by race and Hispanic ethnicity, and by sex. With respect to segregation by race and ethnicity, this work is complementary to a flurry of research studying changes in residential segregation from 1990 to 2000 (Glaeser and Vigdor 2001; Iceland and Weinberg 2002; and McConville and Ong 2001).

As we have suggested elsewhere (and see Estlund 2003), however, workplace segregation may be far more salient for interactions between racial and ethnic groups than is residential segregation. The boundaries used in studying residential segregation may not capture social interactions and are to some extent explicitly drawn to accentuate segregation among different groups; for example, Census tract boundaries are often generated in order to ensure that the tracts are "as homogeneous as possible with respect to population characteristics, economic status, and living conditions."[2] In contrast, workplaces—specifically establishments—are units of observation that are generated by economic forces and in which people clearly do interact in a variety of ways, including work, social activity, labor market networks, and so on. Thus, while it is more difficult to study workplace segregation because of data constraints, measuring workplace segregation may be more useful than measuring residential segregation, as traditionally defined, for describing the interactions that arise in society between different groups in the population.[3] Of course, similar arguments to those about workplaces could be made about other settings, such as schools, religious institutions, and so on (e.g., James and Taeuber 1985), but data constraints truly prevent saying much of anything about segregation along these lines.

Segregation is potentially important for a number of reasons. Aside from general social issues regarding integration between different groups, labor market segregation by race and ethnicity accounts—at least in a statistical sense—for a sizable share of wage gaps between white males and other demographic groups (e.g., Carrington and Troske 1998a; Bayard et al. 1999; King 1992; Watts 1995; Higgs 1977), and the same is true of labor market segregation by sex (Bayard et al. 2003; Blau 1977; and Groshen

1. The 2000 Beta-DEED is an internal U.S. Census Bureau data set that will ultimately become part of an integrated matched employer-employee database at the U.S. Census Bureau. The new integrated data will have characteristics of the Decennial Employer-Employee Database (DEED) and the Longitudinal Employer-Household Dynamics Program (LEHD). Hereafter, the 2000 Beta-DEED will be referred to as the 2000 DEED.
2. See the U.S. Census Bureau, http://www.census.gov/geo/www/GARM/Ch10GARM.pdf (viewed April 27, 2005). Echenique and Fryer (2005) develop a segregation index that relies much less heavily on ad hoc definitions of geographical boundaries.
3. Moreover, industry code, the closest proxy in public-use data to an establishment identifier, is a very crude measure to use to examine segregation. For example, we calculate that racial and ethnic segregation at the three-digit industry level in the DEED is typically on the order of one-third as large as the establishment-level segregation we document in the following.

1991).[4] There has generally been less attention paid to segregation by education, but in our earlier work (Hellerstein and Neumark, forthcoming), we documented rather extensive segregation by education (as well as language, which we do not consider in the present paper) in the 1990 DEED.

Measuring changes in workplace segregation along these lines is of interest for a number of reasons. First, although much attention has been paid to changes in residential segregation—of which there is evidence of modest declines from 1990 to 2000—changes in workplace segregation may be more salient to understanding changing social forces. Second, aside from the relative importance of workplace and residential segregation, in the United States there are extensive efforts to reduce labor market discrimination, and, therefore, measuring changes in workplace segregation by race, ethnicity, and sex provides indicators of the success of these efforts. Finally, increases in the productivity (and pay) of more-educated workers relative to less-educated workers may have led to increased segregation by skill (e.g., Kremer and Maskin 1996).[5] A comparison of education segregation between 1990 and 2000 possibly can shed some light on this hypothesis although relatively more of the run-up in wage inequality occurred prior to 1990 (Autor, Katz, and Kearney 2005).

We measure changes in segregation using the 1990 and 2000 Decennial Employer-Employee Databases (DEEDs). For each year, the DEED is based on matching records in the Decennial Census of Population for that year to a Census Bureau list of most business establishments in the United States. The matching yields data on multiple workers matched to establishments, providing the means to measure workplace segregation (and changes therein) in the United States based on a large, fairly representative data set. In addition, the data from the Decennial Census of Population provides the necessary information on race, ethnicity, and so on. Thus, data from the 1990 and 2000 DEEDs provides unparalleled opportunities to study changes in workplace segregation by skill, race, ethnicity, and sex.[6]

---

4. This segregation may occur along industry and occupation lines, as well as at the more detailed level of the establishment or job cell (occupations within establishments). For example, Bayard et al. (1999) found that, for men, job-cell segregation by race accounts for about half of the black-white wage gap and a larger share of the Hispanic-white wage gap.

5. For example, let the production function be $f(L_1, L_2) = L_1^c L_2^d$, with $d > c$. Assume that there are two types of workers: unskilled workers (L_1) with labor input equal to one efficiency unit, and skilled workers (L_2) with efficiency units of $q > 1$. Kremer and Maskin (1996) show that for low q, it is optimal for unskilled and skilled workers to work together, but above a certain threshold of q (that is, a certain amount of skill inequality), the equilibrium will reverse, and workers will be sorted across firms according to skill. Thus, as the returns to education rise (q increases), there may be increased segregation by education.

6. Carrington and Troske (1998a, b) use data sets much more limited in scope than the ones we use here to examine workplace segregation by race and sex. In general, the paucity of research on workplace segregation is presumably a function of the lack of data linking workers to establishments.

5.2   The 1990 and 2000 DEEDs

The analysis in this paper is based on the 1990 and 2000 DEEDs, which we have created at the Center for Economic Studies at the U.S. Bureau of the Census. We have described the construction of the 1990 DEED in detail elsewhere (in particular, Hellerstein and Neumark 2003). The construction of the 2000 DEED follows the same procedures, and our detailed investigation of the 2000 data thus far has indicated that no new serious problems arise that require different methods for 2000. Thus, in this section we simply provide a quick overview of the construction of the data sets.

The DEED for each year is formed by matching workers to establishments. The workers are drawn from the Sample Edited Detail File (SEDF), which contains all individual responses to the Decennial Census of Population one-in-six Long Form. The establishments are drawn from the Census Bureau's Business Register list (BR), formerly known as the Standard Statistical Establishment List (SSEL); the BR is a database containing information for most business establishments operating in the United States in each year, which is continuously updated (see Jarmin and Miranda 2002).

Households receiving the Decennial Census Long Form were asked to report the name and address of the employer in the previous week for each employed member of the household. The file containing this employer name and address information is referred to as the "Write-In" file, which contains the information written on the questionnaires by Long-Form respondents but not actually captured in the SEDF. The BR is a list of most business establishments with one or more employees operating in the United States. The Census Bureau uses the BR as a sampling frame for its Economic Censuses and Surveys and continuously updates the information it contains. The BR contains the name and address of each establishment, geographic codes based on its location, its four-digit Standard Industrial Classification (SIC) code, and an identifier that allows the establishment to be linked to other establishments that are part of the same enterprise and to other Census Bureau establishment- or firm-level data sets that contain more detailed employer characteristics. We can, therefore, use employer names and addresses for each worker in the Write-In file to match the Write-In file to the BR. Because the name and address information on the Write-In file is also available for virtually all employers in the BR, nearly all of the establishments in the BR that are classified as "active" by the Census Bureau are available for matching. Finally, because both the Write-In file and the SEDF contain identical sets of unique individual identifiers, we can use these identifiers to link the Write-In file to the SEDF. Thus, this procedure yields a very large data set with workers matched to their establishments, along with all of the information on workers from the SEDF.

Matching workers and establishments is a difficult task because we would not expect employers' names and addresses to be recorded identically on the two files. To match workers and establishments based on the Write-In file, we use MatchWare—a specialized record linkage program. MatchWare is comprised of two parts: a name and address standardization mechanism (AutoStan) and a matching system (AutoMatch). This software has been used previously to link various Census Bureau data sets (Foster, Haltiwanger, and Krizan 1998). Our method to link records using MatchWare involves two basic steps. The first step is to use AutoStan to standardize employer names and addresses across the Write-In file and the BR. Standardization of addresses in the establishment and worker files helps to eliminate differences in how data are reported. The standardization software considers a wide variety of different ways that common address and business terms can be written and converts each to a single standard form.

Once the software standardizes the business names and addresses, each item is parsed into components. The value of parsing the addresses into multiple pieces is that we can match on various combinations of these components. We supplemented the AutoStan software by creating an acronym for each company name and added this variable to the list of matching components.[7]

The second step of the matching process is to select and implement the matching specifications. The AutoMatch software uses a probabilistic matching algorithm that accounts for missing information, misspellings, and even inaccurate information. This software also permits users to control which matching variables to use, how heavily to weight each matching variable, and how similar two addresses must be in order to constitute a match. AutoMatch is designed to compare match criteria in a succession of "passes" through the data. Each pass is comprised of "Block" and "Match" statements. The Block statements list the variables that must match exactly in that pass in order for a record pair to be linked. In each pass, a worker record from the Write-In file is a candidate for linkage only if the Block variables agree completely with the set of designated Block variables on analogous establishment records in the BR. The Match statements contain a set of additional variables from each record to be compared. These variables need not agree completely for records to be linked, but are assigned weights based on their value and reliability.

For example, we might assign "employer name" and "city name" as Block variables and assign "street name" and "house number" as Match variables. In this case, AutoMatch compares a worker record only to those establishment records with the same employer name and city name. All employer records meeting these criteria are then weighted by whether and

---

7. For 2000, we also added standard acronyms or abbreviations for cities, such as NY or NYC and LA. However, this added a negligible number of additional matches, so we did not go back and do the same for the 1990 DEED.

how closely they agree with the worker record on the street name and house number Match specifications. The algorithm applies greater weights to items that appear infrequently. The employer record with the highest weight will be linked to the worker record conditional on the weight being above some chosen minimum. Worker records that cannot be matched to employer records based on the Block and Match criteria are considered residuals, and we attempt to match these records on subsequent passes using different criteria.

It is clear that different Block and Match specifications may produce different sets of matches. Matching criteria should be broad enough to cover as many potential matches as possible, but narrow enough to ensure that only matches that are correct with a high probability are linked.[8] Because the AutoMatch algorithm is not exact, there is always a range of quality of matches, and we, therefore, are cautious in accepting linked record pairs. Our general strategy is to impose the most stringent criteria in the earliest passes and to loosen the criteria in subsequent passes, while always maintaining criteria that err on the side of avoiding false matches. We choose matching algorithms based on substantial experimentation and visual inspection of many thousands of records.

The final result is an extremely large data set, for each year, of workers matched to their establishment of employment. The 1990 DEED consists of information on 3.29 million workers matched to around 972,000 establishments, accounting for 27.1 percent of workers in the SEDF and 18.6 percent of establishments in the BR. The 2000 DEED consists of information on 4.09 million workers matched to around 1.28 million establishments, accounting for 29.1 percent of workers in the SEDF and 22.6 percent of establishments in the BR.[9]

In table 5.1, we provide descriptive statistics for the matched workers from the DEED as compared to the SEDF. Columns (1) and (4) report summary statistics for the SEDF for the sample of workers who were elig-

---

8. One might also considering trying to impute matches where this strategy fails by matching based on imputed place of work instead of information in the Write-In file. However, this turns out to be problematic. Even imputing place of work at the level of the Census tract is not easy. For example, there are workers in the SEDF that we are able to match to an employer in the DEED using name and address information whose place of work code actually is allocated in the SEDF. For these workers, the allocated Census tract in the SEDF disagrees with the BR Census tract of the matched establishment in more than half the cases.

9. For both the DEED and SEDF, we have excluded individuals as follows: with missing wages; who did not work in the year prior to the survey year or in the reference week for the Long Form of the Census; who did not report positive hourly wages; who did not work in one of the fifty states or the District of Columbia (whether or not the place of work was imputed); who were self-employed; who were not classified in a state of residence; or who were employed in an industry that was considered "out-of-scope" in the BR. (Out-of-scope industries do not fall under the purview of Census Bureau surveys. They include many agricultural industries, urban transit, the U.S. Postal Service, private households, schools and universities, labor unions, religious and membership organizations, and government/public administration. The Census Bureau does not validate the quality of BR data for businesses in out-of-scope industries.)

Table 5.1   **Means for workers**

	1990			2000		
	SEDF (1)	Full DEED (2)	Restricted DEED (3)	SEDF (4)	Full DEED (5)	Restricted DEED (6)
Age	37.08	37.51	37.53	39.15	39.57	39.53
	(12.78)	(12.23)	(12.13)	(13.03)	(12.51)	(12.33)
Female	0.46	0.47	0.47	0.46	0.50	0.51
Married	0.60	0.65	0.63	0.58	0.62	0.60
White	0.82	0.86	0.84	0.78	0.83	0.79
Hispanic	0.07	0.05	0.06	0.09	0.07	0.08
Black	0.08	0.05	0.06	0.09	0.06	0.08
Full-time	0.77	0.83	0.84	0.78	0.82	0.83
No. of kids (if female)	0.75	0.73	0.69	0.78	0.76	0.74
	(1.04)	(1.01)	(0.99)	(1.07)	(1.04)	(1.03)
High school diploma	0.34	0.33	0.30	0.31	0.29	0.25
Some college	0.30	0.32	0.33	0.33	0.35	0.35
BA	0.13	0.16	0.18	0.15	0.18	0.20
Advanced degree	0.05	0.05	0.06	0.06	0.08	0.09
Ln(hourly wage)	2.21	2.30	2.37	2.55	2.63	2.70
	(0.70)	(0.65)	(0.65)	(0.73)	(0.70)	(0.70)
Hourly wage	12.10	12.89	13.68	17.91	18.83	20.19
	(82.19)	(37.07)	(27.41)	(137.20)	(63.61)	(64.05)
Hours worked in previous year	39.51	40.42	40.55	40.22	40.72	40.90
	(11.44)	(10.37)	(10.10)	(11.74)	(11.09)	(10.85)
Weeks worked in previous year	46.67	48.21	48.46	47.23	48.38	48.56
	(11.05)	(9.34)	(9.05)	(10.58)	(9.27)	(9.05)
Earnings in previous year	22,575	25,581	27,478	33,521	37,244	40,272
	(26,760)	(29,475)	(30,887)	(42,977)	(47,237)	(50,406)
Industry						
Mining	0.01	0.01	0.01	0.01	0.00	0.00
Construction	0.07	0.04	0.03	0.08	0.05	0.04
Manufacturing	0.25	0.34	0.35	0.21	0.26	0.26
Transportation	0.08	0.05	0.05	0.07	0.05	0.05
Wholesale	0.05	0.07	0.08	0.05	0.05	0.05
Retail	0.20	0.17	0.15	0.21	0.21	0.20
FIRE	0.08	0.08	0.09	0.07	0.07	0.07
Services	0.26	0.24	0.24	0.31	0.31	0.32
N	12,143,183	3,291,213	1,828,020	14,057,121	4,089,098	2,209,908

ible to be matched to their establishments, for 1990 and 2000, respectively. Columns (2) and (5) report summary statistics for the full DEED sample. For both years, the means of the demographic variables in the full DEED are quite close to the means in the SEDF across most dimensions. For example, for the 1990 data, female workers comprise 46 percent of the SEDF and 47 percent of the full DEED, and the number of children (for women) is 0.75 in the SEDF and 0.73 in the DEED. Nonetheless, there are cases of somewhat larger differences. Race and ethnic differences are larger in both years; for example, in 2000, the percent white is 78 in the SEDF versus 83 in the DEED, and, correspondingly, the share black (and also Hispanic) is lower in the DEED. In addition, the percent female in the 2000 data is 46 in the SEDF, but 50 in the DEED; this is different than the discrepancy in 1990 where the percent female is 46 in the SEDF and only a slightly higher 47 percent in the DEED.

Part of the explanation for differences in racial and ethnic representation that result from the matching process is that there are many individuals who meet our sample inclusion criteria but for whom the quality of the business address information in the Write-In file is poor, and race and ethnic differences in reporting account for part of the differences in representation. We suspect that the differences in business address information partially reflect weaker labor market attachment among minorities, suggesting that the segregation results we obtain might best be interpreted as measuring the extent of segregation among workers who have relatively high labor force attachment and high attachment to their employers.

The last eight rows of the table report on the industry distribution of workers. We do find some overrepresentation of workers in manufacturing—more so in 1990 when manufacturing comprised a larger fraction of workers to begin with in the SEDF. The reasons for this are given in the following when we discuss establishment-level data.

Columns (3) and (6) report summary statistics for the workers in the DEED who comprise the sample from which we calculate segregation measures. The sample size reductions relative to columns (2) and (5) arise for two reasons. First, for reasons explained in the methods section, we exclude workers who do not live and work in the same Metropolitan Statistical Area/Primary Metropolitan Statistical Area (MSA/PMSA). Second, we exclude workers who are the only workers matched to their establishments, as there are methodological advantages to studying segregation in establishments where we observe at least two workers. The latter restriction effectively causes us to restrict the sample to workers in larger establishments, which is the main reason why some of the descriptive statistics are slightly different between the second and third columns (for example, slightly higher wages and earnings in columns [3] and [6]).

In addition to comparing worker-based means, it is useful to examine the similarities across establishments in the BR and the DEED for each year. Table 5.2 shows descriptive statistics for establishments in each data set. As column (1) indicates, there are 5,237,592 establishments in the 1990 BR, and of these 972,436 (18.6 percent) also appear in the full DEED for 1990, as reported in column (2). For 2000, the percentage in the full DEED is somewhat higher (22.6). Because only one in six workers are sent De-

Table 5.2   **Means for establishments**

	1990			2000		
	BR (1)	Full DEED (2)	Restricted DEED (3)	BR (4)	Full DEED (5)	Restricted DEED (6)
Total employment	17.57	52.68	104.67	18.77	48.74	95.54
	(253.75)	(577.39)	(996.52)	(138.11)	(232.05)	(371.18)
Establishment size						
1–25	0.88	0.65	0.39	0.87	0.66	0.41
26–50	0.06	0.15	0.22	0.06	0.15	0.21
51–100	0.03	0.10	0.19	0.03	0.09	0.17
101+	0.03	0.10	0.21	0.03	0.09	0.20
Industry						
Mining	0.00	0.01	0.01	0.00	0.00	0.00
Construction	0.09	0.07	0.06	0.11	0.08	0.07
Manufacturing	0.06	0.13	0.23	0.06	0.13	0.18
Transportation	0.04	0.05	0.05	0.04	0.05	0.05
Wholesale	0.08	0.11	0.10	0.07	0.07	0.07
Retail	0.25	0.24	0.23	0.25	0.29	0.27
FIRE	0.09	0.10	0.11	0.09	0.08	0.07
Services	0.28	0.26	0.21	0.35	0.30	0.27
In MSA	0.81	0.82	1	0.81	0.79	1
Census region						
North East	0.06	0.06	0.05	0.06	0.05	0.04
Mid Atlantic	0.16	0.15	0.16	0.15	0.14	0.14
East North Central	0.16	0.20	0.21	0.16	0.20	0.21
West North Central	0.07	0.08	0.07	0.08	0.09	0.08
South Atlantic	0.18	0.16	0.15	0.18	0.16	0.16
East South Central	0.05	0.05	0.04	0.06	0.05	0.04
West South Central	0.10	0.10	0.09	0.10	0.10	0.10
Mountain	0.06	0.05	0.05	0.07	0.06	0.06
Pacific	0.16	0.15	0.17	0.16	0.15	0.17
Payroll ($1,000)	397	1,358	2,910	694.44	1,993	4,421
	(5,064)	(10,329)	(16,601)	(69,383)	(115,076)	(198,414)
Payroll/total employment	21.02	24.24	26.70	33.74	35.91	42.27
	(1,385.12)	(111.79)	(181.48)	(772.29)	(1,834.40)	(1,877.29)
Share of employees matched		0.17	0.16		0.16	0.14
Multiunit establishment	0.23	0.42	0.53	0.26	0.40	0.50
N	5,237,592	972,436	317,112	5,651,680	1,279,999	411,300

cennial Census Long Forms, it is more likely that large establishments will be included in the DEED. One can see evidence of the bias toward larger employers by comparing the means across data sets for total employment. (This bias presumably also influences the distribution of workers and establishments across industries, where, for example, the DEEDs overrepresent workers in manufacturing establishments.) On average, establishments in the BRs have eighteen to nineteen employees, while the average in the DEEDs is forty-nine to fifty-three workers. The distributions of establishments across industries in the DEED relative to the BR are similar to those for workers in the worker sample. In columns (3) and (6), we report descriptive statistics for establishments in the restricted DEEDs, corresponding to the sample of workers in columns (3) and (6) of table 5.1. In general, the summary statistics are quite similar between columns (2) and (3) and between columns (5) and (6), with an unsurprising right shift in the size distribution of establishments. Overall, however, the DEED samples are far more representative than previous detailed matched data sets for the United States constructed using just the SEDF and the BR (see Hellerstein and Neumark 2003).[10]

Because the DEED captures larger establishments and because our sample restrictions accentuate this, our analysis focuses on larger establishments. So, for example, the first quartile of the establishment size distribution for workers in our analysis is approximately forty-one workers in 1990 and thirty-six in 2000, whereas the first quartile of the employment-weighted size distribution of all establishments in the BR for each year is nineteen in 1990 and twenty-one in 2001.[11] Although we acknowledge that it would be nice to be able to measure segregation in all establishments, this is not the data set with which to do that convincingly. Nonetheless, most legislation aimed at combating discrimination is directed at larger establishments; Equal Employment Opportunity Commission (EEOC) laws cover employers with fifteen or more workers, and affirmative action rules for federal contractors cover employers with fifty or more workers. Because policy has been directed at larger establishments, examining the extent of and changes in workplace segregation in larger establishments is important.

5.3   Methods

We focus our analysis on a measure of segregation that is based on the percentages of workers in an individual's establishment, or workplace, in different demographic groups. Consider for clarity measuring segregation between white and Hispanic workers. For each white or Hispanic worker in our sample, we compute the percentage of Hispanic workers with which that worker works, excluding the worker him- or herself. Because we exclude

10. These earlier matched data sets—the Worker-Establishment Characteristics Database (WECD), which covers manufacturing only, and the New Worker-Establishment Characteristics Database (NWECD), which covers all industries—were smaller and less representative because the matching algorithm used could only be applied to establishments that were unique in a cell defined by detailed geographic information and industry classification. Thus, for example, manufacturing establishments were much more likely to occupy their own industry-location cell than were retail establishments.
11. In order to adhere to U.S. Census Bureau confidentiality rules, these are "pseudo quartiles" based on averages of observations symmetrically distributed around the actual quartiles.

an individual's own ethnicity in this calculation, our analysis of segregation is conducted on establishments where we observe at least two workers.

We then average these percentages separately for white workers in our sample and for Hispanic workers. These averages are segregation measures commonly used in the sociology literature. The average percentage of coworkers in Hispanic workers' establishments who are Hispanic, denoted H_H, is called the "isolation index," and the average percentage of coworkers in white workers' establishments who are Hispanic, denoted W_H, is called the "exposure index." We focus more on a third measure, the difference between these, or

$$CW = H_H - W_H,$$

as a measure of "coworker segregation." The variable CW measures the extent to which Hispanics are more likely than are whites to work with other Hispanics. For example, if Hispanics and whites are perfectly segregated, then H_H equals 100, W_H is zero, and CW equals 100.[12]

We first report observed segregation, which is simply the sample mean of the segregation measure across workers. We denote this measure by appending an O superscript to the coworker segregation measure—that is, CW^O. One important point that is often overlooked in research on segregation, however, is that some segregation occurs even if workers are assigned randomly to establishments, and we are presumably most interested in the segregation that occurs systematically—that is, that which is greater than would be expected to result from randomness (Carrington and Troske 1997). Rather than considering all deviations from proportional representation across establishments as an "outcome" or "behavior" to be explained, we subtract from our measured segregation the segregation that would occur by chance if workers were distributed randomly across establishments, using Monte Carlo simulations to generate measures of randomly occurring segregation. We denote this random segregation CW^R (and similarly for the isolation and exposure indexes) and then focus on the difference ($CW^O - CW^R$), which measures segregation above and beyond that which occurs randomly.[13] Although theoretically one can have $CW^O <$ CW^R (that is, there is *less* segregation than would be generated randomly) or $CW^O > CW^R$, only the latter occurs in practice in our data. Again following Carrington and Troske, we scale this difference by the maximum

---

12. We could equivalently define the percentages of white workers with which Hispanic or white workers work, H_W and W_W, which would simply be 100 minus these percentages, and $CW' = W_W - H_W$.

13. This distinction between comparing measured segregation to a no-segregation ideal or segregation that is generated by randomness is discussed in other work (see, e.g., Cortese, Falk, and Cohen 1976; Winship 1977; Boisso et al. 1994; and Carrington and Troske 1997). Of course, to build CW^R we also compute the isolation and exposure indexes that would be generated in the case of random allocation of workers, and we report these as well.

segregation that can occur, or $(100 - \mathrm{CW}^R)$, we refer to this measure as "effective segregation." Thus, the effective segregation measure is

$$\left(\frac{\mathrm{CW}^O - \mathrm{CW}^R}{100 - \mathrm{CW}^R} \right) \times 100,$$

which measures the share of the maximum possible segregation that is actually observed.

There are two reasons that we exclude the worker's own ethnicity when computing the fraction of Hispanics with which he or she works. First, this ensures that, in large samples of workers, if workers are randomly allocated across establishments, H_H and W_H both equal the share Hispanic in the population. That is, in the case of random allocation, we expect to have CW^R equal to 0. This is a natural scaling to use and stands in contrast to what happens when the worker is included in the calculations, where CW^R will exceed 0 because Hispanic workers are treated as working with "themselves." Second, and perhaps more important, when the own worker is excluded, our segregation measures are invariant to the sizes of establishments studied. To see this in a couple of simple examples, first consider a simple case of an economy with equal numbers of Hispanics and whites all working in two-person establishments. Establishments can therefore be represented as HH (for two Hispanic workers), HW, or WW. With random allocation, 1/4 of establishments are HH, 1/2 are WH, and 1/4 are WW. Thus, excluding the own worker, $H_H{}^R = (1/2) \cdot 1 + (1/2) \cdot 0 = 1/2$, $W_H{}^R = (1/2) \cdot 1 + (1/2) \cdot 0 = 1/2$, and $\mathrm{CW}^R = 0$.[14] If we count the individual, then $H_H{}^R = (1/2) \cdot 1 + (1/2) \cdot (1/2) = 3/4$, $W_H{}^R = (1/2) \cdot (1/2) + (1/2) \cdot 0 = 1/4$, and $\mathrm{CW}^R = 1/2$. With three-worker establishments and random allocation, 1/8 of establishments are HHH (employing 1/4 of Hispanic workers), 1/8 are WWW (employing 1/4 of white workers), 3/8 are HWW (employing 1/4 of Hispanic and 1/2 of white workers), and 3/8 are HHW (employing 1/2 of Hispanic and 1/4 of white workers). Going through the same type of calculation as in the preceding, if we include the worker, then $H_H{}^R = (1/4) \cdot 1 + (1/4) \cdot (1/3) + (1/2) \cdot (2/3) = 2/3$, $W_H{}^R = (1/4) \cdot 0 + (1/4) \cdot (2/3) + (1/2) \cdot (1/3) = 1/3$ and $\mathrm{CW}^R = 1/3$, whereas if we exclude the worker we again get $H_H{}^R = 1/2$, $W_H{}^R = 1/2$, and $\mathrm{CW}^R = 0$.

Although we just argued that in the case of random allocation Hispanics and whites should work with equal percentages of Hispanic coworkers on average (so that CW^R is zero), this result may not hold in parts of our analysis for two reasons. First, this is a large-sample result, and although the baseline sample size in our data set is large, the samples that we use to calculate some of our segregation measures are not necessarily large enough to generate this asymptotic result. Second, some of our segregation

---

14. For the first calculation, for example, 1/2 of hispanic workers are in HH establishments, for which the share hispanic is 1, and 1/2 are in WH establishments, for which the share Hispanic (excluding the worker) is 0.

measures are calculated conditional on geography (in particular, MSA/PMSA of residence), for reasons explained in the following. When we condition on geography, we calculate the extent of segregation that would be expected if workers were randomly allocated across establishments within a geographic area. If Hispanics and whites are not evenly distributed across geographic borders, random allocation of workers within geographical areas still will yield the result that Hispanics are more likely to have Hispanic coworkers than are white workers because, for example, more Hispanics will come from areas where both whites and Hispanics work with a high share of Hispanic workers. For these reasons, in order to determine how much segregation would occur randomly, in all cases we conduct Monte Carlo simulations of the extent of segregation that would occur with random allocation of workers.

There are, of course, other possible segregation measures, such as the traditional Duncan index (Duncan and Duncan 1955) or the Gini coefficient. We prefer the coworker segregation measure (CW) to these other measures for two reasons. First, the Duncan and Gini measures are scale invariant, meaning that they are insensitive to the proportions of each group in the workforce. For example, if the number of Hispanics doubles but they are allocated to establishments in the same proportion as the original distribution, the Duncan and Gini indexes are unchanged. However, except in establishments that are perfectly segregated, the doubling of Hispanics leads each Hispanic worker in the sample to work with a larger percentage of Hispanic coworkers and also each white worker to work with more Hispanics. In general, this implies that both the isolation and exposure indexes (H_H and W_H, respectively), will increase. But the isolation index will increase by more because establishments with more Hispanics to begin with will have larger increases in the number of Hispanic workers, and, hence, CW will increase.[15] In our view, this kind of increase in the number of Hispanic workers *should* be characterized as an increase in segregation. Second, these alternative segregation measures are also sensitive to the number of matched workers in an establishment (the same issue outlined in the preceding), and because they are measures that are calculated at only the establishment level—unlike the coworker segregation measure we use—there is no conceptual parallel to excluding the own worker from the calculation.[16]

---

15. More generally, W_H will also increase, but not by as much as H_H, and CW will, therefore, rise. For perhaps the simplest such case, start with four establishments as follows: one HHH, one HHW, one HWW, and one WWW. In this case, $H_H = 2/3$, $W_H = 1/3$, and CW = 1/3. Doubling the number of Hispanics and allocating them proportionally, we get the following four establishments: HHHHHH, HHHHW, WWHH, and WWW: In this case H_H rises to 29/36 (increasing by 5/36), W_H rises to 14/36 (increasing by 2/36), and CW rises to 15/36 (increasing by 3/36).

16. We believe this explains why, in Carrington and Troske (1998a, table 3), where there are small samples of workers within establishments, the random Gini indexes are often extremely high.

At the same time, because calculated changes in segregation between 1990 and 2000 based on our coworker segregation index are sensitive to the overall proportions of each group in the workforce, changes over the decade in the proportions of particular demographic groups that are matched to establishments can generate changes in measured segregation. So, for example, the fact that the fraction of workers who are Hispanic grew from 1990 to 2000 should yield a small increase in measured coworker segregation by ethnicity over the decade (even if Hispanics and whites are distributed across establishments in the same proportion in each year). We could avoid this problem by using scale-invariant segregation measures, but then we would fail to capture changes in segregation due to actual changes in workforce composition. That is, the fact that Hispanics make up a growing fraction of the workforce is an important phenomenon to capture.[17] Nonetheless, although we emphasize the coworker segregation measure throughout, we also report our key results based on the Duncan index to see how robust the conclusions are.

We present some "unconditional" nationwide segregation measures, as well as "conditional" measures that first condition on metropolitan area (MSA/PMSA) of residence. In the first, the simulations randomly assign workers to establishments anywhere in the country; not surprisingly, in these simulations the random segregation measures are zero or virtually indistinguishable from zero. For comparability, when we construct these unconditional segregation measures, we use only the workers included in the MSA/PMSA sample used for the conditional analysis.[18] The unconditional estimates provide the simplest measures of the extent of integration by skill, race, ethnicity, or sex in the workplace. However, they reflect the distribution of workers both across cities and across establishments within cities. As such, the unconditional measures may tell us less about forces operating in the labor market to create segregation, whereas the conditional measures—which can be interpreted as taking residential segregation by city as given—may tell us more about these forces. Because we use the same samples for the conditional and unconditional analyses, for these analyses the observed segregation measures are identical. Only the simulations differ, but these differences, of course, imply differences in the effective segregation measures.

17. Some measured changes in the sample composition of workers over time may reflect changes in the match rates of various kinds of workers to establishments rather than a change in the underlying population composition. This is obviously a limitation of matched data sets like ours, one that exists to a much smaller extent in administrative data sets that come closer to capturing fully the universe of workers.

18. The results in this paper are generally robust to measuring unconditional segregation by including all workers in the United States whether they live and work in a metropolitan area. For the unconditional analysis using the full DEEDs versus the MSA/PMSA sample, the changes in segregation are always in the same direction and qualitatively similar although the estimated percentage changes are a bit more moderate than those reported in the following.

For the Monte Carlo simulations that generate measures of random segregation, we need to first define the unit within which we are considering workers to be randomly allocated. This requires a specification of the relevant labor market. We use U.S. Census Bureau MSA/PMSA designations because these are defined to some extent based on areas within which substantial commuting to work occurs.[19] An MSA is a set of one or more counties that contains a population center and the adjacent densely-settled counties, with additional counties included if the share of residents commuting to the population core exceeds a certain threshold.[20] In the case of particularly large MSAs, such as Washington, DC-Baltimore, MD, the entire region meets the criteria to be a MSA, and two or more subsets of the region also meet the MSA definition. In cases such as these, we consider the smaller subsets of counties, called PMSAs. In the Washington, DC-Baltimore, MD example, the larger area (called a Consolidated Metropolitan Statistical Area, or CMSA) is comprised of three PMSAs: Baltimore, MD; Hagerstown, MD; and Washington, DC. Thus, the metropolitan areas on which we focus should be relatively well-defined labor markets, rather than huge areas covering many cities.[21] For example, the 10th percentile of the distribution of MSA/PMSA populations is comprised of smaller metropolitan areas such as Sheboygan, WI, with approximately 100,000 residents, and the 90th percentile is Sacramento, CA, having roughly 1.6 million residents.[22] At the same time, we are certainly not claiming that residential segregation at a level below that of the MSA/PMSA does not influence workplace segregation. However, an analysis of this question requires somewhat different methods. For example, in conducting the simulations, it is not obvious how one should limit the set of establishments within a metropolitan area in which a worker could be employed.

Returning to the simulation procedure, we calculate for each MSA/

19. See the U.S. Census Bureau, http://www.census.gov/geo/lv4help/cengeoglos.html (viewed April 18, 2005).

20. See the Geographic Areas Reference Manual, http://www.census.gov/geo/www/GARM/Ch13GARM.pdf (viewed June 12, 2007). There are a handful of MSAs or PMSAs for which the constituent counties change between 1990 and 2000 or an MSA was abolished or created. The following tables report results using the MSAs/PMSAs present in each year. We constructed a restricted sample that for the most part held MSA/PMSA boundaries fixed by using only counties that were in the same MSA/PMSA in each of the two years; the estimated levels of and changes in segregation were almost identical.

21. Nonetheless, the results in this paper are generally robust to measuring segregation at the level of the MSA/CMSA metropolitan area rather than the MSA/PMSA level. The only difference is that the increase in black-white segregation is about one-quarter smaller in the first case than in the estimates reported in the following. In addition, we examined our main results for cities disaggregated by quartiles of the population-weighted size distribution, and there was no systematic relationship between city size and changes in segregation along the dimensions we study.

22. These are calculated from Summary File 1 for the 2000 Decennial Census. The population-weighted totals reflect slightly larger MSA/PMSAs. The population weighted 10th percentile is Galveston, TX, with approximately 250,000 residents, and the 90th percentile is Chicago, IL, with approximately 8.3 million residents.

PMSA the numbers of workers in each category for which we are doing the simulation—for example, blacks and whites—as well as the number of establishments and the size distribution of establishments (in terms of sampled workers). Within a metropolitan area, we then randomly assign workers to establishments, ensuring that we generate the same size distribution of establishments within a metropolitan area as we have in the sample. We do this simulation 100 times and compute the random segregation measures as the means over these 100 simulations. Not surprisingly, the random segregation measures are very precise; in all cases, the standard deviations were trivially small.

5.4   Changes in Segregation

With the preceding technical material out of the way, the empirical results can be presented quite concisely.

5.4.1   Segregation by Education

The findings for changes in segregation by education are reported in table 5.3. We begin by computing segregation between those with at least some college education and those with at most a high school education. The observed segregation measure for 1990 indicates that, on average, low-education workers are in workplaces in which 54.2 percent of their coworkers are low education, while high-education workers are in workplaces in which only 34.5 percent are low education, for a difference of 19.7. This is also the effective segregation measure for the national sample because random allocation of workers to establishments anywhere in the country leads to a random coworker segregation measure of zero. When we look within MSAs/PMSAs, randomness generates a fairly small amount of segregation, so the effective segregation measure declines only a little, to 17.3.

In the 2000 data, observed segregation is 1.4 percentage points higher (21.1), while random segregation is lower. In combination, then, looking within MSAs/PMSAs, effective segregation by education rises two percentage points, or by 11.3 percent, from 1990 to 2000. In the national data, the increase is smaller, from 19.7 to 21.1 percent, or 7.0 percent.[23] The next two panels of table 5.3 report results for two alternative education cutoffs: high school dropouts versus at least a high school degree; and less than a bachelor's degree versus at least a bachelor's degree. For the high school dropouts versus at least a high school degree breakdown, the overall national figures indicate an increase in segregation similar to that seen in the first panel of the table; educational segregation increased by 1.7 percentage points (11.1 percent nationally) and by 1.9 percentage points (13.6 percent) within MSAs/PMSAs. When we instead classify workers by whether

23. We remind that reader that when we say "national," we refer to the MSA/PMSA sample.

Table 5.3 **Segregation by education (% low education)**

	1990 U.S. MSA/PMSA sample (1)	1990 Within MSA/PMSA sample (2)	2000 U.S. MSA/PMSA sample (3)	2000 Within MSA/PMSA sample (4)
Coworker segregation				
High school degree or less vs. more than high school				
Observed segregation				
Low-education workers	54.2	54.2	49.3	49.3
High-education workers	34.5	34.5	28.2	28.2
Difference	19.7	19.7	21.1	21.1
Random segregation				
Low-education workers	42.9	44.6	35.8	37.3
High-education workers	42.9	41.7	35.8	35.0
Difference	0	2.9	0	2.3
Effective segregation	19.7	17.3	21.1	19.2
Percentage point (percent)				
change, 1990–2000			1.4 (7.0)	2.0 (11.3)
Less than high school vs. high school degree or more				
Observed segregation				
Low-education workers	26.0	26.0	25.5	25.5
High-education workers	10.8	10.8	8.6	8.6
Difference	15.2	15.2	16.9	16.9
Random segregation				
Low-education workers	12.7	13.8	10.4	11.3
High-education workers	12.7	12.6	10.4	10.3
Difference	0	1.3	0	1.0
Effective segregation	15.2	14.1	16.9	16.0
Percentage point (percent)				
change, 1990–2000			1.7 (11.1)	1.9 (13.6)
Less than bachelor's degree vs. bachelor's degree or more				
Observed segregation				
Low-education workers	80.7	80.7	77.7	77.7
High-education workers	60.6	60.6	54.3	54.3
Difference	20.2	20.2	23.4	23.4
Random segregation				
Low-education workers	75.9	76.6	70.8	71.9
High-education workers	75.9	73.5	70.8	68.2
Difference	0	3.1	0	3.8
Effective segregation	20.2	17.6	23.4	20.4
Percentage point (percent)				
change, 1990–2000			3.3 (16.2)	2.8 (16.0)
No. of workers	1,828,020	1,828,020	2,209,908	2,209,908
No. of establishments	317,112	317,112	411,300	411,300

they have a bachelor's degree, the increases in segregation are somewhat larger, between 2.8 and 3.3 percentage points, or 16 to 16.2 percent.[24]

These figures strike us as modest but measurable increases in segregation by education. The direction of change is consistent with the conjecture of Kremer and Maskin (1996), and it is possible that the decade of the 1980s might have experienced even a greater increase in segregation by education, given the sharper increase in schooling-related earnings differentials in that period, although the workforce adjustments may occur relatively slowly. Nonetheless, we may want to be cautious in inferring that the increase in segregation by education is attributable to increased returns to skill. One of the mechanisms for this increase in segregation by education is the decline over the decade in the fraction of workers in the sample with low levels of education—for example, the fraction with at most a high school degree drops from 42.9 percent in 1990 to 35.8 percent in 2000. It is also possible, then, that segregation by skill (rather than measured education) is actually unchanged, but more workers with high unobserved skills have higher education in the 2000 data.

5.4.2   Segregation by Race

Evidence on changes in segregation by race is reported in table 5.4. In 1990, the observed segregation measures indicate that blacks, on average, worked with workforces that were 23.7 percent black, whereas the comparable figure for whites was only 5.8 percent, for an observed segregation measure of 17.8. This rose between 1990 and 2000 to 21.8, driven mainly by an increase in the average share black in workplaces where blacks were employed. Nationally, black-white segregation rose 4 percentage points, from 17.8 to 21.8, or an increase of 22.3 percent. Within MSAs/PMSAs, the increase is slightly smaller, at 2.8 percentage points, or 20.3 percent. We interpret these magnitudes as indicating a relatively large increase in workplace segregation by race from 1990 to 2000.

5.4.3   Hispanic-White Segregation

Next, table 5.5 reports results for Hispanic-white segregation.[25] Observed Hispanic-white segregation is pronounced. In 1990, Hispanic workers, on average, worked in establishments with workforces that were 39.4 percent Hispanic, compared with a 4.5 percent figure for whites. Both of these numbers increased slightly as of 2000, to 40.7 percent and 6 percent, respectively, so that the observed segregation measure remained roughly constant—34.9 percent in 1990 and 34.7 percent in 2000.

---

24. In Hellerstein and Neumark (forthcoming), we report bootstrapped standard errors for differences in estimates of effective segregation. Differences considerably smaller than the types of increases we find in this paper were strongly significant.

25. Using the 1990 data only, Hellerstein and Neumark (forthcoming) go into considerable detail regarding Hispanic-white segregation, finding that differences in English language skills account for about one-third of this segregation.

Because of relatively sharp differences in the Hispanic composition of urban areas across the United States, randomness generates a considerable amount of Hispanic-white segregation. This is indicated in the table, where random segregation equals 18.8 in 1990 and 18.0 in 2000. However, again the changes are small so that the change in effective Hispanic-white segregation appears to be relatively minor. Segregation declines in the national

Table 5.4	Black-White segregation (% Black)			
	1990 U.S. MSA/PMSA sample (1)	1990 Within MSA/PMSA sample (2)	2000 U.S. MSA/PMSA sample (3)	2000 Within MSA/PMSA sample (4)
Coworker segregation				
Observed segregation				
Black workers	23.7	23.7	28.7	28.7
White workers	5.8	5.8	6.9	6.9
Difference	17.8	17.8	21.8	21.8
Random segregation				
Black workers	7.1	11.2	8.8	14.2
White workers	7.1	6.8	8.8	8.3
Difference	0	4.4	0	5.9
Effective segregation	17.8	14.0	21.8	16.8
Percentage point (percent) change, 1990–2000			4.0 (22.3)	2.8 (20.3)
No. of workers	1,618,876	1,618,876	1,893,034	1,893,034
No. of establishments	285,988	285,988	360,072	360,072

Table 5.5	Hispanic-White segregation (% Hispanic)			
	1990 U.S. MSA/PMSA sample (1)	1990 Within MSA/PMSA sample (2)	2000 U.S. MSA/PMSA sample (3)	2000 Within MSA/PMSA sample (4)
Coworker segregation				
Observed segregation				
Hispanic workers	39.4	39.4	40.7	40.7
White workers	4.5	4.5	6	6
Difference	34.9	34.9	34.7	34.7
Random segregation				
Hispanic workers	6.9	24.4	9.2	25.5
White workers	6.9	5.6	9.2	7.5
Difference	0	18.8	0	18.0
Effective segregation	34.9	19.8	34.7	20.4
Percentage point (percent) change, 1990–2000			−0.2 (−0.4)	0.6 (3.0)
No. of workers	1,625,953	1,625,953	1,906,878	1,906,878
No. of establishments	293,989	293,989	373,006	373,006

data by 0.2 percentage point, or by less than 1 percent. And within urban areas, segregation increases slightly, from 19.8 to 20.4, or by only 3 percent. Overall, then, both the small magnitudes and the differences in results across and within urban areas lead us to conclude that little changed with respect to Hispanic-white workplace segregation between 1990 and 2000.

5.4.4   Sex Segregation

Finally, we turn to segregation by sex. A priori, we might expect to find substantial declines in this form of segregation because of the declining differences in the types of jobs done by men and women (Wells 1998). As table 5.6 reports, in 1990 women, on average, worked in establishments with workforces that were 59.9 percent female, as compared with establishments in which men worked, which were 36.2 percent female. Thus, observed segregation was 23.6. As of 2000, the increase in the share female with which men work increased relatively sharply, from 36.2 to 40.2, and as a result observed segregation fell to 20.4. Random segregation by sex is relatively trivial because neither men nor women constitute a very small share of the workforce. As a result, the change in effective segregation is close to the change in observed segregation. In particular, effective segregation by sex declined from 23.6 to 20.4, or 13.7 percent, on a national basis. And virtually the same decline, 3.2 percentage points or 13.6 percent, is estimated within urban areas because, of course, the distributions of men and women across cities are similar. We view the magnitude of these changes in sex segregation as suggesting a substantive decline over the decade.

One possible explanation for the overall decline in sex segregation is convergence in the occupational distributions of men and women, rather than a reduction in segregation across workplaces even for men and women in the same occupation. To address this possibility, following the methods in Hellerstein and Neumark (forthcoming), we construct "conditional" random segregation measures, where we simulate segregation holding the distribution of workers by occupation fixed across workplaces. So, for example, if an establishment in our sample is observed to have three workers in occupation A, then three workers in occupation A will be randomly allocated to that establishment. As before, we compute the average (across the simulations) simulated fraction of coworkers who are female for females, denoting this F_F^C, and the average (across the simulations) simulated fraction of coworkers who are female for males, denoting this M_F^C. The difference between these two is denoted CW^C, and we define the extent of "effective conditional segregation" to be

$$\frac{CW^O - CW^C}{100 - CW^R} \times 100,$$

where CW^R is the measure of random segregation obtained when not conditioning on occupation. A conditional effective segregation measure of

Table 5.6 Segregation by sex (% female)

	Unconditional				Conditional on 3-digit occupation	
	1990 U.S. MSA/PMSA sample (1)	1990 Within MSA/PMSA sample (2)	2000 U.S. MSA/PMSA sample (3)	2000 Within MSA/PMSA sample (4)	1990 Within MSA/PMSA sample (5)	2000 Within MSA/PMSA sample (6)
Coworker segregation						
Observed segregation						
Female workers	59.9	59.9	60.6	60.6	59.9	60.6
Male workers	36.2	36.2	40.2	40.2	36.2	40.2
Difference	23.6	23.6	20.4	20.4	23.6	20.4
Random segregation						
Female workers	47.4	47.7	50.5	50.7	54.4	56.8
Male workers	47.4	47.2	50.5	50.3	41.1	44.1
Difference	0	0.5	0	0.4	13.3	12.6
Effective segregation	23.6	23.3	20.4	20.1	10.4	7.8
Percentage point (percent) change, 1990–2000			−3.2 (−13.7)	−3.2 (−13.6)		−2.6 (−24.8)
Fraction of sex segregation accounted for by occupation					55.4	61.2
No. of workers	1,828,020	1,828,020	2,209,908	2,209,908	1,828,020	2,209,908
No. of establishments	317,112	317,112	411,300	411,300	317,112	411,300

zero would imply that all of the effective segregation between women and men can be attributed to differences in the occupations employed by various establishments ("occupational segregation"), coupled with differences in the occupational distributions of women and men. Conversely, a conditional effective segregation measure equal to that of the (unconditional) effective segregation measure would imply that none of the effective segregation between women and men can be attributed to occupational segregation across workplaces.

Columns (5) and (6) of table 5.6 report the results of doing this calculation based on a consistent occupation classification across 1990 and 2000, as developed in Meyer and Osborne (2005), which is approximately at the three-digit level.[26] We do this only for the within MSA/PMSA sample because central to this analysis is the ability to randomly distribute workers to different establishments, and it makes more sense to do this within the urban areas in which workers commute. The estimates for 1990, in column (5), indicate that a substantial fraction (nearly 50 percent) of the effective segregation of women from men is attributable to differences in the occupational distribution; conditional on occupation, effective segregation by sex falls from 23.3 (column [2]) to 10.4. In the 2000 data, reported in column (6), the effect of occupation is a little bit more pronounced, accounting for 61.2 percent of effective segregation. Finally, conditional on occupation, sex segregation within MSAs/PMSAs declines over time by 2.6 percentage points (from 10.4 to 7.8); in absolute terms, this is similar to the decline in unconditional segregation, but because effective segregation conditional on occupation (in 1990) was only about 45 percent as large as the unconditional effective segregation measure, the decline in conditional segregation between columns (5) and (6) represents a much larger percentage decline—24.8 percent. Altogether, these results suggest that the decline in sex segregation over the decade is not being driven by the increased propensity of women to work in the same occupations as men.

5.5   The Impact of Changing Establishment and Industry Composition

Changes in segregation can arise due to a multitude of factors, some of them compositional, such as the changing occupational distribution of women as discussed in the previous section. In this section, we explore the robustness of our full-sample results to two other types of potentially important compositional changes. First, we explore whether the changes in segregation are due to the changing composition of establishments by recalculating our segregation indexes for only the sample of establishments

---

26. There are nontrivial differences in occupation codes at the three-digit level between 1990 and 2000. The structure of occupation codes at the one-digit level changed even more dramatically between 1990 and 2000, so we do not attempt a concordance at this higher level of aggregation.

that exist in both the 1990 and 2000 Restricted DEED samples (corresponding to columns [3] and [6] of table 5.1).[27] Ideally, we would like to isolate the separate roles of establishment entry and exit—that is, births of new establishments and deaths of existing ones. However, given that we only match some establishments, we cannot necessarily distinguish births and deaths from matches and nonmatches. But assuming that matching is random with respect to segregation, focusing on the set of establishments that are in both samples is informative about the combined roles of establishment entry and exit.

Second, we explore the robustness of our changes in segregation to changes in the industry mix of employment over the decade by reweighting the segregation indexes for 2000 to reflect the industrial composition of employment at the one-digit level that exists in our 1990 data. This is a little more complicated. First, because we are interested in calculating within-MSA indexes, it is actually the within-MSA industry composition that we need to hold fixed at 1990 levels. As a result, we include in the sample only MSAs that exist in both years. Second, we exclude mining because mining makes up such a trivial proportion of employment that there are some MSAs that have matched workers in mining in 1990 but not in 2000.

To understand how we construct changes in segregation over the decade while holding the distribution of employment across industries within MSAs fixed at 1990 levels, consider again the example of ethnic segregation we discussed in section 5.3. Obviously, we compute H_H (the isolation index) and W_H (the exposure index) for 1990 in the same way we did previously because no adjustment needs to be made when accounting for the 1990 industry composition. In order to compute H_H for 2000 with industry composition fixed as of 1990, we compute the isolation index separately for each industry/MSA pair in 2000.[28] We then take a weighted average across industries of these isolation indexes, where the weight is the product of two components: the fraction of total Hispanic employment (in this example) that works in that industry/MSA pair in 2000, and the ratio of the employment share in the industry/MSA pair in 1990 relative to 2000. The fraction of Hispanic employment serves to aggregate up the industry/MSA-specific isolation indexes to the full-sample isolation index (and, if used alone to weight up the industry/MSA-specific indexes would yield the 2000 unadjusted isolation index), while the ratio of the employment shares adjusts the data appropriately to reflect the composition of employment in 1990 across industries. For the exposure index, W_H, we do the same thing, calculating a

---

27. By restricting the sample to establishments that exist in the Restricted DEED samples in both years, we drop some very small MSAs from some of the samples we used to calculate segregation indexes in earlier tables, in cases where there are no matched workers for whom to calculate indexes across the two years.

28. For the random segregation indexes, the industry used is the random industry to which the worker is assigned.

separate exposure index for each industry/MSA pair and then weighting by the product of the industry employment share ratio times the fraction of white employment in that pair in 2000. Because the fraction Hispanic in an industry MSA/pair may differ from the fraction white in that same industry/MSA pair, the reweighting may have differential effects on the exposure and isolation indexes. As a consequence, adjusting for industry employment changes over the decade will have the largest impact on measured changes in segregation when there has been differential employment growth in industries with a large share Hispanic coupled with a large difference between the share of Hispanic and the share of white employment in the industry (or if there is a large difference between the isolation and exposure indexes).[29]

The results of these alternative computations are presented in condensed form in table 5.7, where we report only the within-MSA effective segregation measures in each year and the changes over the decade. In the first panel of table 5.7, we report results for coworker segregation by high school degree status. In column (1), we first report the within-MSA effective segregation measure in 1990 of 17.3 (from table 5.3). Following that number, we report the corresponding figure for the sample of establishments that existed both in 1990 and 2000, finding that coworker segregation by high school degree status in 1990 is somewhat lower, at 15.7. The fixed-industry-composition coworker segregation measure for 1990 is 17.3, identical to that for the full sample.[30] In column (2), we report the coworker segregation measures for 2000. For the fixed-establishment sample, coworker segregation by high school degree status is 17.0, 2.2 percentage points lower than for the full sample, and for the results holding industry composition fixed, the coworker measure is slightly higher, at 20.3. Overall, the change over the decade of 2 percentage points for the full sample is close to the 1.4 percentage point increase for the fixed-establishment sample, and the increase holding industry composition fixed is a bit larger, at 3.1 percentage points. In general, though, the observed increase in coworker segregation for the full sample over the decade is robust to the changing mix of establishments and industries.

In the second and third panels of table 5.7, we report the results for the alternative education cutoffs. The results again reflect some small differences across the sample of establishments and mix of industries, and the overall qualitative results again point to increases in segregation by education over the decade.

---

29. This turns out to be quite significant in our calculations for changes in sex segregation holding the industry composition of employment fixed, where the services industry grew rapidly and is also heavily female.

30. Because we exclude workers in mining and workers in MSAs that were not defined as such in 1990 and 2000, the results for 1990 can be slightly different than we report in the full sample in table 5.3.

Table 5.7   **Alternative coworker segregation calculations**

	1990 Within MSA/PMSA sample, effective segregation (1)	2000 Within MSA/PMSA sample, effective segregation (2)	Percentage point (percent) change, 1990–2000 (3)
Segregation by education			
High school degree or less vs. more than high school			
Full sample, table 5.3	17.3	19.2	2.0 (11.3)
Establishments present in 1990 and 2000	15.7	17.0	1.4 (8.9)
Fixed industry composition	17.3	20.3	3.1 (17.8)
Less than high school vs. high school degree or more			
Full sample, table 5.3	14.1	16.0	1.9 (13.6)
Establishments present in 1990 and 2000	11.4	12.7	1.2 (10.7)
Fixed industry composition	13.8	15.8	2.0 (14.3)
Less than bachelor's degree vs. bachelor's degree or more			
Full sample, table 5.3	17.6	20.4	2.8 (16.0)
Establishments present in 1990 and 2000	15.4	17.4	2.0 (12.8)
Fixed industry composition	17.6	21.8	4.2 (24.0)
Black-White segregation			
Full sample, table 5.4	14.0	16.8	2.8 (20.3)
Establishments present in 1990 and 2000	11.2	12.6	1.4 (12.7)
Fixed industry composition	14.1	14.7	0.6 (4.6)
Hispanic-White segregation			
Full sample, table 5.5	19.8	20.4	0.6 (3.0)
Establishments present in 1990 and 2000	16.5	15.6	−0.9 (−5.6)
Fixed industry composition	19.1	22.0	2.9 (15.3)
Segregation by Sex			
Unconditional			
Full sample, table 5.6	23.3	20.1	−3.2 (−13.6)
Establishments present in 1990 and 2000	25.2	23.0	−2.3 (−8.9)
Fixed industry composition	23.4	14.4	−9.0 (−38.3)

Note: Mining is excluded for "Full sample" and "fixed industry composition."

Racial segregation increased over the decade for the full sample by 2.8 percentage points (20.3 percent), but increased by only about half that much for the sample of establishments that exist in both years. This means that new establishments in 2000 are characterized by more racial segregation than establishments that existed in 1990. Moreover, holding the industry composition of employment fixed at 1990 levels, racial segregation increased by a much smaller amount over the decade—0.6 percentage points (4.6 percent). The fact that newer establishments and the industries that are gaining in employment over the decade are also more segregated by race in 2000 than older establishments and declining industries could portend continuing increases in racial segregation.

Interestingly, the results are somewhat different for Hispanic-white segregation, as we report in the fifth panel of table 5.7. In the overall sample, coworker segregation increased relatively little over the decade, by only 0.6 percentage points (3 percent). For the sample of establishments that exist in both years, coworker segregation actually fell a little, from 16.5 to 15.6, whereas for the fixed-industry-composition, the coworker segregation measure rose over the decade from 19.1 to 22.0. While none of these results point to major differences, it appears that the changing industry mix served to decrease Hispanic-white segregation, while the entry and exit of establishments seems to have worked in the opposite direction.

As reported in the last panel of table 5.7, the results are most notably different for sex segregation—in particular, with respect to the role of industry composition. First, for the full sample, coworker segregation fell by 3.2 percentage points over the decade, whereas for the sample of continuing establishments, it fell by 2.3 percentage points. Because the baseline coworker segregation measure in 1990 for the continuing establishments sample is slightly higher (25.2) than for the full sample (23.3), on a percentage basis segregation actually declined somewhat more for the full sample, but the difference is small. However, a much sharper difference arises when comparing the change over the decade to that obtained holding the distribution of employment across industries fixed at 1990 levels. In particular, coworker segregation in 2000 is 20.1 in the full sample, but only 14.4 in the fixed-industry-composition results. As a result, coworker segregation for the fixed-industry-composition calculation falls over the decade by a full 9 percentage points, or 38.3 percent.

Industry composition has such a strong influence on changes in measured sex segregation because there was very sharp employment growth in services, which is a highly sex segregated industry with a high share of female employment. Thus, absent the growth in services (which is what we mimic by holding the industry composition of employment fixed), sex segregation would have declined by considerably more. To see this, table 5.8 presents detailed information on isolation and exposure indexes and observed segregation by industry, as well as the distribution of employment of men and women across industries, and industry employment growth over the decade. The table shows, first, that with the exception of transportation, which is a relatively small industry, services is the most segregated industry in both years. The percentage point decline in observed segregation is relatively similar across industries, with the exception of wholesale. In addition, the services industry was the largest employer of women in both years, accounting for 35 percent of female employment in

Table 5.8   Observed sex segregation, by industry, within MSA/PMSA

	Observed segregation		Percentage point (percent) change, 1990–2000	Share of female or male employment in industry		Ratio of 1990 to 2000 industry employment
	1990 (1)	2000 (2)	(3)	1990 (4)	2000 (5)	(6)
Construction						
Female	23.7	21.6		0.02	0.02	0.92
Male	21.1	23.9		0.05	0.06	
Difference	2.5	–2.3	–4.9 (–191.4)			
Manufacturing						
Female	43.7	41.2		0.24	0.17	1.29
Male	28.2	29.8		0.44	0.35	
Difference	15.5	11.4	–4.1 (–26.3)			
Transportation						
Female	49.0	48.8		0.04	0.04	1.05
Male	29.4	32.2		0.07	0.07	
Difference	19.6	16.7	–3.0 (–15.1)			
Wholesale						
Female	40.2	38.6		0.06	0.03	1.50
Male	31.9	31.6		0.10	0.07	
Difference	8.3	6.9	–1.4 (–16.3)			
Retail						
Female	59.3	57.1		0.17	0.20	0.80
Male	42.9	44.7		0.14	0.20	
Difference	16.4	12.4	–4.0 (–24.3)			
FIRE						
Female	69.3	69.1		0.12	0.09	1.24
Male	61.3	63.7		0.05	0.05	
Difference	8.0	5.4	–2.6 (–32.7)			
Services						
Female	74.2	72.7		0.35	0.44	0.76
Male	55.1	58.4		0.15	0.21	
Difference	19.2	14.3	–4.8 (–25.1)			

1990 and 44 percent of female employment in 2000. So, for example, services alone accounts for half of the isolation index in 2000.[31] Services was also the second largest employer of men in both years, but well behind manufacturing. Employment of both men and women in services grew sharply over the decade. This is reflected in the distribution of men and women across industries by year (columns [4] and [5]), as well as in the ratio of overall employment in 1990 relative to 2000, as reported in column (6); services has the lowest ratio (0.76), corresponding to the sharpest growth.

31. This can be seen by multiplying the isolation index for services of 72.7 percent by the employment share of services in female employment of 44 percent, as reported in table 5.8, accounting for 53 percent of the overall isolation index in 2000 of 60.7 corresponding to the sample used in that table.

Table 5.9   Sex segregation including and excluding services, within MSA/PMSA

	1990	2000	2000, fixed industry composition
Including services			
Observed segregation			
Female	59.9	60.7	55.1
Male	36.2	40.2	40.3
Difference	23.7	20.5	14.7
Random segregation			
Female	47.7	50.7	50.7
Male	47.2	50.4	50.4
Difference	0.5	0.4	0.4
Effective segregation	23.4	20.2	14.4
Percentage point (percent) change, 1990–2000		−3.2 (−13.5)	−9.0 (−38.3)
No. of workers	1,739,063	2,151,566	2,151,566
No. of establishments	301,029	398,958	398,958
Excluding services			
Observed segregation			
Female	52.1	51.2	48.9
Male	32.9	35.4	35.1
Difference	19.2	15.9	13.8
Random segregation			
Female	41.0	42.2	42.2
Male	40.5	41.9	41.9
Difference	0.5	0.3	0.3
Effective segregation	18.8	15.7	13.6
Percentage point (percent) change, 1990–2000		−3.1 (−16.5)	−5.2 (−27.7)
No. of workers	1,310,125	1,450,311	1,450,311
No. of establishments	236,412	289,206	289,206

Note: Mining is excluded.

As a result of the fact that services is a relatively highly sex segregated industry, coupled with the fact that it is a heavily female industry that grew tremendously over the decade, the services industry plays a large role in overall changes in sex segregation. To reinforce the importance of the growth in services employment in mitigating the decline in sex segregation, table 5.9 shows our calculations of effective sex segregation and how it changed over the decade, with and without holding the industry composition of employment fixed and with and without including services. The top panel shows calculations for all industries, echoing the earlier results.[32] In

32. As noted earlier, the estimates allowing the industry composition to change are slightly different from in table 5.6 because of changes in the sample to do the calculation holding industry composition fixed.

the bottom panel, however, services is simply dropped from the calculation, and the difference in the change in segregation from holding industry composition fixed is only about half as large.[33]

5.6   Robustness to Alternative Segregation Measures

Finally, table 5.10 compares the estimates for the key results using the coworker segregation measure and the Duncan index to see how robust the results are to alternative segregation measures. For segregation by education, the measure of effective segregation in each year and for each educational split is quite similar. The changes in segregation are also similar, with the only exception that the Duncan index points to a larger increase in segregation between those with less than a high school degree versus those with a high school degree or more. The results for black-white and Hispanic-white segregation all show increases over the decade, although the increase in the Duncan index relative to the coworker measure is a little smaller for black-white segregation and a little larger for Hispanic-white segregation. The estimates for sex segregation corresponding to table 5.6 (i.e., unconditional, and conditional on occupation), are very similar for the two measures, with both showing marked declines, and of similar magnitudes. However, holding industry composition fixed appears to have much less impact using the Duncan index. Given that the importance of industry composition using the coworker segregation measure is derived in part from the large share female in services coupled with the strong growth of that industry, it is not surprising that the effect of holding industry constant has less of an impact when using the Duncan index because this index is not sensitive to simple changes in a group's representation in the workforce that are distributed across establishments in proportion to their original distribution.

We argued earlier that we have some preference for the coworker measure over indexes like the Duncan index, most importantly because we think the variation in the coworker measure in response to simple changes in the share of a particular group in the workforce represents meaningful changes in workplace segregation, but also for the more technical reasons discussed in section 5.3. In general, though, the conclusions that can be drawn from the two segregation measures are qualitatively similar and, in particular, the directions of the changes across the decade are always the same. Given the differing properties of the two measures, however, the quantitative answers obviously differ somewhat. Nonetheless, as a summary measure of the comparability of the estimates, the last row of the table shows that the estimated percentage point and percent changes are highly correlated across the two indexes (0.78 and 0.83, respectively), computed across all of the estimates reported in the tables.

---

33. Note that there was also strong growth in retail, another industry that is relatively sex-segregated.

Table 5.10   **Comparisons of results for coworker segregation and Duncan Indexes, effective segregation, within MSA/PMSA**

	Effective segregation		Percentage point change, 1990–2000	Percent change, 1990–2000
	1990 (1)	2000 (2)	(3)	(4)
Table 5.3				
High school degree or less vs. more than high school				
Coworker	17.3	19.2	2.0	11.3
Duncan	25.3	28.6	3.3	13.0
Less than high school vs. high school degree or more				
Coworker	14.1	16.0	1.9	13.6
Duncan	29.8	37.5	7.7	25.7
Less than bachelor's degree vs. bachelor's degree or more				
Coworker	17.6	20.4	2.8	16.0
Duncan	26.3	28.5	2.2	8.5
Table 5.4				
Black-white				
Coworker	14.0	16.8	2.8	20.3
Duncan	18.4	20.9	2.5	13.5
Table 5.5				
Hispanic-white				
Coworker	19.8	20.4	0.6	3.0
Duncan	19.8	23.2	3.5	17.5
Table 5.6				
Male-female				
Unconditional				
Coworker	23.3	20.1	−3.2	−13.6
Duncan	31.6	28.4	−3.2	−10.2
Conditional on 3-digit occupation				
Coworker	10.4	7.8	−2.6	−24.8
Duncan	11.3	8.5	−2.8	−24.7
Table 5.7				
Male-female				
Unconditional, fixed industry composition				
Coworker	23.4	14.4	−9.0	−38.3
Duncan	31.7	28.5	−3.2	−11.3
Correlation between indexes			.78	.83

Note: See notes to corresponding tables.

5.7   Conclusions

We present evidence on changes in workplace segregation by education, race, ethnicity, and sex. For this analysis, we use the newly-constructed 2000 Decennial Employer-Employee Dataset (DEED). The 2000 DEED, like the 1990 DEED, provides new opportunities to study workplace segregation at the establishment level. More significantly, by pairing the two we are able to present what we believe are the first estimates of changes in workplace segregation based on 2000 Census data. These estimates provide evidence that is complementary to that on changes in residential segregation in the decade between the Censuses. Moreover, we believe that evidence on workplace segregation and how it has changed is likely to be more informative about social interactions between groups (with reference to race, ethnicity, and sex), and directly informative about hypotheses regarding changes in workplace segregation by skill.

The evidence indicates that racial and ethnic segregation at the workplace level remains quite pervasive. For example, if we compare black and white workers, the difference in the share black among the workforce at the establishments where they work is around 22 percentage points. If we compare Hispanics and whites, the difference is about 50 percent larger. At the same time, there is fairly substantial segregation by skill, as measured by education. In other work (Hellerstein and Neumark [forthcoming], using only the 1990 DEED), we explore the extent to which racial and ethnic segregation is attributable to skill differences between blacks and whites or Hispanics and whites; in the latter case, we focus on language skills. Only for the latter is there evidence that skill differences play a substantial role, explaining about one-third of Hispanic-white segregation.

More significantly, putting together the 1990 and 2000 data, we find *no* evidence of declines in workplace segregation by race and ethnicity. Hispanic-white segregation was largely unchanged, while black-white segregation increased by about 3 to 4 percentage points, or about 20 percent. This increase in racial segregation was reinforced by the entry and exit of establishments and by the changing industry composition of employment, suggesting that there may be forces at work that will lead to the persistence of or even increases in racial segregation. Over this decade, segregation by education also increased, by about 2 to 3 percentage points, or 11 to 16 percent. This increase is consistent with conjectures that rising returns to skill might generate more segregation by skill, although it could also be attributable to rising education levels among workers with more unobserved skills but with an unchanging pattern of segregation based on these skills.[34]

---

34. Coupled with the earlier findings suggesting that black-white segregation is largely unrelated to education differences, this likely has little if anything to do with the increase in workplace segregation by race.

To the extent that declines in segregation are positive developments, the one bright spot is the decline in workplace segregation by sex, which fell about 3 percentage points, or 14 percent, from 1990 to 2000. Changes in the occupational distribution of men and women did not play a major role in this decline in segregation. If we hold the distribution of men and women across three-digit occupations fixed, the absolute decline in segregation is roughly the same, although it is larger in percentage terms. On the other hand, shifts in the industry composition of employment worked *against* the decline in sex segregation, as the fastest-growing industry was services, which is also one of the most sex-segregated and most heavily female industries. What this implies for future changes in sex segregation depends on whether the shifts in industrial composition continue as in the recent past or change course, on changes in the distribution of women across industries, and on changes in sex segregation across establishments within industries.

References

Autor, David H., Lawrence F. Katz, and Melissa S. Kearney. 2005. Trends in U.S. wage inequality: Re-assessing the revisionists. NBER Working Paper no. 11627. Cambridge, MA: National Bureau of Economic Research.

Bayard, Kimberly, Judith Hellerstein, David Neumark, and Kenneth Troske. 1999. Why are racial and ethnic wage gaps larger for men than for women? Exploring the role of segregation using the New Worker-Establishment Characteristics Database. In *The creation and analysis of employer-employee matched data,* ed. J. Haltiwanger, J. Lane, J. R. Spletzer, J. Theeuwes, and K. Troske, 175–203. Amsterdam: Elsevier Science.

———. 2003. New evidence on sex segregation and sex differences in wages from matched employee-employer data. *Journal of Labor Economics* 21 (4): 887–922.

Blau, Francine D. 1977. *Equal pay in the office* Lexington, MA: Heath.

Boisso, Dale, Kathy Hayes, Joseph Hirschberg, and Jacques Silber. 1994. Occupational segregation in the multidimensional case. *Journal of Econometrics* 61 (1): 161–71.

Carrington, William J., and Kenneth Troske. 1997. On measuring segregation in samples with small units. *Journal of Business and Economic Statistics* 15 (4): 402–9.

———. 1998a. Interfirm racial segregation and the black/white wage gap. *Journal of Labor Economics* 16 (2): 231–60.

———. 1998b. Sex segregation in U.S. manufacturing. *Industrial and Labor Relations Review* 51:445–64.

Cortese, Charles F., R. Frank Falk, and Jack K. Cohen. 1976. Further considerations on the methodological analysis of segregation indices. *American Sociological Review* 51 (4): 630–7.

Duncan, Otis D., and Beverly Duncan. 1955. A methodological analysis of segregation indices. *American Sociological Review* 20 (2): 210–7.

Echenique, Federico, and Roland Fryer. 2005. On the measurement of segregation. NBER Working Paper no. 11258. Cambridge, MA: National Bureau of Economic Research.

Estlund, Cynthia. 2003. Working together: How workplace bonds strengthen a diverse democracy. New York: Oxford University Press.

Foster, Lucia, John Haltiwanger, and C. J. Krizan. 1998. Aggregate productivity growth: Lessons from microeconomic evidence. NBER Working Paper no. 6803. Cambridge, MA: National Bureau of Economic Research.

Glaeser, Edward L., and Jacob L. Vigdor. 2001. Racial segregation in the 2000 Census: Promising news. The Brookings Institution Survey Series. Washington, DC: Brookings Institution, April.

Groshen, Erica L. 1991. The structure of the female/male wage differential: Is it who you are, what you do, or where you work? *Journal of Human Resources* 26 (3): 457–72.

Hellerstein, Judith, and David Neumark. 2003. Ethnicity, language, and workplace segregation: Evidence from a new matched employer-employee data set. *Annales d'Economie et de Statistique* 71–72:19–78.

———. 2007. Production function and wage equation estimation with heterogeneous labor: Evidence from a new matched employer-employee data set. In *Hard to Measure Goods and Services: Essays in Honor of Zvi Griliches*, eds. E. R. Berndt and C. R. Holten, 31–71. Chicago: University of Chicago Press.

———. Forthcoming. Workplace segregation in the United States: Race, ethnicity, and skill. *Review of Economics and Statistics.*

Higgs, Robert. 1977. Firm-specific evidence on racial wage differentials and workforce segregation. *American Economic Review* 67 (2): 236–45.

Iceland, John, and Daniel H. Weinberg. 2002. Racial and ethnic segregation in the United States: 1980–2000. U.S. Census Bureau, Census 2000 Special Reports. http://www.census.gov/hhes/www/housing/housing_patterns/pdf/censr-3.pdf.

James, Daniel R., and Karl E. Taeuber. 1985. Measures of segregation. In *Sociological methodology,* ed. N. B. Tuma, 1–32. San Francisco: Jossey-Bass.

Jarmin, Ron S., and Javier Miranda. 2002. The longitudinal business database. CES Working Paper no. CES-WP-02-17. Washington, DC: Center for Economic Studies.

King, Mary C. 1992. Occupational segregation by race and sex, 1940–1988. *Monthly Labor Review* 115 (4): 30–7.

Kremer, Michael, and Eric Maskin. 1996. Wage inequality and segregation by skill. NBER Working Paper no. 5718. Cambridge, MA: National Bureau of Economic Research.

McConville, Shannon, and Paul Ong. 2001. Examining residential segregation patterns. The Ralph and Goldy Lewis Center for Regional Policy Studies, Discussion Paper, The University of California at Los Angeles.

Meyer, Peter B., and Anastasiya M. Osborne. 2005. Proposed category system for 1960–2000 Census occupations. BLS Working Paper no. 383. Washington, DC: Bureau of Labor Statistics, September.

Watts, Martin J. 1995. Trends in occupational segregation by race and gender in the U.S.A., 1983–92: A multidimensional approach. *Review of Radical Political Economics* 27 (4): 1–36.

Wells, Thomas. 1998. Change in occupational sex segregation during the 1980s and 1990s. Center for Demography and Ecology. Working Paper no. 98-14. Madison: University of Wisconsin.

Winship, Christopher. 1977. A revaluation of indexes of residential segregation. *Social Forces* 55 (4): 1058–66.

The Effect of Tuition
Reimbursement on Turnover
A Case Study Analysis

Colleen Flaherty Manchester

6.1 Introduction

Becker's (1964) seminal work on investment in human capital makes a fundamental distinction between general and firm-specific skills, which has implications for investment and employee turnover. Firm-specific human capital is defined as having value only to the current employment relationship, while general human capital is valuable to both current and potential employers. Becker's theory predicts that employees will bear the full cost of general skills training—either by paying for training directly or by accepting lower wages during training periods—because employers face the threat of not capturing the return on their investment due to "poaching" of trained employees by other employers. In a competitive labor market, workers have the incentive to invest efficiently in general human capital because they receive a wage equal to the value of their marginal

Colleen Flaherty Manchester is an assistant professor at the Carlson School of Management, University of Minnesota.

I would like to thank the participants at the Conference for the Analysis of Firms and Employees (CAFE) for their comments and suggestions as well as the editors and reviewers of this conference volume. In addition to the conference sponsors, this research was made possible by the Hawley-Shoven Fellowship Fund, through a grant to the Stanford Institute for Economic Policy Research. I would like to thank my advisors, John Shoven, Michael Boskin, John Pencável, and Edward Lazear, as well as members of the labor reading group at Stanford University for their comments and feedback. I would also like to thank Harley Frazis, Merrisa Piazza, Maury Gittleman, and James Spletzer at the U.S. Bureau of Labor Statistics as well as the Human Resource Department at the case study institution for access to the data used in this analysis. The views presented in this paper are mine alone and do not reflect those of my advisors, the aforementioned organizations, or the National Bureau of Economic Research.

product. In the case of investment in firm-specific human capital, employers and employees share the costs. Neither party is willing to bear the full amount due to the risk of opportunistic behavior by the other. The employer and the employee share the surplus, or rents, from the investment; the relative bargaining power of the two parties determines how these rents are allocated.

This standard theory on investment in human capital has implications for turnover. Investment in firm-specific human capital reduces turnover because rents accrue only if the employment relationship is maintained. However, this result does not hold for investments in general human capital because these skills are transferable across employers. According to standard theory, offering employees general skills training would increase turnover.

Despite the predictions of this theory, recent empirical studies show that firms provide general training to their workers and often argue that firms bear part of the cost.[1] Tuition reimbursement programs are an example of general skills training provided by firms. Employers reimburse employees for direct costs of coursework taken at accredited academic institutions. Because instruction and degree accreditation occur at third-party institutions, skills acquired are transferable—as well as observable—to many potential employers. Hence, tuition reimbursement programs closely resemble general skills training as described by Becker (1964).

A primary reason firms give for offering these programs is to reduce turnover, which challenges standard human capital theory.[2] This chapter examines empirically whether employees who participate in tuition reimbursement have higher retention rates than nonparticipants using a case study analysis of workers at a nonprofit institution. Results from the case study indicate that participation reduces employee turnover. Hence, the firm's motivation for offering this program is supported by this analysis: general skills training increases retention.

The remainder of this chapter is organized as follows. Section 6.2 documents the prevalence of tuition reimbursement programs using the Survey of Employer-Provided Training, 1995 (SEPT95) and describes the typical characteristics of these programs. Section 6.3 reviews previous studies of tuition reimbursement programs, while the case study analysis is presented in section 6.4. Section 6.5 discusses the results from the case study, and section 6.6 concludes the chapter.

1. These include, but are not limited to, Loewenstein and Spletzer (1999a, b), Acemoglu and Pischke (1998, 1999a, b), Autor (2001), and Cappelli (2004).
2. Increased retention is a response given by human resource professionals in interviews with the author. Cappelli (2004) and the Corporate Leadership Council (2003) report the same finding.

6.2   Background on Tuition Reimbursement Programs

6.2.1   Program Prevalence

Employer-provided tuition reimbursement programs are widespread and constitute a nontrivial part of nonwage compensation. One of the few data sets that collects information on tuition reimbursement programs is SEPT95. This survey collects information on employer-provided training practices for a cross section of establishments. The survey was conducted by the Bureau of Labor Statistics (BLS), part of the U.S. Department of Labor, from May to August of 1995, with the purpose of collecting nationally representative data (Bureau of Labor Statistics 1996). The sample represents private, nonagriculture establishments employing fifty or more workers. The results from SEPT95 show that a substantial fraction of firms offer tuition reimbursement: 61 percent of establishments employing fifty or more workers offer tuition reimbursement programs. Using the 1994 National Employer Survey of Educational Quality in the Workforce (NES-EQW), Black and Lynch (1998) report that 47 percent of firms employing twenty or more employees offer tuition reimbursement programs. The estimates from SEPT95 and 1994 NES-EQW are comparable because larger establishments are more likely to offer a tuition reimbursement program (Frazis et al. 1998; Frazis, Gittleman, and Joyce 2000). Examining the access of workers to this program, over three-quarters of the employees who work in establishments represented in SEPT95 are offered tuition reimbursement by their employer.

In addition, the amount spent on these programs is substantial: establishments represented in SEPT95 spent $2.8 billion in 1994 on tuition reimbursement.[3] The trade magazine *Workforce Management* estimates that companies paid $10 billion toward tuition reimbursements in 2003.[4] Hence, expenditures on tuition reimbursement programs represent a significant source of investment in general skills of employees and appear to be on the rise. However, these programs are relatively unexamined in the academic literature. This chapter examines the effect of participation in the tuition reimbursement program offered by the case study institution on the propensity of an employee to separate from his or her employer.

6.2.2   Program Characteristics

Tuition reimbursement programs typically consist of three components: (1) a maximum reimbursement amount; (2) an eligibility requirement; and (3) a reimbursement policy based on academic performance. The first

---

3. The confidence interval for this estimate ranges from $2.6 billion to $3.0 billion (1994 U.S. dollars).
4. See *Workforce Management,* May 1, 2004.

characteristic is affected by the tax-advantage status of these programs. Reimbursements from employer-provided programs are exempt from income taxation under Section 127 of the U.S. Internal Revenue Code.[5] The maximum income exclusion for a single calendar year is $5,250, and reimbursements under this level are exempt from federal income tax, payroll tax, and state income tax. A 2002 survey by Eduventures of human resource professionals and managers at over 500 firms finds that 70 percent of firms offering a tuition reimbursement program cap annual reimbursement, and over half of these firms (57 percent) have maximums that exceed $4,000 (Newman and Stein 2003).[6] Table 6.1 shows the distribution of reimbursement maximums from the Eduventures' survey. The majority of firms choose maximums below or equal to the maximum annual tax exclusion, $5,250, but a sizable fraction of firms have reimbursement maximums that exceed the tax exempt limit or have no maximum reimbursement amount. Among firms offering tuition benefits, nearly 40 percent offer reimbursements beyond the level that receives tax-advantaged status (i.e., amounts greater than $5,250). The fact that firms set annual limits in excess of the tax exempt amount provides evidence that these programs are not solely offered because of their tax-advantaged status.[7]

Most firms in the Eduventures' survey allow employees to become eligible for the program after six months of service; rarely do eligibility requirements exceed one year. Twenty percent of firms in the survey impose service requirements after participation. Service requirements after participation are more common in plans that have unlimited tuition reimbursement. The survey also reports that over 90 percent of programs have a minimum grade standard for reimbursement, typically set at a "C" or better. Many companies tie grades directly to reimbursement percentages, making the cost of participation higher for workers who receive lower grades. The tuition reimbursement program offered at the case study insti-

---

5. Section 127 of the Internal Revenue Code outlines the tax-advantaged status of educational assistance plans provided by employers: "Gross income of an employee does not include amounts paid or expenses incurred by the employer for educational assistance to the employee if the assistance is furnished pursuant to a [educational assistance] program" (26 U.S.C.§ 127).

6. The survey was sponsored by Cenquest, a provider of managed education solutions, which helps companies create and manage tuition assistance programs (http://www.cenquest.com). Eduventures, who conducted the survey, is an independent research and advisory firm of corporate, postsecondary, and pre–K-12 learning markets (http://www.eduventures.com).

7. A common reaction to tuition reimbursement programs is to only attribute their provision by firms to their tax-advantaged status. However, this overlooks the trade-off between wage and nonwage compensation. If total compensation reflects the value of a worker's marginal product, then benefits and wages are substitutes at the margin. Firms offer tuition reimbursement program instead of additional wages or other benefits if tuition benefits are more effective at attracting or retaining a certain type of worker. The tax-advantaged status of tuition reimbursement programs increases the value of these benefits to a worker facing a positive tax rate, but it cannot explain the effect of these programs on recruitment or turnover.

Table 6.1   **Distribution of maximum reimbursements for tuition programs**

Amount	% of sample
<$1,000	6.2
$1,001–$2,500	19.1
$2,501–$4,000	15.7
$4,001–$5,250	19.8
$5,251–$7,000	4.8
$7,000+	3.7
No maximum	30.7
No. of observations	434

Source: Newman and Stein (2003).

tution has an eligibility requirement of one year of service and does not have a service requirement after participation. The maximum reimbursement amount is $5,250 for a single year, and the program only reimburses costs of tuition for participants obtaining a "C" grade or better. Hence, the case study program is typical in its reimbursement amount and requirements, making it a good candidate for case study analysis.

6.3   Literature on Tuition Reimbursement Programs

The primary reasons given by firms as to why they offer tuition reimbursement programs are recruitment and employee retention. The first reason suggests that tuition reimbursement is a nonwage benefit that affects the type of workers attracted to the firm. One potential mechanism behind the second reason is that tuition reimbursement programs increase employee retention by making the worker more productive at the current firm relative to outside employers. The remainder of this section outlines the existing literature on these two given motivations and discusses the handful of studies on tuition reimbursement.

6.3.1   Tuition Reimbursement Programs and Recruitment

The use of benefits as a recruiting device is prevalent in labor and personnel economics. Rosen's (1986) work on "equalizing differences" establishes a theory for how nonwage benefits affect the composition of workers attracted to a firm. In the case of tuition reimbursement, workers who value continuing education are willing to trade off wages (at some rate) for tuition payments. This trade-off implies that at least part of the incidence of tuition reimbursement is on the worker. Employers may find it profitable to attract such workers if a preference for continued education is correlated with unobservable characteristics, such as ability or motivation.

Cappelli (2004) addresses the effect of tuition reimbursement programs on recruitment by developing a model such that provision of these programs generates a separating equilibrium in which only high-ability workers choose to work at firms with a tuition program. His model includes two types of agents, low-ability and high-ability, in which ability is known to the worker, but unknown to the firm. Participation in a tuition reimbursement program is assumed to reveal the worker's type to all potential employers because certification takes place outside the firm. Because participation is assumed to be more costly to workers of low ability, wages can be set such that all high-ability types participate and no low-ability types participate. Hence, in his model, firms use tuition reimbursement programs as a screening device to attract high-ability workers. Using educational attainment as a proxy for ability, Cappelli tests his theory using the 1997 NES-EQW and finds that the average education attainment of new hires is higher for firms with tuition reimbursement programs, which is consistent with his theory if educational attainment is a direct measure of ability.

However, the sharp prediction of his model—all high-ability types participate—is inconsistent with empirical participation rates. Participation rates in tuition reimbursement programs by employees are typically around 5 percent.[8] The Corporate Leadership Council (CLC; 2003) reports that low participation rates could be due to a lack of marketing by firms. If employees lack information about the program, it cannot influence an employee's selection of an employer.

Aside from the sharp predictions and possible shortcoming listed in the preceding paragraph, the general idea of Cappelli's (2004) model is attractive because it is consistent with Rosen's (1986) prior work. The low participation rates found empirically could be reconciled in his model by thinking of workers as attaching an option value to participation: nonparticipants at firms that offer the program could be systematically different (i.e., of higher ability) than workers at firms that do not offer this program if high-ability workers are willing to trade off wages for the option of participating in the future. Data on how implementation of a tuition reimbursement program affects the applicant pool would be ideal to test the effect of these programs on recruitment. However, this type of data is difficult to obtain. Results from the case study in section 6.4 provide some evidence that implementation of a tuition reimbursement program affects employee composition because both the determinants of participation and the effect of participation on retention are different for new hires relative to those employees hired before the program was implemented.

6.3.2   Tuition Reimbursement and Retention

In contrast to using tuition benefits as a recruiting device, the claim by firms that they use tuition reimbursement programs to reduce turnover does not have support in the theoretical literature. Rather, the theoretical

---

8. References include the Corporate Leadership Council (2003), statistics from Watson Wyatt, and conversations with human resource (HR) personnel at firms with a program.

literature predicts the opposite: provision of general skills training would increase turnover. Becker's (1964) theory of investment in human capital argues that, because general skills are fully transferable (by definition), firms risk having their trained employees poached or "cherry-picked" by outside firms if they provide workers with general skills training. The labor market is assumed to be competitive with the worker's wage set equal to the value of her marginal product. Becker's theory implies that the worker bears the full cost of general training because she captures the full return on the investment. Because the market is competitive and skills are transferable, the worker is indifferent between employers. Therefore, even if the incidence of general skills training falls on the worker, turnover would be nondecreasing in the provision of general skills training. This disconnect between the theoretical literature and the intended use of these programs by firms presents an opportunity to analyze empirically the effect of tuition reimbursement programs on retention.

There are a handful of studies that examine the tuition reimbursement programs offered by the U.S. Department of Defense.[9] The two studies most similar in their econometric methodology to the case study analysis in this paper are Arkes, Garcia, and Trost (2000) and Buddin and Kapur (2005), which both examine the impact of tuition reimbursement on retention in the U.S. Navy. Arkes, Garcia, and Trost (2000) follow a cohort of enlistees who began service in 1992 and study the effect of participation on the probability of remaining with the Navy for at least six years. They find that participation increases the probability of staying in the Navy by nearly 13 percentage points.

Buddin and Kapur (2005) find the opposite: participation in tuition reimbursement decreases the probability of reenlisting after four years by 16.5 percentage points. Buddin and Kapur criticize Arkes, Garcia, and Trost's (2000) definition of retention and instead use reenlistment after the end of a four-year contract as the relevant measure. Buddin and Kapur (2005) argue that the time window for which enlistees have access to participation in tuition reimbursement should be held fixed, so they limit their sample only to those enlistees who served a full four-year contract. These two studies also differ in the variables used as exclusion restrictions in their bivariate probit estimation: Arkes, Garcia, and Trost (2000) use participation in the orientation session for educational opportunities offered to enlistees, while Buddin and Kapur (2005) use the enlistee's proximity to a four-year college before enlistment and an interaction between the number of courses offered on base and the size of the base. Buddin and Kapur argue that the instrument used by Arkes, Garcia, and Trost (2000) fails the exogeneity test.[10]

---

9. These include Boesel and Johnson (1988), Garcia, Joy, and Reese (1998), Arkes, Garcia, and Trost (2000), Buddin and Kapur (2002), and Buddin and Kapur (2005).

10. Participation in the orientation session is not random; it is positively correlated with an individual's intention to use the program. Therefore, Buddin and Kapur (2005) argue that it is correlated with the probability of staying in the Navy.

While the exclusion restriction in Arkes, Garcia, and Trost (2000) is untenable, this chapter does not agree with Buddin and Kapur's (2005) criticism that the window of opportunity for participation needs to be held constant for "leavers" and "stayers." If enlistees jointly determine their participation and retention decisions, constraining the duration of service to be the same across participants and nonparticipants imposes restrictions on the effect of the program. By using different criteria for their samples, Arkes, Garcia, and Trost (2000) and Buddin and Kapur (2005) are addressing slightly different research questions. Arkes, Garcia, and Trost (2000) examine the effect of participation on the probability of staying six years, while Buddin and Kapur (2005) analyze the effect of participation on the probability of staying a fifth year after already completing four years with the Navy. Even in the absence of these complications, generalizing results from the Armed Services to civilian workers is difficult due to the fundamentally different employment relationship.

Benson, Finegold, and Mohrman (2004) present an analysis of the impact of participation in tuition reimbursement on retention using a case study of a large U.S. manufacturing firm (roughly 10,000 civilian employees). Employees at this firm have a high participation rate in the tuition program—nearly 60 percent—which may be due to the program's unlimited reimbursement of tuition, stock rewards for degree completion, and the fact that the firm strives to be a leader in the provision of continued education for its workers. This number is also inflated because it includes individuals who took only a single course rather than limiting the sample to those enrolled in a degree program. Hence, their study examines an atypical tuition reimbursement program in terms of characteristics and participation rates.

Benson, Finegold, and Mohrman (2004) use a Cox-proportional hazard model to analyze how participation and degree completion affect the probability of leaving the firm between January 1996 and June 2000. They propose a theory in which promotion after degree completion would reduce the probability of leaving because it produces a better match between responsibilities and skill sets. However, their theory falls short of fully explaining their empirical findings. They find that promotion decreases the probability of leaving for employees who obtain a graduate degree. However, these individuals still have a greater probability of leaving the firm than nonparticipants, and promotion does not affect the turnover propensity for those employees earning either a bachelor's or an associate's degree. Another possible source for concern is the authors' assumption that the effect of participation on the separation hazard is proportional because the authors make note of a sharp increase in the hazard upon degree completion. In addition, their analysis assumes that participation in the tuition program is exogenous to the employee's retention decision. A major advantage to the Benson, Finegold, and Mohrman study is the data used in their analysis because it allows current participants to be distinguished from those who have completed degree programs. Overall, however, it is difficult to generalize their findings to other establishments because the institution they analyze is an outlier in terms of program characteristics and due to the methodological shortcomings.

While few studies examine tuition reimbursement programs, there have been many studies that examine the provision of general skills training by employers. These studies develop models in which a variety of mechanisms, such as asymmetric information or mobility costs, create a wedge between wages and productivity. This wedge provides firms with an incentive to offer and pay for general skills training.[11] These studies, however, do not focus on the effect of general training on employee retention.

This chapter empirically evaluates the effect of employer-provided general training—provided through tuition reimbursement programs—on employee attachment to the firm. It contributes to the literature by examining the effect of these programs on the retention of civilian workers using a program that is typical in terms of its characteristics. Additionally, this analysis accounts for the interdependence between an employee's participation and retention decisions.

6.4   Case Study Program (CSP)

To examine the impact of tuition reimbursement programs on employee retention, this chapter analyzes data from a single employer. This section presents the program characteristics, an econometric framework, and the results from analyzing the case study program. The data were obtained from a nonprofit institution that implemented a tuition reimbursement program in September 1999. The case study program will be referred to as CSP in the remainder of this chapter. Employees included in this analysis are staff members in supervisory and nonsupervisory positions who were employed on December 15, 1999, and those who were hired between December 15, 1999, and September 1, 2001. There are nearly 8,000 employees in total. A panel of observations was constructed based on seven "point-in-time" observations from administrative records. Individuals are observed on December 15 of each year from 1999 to 2005. The data include information on gender, age, and race as well as start date, job characteristics, and annual wage rates. One shortcoming of the data is that those employees who start and end employment between December 15 of one year and December 15 of the subsequent year are not included in the sample. An additional shortcoming is that the data do not distinguish voluntary separations from involuntary separations.[12] Individual records of partici-

---

11. These include, but are not limited to, Black and Lynch (1998), Loewenstein and Spletzer (1999a, b) and Acemoglu and Pischke (1998, 1999a, b), and Autor (2001).

12. Being able to distinguish between the two would improve our understanding of how these programs affect employee attachment; however, this is not possible using these data. Historically, this employer has not used mass layoffs, and most separations appear to have been voluntary.

pation in CSP include the amount reimbursed, the degree type, and the major or area of concentration for those participating from September 1, 1999, to August 31, 2004.[13] The amount reimbursed over these five years totaled nearly two million dollars (in 2001 U.S. dollars), with a participation rate of 5.0 percent.[14]

6.4.1   CSP Characteristics and Data

As mentioned in section 6.2, employees are required to have one year of service to be eligible for CSP. Employees need to be admitted into a degree program, but the program does not need to be job-related. The employee's supervisor must approve the request to participate in CSP, but this is not a binding constraint because the employee can appeal directly to the benefits department for reimbursement if his or her supervisor does not grant the request. A staff member working full time (more than thirty hours per week) qualifies for $5,250 in reimbursement per year; this amount is prorated for members working part time. The maximum reimbursement amount was $2,000 for the first two years of the program, September 1, 1999, through August 31, 2001, but was increased to $5,250 as of September 1, 2001. CSP qualifies under Section 127 of the Internal Revenue Code, allowing reimbursements to be exempt from income and payroll taxation. Under CSP, reimbursements are only allowable for the cost of tuition. Tuition reimbursements are made directly to the institution prior to the quarter or semester. The employee assumes responsibility of satisfactory completion of the course (grade of C or better); if not, the funds must be repaid in total to the employer.

Table 6.2 displays descriptive statistics of worker characteristics for those used in the analysis. Participants in CSP differ from nonparticipating employees in terms of observable demographic and employment characteristics. Participants are younger, are more likely to identify themselves as black, have a lower starting wage, and are less likely to be in a supervisory role.[15] Of those who participated between September 1, 1999, and August 31, 2004, the average total reimbursement amount was nearly $5,200, and participants spent an average of two years in the program.

The participation rate of an employee's peers is also higher for participants. Peer groups were constructed using both the location of an em-

---

13. Major, or area of study, was not available for twenty-two participants.
14. Participation is measured as having ever participated in the program. It is important to note that data on participation in CSP is only available through August 31, 2004; therefore, this rate likely underestimates actual participation. In particular, this participation rate only includes two years of participation behavior for employees hired in 2001.
15. Workers are categorized as supervisors if they are "exempt," while "nonexempt" workers are those in nonsupervisory positions. Exempt and nonexempt refer to whether the employee is subject to the U.S. Fair Labor Standards Act of 1938 (FLSA), which establishes minimum wage and overtime pay laws for full-time and part-time workers in the private and government sectors. Workers who are nonexempt from FLSA are those paid on an hourly basis and occupy nonsupervisory positions; the salary of exempt workers must also meet the minimum wage.

Table 6.2   Comparing nonparticipants to participants

Employee characteristics	Nonparticipants	Participants
Female (%)	70.6	73.8
Age	40.7	34.5**
White (%)	68.3	62.8**
Black (%)	5.4	10.7**
Hispanic (%)	7.9	9.7
Asian (%)	18.4	16.8
Initial weekly wage ($2001)	1,393	1,225**
Nonsupervisor (nonexempt, %)	41.9	52.1**
Supervisor (exempt, %)	58.1	47.1**
Leave before 5 years (%)	47.1	33.2**
Years in tuition program		1.96
Tuition spending (nominal, $)		5,169
Participation rate of peers (%)	2.8	3.2**
No. of observations	7,291	382

**Statistically different at the 5 percent significance level.

ployee's division and the general classification of his or her job to define a group of workers whose participation behavior could influence an individual employee's participation decision, such as through the dissemination of information about the program. The peer participation rate assigned to each employee does not include that particular employee's participation behavior. This variable is used later in the paper as an exclusion restriction in the econometric analysis of the effect of participation on retention.

Tables 6.3 and 6.4 show the (unconditional) retention behavior of nonparticipants and participants. The raw data show that participants have higher retention rates than nonparticipants for each year of service. The largest difference in the separation percentages occurs at the three-year mark, but the difference still persists at the five-year mark. Whether the worker separates from the institution before five years is the primary outcome evaluated in this study. Unfortunately, the data do not contain information on degree completion, so the retention behavior of participants after completing their coursework cannot be directly examined. The five-year time window is used as an approximation for degree completion.

Figure 6.1 graphically displays the difference between participants and nonparticipants in their propensities to separate from the institution by plotting Kaplan-Meier survival functions. These survival functions use actual employment start dates, but the end dates are randomly assigned to a date in the year in which the employee leaves the institution, which produces a relatively smooth curve.[16] The survival function of participants lies

16. For employees hired before September 1999, length of service is measured as the difference between implementation of the program (September 1, 1999) and the employee's end date or censoring date (December 15, 2005) when applicable.

Table 6.3   Retention of participants (unconditional)

Year hired	Number	% leave before:		
		3 years	4 years	5 years
Before Sept. 1999[a]	242	14.5	21.5	30.2
Sept. 1999–Dec. 1999	11	0.0	9.1	36.4
2000	72	12.5	20.8	33.3
2001	57	24.6	31.6	45.6

[a]Service length is measured as of first year observed (Dec. 15, 1999).

Table 6.4   Retention of nonparticipants (unconditional)

Year hired	Number	% leave before:		
		3 years	4 years	5 years
Before Sept. 1999[a]	4,980	31.7	37.3	42.3
Sept. 1999–Dec. 1999	264	48.5	9.1	63.6
2000	1,199	40.6	20.8	57.8
2001	848	43.4	53.1	59.2

[a]Service length is measured as of first year observed (Dec. 15, 1999).

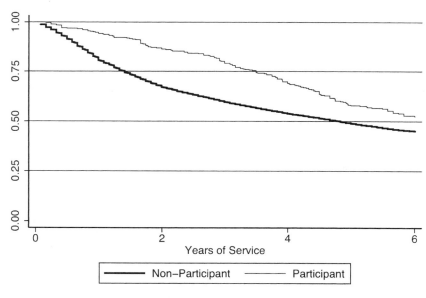

Fig. 6.1 Kaplan-Meier survival function plots by participation status (all hires)

to the right of nonparticipants, meaning that for any year of service, participants are more likely to still be employed at the institution. Differences in survival rates are largest just before three years of service. Figure 6.2 charts the survival functions for workers hired after September 1999 (i.e., hired after CSP was introduced).

Figures 6.3 and 6.4 graph the survival function by degree type and major pursued. Survival rates differ by the type of degree pursued: participants enrolled in undergraduate programs have higher survival rates than those in graduate programs (figure 6.3). The analysis in the next section examines whether this difference between degrees persists after controlling for individual characteristics.

While not a part of the administrative record, the relevance of the participant's major to their current job title was imputed. Participants were classified as pursuing a job-related major unless the discrepancy was large (i.e., a computer technician pursuing a major in art history) in an attempt to uncover a "lower bound" for the effect of participation on separation, meaning the effect of participation on retention that can be attributed to the service length requirement prior to eligibility and the fact that the worker needs to continue employment through the completion of his or her course in order to receive reimbursement. As seen in figure 6.4, the survival rate of participants is higher for the first few years of service even for those pursuing majors that are vastly unrelated to their job. The survival function for those pursuing majors that are at least *somewhat* job-related is to

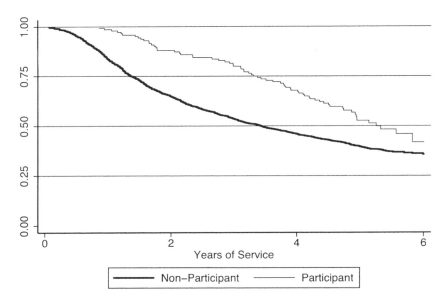

Fig. 6.2   Kaplan-Meier survival function plots by participation status (new hires)

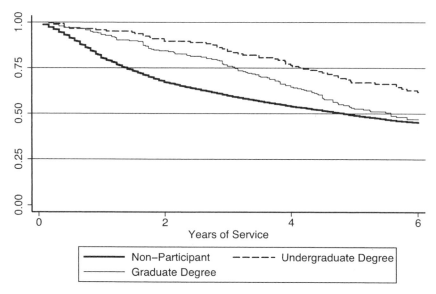

Fig. 6.3   Kaplan-Meier survival function plots by degree pursued (all hires)

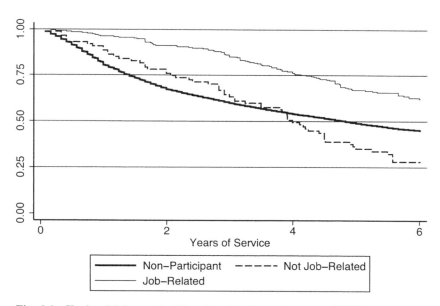

Fig. 6.4   Kaplan-Meier survival function plots by major pursued (all hires)

the right of the survival function of nonparticipants; the right shift persists beyond five years of service.

6.4.2 Estimation

This section models the event of an employee leaving the institution using a latent variable framework. The individual compares the utility from staying with the employer to that obtained from separating. The propensity to separate from the employer is a continuous variable, but the observed outcome is binary, taking a value equal to 1 if the individual separates, and equal to 0 otherwise. The likelihood of leaving depends on observable characteristics, X, participation in CSP, P, and factors unobservable to the researcher, ε. Let S^* be the underlying index—unobservable to the researcher—that determines whether the individual separates from the employer within a specified time frame:

$$(1) \qquad\qquad S^* = X'\,\beta + \alpha P + \varepsilon$$

$$(2) \qquad\qquad S = \begin{cases} 1 \text{ if } S^* \geq 0 \Leftrightarrow X'\beta + \alpha P \geq -\varepsilon \\ 0 \text{ if } S^* < 0 \Leftrightarrow X'\beta + \alpha P < -\varepsilon \end{cases}$$

If we assume ε to have a standard normal distribution, then we can estimate how worker characteristics affect the probability of separating from the institution using a probit model.

The same framework can be applied to participation in CSP because participation is also a binary outcome. Let P^* be the underlying latent variable that determines whether the individual participates, while Z represents individual characteristics, and let u be unobservable characteristics. Again, the individual compares the utility from participating to that from not participating:

$$(3) \qquad\qquad P^* = Z'\gamma + u$$

$$(4) \qquad\qquad P = \begin{cases} 1 \text{ if } P^* \geq 0 \Leftrightarrow Z'\gamma \geq -u \\ 0 \text{ if } P^* < 0 \Leftrightarrow Z'\gamma < -u. \end{cases}$$

As with the analysis of the probability of separation, determinants of participation can be examined using a probit model if u has a standard normal distribution.

If participation in CSP were exogenous in equation (1), then α would measure the effect of participation in CSP on the probability of separation. For participation to be exogenous, the decision to participate cannot be related to the decision to leave the employer in terms of unobservable characteristics, or $\text{cov}(\varepsilon, u) = 0$. However, because participation in CSP affects employment and promotion opportunities due to an increase in general skills, arguing that the two decisions are uncorrelated is tenuous. This chapter models the two decisions jointly, allowing for participation in CSP to be endogenous in equation (1), or that $cov(\varepsilon,u) \neq 0$. The distribution of (ε,u) is assumed to be bivariate standard normal with $cov(\varepsilon,u) = corr(\varepsilon,u) = \rho$, or that:

(5)
$$\begin{pmatrix} \varepsilon \\ u \end{pmatrix} \sim \text{BVN} \left[\begin{pmatrix} 0 \\ 0 \end{pmatrix}, \begin{pmatrix} 1 & \rho \\ \rho & 1 \end{pmatrix} \right].$$

Equations (1) and (2) are estimated jointly using bivariate probit maximum likelihood estimation. Arkes, Garcia, and Trost (2000) and Buddin and Kapur (2005) use this technique in their studies of the U.S. Navy. In order to estimate the model, Z in equation (3) should include a variable that affects the probability of participating, but does not affect the probability of leaving (i.e., not contained in X from equation [1]). This chapter uses an information effect or knowledge "spillover," measured by the participation rate of peers, to satisfy this exclusion restriction. Peer groups were created based on the division (eighteen in total) in which the employee worked and a broadly defined job classification (administrative, professional, or manager). The participation rate of peers attached to each individual does not include the participation decision of that particular individual. This rate is used as a measure of how informed an individual is about CSP.[17]

Because the sample consists of both employees hired before and after the implementation of CSP, the empirical analysis will be conducted on two groups: (1) employees hired before September 1, 1999; and (2) employees hired on or after September 1, 1999. The groups need to be separated because, as discussed in section 6.3.1, implementation of CSP could affect the applicant pool. The effect of CSP on retention for future hires will be determined based on results collected from the second group, which is the measure most applicable to firms who have an established program. If a firm is considering implementing a tuition reimbursement program, the effect of CSP on current and future workers is relevant.

6.4.3   Results from Case Study

Before analyzing the probability of separating from the establishment, this section first examines determinants of participation. Table 6.5 shows the marginal effects from estimating the probability of participating in CSP using a probit model. The estimates in column (1) are for workers hired before CSP was implemented (i.e., before September 1, 1999). For workers in

---

17. The direction of the effect in unclear: Does the participation of peers inform the individual or does participation by the individual inform her peers? To address this, a robustness check was performed that assigned the current year's participation rate to newly hires employees by peer group. Because these new workers were not eligible to participate in the first year due to the one-year service requirement, the direction of this information effect is clear. This alternative measure of peer participation rates does not affect the results.

Table 6.5   Determinants of participating in case study program (CSP)

Probit model (LHS: Pr[P = 1])	Hired before Sept. 1999 (1)	Hired after Sept. 1999 (2)
Female	0.011	−0.005
	(0.005)**	(0.010)
Age	0.000	0.001
	(0.002)	(0.003)
Age^2	0.000	0.000
	(0.000)	(0.000)
Black	0.030	0.027
	(0.014)**	(0.023)
Hispanic	0.005	−0.011
	(0.010)	(0.014)
Asian	−0.016	0.008
	(0.007)**	(0.011)
Nonsupervisor	0.005	0.038
	(0.007)	(0.012)***
Ln of weekly wage (in thousands), $2001	−0.012	0.037
	(0.011)	(0.017)**
Log-likelihood	−922.3	−517.9
No. of observations	5,222	2,451

Note: Numbers reflect dF/dX values; standard errors in parentheses.
***Significant at the 1 percent level.
**Significant at the 5 percent level.

this group, women are more likely to participate than men as well as are individuals identifying themselves as black (relative to those identifying themselves as white); individuals identifying themselves as Asian are less likely to participate. While the magnitudes for the marginal effects seem small, they are substantial when compared to the participate rate: 4.6 percent of workers hired before September 1, 1999, participate, while 5.7 percent of those hired on or after September 1, 1999, participate in CSP (this difference is significant at the 5 percent level).

For workers hired after the introduction of CSP, the probability of participation is increasing in the starting wage rate and workers in nonsupervisory positions are more likely to participate than those in supervisory roles. An additional method for examining determinants of participation is to look at reimbursement amounts, such as the highest annual fraction of reimbursement received by workers (nonparticipants are given a value of zero). Table 6.6 shows the results from using a tobit model; the findings closely resemble those in table 6.5.

The next set of results estimate the effect of participation in CSP on the probability of separating from the employer (voluntarily or involuntarily) within five years when participation is treated as exogenous. Table 6.7 lists the marginal effects from estimating a probit model on the decision to sep-

Table 6.6   Determinants of case study program (CSP) reimbursement amount

Tobit model (LHS: Maximum Annual Reimbursement [fraction])	Hired before Sept. 1999 (1)	Hired after Sept. 1999 (2)
Female	0.437	−0.109
	(0.218)**	(0.166)
Age	0.012	0.016
	(0.067)	(0.059)
Age^2	−0.001	−0.001
	(0.001)	(0.001)
Black	0.930	0.370
	(0.32)***	(0.293)
Hispanic	0.202	−0.178
	(0.310)	(0.285)
Asian	−0.613	0.056
	(0.269)**	(0.184)
Nonsupervisor	0.178	0.618
	(0.240)	(0.208)***
Ln of weekly wage (in thousands), $2001	−0.325	0.650
	(0.401)	(0.300)**
Constant	−3.899	−2.798
	(1.334)***	(1.079)***
Log-likelihood	−1,098.0	−598.9
No. of observations	5,222	2,451

Note: Numbers reflect value of coefficient; standard errors in parentheses.
***Significant at the 1 percent level.
**Significant at the 5 percent level.

arate from the case study institution. For workers hired before CSP was implemented, $S = 1$ if they separate within five years measured from September 1, 1999 (start date of CSP); and $S = 0$ otherwise. For workers hired after implementation, $S = 1$ if they separate within five years of their hire date; and $S = 0$ otherwise. Individual and employment characteristics, such as age, weekly wage, and years of service, are taken as of December 15 of the first year observed. Participation in CSP, P is equal to 1 if the individual ever participated in the program beginning September 1, 1999, through August 31, 2004. This binary variable definition is used most often in this analysis because of the intensity at which workers use the program. Table 6.7 also includes results from using the maximum fraction of annual reimbursement received as a measure of participation; the findings are similar to those using the binary definition.

As seen in table 6.7, if participation in CSP were exogenous, participation would lower the probability of separating by over 20 percentage points for employees hired before or after September 1, 1999. This impact on retention is equivalent to the effect of being three and a half years older, or having six additional years of experience (as of December 15, 1999) for

Table 6.7   **Determinants of separating from firm within 5 years**

Probit model (LHS: Pr[S = 1])	Hired before Sept. 1999		Hired after Sept. 1999	
	(1)	(2)	(3)	(4)
Participation in CSP	−0.207		−0.218	
	(0.027)***		(0.043)***	
Maximum annual reimbursement (fraction)		−0.303		−0.238
		(0.044)***		(0.065)***
Female	0.029	0.029	0.003	0.003
	(0.016)*	(0.016)*	(0.023)	(0.023)
Age	−0.066	−0.066	−0.048	−0.048
	(0.005)***	(0.005)***	(0.007)***	(0.007)***
Age^2	0.001	0.001	0.001	0.001
	(0.000)***	(0.000)***	(0.000)***	(0.000)***
Black	0.042	0.044	−0.024	−0.026
	(0.032)	(0.032)	(0.047)	(0.047)
Hispanic	−0.060	−0.060	−0.096	−0.095
	(0.026)**	(0.026)**	(0.039)**	(0.039)**
Asian	−0.092	−0.091	−0.117	−0.120
	(0.019)***	(0.019)***	(0.026)**	(0.026)***
Service length^a	−0.034	−0.034	0.048	0.042
	(0.003)***	(0.003)**	(0.158)	(0.158)
Service length^2	0.001	0.001	−0.182	−0.177
	(0.000)***	(0.000)***	(0.153)	(0.153)
Nonsupervisor	−0.024	−0.023	−0.142	−0.144
	(0.019)	(0.019)	(0.028)***	(0.028)***
Ln of weekly wage (in thousands), $2001	−0.002	0.001	−0.293	−0.295
	(0.027)	(0.027)	(0.042)***	(0.042)***
Log-likelihood	−3,165.9	−3,162.9	−1,550.3	−1,555.6
No. of observations	5,222	5,222	2,451	2,451

Note: Numbers reflect dF/dX values; standard errors in parentheses.
^{a}Measured as of Dec. 15 of initial year observed.
***Significant at the 1 percent level.
**Significant at the 5 percent level.
*Significant at the 10 percent level.

those employees hired before September 1999. For recent hires, the effect is similar to being four and half years older or having a $750 increase in the worker's starting weekly wage.

Table 6.8 shows the results from examining the effect of participation on retention separately for undergraduate and graduate degrees while still treating participation as exogenous. The effect of pursuing an undergraduate degree in CSP is roughly one and a half times as large as the effect of pursuing a graduate degree across the two groups. However, if participation is endogenous, these estimates of how participation in CSP affects retention are inconsistent.

To allow for interdependence between participation and retention deci-

Table 6.8   Determinants of separating from firm within 5 years, by degree

Probit model (LHS: Pr[S = 1])	Hired before Sept. 1999 (1)	Hired after Sept. 1999 (2)
Graduate degree in CSP	−0.169	−0.182
	(0.036)***	(0.053)***
Undergrad degree in CSP	−0.258	−0.286
	(0.036)***	(0.067)***
Female	0.029	0.004
	(0.016)	(0.023)
Age	−0.066	−0.048
	(0.005)***	(0.007)***
Age^2	0.001	0.001
	(0.000)***	(0.000)***
Black	0.042	−0.020
	(0.032)	(0.047)
Hispanic	−0.060	−0.094
	(0.026)**	(0.039)**
Asian	−0.091	−0.116
	(0.019)***	(0.026)***
Service length[a]	0.034	0.047
	(0.003)***	(0.158)
Service length^2	0.001	−0.181
	(0.000)***	(0.153)
Nonsupervisor	−0.022	−0.140
	(0.019)	(0.028)***
Ln of weekly wage (in thousands), $2001	−0.001	−0.292
	(0.027)	(.042)***
Log-likelihood	−3,164.4	−1,549.6
No. of observations	5,222	2,451

Note: Numbers reflect dF/dX values; standard errors in parentheses.

[a]Measured as of Dec. 15 of initial year observed.

***Significant at the 1 percent level.

**Significant at the 5 percent level.

sions, bivariate probit maximum likelihood estimation is used and the correlation between the unobservable characteristics affecting these decisions is estimated. As mentioned in section 6.4.2, the participation rate of an individual's peer group is used for the exclusion restriction that is required for the estimation. One concern is that the members of peer group could all be affected by some exogenous shock that affects both their participation and retention behavior (such as a "supervisor effect").[18] However, because applications for reimbursement through CSP are handled by a central pro-

18. The type of exogenous shock that would be problematic is one that affects both the participation and separation propensities of the group, such that the participation behavior of peers could not be excluded from the individual's separation decision.

gram administrator, this shock is less of a concern. In addition, there is an opportunity to switch departments within the institution in the event of a poor supervisor-worker paring—over 18 percent of individuals made moves that landed them in a different peer group in a span of five years. Furthermore, peer groups were also constructed at the department level (twenty-three groups instead of the original seventy-one) to mitigate the effect of an exogenous shock; the findings are robust to this different specification.

Table 6.9 displays the marginal effects from the estimation on those employees hired before September 1, 1999. As reported earlier, the probability of participation is significantly higher for females relative to males and for blacks (relative to those identifying themselves as white); workers identifying themselves as Asian are less likely to participate. In addition to these individual characteristics, the participation rate by peers is included as a determinant of participating in CSP, but not included as a factor that affects the probability of separating from the employer. The probability of participating in CSP increases in step with the participation rate of peers: a 1 percent increase in the participation rate of peers increases an individual's probability of participating by 0.9 percentage points. The second set of estimates in table 6.9 corresponds to the probability of separating from the firm. The probability of separating is decreasing (at a decreasing rate) in age and experience and is significantly lower for Hispanics and Asians (relative to white workers). As opposed to the estimates in table 6.7, where participation was assumed to be exogenous, the effect of participation in CSP on turnover is positive, but not significantly different from zero for this group. The change in the magnitude of the estimate can be attributed to the negative correlation between the unobservable characteristics. A negative correlation implies that individuals (hired before September 1, 1999) who participated in CSP were predisposed to staying at the institution and, thus, the program did not significantly affect their retention behavior.

Table 6.10 presents the results from the joint estimation of the probability of participating in CSP and separating from the employer within five years for workers hired on or after September 1, 1999. For these workers, participation in CSP is significantly higher for workers in a nonsupervisory role and is increasing in the starting wage: a $100 higher starting weekly wage corresponds to a 0.43 percentage point increase in the probability of participating in CSP. The participation rate of peers positively affects an individual's probability of participation: a 2 percentage point increase in the participation rate of one's peers increases an individual's probability of participating by 1 percentage point. As for the probability of separating from the employer, workers identifying themselves as Hispanic are nearly 10 percentage points more likely to separate than those identifying themselves as white; workers of Asian descent are over 11 percentage points less

Table 6.9   Determinants of participating in CSP and separating from firm within 5 years (existing hires)

Bivariate probit model	Hired before Sept. 1999	
	Pr(P = 1)	Pr(S = 1)
Participate in CSP		0.098
		(0.183)
Female	0.011	0.024
	(0.005)**	(0.017)
Age	0.001	−0.063
	(0.002)	(0.005)***
Age²	0.000	0.001
	(0.000)	(0.000)***
Black	0.030	0.030
	(0.013)**	(0.032)
Hispanic	0.005	−0.062
	(0.009)	(0.026)***
Asian	−0.014	−0.085
	(0.006)**	(0.019)***
Service length[a]		−0.033
		(0.003)***
Service length²		0.001
		(0.000)***
Nonsupervisor	0.002	−0.142
	(0.007)	(0.028)***
Ln of weekly wage (in thousands), $2001	−0.009	−0.027
	(0.012)	(0.019)
Participation in CSP by peers (%)	0.009	
	(0.003)***	
Correlation between Errors	−0.387	
	(0.200)*	
Log-likelihood	−4,081.7	
Observations	5,222	

Note: Numbers reflect dF/dX values; standard errors in parentheses.
[a]Measured as of Dec. 15 of initial year observed.
***Significant at the 1 percent level.
**Significant at the 5 percent level.
*Significant at the 10 percent level.

likely to separate relative to white workers. Employees in nonsupervisory positions are over 14 percentage points less likely to separate than those in supervisory roles. Participation in CSP has the largest effect on retention: it reduces the probability of separating within five years by nearly 48 percentage points. The correlation between the error terms is positive and marginally significant (*p*-value of 0.15). A positive correlation implies that those individuals who are more likely to participate in CSP are also more inclined to separate from the employer within five years. Hence, by failing

Table 6.10   **Determinants of participating in CSP and separating from firm within 5 years (new hires)**

Bivariate probit model	Hired after Sept. 1999	
	Pr(P = 1)	Pr(S = 1)
Participate in CSP		−0.479
		(0.115)***
Female	−0.004	0.002
	(0.010)	(0.023)
Age	0.001	−0.048
	(0.003)	(0.007)***
Age^2	0.000	0.001
	(0.000)	(0.000)***
Black	0.025	−0.013
	(0.023)	(0.047)
Hispanic	−0.012	0.098
	(0.014)	(0.039)**
Asian	0.006	−0.114
	(0.011)	(0.027)***
Service length[a]		0.053
		(0.155)
Service length^2		−0.183
		(0.155)
Nonsupervisor	0.034	−0.142
	(0.012)***	(0.028)***
Ln of weekly wage (in thousands), $2001	0.043	−0.027
	(0.017)**	(0.019)
Participation in CSP by peers (%)	0.005	
	(0.002)***	
Correlation between Errors	0.435	
	0	
Log-likelihood	−2,063.7	
No. of observations	2,451	

Note: Numbers reflect dF/dX values; standard errors in parentheses.
[a]Measured as of Dec. 15 of initial year observed.
***Significant at the 1 percent level.
**Significant at the 5 percent level.

to account for endogenous participation behavior, the effect of participation on retention is underestimated.

The estimated effect of participation in CSP on retention in tables 6.9 and 6.10 uses a specification in which the type of degree pursued does not matter for separation rates. A second specification is found in tables 6.11 through 6.14, which allows the effect to vary by degree pursued. Tables 6.11 and 6.12 give the estimates for how pursuing an undergraduate in CSP affects retention. The effect is negative for both groups of hires: the probability of leaving within five years is reduced by 11 percentage points for

Table 6.11   Determinants of pursuing an undergraduate degree and separating from
                    firm within 5 years (existing hires)

	Hired before Sept. 1999	
Bivariate probit model	Pr(P = 1)	Pr(S = 1)
Undergraduate degree in CSP		−0.114
		(0.406)
Female	0.005	0.027
	(0.003)	(0.017)
Age	0.001	−0.064
	(0.001)	(0.005)***
Age^2	0.000	0.001
	(0.000)	(0.000)***
Black	0.016	0.035
	(0.009)*	(0.033)
Hispanic	0.007	−0.061
	(0.006)	(0.027)**
Asian	0.000	−0.087
	(0.004)	(0.019)***
Service length^a		−0.034
		(0.003)***
Service length^2		0.001
		(0.000)***
Nonsupervisor	0.016	−0.023
	(0.005)***	(0.021)
Ln of weekly wage (in thousands), $2001	0.005	0.001
	(0.007)	(0.027)
Participation in CSP by peers (%)	0.003	
	(0.001)*	
Correlation between errors	−0.194	
	0.474	
Log-likelihood	3,642.4	
No. of observations	5,222	

Note: Numbers reflect dF/dX values; standard errors in parentheses.
^{a}Measured as of Dec. 15 of initial year observed.
***Significant at the 1 percent level.
**Significant at the 5 percent level.
*Significant at the 10 percent level.

those hired before September 1, 1999, and 56 percentage points for the
group of new hires. However, the effect is not statistically significant for
those hired before September 1, 1999. For those hired after the introduction
of CSP, the correlation between the error terms is positive and significant.

The effects of pursuing a graduate degree in CSP on retention for the two
cohorts of employees are listed in tables 6.13 and 6.14. Again, the effect of
pursuing a graduate degree differs across the two cohorts of employees. For
those hired before CSP was implemented, pursuing a graduate degree increases the probability of separating from the institution by nearly 28 per-

Table 6.12   Determinants of pursuing an undergraduate degree and separating from firm within 5 years (new hires)

Bivariate probit model	Hired after Sept. 1999	
	Pr(P = 1)	Pr(S = 1)
Undergraduate degree in CSP		−0.562
		(0.237)***
Female	0.005	0.007
	(0.004)	(0.023)
Age	0.000	−0.047
	(0.002)	(0.007)***
Age^2	0.000	0.001
	(0.000)	(0.000)***
Black	0.037	0.011
	(0.018)**	(0.046)
Hispanic	0.007	−0.081
	(0.009)	(0.039)**
Asian	0.003	−0.111
	(0.006)	(0.026)**
Service length^a		0.030
		(0.155)
Service length^2		−0.166
		(0.150)
Nonsupervisor	0.024	−0.127
	(0.008)***	(0.028)***
Ln of weekly wage (in thousands), $2001	0.013	−0.283
	(0.009)	(0.042)***
Participation in CSP by peers (%)	0.001	
	(0.001)*	
Correlation between errors	0.894	
	(0.435)**	
Log-likelihood	1,760.1	
No. of observations	2,451	

Note: Numbers reflect dF/dX values; standard errors in parentheses.
^{a}Measured as of Dec. 15 of initial year observed.
***Significant at the 1 percent level.
**Significant at the 5 percent level.
*Significant at the 10 percent level.

centage points (statistically significant at the 10 percent level). The correlation between the errors is negative for this group and statistically significant, meaning that those who are more likely to pursue a graduate degree are also more likely to remain with the employer. For workers hired on or after September 1, 1999, pursuing a graduate degree reduces the probability of leaving within five years by 49 percentage points. Similar to workers in this cohort who pursued an undergraduate degree, the correlation between the errors is positive.

These results indicate that participation in CSP substantially increases

Table 6.13   Determinants of pursuing a graduate degree and separating from firm within 5 years (existing hires)

Bivariate probit model	Hired before Sept. 1999	
	Pr(P = 1)	Pr(S = 1)
Graduate degree in CSP		0.277
		(0.161)*
Female	0.005	0.023
	(0.003)	(0.016)
Age	0.001	−0.062
	(0.001)	(0.005)***
Age²	0.000	0.001
	(0.000)	(0.000)***
Black	0.016	0.031
	(0.009)*	(0.031)
Hispanic	0.007	−0.06
	(0.006)	(0.026)**
Asian	0.000	−0.082
	(0.004)	(0.019)***
Service length[a]		−0.033
		(0.003)***
Service length²		0.001
		(0.000)***
Nonsupervisor	0.013	−0.023
	(0.005)***	(0.019)
Ln of weekly wage (in thousands), $2001	−0.013	0.002
	(0.009)	(0.027)
Participation in CSP by peers (%)	0.006	
	(0.002)***	
Correlation between errors	−0.497	
	(0.182)**	
Log-likelihood	−3,796.7	
No. of observations	5,222	

Note: Numbers reflect dF/dX values; standard errors in parentheses.
[a]Measured as of Dec. 15 of initial year observed.
***Significant at the 1 percent level.
**Significant at the 5 percent level.
*Significant at the 10 percent level.

the retention of those employees hired after the program was implemented; however, participation has a weak negative effect on retention for those employees hired before the introduction of CSP. The differential effect across the two cohorts suggests that the introduction of the program affected the pool of workers attracted to and hired by the employer. The results from tables 6.5 and 6.6 show that the observable individual factors that affect participation are different across the two groups. More important for estimating the effect of participation on separation rates, the two

Table 6.14   Determinants of pursuing a graduate degree and separating from firm within 5 years (new hires)

	Hired after Sept. 1999	
Bivariate probit model	Pr(P = 1)	Pr(S = 1)
Graduate degree in CSP		−0.489
		(0.137)***
Female	−0.007	−0.001
	(0.008)	(0.023)
Age	0.001	−0.048
	(0.003)	(0.007)***
Age²	0.000	0.001
	(0.000)	(0.000)***
Black	−0.017	−0.041
	(0.011)	(0.047)
Hispanic	−0.020	−0.105
	(0.009)**	(0.039)***
Asian	0.002	−0.115
	(0.009)	(0.039)***
Service length[a]		0.044
		(0.155)
Service length²		−0.176
		(0.150)
Nonsupervisor	0.007	−0.140
	(0.009)	(0.029)***
Ln of weekly wage (in thousands), $2001	0.024	−0.282
	(0.013)*	(0.044)***
Participation in CSP by peers (%)	0.003	
	(0.001)**	
Correlation between errors	0.497	
	0.361	
Log-likelihood	−1,940.9	
No. of observations	2,451	

Note: Numbers reflect dF/dX values; standard errors in parentheses.

[a]Measured as of Dec. 15 of initial year observed.

***Significant at the 1 percent level.

**Significant at the 5 percent level.

*Significant at the 10 percent level.

groups differ in terms of the correlation between the unobservable factors that affect the participation and retention decisions. For those hired on or after September 1, 1999, there is a strong positive correlation between the probability of participating in CSP and separating from the employer. Hence, estimating the effect of CSP on the probability of separation in a single-equation framework underestimates the impact of participation on retention. Participation in CPS decreases the probability of separating from the employer within five years by 48 percentage points when participation is treated as endogenous, substantially higher than the 22 percentage point decrease in the probability of separation when participation is treated as exogenous.

For employees hired before CSP was implemented, the correlation between the unobservable factors affecting participation in CSP and separation from the employer is negative, meaning that those workers who are more likely to participate have higher attachment to the institution. Hence, the estimated effect of participation on separation rates treating participation as exogenous overestimates the effect on retention. The effect of participating in CSP using a single-equation framework is a 21 percentage point decrease in the probability of separating from the employer; however, when we treat participation as endogenous, the effect changes signs (becomes a 10 percentage point increase) and loses statistical significance.

This case study finds that tuition reimbursement programs substantially increase the retention of new hires. Hence, this chapter finds empirical support for the explanation given by firms for providing tuition reimbursement programs—to increase employee retention—despite the predictions of the standard theory of human capital that provision of general training would increase turnover. It is important to note that implementation of a program appears to affect current and future employees differentially; this difference provides some evidence that tuition programs affect the composition of a firm's applicant pool. Because of the prevalence of these programs, the results regarding new hires are likely to be most useful to employers.

6.5   Interpreting the Results

The result that participation in employer-provided general training programs increases worker retention contradicts the predictions of Becker's standard model of investment in human capital. However, there are possible mechanisms by which this result can be reconciled within standard theory. The first is the structure of tuition reimbursement programs, which Cappelli (2004) takes note of in his analysis.[19] Recall that eligibility for CSP is subject to a one-year service length requirement, which mechanically reduces the turnover rate for participants relative to nonparticipants in the first year. In addition, the duration of coursework increases attachment while the employee is participating because he or she needs to successfully complete the course, as well as continue employment, to receive his or her reimbursement. After course completion, however, this mechanism is no longer operative, and the worker's propensity to separate would increase. If this is the primary mechanism creating increased retention, then Becker's theory would be applicable following course completion.

The raw plots of the survival functions begin to address this concern. As

---

19. This point was also rightly emphasized by one of the referees for this volume.

discussed in section 6.4.1, figure 6.4 plots the Kaplan-Meier survival functions for participants relative to nonparticipants, separating those participants who are pursuing majors vastly unrelated to their jobs (Not Job-Related) from the remaining participants (Job-Related). The survival function of the Not Job-Related group can be interpreted as showing the pure mechanical retention effect attributable to the tuition program's structure: the survival rate for this group is initially higher than nonparticipants, but then drops below after three years of service. The survival function of participants in the Job-Related group starts above that of nonparticipants and remains above throughout the duration of the data. While these results are not definitive, they suggest that the retention effect is stronger than that simply implied by the program's structure.

An alternative explanation is that the general skills acquired through tuition reimbursement programs make the worker more productive at the current firm relative to outside employers through complementarities between firm-specific and general human capital. If complementarities exist between general and firm-specific human capital in production, general skills acquired through participation in tuition reimbursement could increase the productivity of firm-specific human capital, thereby increasing employee retention. Acemoglu and Pischke (1999a, b) argue that if general and firm-specific human capital are complements, wage structures could become compressed, thereby giving firms an incentive to provide general skills training.[20] The complementarities mechanism implies that the effect of participation on retention would persist after coursework has been completed.

It is important to note that complementarity between general and firm-specific skills is not necessary for tuition programs to have a continued effect on retention after courses are completed. Other mechanisms could result in this effect in there is investment in firm-specific human capital. For tuition reimbursement programs, participation would increase the amount of firm-specific skills if these skills are acquired over calendar time (or tenure) because coursework takes several semesters to complete. Service length requirements before and after participation would result in additional investment (Cappelli 2004). Alternatively, Lazear (2005) presents a model in which all skills are general, but how these skills are combined in production is specific to the firm. Hence, in his model, providing general skills training is essentially equivalent to investing in firm-specific skills, which would result in increased retention. In addition, firms could use general training as an insurance mechanism: if workers are reluctant to work at a firm that requires investment in firm-specific human capital due to the

---

20. Acemoglu and Pischke (1999a, b) define compression in the wage structure to mean that profits from trained workers are higher than those from untrained workers. They list several other market imperfections that could result in compressed wages, including search costs, mobility costs, and minimum wage laws.

risk of wage loss in the event of involuntary separation, firms could offer general training as a way to mitigate this risk and thereby encourage investment in firm-specific skills (Feuer, Glick, and Desai 1987).

Examining the effect of participation on retention after course completion is one way to test the role of firm-specific human capital relative to the mechanical effect due to the structure of these tuition programs. However, the data used in this analysis are not well suited for this test because they do not include exact course dates or departure dates, just the year in which participation and separation occur. This analysis attempts to capture the effect on retention following degree completion by using a five-year window for the separation outcome, but this measure is not ideal. Future work should examine the effect on retention following course completion as well as the firm-level determinants of providing these programs to improve our understanding of the role played by firm-specific skills.

6.6   Conclusion and Future Research

Tuition reimbursement programs are a type of general training program commonly offered by employers. Counter to the prediction of Becker's theory of investment in human capital, firms claim that they use these programs to increase employee retention. Results from the case study show that participation in tuition reimbursement substantially reduces the probability of separating from the employer: participation by those employees hired after the program was implemented reduced their probability of separating from the employer within five years by nearly 50 percentage points. This result challenges the prediction of standard theory that investment in general human capital by firms increases employee turnover. However, there are several mechanisms that can explain this result within standard theory, such as by allowing for an interaction between firm-specific and general human capital. To evaluate the merits of this hypothesis relative to others, such as the mechanical effect on turnover due the structure of tuition programs, future work should analyze the effect of participation on retention using data that include course and degree completion dates.

This case study analysis also provides evidence that offering tuition reimbursement affects the type of worker attracted to the firm. The participation rate in the program is significantly higher for new hires relative to existing hires, and the determinants of participation also vary across the two cohorts. After taking into account the interdependence between participation and retention decisions, the effect of the program on the probability of separation differs across the cohorts as well. Future work could examine the effect of this program on retention rates over a longer time horizon to see if the difference between the two cohorts persists.

A shortcoming of the case study analysis is whether the findings can be generalized to other employers and programs. While the tuition reimbursement program is typical in terms of its program characteristics, future work should examine the effect of tuition reimbursement programs on turnover rates using the cross section of firms, such as those surveyed in the SEPT95.

References

Acemoglu, Daron, and Jorn-Steffen Pischke. 1998. Why do firms train? Theory and evidence. *Quarterly Journal of Economics* 113:1: 79–119.
————. 1999a. Beyond Becker: Training in imperfect labour markets. *The Economic Journal* 109 (February): F112–F142.
————. 1999b. The structure of wages and investment in general training. *Journal of Political Economy* 107 (3): 539–72.
Arkes, Jeremy, Federico Garcia, and Robert Trost. 2000. Does employer-financed general training pay? Evidence from the US Navy. *Economics of Education Review* 21:19–27.
Autor, David H. 2001. Why do temporary help firms provide general skills training? *Quarterly Journal of Economics* 116 (4): 1408–48.
Becker, Gary S. 1964. *Human capital.* Chicago: University of Chicago Press.
Benson, George S., David Finegold, and Susan Albers Mohrman. 2004. You paid for the skills, now keep them: Tuition reimbursement and voluntary turnover. *Academy of Management Journal* 4 (3): 315–33.
Black, Sandra E., and Lisa M. Lynch. 1998. Beyond the incidence of employer-provided training. *Industrial and Labor Relations Review* 52 (1): 64–81.
————. 2001. How to compete: The impact of workplace practices and information technology on productivity. *The Review of Economics and Statistics* 83 (3): 434–45.
Buddin, Richard, and Kanika Kapur. 2002. Tuition assistance usage and first-term military retention. Santa Monica, CA: RAND.
————. 2005. The effect of employer-sponsored education on job mobility: Evidence from the U.S. Navy. *Industrial Relations* 44 (2): 341–63.
Boesel, David, and Kyle Johnson. 1988. The DoD Tuition Assistance Program: Participation and outcomes. Arlington, VA: Defense Manpower Data Center.
Bureau of Labor Statistics (BLS). 1996. BLS reports on the amount of employer-provided formal training. *United States Department of Labor News,* July 10.
Cappelli, Peter. 2004. Why do employers pay for college? *Journal of Econometrics* 121:213–41.
Corporate Leadership Council (CLC). 2003. Trends in tuition aid programs. Corporate Executive Board Catalogue no. CLC1-1100OH. Washington, DC: Corporate Leadership Council.
Feuer, Michael J., Henry A. Glick, and Anand Desai. 1987. Is firm-sponsored education viable? *Journal of Economic Behavior and Organization* 8:121–36.
Frazis, Harley, Maury Gittleman, Michael Horrigan, and Mary Joyce. 1998. Result from the 1995 Survey of Employer-Provided Training. *Monthly Labor Review* 121 (6): 3–11.
Frazis, Harley, Maury Gittleman, and Mary Joyce. 2000. Correlates of training: An analysis using both employer and employee characteristics. *Industrial and Labor Relations Review* 53 (3): 443–62.
Garcia, Federico, Ernest H. Joy, and David L. Reese, 1998. Effectiveness of the vol-

untary education program. Report no. CRM-98-40. Alexandria, VA: Center for Naval Analyses.

Lazear, Edward P. 2005. Firm-specific human capital: A skill-weights approach. NBER Working Paper no. 9679. Cambridge, MA: National Bureau of Economic Research.

Loewenstein, Mark, and James R. Spletzer. 1999a. Formal and informal training: Evidence from the NLSY. In Research in labor economics. Vol. 18, ed. John Robst, 403–38. Stamford, CT: JAI Press.

————. 1999b. General and specific training: Evidence and implications. *Journal of Human Resources* 34 (4): 710–33.

Newman, Adam, and Matt Stein. 2003. Tuition assistance plan benchmark: Managing TAP as a strategic asset. Boston: Eduventures.

Rosen, Sherwin. 1986. The theory of equalizing differences. In *Handbook in labor economics.* Vol. 1, ed. Orley Ashenfelter and Richard Layard, 641–92. Amsterdam: North-Holland.

Ownership and Wages
Estimating Public-Private and Foreign-Domestic Differentials with LEED from Hungary, 1986 to 2003

John S. Earle and Álmos Telegdy

7.1 Introduction

Wages in the transition economies of Eastern Europe have changed dramatically in the fifteen years since the collapse of central planning. Average wages tended to decline in the first few years of transition and to rise more recently.[1] At the same time, the economies of the region have experienced massive organizational changes, most prominently large-scale privatization and opening to the global economy, including foreign direct investment.

These rapid changes provide a useful context for investigating the relationship between firm ownership and the level of wages. The transfers from the state to new domestic and foreign owners took place not only quickly but

John S. Earle is a senior economist at the Upjohn Institute for Employment Research, and a professor of economics at Central European University. Álmos Telegdy is codirector of the Labor Project at Central European University, and a senior research fellow at the Institute of Economics of the Hungarian Academy of Sciences.

The research on this paper was supported by a grant from the National Council for East European and Eurasian Research. The paper was presented at the Conference on Firms and Employees (CAFE) in September 2006 in Nuremberg, Germany, supported by the Institute for Employment Research (IAB), the Data Access Center (FDZ-BA/IAB), the Deutsche Forschungsgemeinschaft, the Research Network "Flexibility in Heterogeneous Labour Markets," the Alfred P. Sloan Foundation, and the National Science Foundation. For helpful comments, we thank Alan de Brauw, Susan Helper, Joanne Lowery, John Pencavel, two anonymous referees, and participants in the 2006 AEA, CAFE, and SOLE meetings and in seminars at the Upjohn and Ente Einaudi Institutes. We are also grateful to Gábor Antal for outstanding research assistance, to Mónika Bálint, Judit Máthé, Anna Lovász, and Mariann Rigó for conscientious help with data preparation, to János Köllö for advice on the Wage Survey data, to Gábor Békés for helping to improve the longitudinal linkages, and to Philipp Jonas for programming some of the specification tests. We thank the Hungarian National Bank for cooperation and data support. All errors are our own.

1. Commander and Coricelli (1995) and World Bank (2005) document average real wage changes in a number of transition economies.

also broadly across nearly all sectors. The tightly controlled wages of the centrally planned systems were abruptly liberalized, permitting organizations to set their own wages and to increase skill differentials, which were compressed under socialism (e.g., Kornai 1992). But how these changes might be related is unclear a priori. If firms maximize profits, labor markets are perfectly competitive, and there are no differences in nonwage compensation and work conditions, then wages should be correlated with ownership only through compositional differences in types of employees. Shifts in labor demand may lead to temporary wage differentials for the same type of worker, but these should disappear as workers move from lower to higher return activities. However, if ownership is associated with differences in the firm's objectives, competitive environment, or provision of fringe benefits and work conditions, then differences in wages across these types may persist even beyond the time required for workers to overcome mobility frictions.

In this paper, we estimate the relationship between the level of wages and ownership using linked employer-employee panel data for Hungary. Hungary is a particularly appropriate country for the analysis, not only because it underwent sweeping ownership changes, similar to some of its neighbors, but also because its privatization policies tended to result in ownership structures more akin to those in market economies, with more outside investor control and with much more foreign involvement than other transition economies. Moreover, the available data for Hungary are exceptional in size and quality. The data include observations on some 1.35 million worker years at 21,238 employers that we follow over a long time period, from 1986 to 2003. The worker characteristics in the data are useful for controlling for the composition of employment at each firm, and the firm-side information permits us to measure ownership changes, control for firm characteristics, and control for some types of selection bias into ownership type. However, the data allow us to distinguish only three types of ownership: state (public), domestic private, and foreign. They also do not enable us to follow individual workers over time, nor do they include information on working hours, nonmonetary benefits, and other work conditions. We thus cannot control for unobserved differences across workers, nor can we rule out the possibility that observed wages reflect compensating variations with respect to differences along other dimensions of the employer-employee relationship.

Nevertheless, these data help overcome a number of drawbacks in previous research. Studies relying on firm-level data usually have small samples, short time series, and no worker characteristics, and they sometimes lack a comparison group. Identification may depend on observing ownership changes, but few studies analyze the effects of privatization on wages.[2]

---

2. The lack of research on the wage impact of privatization contrasts with the large literature on firm performance, already the subject of multiple survey articles (e.g., Megginson and Netter 2001; Djankov and Murrell 2002).

Haskel and Szymanski (1993) is the earliest systematic study, and it analyzed fourteen British publicly owned companies, of which only four were actually privatized. Martin and Parker (1997) study fourteen large British privatizations, while Kikeri (1998) and Birdsall and Nellis (2003) summarize a number of case studies and small sample surveys of privatization effects on labor in several developing economies. La Porta and Lopez-de-Silanes (1999) analyze 170 privatized firms in Mexico, although the post-privatization information is limited to a single year. The small sample size problem is overcome in Brown, Earle, and Telegdy (2005), who study nearly comprehensive panels of manufacturing firms in Hungary, Romania, Russia, and Ukraine, finding a zero or very small negative effect of privatization.[3] But a fundamental problem with all of this work using firm-level data is the inability to measure worker characteristics and thus to control for composition of the workforce, particularly if changes in composition are correlated with changes in ownership.

A similar problem is evident with most studies of relative wages at foreign-owned firms. For example, Feliciano and Lipsey (1999) study wage differentials between foreign and domestically owned establishments in the United States. Aitken, Harrison, and Lipsey (1996) analyze the same topic but extend the analysis with wage spillovers between foreign and domestic firms. Conyon et al. (2002) study wage changes following foreign acquisitions in manufacturing firms in the United Kingdom. Lipsey and Sjöholm (2004) study these wage differentials in Indonesian manufacturing, although in this case they do control for the composition of workforce at the firm level. Brown, Earle, and Telegdy (2005) analyze the wage effects of privatization to foreign intervention. All these studies tend to find a wage premium in foreign firms.

However, a second, equally serious problem is that most studies do not account for ownership selection effects. If firms experiencing an ownership change are not randomly selected with respect to their wage behavior and the researcher does not take this into account, the estimated effect of ownership change will generally be biased. Indeed, some recent studies demonstrate this possibility.[4]

Instead of using firm-level data, another category of research has employed individual data that include information on employer ownership as well as wages. There is a sizable literature on public-private wage differentials, surveyed by Gregory and Borland (1999). In the Western context,

---

3. A related line of research analyzes effects of all types of ownership change on wages: for example, Lichtenberg and Siegel (1990) on leveraged buyouts, Gokhale, Groshen, and Neumark (1995) on hostile takeovers, and McGuckin and Nguyen (2001) on mergers and acquisitions. Our data do not contain information on all ownership changes, but only on transitions between state, domestic private, and foreign ownership types, which are thus our focus in this paper.

4. Conyon et al. (2002) employ firm fixed effects to study foreign acquisitions in Britain. Almeida (2003) discusses selection of foreign acquisitions, and Brown, Earle, and Telegdy (2005, 2006) discuss selection in privatization programs.

however, this research amounts to an analysis of interindustry differentials with little possibility of taking into account unobserved differences in ownership types that are correlated with wages. Concerning foreign wage differentials, Peoples and Hekmat (1998) carry out an analysis for the United States, but they use only industry-level ownership information. In the transition context, Brainerd (2002) estimates wage effects of Russian mass privatization using worker-level data. A problem with these studies is possibly inaccurate measures of ownership, which are reported by workers who may not be fully informed about the progress of the privatization process. More importantly, worker-level data do not permit controls for firm selection into ownership type.[5]

The advantages of both firm- and worker-level data can be exploited only if one combines the two data types into linked employer-employee data. But only two previous studies, both of them recent working papers, use linked data for a similar purpose, and both focus on the effects of foreign acquisitions on wages in Portugal: Almeida (2003) estimates the effect of 103 foreign acquisitions and finds higher wages in foreign firms, but Martins (2004), using a data set with 231 acquisitions, reports a negative effect. These studies share the problem, common to most Western data sets, of relatively few ownership changes, so that the ownership effect is identified only on a small sample of firms. In our Hungarian data, by contrast, we observe thousands of ownership changes, including 3,550 involving domestic private ownership and 926 involving foreign ownership (some of which overlap). The Hungarian data also contain substantial numbers of observations of each ownership type for each industry, so we can avoid the usual pitfall, particularly common in the public-private wage literature, of attempting to infer ownership differentials from industry differentials. Unlike other transition economies, moreover, the Hungarian ownership structure emerging from the transition process is more similar to developed market economies than elsewhere in Eastern Europe. By contrast with other transition economies of the region, Hungary emerged with very little worker ownership and frequently with strong outside blockholders, particularly foreign investors.

While we believe that our data, context, and methods provide the possibility for significant progress in identifying ownership effects, it is, of course, still possible that the differentials we estimate may not equal the causal effects of ownership. First, it is likely that selection of firms and workers into ownership types is nonrandom with respect to unobserved factors, such as quality of the firm or the worker. We exploit the longitudinal structure of the firm side of the data to control for fixed and trending

---

5. An identification approach in analyzing wage differentials across sectors examines wage changes of workers who switch sectors (Krueger and Summers 1988). Our firm fixed effects and firm-specific trends methods in the following rely on firms switching sectors.

differences across firms, but because we do not know the form taken by the heterogeneity, we cannot be sure that these methods fully account for selection bias. Moreover, we cannot control for unobserved heterogeneity at the worker level. A second issue in interpreting our estimates on domestic private and foreign ownership is that we do not observe wage outcomes in state firms under a counterfactual of no privatization and no liberalization of foreign entry into the Hungarian economy. Indeed, wage behavior of each ownership type may well be influenced by each of the others through labor market interactions. Analyzing such spillover effects could be interesting, but we leave it for future research.

The next section describes the construction of the employer and employee components of our data and how we link them into a single database. In section 7.3, we briefly explain the changes in the ownership structure during the period studied and summary statistics for all variables. We also provide some initial analysis of the evolution of wage levels. Section 7.4 describes regression estimates of the impact of ownership on the level and structure of wages, including specifications that control for selection bias into ownership type based on firm-specific time-invariant and time-trending heterogeneity. An important issue in estimating such impacts is the appropriate unit of analysis, and we provide some comparisons of results where the observation is a worker year with others where the observation is a firm year. Our data measure wages at both levels, but the worker-year observations permit us to analyze worker heterogeneity in wages and to control for worker characteristics, while the firm-year approach is more closely aligned with our variable of interest, firm ownership. Section 7.5 concludes with a summary and suggestions for further research.

7.2   Data Sources and Sample Construction

We study a linked employer-employee data set from two sources. The first is the Hungarian Wage Survey, which gathers information on individual worker characteristics and wages. The Wage Survey was carried out in 1986, 1989, and annually since 1992, with the last available round in 2003. Our analysis thus uses information on workers from 1986, four years before the Communist Party lost power, until 2003, the year just prior to European Union accession. Until 1995, the sampling frame for firms each year includes every tax-paying legal entity using double-sided balance sheets with at least twenty employees; after 1995, the size threshold for inclusion is ten employees, and a random sample of smaller firms is also included. To maintain consistency across years, we restrict attention to firms with at least twenty employees in at least one year.

From this sampling frame, employers are included in the Wage Survey according to whether their employees are selected by a second-level procedure. In 1986 and 1989, workers were selected by using a systematic random design with a fixed interval of selection: in 1986, every seventh production worker and every fifth nonproduction worker, while in 1989 every tenth worker, regardless of skill; in addition, each manager of the company was included. In these two years, therefore, every Hungarian firm using double-sided accounting should be included, except for nonresponses. From 1992 the worker sampling design changed: production workers were selected if born on the 5th or 15th of any month, while nonproduction workers were chosen if born on the 5th, 15th, or 25th of any month. In these years, firms are included only if they have employees born on these dates; they are excluded if they do not have such employees or if they do not respond to the survey. Leaving aside nonresponse, this selection procedure provides a random sample of workers within firms and includes, on average, about 6.5 percent of production workers and 10 percent of nonproduction workers. Assuming birthdates and nonresponses are randomly distributed across firms, the sample of firms is related to size (the probability of having employees with the given birthdates), but otherwise random.[6]

We constructed two types of weights to reproduce the universe of workers of Hungarian firms with more than twenty employees. The first type of weight adjusts for within-firm oversampling of nonproduction workers and worker nonresponse using separately available information on the number of production and nonproduction workers in each sampled firm, available for May of each year. The second set of weights corrects for undersampling of smaller firms and firm nonresponse to the Wage Survey. These weights are constructed using a second database, drawn from the Hungarian Tax Authority, which consists of annual firm-level information between 1992 and 2003 on every firm that used double-entry bookkeeping. The weights are computed for various size classes as the ratio between total employment in this universal data to total employment in the sampled firms in the Wage Survey.[7]

We also use the Tax Authority data to generate some of the firm characteristics in our analysis. The Wage Survey and Tax Authority data are linked using some common variables.[8] The information includes the balance sheet and income statement, the proportion of share capital held by different types of owners, and some basic variables, such as average yearly employ-

---

6. For example, a firm with twenty production workers has a probability of about 0.11 to be excluded from the sample, while for a similar firm with 100 employees, this probability is only 0.012. In addition to weighting to account for the size-probability relationship, we have also estimated all equations restricting the sample to employees of firms with more than 100 workers, with results qualitatively similar to what we report for the larger sample.

7. The size categories are groups of ten from 20 to 100 employees, 101 to 250, 251 to 500, 501 to 1000, and larger than 1,000. The few cases where the sum of sample employment exceeded universal employment were assigned weights of one.

8. Neither data set contains firm names, exact addresses, or identification codes, and we constructed the links using an exact one-to-one matching procedure for the following variables: county, detailed industry, employment, and financial indicators such as sales and profits.

ment, location, and industrial branch of the firm. We use the share capital variables to construct the ownership structure. For the two early years—1986 and 1989—the Tax Authority data are not available, and for these years we use the firm information from the Wage Survey; ownership in these years is always state, so the share capital variables are not necessary.

We cleaned firm ownership data extensively, checking for miscoding and dubious changes (e.g., firms that switch back and forth between ownership types). Our procedures also paid a great deal of attention to longitudinal links, for which we used a data set from the Central Statistical Office of Hungary providing information on reregistration and boundary changes. As this data set is not comprehensive, we also tried to find spurious entries and exits by looking for matches of exits among the entries on the basis of headquarter settlement, county, industry, and employment. Unfortunately, the Wage Survey data do not provide identification codes for workers, so it is not possible to track them across years.

Table 7.1 shows the number of workers with full information on characteristics, the number of firms with information on ownership, and the total number of employees in these firms.[9] The data set we work with is a panel of 21,238 firms linked with a within-firm random sample of 1.35 million workers.

7.3   Evolution of Ownership, Variable Definitions, and Summary Statistics

Compared with its neighbors in Eastern Europe, Hungary began corporate control changes relatively early. Starting with a more relaxed planning regime in 1968, the socialist government gradually permitted state-owned enterprises to operate with increased autonomy, and the decentralization process accelerated during the 1980s (e.g., Szakadat 1993). Movement of assets out of state ownership began at the very end of the 1980s in the form of so-called spontaneous privatization, which usually involved spin-offs initiated by managers, who were also usually the beneficiaries, sometimes in combination with foreign or other investors (see, e.g., Voszka 1993). After the first free elections in May 1990, procedures became more regularized, involved sales of entire going concerns, and generally relied upon competitive tenders open to foreign participation. Unlike the programs in many other countries, the Hungarian policies did not grant workers significantly discounted prices at which they could acquire shares in their companies, with the exception of about 350 management-employee buyouts. Nor did Hungary carry out a mass distribution of shares aided by vouchers, as was common in most other countries of the region. On the other hand, Hungary was much more open to foreign investors than else-

---

9. Firm-year observations with no information on sales and employment are dropped from the sample.

Table 7.1   Sample size by year

Year	No. of workers	No. of firms	Total employment
1986	100.5	3,236	2,633.5
1989	106.3	3,946	2,268.2
1992	64.8	4,393	1,198.4
1993	67.8	5,158	1,096.9
1994	95.7	7,128	1,351.4
1995	99.2	7,428	1,369.6
1996	97.6	7,421	1,292.1
1997	88.0	7,476	1,258.0
1998	99.0	7,459	1,282.2
1999	99.4	8,020	1,220.8
2000	109.5	9,149	1,257.6
2001	107.7	9,138	1,222.0
2002	102.8	5,630	1,049.2
2003	103.8	5,106	997.0

Notes: No. of workers = thousands of workers in the sample with information on education, experience, and gender. No. of firms = number of firms with information on ownership and with at least one worker in the given year with information on education, experience, and gender. Total employment = total employment of firms in the sample in thousands (i.e., including nonsampled workers).

where. As a consequence, Hungarian privatization resulted in very little worker ownership, very little dispersed ownership, and high levels of block-holdings by managers and both domestic and foreign investors.[10]

Our database provides the ownership shares of the state, domestic, and foreign owners at the end of each year (the reporting date). We define a firm as domestic private if it is majority private and the domestic ownership share is higher than that of foreign ownership. If the foreign share is larger than the domestic, the firm is foreign-owned for the purposes of this chapter.[11] The evolution of the ownership structure among the firms in our sample is presented in figure 7.1, clearly reflecting the early start and the heavy presence of foreign ownership in Hungarian privatization. Although there was only negligible privatization and new private entry by 1989, already in 1992 about 40 percent of the workers in our sample worked in private enterprises. The share of domestically privatized firms grew steadily until 1998, when 54 percent of the employees worked for domestic owners. Thereafter, it ceased growing and even shrank slightly (because of attrition from the sample). The proportion of employees in foreign-owned

10. Frydman, et al. (1993) and Hanley, King, and Toth (2002) contain descriptions of the Hungarian privatization process. Earle, Kucsera, and Telegdy (2005) study ownership of firms listed on the Budapest Stock Exchange.

11. This definition has the advantage over definitions that would involve majority ownership that all privatized firms can be categorized as domestic- or foreign-owned.

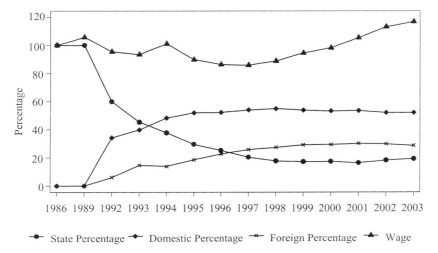

Fig. 7.1   Evolution of the ownership structure and average wages

Notes: Number of observations = 1,342,158. State % = percent of employees of firms majority state owned. Domestic % = percent of employees of firms majority private where domestic is the largest private employer type. Foreign % = percent of firms majority private where foreign is the largest private owner type. The evolution of the average real wage is presented as estimated year effects from a regression including firm fixed effects to control for sample changes (dependent variable = log real wage, normalized at 100 in 1986). Data are weighted by the numbers of blue-collar and white-collar workers within each firm, and each firm is weighted using total employment by firm size category.

firms grows steadily in our sample, reaching 29 percent by 2003. At the same time, about 20 percent of the employees worked for the state. The firm-level figures are different from the worker-level figures, as about three-quarters and one-fifth of the firms are controlled by domestic and foreign owners, respectively, but even by this measure the state has a controlling stake in at least 5 percent of the firms, thus providing a comparison group for the effects of privatization.

Table 7.2 shows the incidence of various types of changes in ownership type. The transition process resulted in many more changes from state to private than could ever be observed in a nontransition economy, and the number of changes involving foreign ownership in Hungary are probably the largest that could be found in Eastern Europe. In our data, 3,115 ownership changes involve domestic private ownership, and about 600 involve foreign ownership. We will exploit these ownership changes when we control for unobserved heterogeneity in estimating wage differentials, as described in the following.

The wage variable in our data is gross monthly cash earnings in May plus one-twelfth of previous year's bonuses, which we have deflated by the an-

Table 7.2   Firms by ownership type and switches

	No. of firms
Nonswitchers	17,295
Always State	3,167
Always Domestic	11,844
Always Foreign	2,284
Ownership switchers	3,694
State—Domestic	2,768
State—Foreign	144
Domestic—Foreign	435
Foreign—Domestic	347

Notes: No. of firms = 21,238. State = 1 if the firm is at least 50 percent owned by the state in $t - 1$. Domestic = 1 if the firm is majority private and domestic owner shareholding is larger than foreign in $t - 1$. Foreign = 1 if the firm is majority private and foreign owner shareholding is larger than domestic in $t - 1$. The numbers of switchers and nonswitchers do not sum to the number of firms as 201 firms have multiple changes in ownership type.

nual Consumer Price Index (CPI).[12] Figure 7.1 shows the evolution of real wages from 1986 to 2003: an initial decline of around 10 percent and subsequent rise of about 25 percent.[13] The steady, substantial growth in the Hungarian real wage since the mid-1990s is unusual among the transition economies, and an interesting question is whether Hungary's relatively rapid privatization and large foreign component may have contributed to this performance. The reliability of the real wage measure is, of course, strongly influenced by the quality of the deflator (in this case, the CPI), and the large changes in quality and availability of goods suggest caution should be exercised when interpreting these figures. When we estimate wage differences by ownership, however, we include year effects, so our comparisons are not influenced by these measurement problems.

Table 7.3 provides calculations of differences in mean wages by type of owner, presenting information for 1992 and 2003—the first and the last year in our panel when each ownership type is present. In both years, the unconditional mean wage is smallest in domestic private firms, largest in foreign-owned firms, and intermediate under state-ownership. Average worker characteristics also vary, however, with higher rates of female and university employment in foreign-owned firms, higher rates of vocational employment in domestic private firms, and higher rates of high school em-

12. Most studies of wages in Eastern Europe (and many in Western Europe) analyze monthly rather than hourly or weekly earnings; this is because of institutional differences such as the custom of reporting wages on a monthly basis, the lower incidence of part-time employment and greater standardization of full-time hours, and the frequent unavailability of hours information (even for production workers). In our data, hours of work are available only for the most recent years, so we cannot analyze changes using them.

13. To maintain comparability over time, the evolution of the average real wage is estimated as the year effects in a ln(real wage) equation that controls for firm fixed effects.

Table 7.3   Characteristics of workers in the sample, 1992 and 2003

	State		Domestic		Foreign	
	1992	2003	1992	2003	1992	2003
Real wage	102.6	130.9	79.2	111.2	122.3	189.6
	(64.5)	(99.0)	(54.9)	(109.8)	(96.3)	(210.4)
Female (%)	37.9	33.7	36.3	38.7	44.4	47.1
Education (%)						
Elementary or less	31.8	19.9	35.7	22.2	30.3	17.0
Vocational	30.3	30.9	38.3	39.6	36.3	30.9
High school	30.2	40.9	20.3	28.6	24.5	33.6
University	7.8	8.2	5.7	9.6	8.9	18.5
Potential experience (yrs)	22.2	26.1	22.5	25.4	20.5	21.8
	(10.6)	(10.6)	(10.5)	(11.5)	(10.7)	(11.3)
Occupation (%)						
Managers	5.2	9.3	6.9	8.8	4.5	7.9
Professionals	7.0	3.2	5.0	3.5	7.5	8.9
Assoc. professionals	14.9	18.1	7.8	11.1	9.4	18.2
Skilled nonmanual	6.9	6.5	6.9	5.9	6.1	5.9
Service	10.5	16.1	7.9	9.2	8.3	5.4
Skilled manual	44.5	39.1	53.9	50.5	53.4	47.8
Unskilled	11.0	7.7	11.6	11.1	10.8	5.9
No. of observations	42,089	17,119	17,773	60,134	4,093	26,544

Notes: Real wage measured in thousands of 2003 HUF, deflated by CPI. State = 1 if the firm is at least 50 percent owned by the state in $t-1$. Domestic = 1 if the firm is majority private and domestic owner shareholding is larger than foreign in $t-1$. Foreign = 1 if the firm is majority private and foreign owner shareholding is larger than domestic in $t-1$. Standard deviations are shown in parentheses for continuous variables. Data are weighted by the numbers of blue-collar and white-collar workers within each firm, and each firm is weighted using total employment by firm size category.

ployment under state ownership.[14] Potential experience tends to be lower in foreign-owned firms, a difference that becomes much more pronounced by 2003. The composition of the workforce by occupation also varies considerably, with a much higher rate of employment of professionals under foreign ownership, and a high rate of skilled manual employment in domestic private firms. Such factors likely influence average wage differentials by ownership type and can be taken into account by multivariate analysis.

Firm characteristics also vary by ownership, as table 7.4 documents. Measured by employment size, state-controlled firms are the largest, with an average size of 284 employees in 1992 and 400 in 2003. Foreign-owned firms are also quite large, on average, over 150 employees in 1992 and 220 in 2003, while domestic firms are much smaller, with an average size under

14. Wages and educational composition for the categories never privatized and eventually domestic and foreign privatized firms are much more similar in 1986 than in table 7.2, indicating that the different composition and wages in 1992 are probably due at least partly to privatization.

Table 7.4   Characteristics of firms in the sample, 1992 and 2003

	State		Domestic		Foreign	
	1992	2003	1992	2003	1992	2003
Employment	284.0	401.4	85.9	61.8	155.8	224.2
	(2,076.5)	(2,899.9)	(101.7)	(152.6)	(301.0)	(904.0)
Labor productivity	9.8	10.0	7.8	20.7	18.8	39.4
	(21.7)	(42.1)	(17.4)	(172.7)	(53.6)	(86.3)
Industry (%)						
Agriculture	6.1	9.4	25.1	13.1	2.0	2.6
Mining	0.7	0.2	0.2	0.5	0.6	1.2
Manufacturing	32.5	7.2	33.7	34.5	64.5	55.2
Energy and water supply	1.4	24.7	0.0	0.6	0.0	1.1
Construction	8.8	8.9	16.2	10.4	5.3	2.3
Trade	22.1	1.9	16.4	18.2	18.8	17.4
Hotels and restaurants	5.1	0.4	3.0	3.4	4.0	2.7
Transportation	5.6	7.7	1.2	3.6	0.2	3.3
Telecom	0.1	0.4	0.0	0.4	0.0	0.8
FIRE	13.1	20.6	3.7	13.3	4.6	11.4
Other services	4.5	18.4	0.4	2.1	0.0	2.1
No. of observations	1,538	346	2,572	3,701	276	1,057

Notes: Labor productivity is measured as the value of sales (in millions of 2003 HUF) over average number of employees. State = 1 if the firm is at least 50 percent owned by the state in $t-1$. Domestic = 1 if the firm is majority private and domestic owner shareholding is larger than foreign in $t-1$. Foreign = 1 if the firm is majority private and foreign owner shareholding is larger than domestic in $t-1$. FIRE = finance, insurance, and real estate. Standard deviations are shown in parentheses for continuous variables. Data are weighted by the numbers of blue-collar and white-collar workers within each firm, and each firm is weighted using total employment by firm size category.

100 in both years. Labor productivity (measured as the value of real sales over the average number of employees) varies dramatically by ownership type: the least productive firms were domestically owned in 1992, followed by state-owned firms. The productivity difference between these two ownership types is quite small, at least compared to the productivity of foreign-owned firms, which were about twice as productive as state-owned firms, and three times as productive as the domestically owned ones. The productivity of both types of private firms increased greatly by 2003 and remained practically unchanged for state-owned firms.[15] Finally, the industrial composition of firms in the sample also varies by ownership. In both years presented in the table, foreign firms had a high presence in manufacturing, while the share of state-owned firms in this sector dropped dramatically. Energy and water supply was mostly controlled by the state, and do-

15. These results should be treated with caution, as the sample within each ownership type varies considerably. For a multivariate analysis of the productivity effects of domestic and foreign privatization in four transitional countries (among them Hungary), see Brown, Earle, and Telegdy (2006).

mestic firms had a large proportion of firms in agriculture. The presence of state ownership in all sectors of the economy helps in identifying the wage effect of state ownership, which is often confused with interindustrial wage differentials when data from developed countries are analyzed.

To summarize the discussion of selection of workers into different ownership types, we ran multinomial logit regressions, where we test how individual characteristics influence the ownership type of the employer. As shown in table 7.5, longer potential experience and only basic education (eight years or less) make it more likely that the worker is employed in a firm controlled by the state; vocational education increases the probability that the employer is a domestic private owner; females and more-educated workers are more likely to work for foreign owners.

In the next step toward the analysis of wages and ownership, table 7.6 contains calculations of mean wages by ownership type and educational attainment in 1992 and 2003. For both years and all four educational categories, the ownership types are clearly ranked in wage levels, with foreign highest, state second, and domestic private lowest. At this level of analysis, there are clearly large differences among the three ownership types in both the level and the structure of wages they pay. It is interesting that the mean wages of the two types of private ownership—domestic and foreign—are much more different from each other than from state ownership.

Table 7.5   **Selection into forms of ownership**

	State	Domestic	Foreign
Vocational	−0.168***	0.125***	0.043***
	(0.008)	(0.007)	(0.007)
High school	−0.070***	0.012	0.058***
	(0.016)	(0.012)	(0.013)
University	−0.157***	0.009	0.148***
	(0.014)	(0.018)	(0.017)
Experience	−0.000	0.003***	−0.002***
	(0.000)	(0.000)	(0.000)
Female	−0.046**	0.004	0.042***
	(0.020)	(0.015)	(0.008)
Predicted probability	0.455	0.380	0.165

Notes: $N = 1,342,158$. Multinomial logit estimates, marginal effects reported. The dependent variable is ownership type: State if the firm is majority state in $t - 1$; Domestic if the firm is majority private and domestic shareholding is larger than foreign in $t - 1$; Foreign if the firm is majority private and foreign shareholding is larger than domestic in $t - 1$. Standard errors (corrected for firm clustering) are shown in parentheses. The regressions are weighted by the numbers of blue-collar and white-collar workers within each firm, and each firm is weighted using total employment by firm size category.

***Significant at the 1 percent level.

**Significant at the 5 percent level.

Table 7.6   **Average real wages by ownership type and education**

	State		Domestic		Foreign	
	1992	2003	1992	2003	1992	2003
Elementary or less	78.7	92.4	63.4	76.9	86.4	96.4
	(34.2)	(43.9)	(32.7)	(33.7)	(37.3)	(41.4)
Vocational	91.2	112.0	72.0	88.2	103.2	122.1
	(41.8)	(43.3)	(34.8)	(43.4)	(48.7)	(61.1)
High school	114.3	132.6	95.6	121.3	137.8	174.1
	(57.2)	(70.5)	(66.7)	(91.8)	(79.3)	(130.0)
University	199.6	286.6	167.2	256.0	280.0	416.3
	(128.8)	(231.6)	(107.1)	(253.4)	(203.2)	(365.1)
No. of observations	42,089	17,119	17,773	60,134	4,093	26,544

Notes: Real wage (deflated by CPI) measured in thousands of 2003 HUF. Standard deviations in parentheses. State = 1 if a majority of the firm's shares are owned by the state. Domestic = 1 if the firm is majority private and domestic owner shareholding is larger than foreign in $t - 1$. Foreign = 1 if the firm is majority private and foreign owner shareholding is larger than domestic in $t - 1$. Data are weighted by the numbers of blue-collar and white-collar workers within each firm, and each firm is weighted using total employment by firm size category.

7.4 Regression Estimates

To estimate the systematic impact of ownership on wages, we turn to regressions. We are interested not only in controlling for worker characteristics in various combinations—and in assessing the robustness of our results to such controls—but also in attempting to remove some types of selection bias in the determination of ownership type. For example, if state-owned enterprises that already pay higher wages are more likely to be purchased by foreigners (perhaps because of higher unobserved skill, better technology, or, indeed, for any reason), then the foreign wage premium we have documented may be due to the systematic selection of high-wage firms into foreign ownership. The privatization process involving either domestic or foreign owners may not be random because politicians, frequently together with employees, choose whether a state-owned firm can be acquired. Most arguments imply that firms with better prospects tend to be privatized earlier: politicians may try to demonstrate the success of their reform programs, to protect workers in poorly performing firms from layoffs and wage cuts (in which case the employees are also likely to oppose privatization), or to collect bribes in a corrupt privatization process. If firm quality and worker wages are positively correlated, these mechanisms would impart positive selection biases to wages in domestic and foreign private firms relative to the state sector.

Of course, we cannot entirely eliminate all possibility of bias, but a great advantage of our data is that we can exploit a large number of ownership changes together with the longitudinal dimension to check whether the differentials implied by our analysis so far are robust to some simple attempts to account for selection bias. For this purpose, we employ methods developed for the evaluation of training programs in the United States. The first method is the standard correlated effects model that controls for time-invariant unobserved heterogeneity at the firm level; this is a regression-adjusted difference-in-differences approach, where firms that do not change ownership (both firms that are always state-owned and those always either domestic or foreign private throughout the sample period) are the comparison group. A second is the random growth model, which includes a firm-specific linear time trend.[16] Such a model may be appropriate if, for example, foreign investors are more likely to acquire firms that for some intrinsic reason (unobservable to the researcher but not caused by ownership) are raising their wages or increasing the premiums paid to more highly educated workers. Higher-order parameterizations of heterogeneity are of course possible, but we do not take them into account, and identification of the effect of ownership in our analysis assumes that any other heterogeneity is uncorrelated with either ownership or wages. Both of these estimators rely on ownership changes to identify the coefficients of interest; indeed, the random growth model measures changes in the growth rate before and after an ownership change. A resulting disadvantage is that the results pertain to firms that experience such changes, not to the broader sample.[17] Finally, we use some specification tests to evaluate the performance of the estimators.

All equations control for year of observation and region of the establishment. We report standard errors in all cases permitting general within-firm correlation of residuals using Arellano's (1987) clustering method so that our test statistics are robust to both serial correlation and heteroskedasticity.[18] Standard errors are also adjusted for loss of degrees of freedom in specifications when the data are demeaned and detrended.

16. Ashenfelter and Card (1985) and Heckman and Hotz (1989) use random trend models to evaluate training, while Jacobson, LaLonde, and Sullivan (1993, 2005) apply it to the wage effects of job displacement and community colleges. Brown, Earle, and Telegdy (2005, 2006) use the model to estimate the impact of privatization on employment, wages, and productivity at the firm level. Our paper is the first to our knowledge that uses firm-level trends in any analysis of worker-level wages, and it is the first that uses firm fixed effects in a study of ownership and worker-level wages.

17. Another potential disadvantage is that these estimators may raise the noise-to-signal ratio, eliminating relevant between-firm variation while exacerbating the effects of measurement error in ownership. On the other hand, misclassification error is unlikely to be a problem in our case of official firm reports to the Tax Authority on the firm's ownership—a clear, measurable concept reported by professional accountants. This contrasts with the standard cases studied by economists of changes in industry of employment, union membership, or labor force status. In these cases, switching is usually measured in a household survey context by differing answers over time from (potentially different) family members who happen to be home and who are asked questions about one family member's job search, availability, union status, and other employment-related activities.

18. Kézdi (2003) contains a detailed analysis of autocorrelation and the robust cluster estimator in panel data models.

Table 7.7   Estimated impacts of state and foreign ownership

	OLS	OLS	FE	FE&FT
State	0.238***	0.197***	0.065***	0.078***
	(0.024)	(0.017)	(0.015)	(0.016)
Foreign	0.398***	0.386***	0.137***	0.073***
	(0.020)	(0.014)	(0.015)	(0.013)
Vocational		0.127***	0.132***	0.137***
		(0.005)	(0.003)	(0.004)
High school		0.373***	0.314***	0.330***
		(0.009)	(0.006)	(0.006)
University		0.950***	0.840***	0.872***
		(0.016)	(0.010)	(0.011)
Experience		0.027***	0.027***	0.026***
		(0.001)	(0.000)	(0.000)
Experience^2 • 100		−0.040***	−0.039***	−0.037***
		(0.001)	(0.001)	(0.001)
Female		−0.222***	−0.203***	−0.194***
		(0.006)	(0.005)	(0.005)
Firm-specific intercepts (FE)	no	no	yes	yes
Firm-specific trends (FT)	no	no	no	yes
R^2	0.139	0.413	0.630	0.354

Notes: No. of observations = 1,342,158. Dependent variable = ln(real gross wage). State = 1 if the firm is majority state in $t - 1$. Foreign = 1 if the firm is majority private and foreign shareholding are larger than domestic in $t - 1$. The regressions are weighted by the numbers of blue-collar and white-collar workers within firm and the total employment by firm-size categories. Elementary is the omitted educational category. OLS = ordinary least squares; FE = specification including firm fixed effects; FT = all variables have been detrended using individual firm trends. All equations include year and region fixed effects. The regressions are weighted by the numbers of blue-collar and white-collar workers within each firm, and each firm is weighted using total employment by firm size category. Standard errors (corrected for firm clustering and for loss of degrees of freedom when detrending) are shown in parentheses. R^2: overall for OLS, within for FE and FE&FT. The difference between the foreign and state effect is statistically significant in OLS and FE, and insignificant in FE&FT.

***Significant at the 1 percent level.

Table 7.7 displays estimates by pooled ordinary least squares (OLS), firm fixed effects estimations (FE), and firm fixed effects and trends (FE&FT). The first OLS column includes no controls beyond year and region, and the estimates demonstrate that the raw ownership differences are large (0.24 for state and 0.40 for foreign), and they are precisely estimated. The next column adds standard worker characteristics—education, experience, and gender—to construct a Mincer earnings function, but with little qualitative change in the results: a slight decline in the estimated foreign coefficient and somewhat larger decline for state ownership (to 0.39 and 0.20, respectively). The small difference between the unconditional estimates and those controlling for worker characteristics is somewhat surprising given that worker characteristics are highly correlated with both wages and ownership, as we documented in the previous section.[19]

Adding firm-specific intercepts, however, greatly diminishes the magnitude of both coefficients, while hardly affecting the estimated wage structure by worker characteristics. The state coefficient estimate is 0.07 and the foreign is 0.14. Further adding firm-specific trends increases slightly the state effect, but halves the foreign coefficient. Both coefficients in the FE&FT specification have similar standard errors to those in the other specifications, so the issue is not one of precision. Evidently, the estimates are not at all robust to these controls for selection bias into ownership type. The hypothesis that the state and foreign effects are equal is rejected in OLS and FE specifications, but not in the FE&FT, where the point estimates (0.078 for state and 0.073 for foreign) are strikingly similar.

Table 7.8 provides additional estimates that include controls for occupational group of the worker. The estimated coefficients on worker characteristics are somewhat affected by these variables, but they matter little for the estimated impacts of state and foreign ownership. At the same time, the ownership coefficients are highly sensitive to the controls for selection bias, but the worker characteristic coefficients are not. The wage structure by worker characteristics that we described in the previous section appears not to result from systematic sorting of workers across firms that pay different wage levels because any time-invariant firm heterogeneity in wage levels is controlled for in the FE specification, while any time-trending heterogeneity across firms is controlled for in the FE&FT.[20]

In table 7.9, we further exploit the nature of our data and control for firm characteristics (industry, size, and productivity) in addition to worker characteristics. The coefficient on log employment is highly significant and positive in OLS and FE, showing that wages increase by 0.5 percent for each 10 percent increase in the size of the OLS. This effect is only 0.2 percent in FE, and negative and insignificant when firm-specific trends are controlled for. The wage effect of average labor productivity is always highly significant and positive, with a magnitude of 0.11 in OLS, 0.07 in FE, and 0.035 in FE&FT.

Concerning the ownership type coefficients in table 7.9, including industry controls in the OLS specification decreases the state coefficient to 0.16

19. These results are little changed by adding interactions between education categories and experience, by estimating separately by gender, or by employing a number of other alternative approaches to estimating earnings functions.

20. A referee has pointed out that our use of the conventional log-linear specification may result in an understated foreign coefficient if log wage variability is higher in foreign firms. Our data, however, do not imply large differences in variance: the estimated variance of the residuals from the FE&FT specification in table 7.7 is 0.11 for state ownership, 0.12 for domestic private, and 0.14 for foreign firms. The coefficients on ownership are small and statistically insignificant in the FE and FE&FT specifications of regressions using squared residuals as the dependent variable.

Table 7.8   Estimated impacts of state and foreign ownership, with controls
             for occupation

	OLS	FE	FE&FT
State	0.208***	0.068***	0.079***
	(0.016)	(0.013)	(0.016)
Foreign	0.384***	0.139***	0.072***
	(0.014)	(0.015)	(0.013)
Skilled manual	0.219***	0.203***	0.203***
	(0.007)	(0.006)	(0.008)
Service	0.072***	0.111***	0.115***
	(0.022)	(0.019)	(0.023)
Skilled nonmanual	0.234***	0.212***	0.220***
	(0.012)	(0.009)	(0.011)
Assoc. professional	0.334***	0.307***	0.321***
	(0.017)	(0.013)	(0.015)
Professional	0.425***	0.393***	0.403***
	(0.011)	(0.008)	(0.009)
Manager	0.650***	0.685***	0.705***
	(0.010)	(0.010)	(0.012)
Firm-specific intercepts (FE)	no	yes	yes
Firm-specific trends (FT)	no	no	yes
R^2	0.462	0.676	0.442

Notes: No. of observations = 1,342,158. The specifications are the same as in Table 7.7 except for the addition of occupational categories. Unskilled manual is the omitted occupation. All equations include year and region fixed effects. The regressions are weighted by the numbers of blue-collar and white-collar workers within each firm, and each firm is weighted using total employment by firm size category. Standard errors (corrected for firm clustering and for loss of degrees of freedom when detrending) are shown in parentheses. R^2: overall for OLS, within for FE and FE&FT. The difference between the foreign and state effect is statistically significant in OLS and FE, and insignificant in FE&FT.
***Significant at the 1 percent level.

and the foreign coefficient to 0.34. Further addition of labor productivity slightly increases the estimated state effect and further diminishes the estimated foreign effect. Controlling for employment size (but not productivity) has a large effect on the state coefficient (decreasing it to 0.07) but a smaller effect on the foreign coefficient (decreasing it to 0.28). These observable characteristics of firms thus account for more of the raw state-private gap than of the foreign differentials. By contrast, the FE and FE&FT estimates are unaffected by the addition of firm size or productivity.[21] Once we control for selection into ownership, these estimations show that inclusion of firm characteristics do not change the main results.

An important and somewhat neglected issue in analyzing the relationship between worker wages and firm characteristics such as ownership is the question of the appropriate unit of observation: the worker or the firm.

21. As firms rarely change industry in our data, we do not control for industry in the FE and FE&FT specifications.

Table 7.9   **Estimated impacts of state and foreign ownership, with firm-level controls**

	OLS			FE		FE&FT	
	1	2	3	1	2	1	2
State	0.156***	0.162***	0.069***	0.067***	0.063***	0.081***	0.079***
	(0.019)	(0.013)	(0.017)	(0.011)	(0.012)	(0.015)	(0.016)
Foreign	0.341***	0.269***	0.283***	0.126***	0.137***	0.071***	0.072***
	(0.014)	(0.013)	(0.015)	(0.014)	(0.015)	(0.013)	(0.013)
Labor productivity		0.108***		0.067***		0.035***	
		(0.009)		(0.004)		(0.007)	
Employment			0.050***		0.021***		–0.009
			(0.005)		(0.005)		(0.007)
Industry intercepts	yes	yes	yes	no	no	no	no
Firm-specific intercepts	no	no	no	yes	yes	yes	yes
Firm-specific trends	no	no	no	no	no	yes	yes
R^2	0.479	0.511	0.495	0.677	0.676	0.442	0.442

Notes: No. of observations = 1,342,158. The specifications are the same as in Table 7.8 except for the addition of firm-level controls. The regressions are weighted by the numbers of blue-collar and white-collar workers within each firm, and each firm is weighted using total employment by firm size category. Standard errors (corrected for firm clustering and for loss of degrees of freedom when detrending) are shown in parentheses. R^2: overall for OLS, within for FE and FE&FT. The difference between the foreign and state effect is statistically significant in OLS and FE, and insignificant in FE&FT.
***Significant at the 1 percent level.

Analyzing workers exploits the variation in wages among workers and allows their characteristics to be controlled for so that the composition of employment is held constant. Analyzing firms is appropriate because ownership is an attribute of the firm, and it may be advantageous if the firm-level wage is better measured than wages at the individual level. Table 7.10 presents a comparison of some alternative approaches along a number of dimensions: unit of observation (firm or worker), source of dependent variable (firm reports to the Tax Authority, average firm wage constructed from worker data, and individual worker data), and weights on workers when constructing firm-level average wages. The last row in table 7.10 reproduces our results from table 7.7 for comparison purposes. The other rows show the results of various changes in the specification and sample. Regardless of the choice of specification, the coefficients on state and foreign are always positive and statistically significant (except in one case), and the estimates are highly sensitive to the selection control method applied, similar to our previous results. The magnitude of the estimated effects, however, varies relatively little by the choice of unit of observation, wage measurement, controls for composition of workforce, and weighting.[22]

22. A similar issue about the appropriate level of observation arises in research on union wage differentials, as discussed by Pencavel (1991), who notes that the few establishment-level studies tend to find lower differentials than those based on individual data. See also DiNardo and Lee (2004), who find no union wage differential using firm-level data on union elections.

Table 7.10   **Firm-level versus worker-level estimates**

Dependent variable	Composition controls	Employment weights	State			Foreign		
			OLS	FE	FE&FT	OLS	FE	FE&FT
AW_F	no	no	0.237***	0.040***	0.030***	0.550***	0.093***	0.046***
AW_F	no	yes	0.222***	0.031	0.033	0.486***	0.186***	0.050
AW_F	yes	no	0.194***	0.039***	0.029***	0.486***	0.091***	0.045***
AW_F	yes	yes	0.136***	0.029	0.032	0.399***	0.176***	0.048
AW_I	no	no	0.233***	0.073***	0.159***	0.527***	0.091***	0.082***
AW_I	no	yes	0.278***	0.065***	0.102***	0.471***	0.168***	0.085***
AW_I	yes	no	0.182***	0.069***	0.149***	0.468***	0.082***	0.070***
AW_I	yes	yes	0.198***	0.063***	0.101***	0.396***	0.141***	0.078***
W_I	n.a.	n.a.	0.197***	0.065***	0.078***	0.386***	0.137***	0.073***

Notes: These are regression coefficients (standard errors clustered on firms) for alternative specifications in which the unit of observation is the firm in the first eight and the worker in the last row (which is the reproduction of the coefficients in Table 7.7), the log wage dependent variable is taken from firm financial reports or the worker survey, region and year controls are added, the methods of estimation are OLS, FE (firm fixed effects), and FE&FT (firm-specific intercepts and trends). AW_F = average wage constructed from firm-level data (wage bill/number of employees); AW_I = average wage constructed from individual wages, weighted by production and nonproduction worker weights; W_I = individual wages. Composition controls are the proportion of females, proportion of workers in different educational groups, average potential experience and its square, weighted by the number of blue- and white-collar workers. All regressions are weighted by firm weights, those where "employment weights" are indicated are in addition weighted by the number of workers. The last row reproduces the results from Table 7.7, for comparison purposes. n.a. = not applicable.
***Significant at the 1 percent level.

Because the FE and FE&FT specifications produce such different results from the OLS, it is useful to carry out some specification tests. First, we assess the joint statistical significance of the fixed effects, and then, conditional on including the fixed effects, of the firm-specific trends. The F-tests in each case reject the exclusion of the FE and the FT at significance levels of 0.0001. Next, we carry out Hausman tests of the vector of coefficients of the FE model relative to the OLS, and of the FE&FT relative to the FE. Again, these chi-square tests reject the restricted model in each case.

7.5   Conclusion

Do foreign-owned and state-owned organizations pay higher wages than domestic private firms? Economists have devoted considerable attention to estimating these wage differentials, usually finding positive foreign and state (public) premiums. But the existing research suffers from profound difficul-

---

Although there has been much more research on union than ownership wage differentials, apparently no study of unions uses linked employer-employee data to investigate such differences.

ties. In the foreign-ownership literature, estimates are usually identified from cross-sectional variation across firms of different types. Few studies use worker-level data on wages and characteristics, so they cannot control for observable worker heterogeneity, and still fewer analyze firms that change ownership type, so they cannot control for unobserved firm-level heterogeneity. In research on state-private differentials, usually referred to as the literature on the public-sector wage premium, estimation is typically at the worker level, and sometimes identification uses worker switching across organizations. But the state and private organizations in these studies typically operate in very different industries, so that the estimation essentially concerns interindustry differentials, which may be conflated with differences in work conditions and other unobservables. In both cases, there is reason to doubt that the causal effect of ownership has been identified.

In this paper, we have analyzed linked employer-employee data available for a long panel of firms during the unusual context of economic transition in Hungary, and we have applied new econometric methods that exploit the context and data to try to make progress on estimating foreign and state ownership wage differentials. The data cover nearly every tax-paying entity of at least twenty employees in Hungary from 1986 to 2003, and they include many more switches of ownership type than in previous research: nearly 1,000 involving foreign firms and nearly 3,500 involving state-owned organizations. The employee side of the data enables us to measure individual worker wages (rather than rely on a firm-level average as in some previous research) and to control for individual worker characteristics and changes in the composition of employment that may be correlated with ownership. The employer side of the data allows us to measure ownership reliably and to control for firm characteristics, and the longitudinal linking of employers facilitates some controls for selection bias into ownership type.

We find that simple OLS models imply substantial ownership effects in our data: an approximately 0.39 premium for working in a foreign-owned firm compared to a domestic private company, and a 0.20 premium for state enterprise employees versus those under domestic private ownership. These results control for other worker characteristics, including gender and experience, and for region and year fixed effects, but they assume no biased selection into ownership types, consistent with much of the literature.

We also estimate models that control for selection based on unobserved heterogeneity through firm fixed effects and firm-specific trend growth in wages. The latter specifications (usually referred to as "random trend models") permit not only idiosyncratic wages at each firm (as in the fixed effects model) but also allow wages to evolve independently at each firm in a way that is correlated with ownership and with worker characteristics. For example, they permit compensating differentials due to fringe benefits or other work conditions not only to vary across firms as a fixed fraction of total compensation, but also to evolve over time according to an idiosyncratic trend for each firm.

Our results imply statistically significant wage premiums under both state and foreign ownership, relative to domestic private. The estimated magnitudes of the differentials vary little with controls for observable worker and firm characteristics, and there is relatively little variation with the unit of observation (firm or worker). But the magnitudes vary considerably with the controls for unobserved firm heterogeneity. We find that inclusion of firm fixed effects more than halves the state-domestic and foreign-domestic wage differential implied by the OLS estimates and that inclusion of firm-specific trends further reduces the estimates. While we find significant differences of both state and foreign wages relative to domestic private, it is striking that these differentials are quite similar in magnitude, particularly when we add firm fixed effects, and even more so with firm-specific trends. Taken at face value, this last specification implies there may be no difference in the wage behavior of foreign-owned and state-owned firms.

The large variation in estimated coefficients across specifications with different controls for unobserved firm heterogeneity motivates us to carry out specification tests. F-tests on the firm fixed effects and firm-specific trends are always highly significant, and Hausman tests reject the more parsimonious models in each case. These results imply that the fixed effects specification is strongly preferred to the OLS, and the specification with trends to the one without trends.

The results also carry implications for the nature of systematic selection of organizations into ownership types. The finding that the OLS estimate of the foreign premium is reduced substantially when firm fixed effects and trends are added suggests that foreign investors may systematically acquire firms already paying relatively high and more quickly growing wages. The estimated state-private premium also falls with these controls, but it is smaller under OLS, implying a similar direction of selection bias but one that is smaller in magnitude compared to foreign ownership. For domestic private firms, on the other hand, the estimates imply selection of firms with relatively low and more slowly growing wages. More broadly, the results demonstrate that taking into account possible selection biases of firms into different ownership types can be essential for estimating differences in their behavior.

References

Aitken, Brian, Ann Harrison, and Robert E. Lipsey. 1996. Wages and foreign ownership: A comparative Study of Mexico, Venezuela and the United States. *Journal of International Economics* 40 (3–4): 345–71.

Almeida, Rita. 2003. The effects of foreign owned firms on the labor market. IZA Discussion Paper no. 785. Bonn, Germany: Institute for the Study of Labor.

Arellano, Manuel. 1987. Computing robust standard errors for within-groups estimators. *Oxford Bulletin of Economics and Statistics* 49 (4): 431–34.

Ashenfelter, Orley, and David Card. 1985. Using the longitudinal structure of earnings to estimate the effect of training programs. *Review of Economics and Statistics* 67 (4): 648–60.

Birdsall, Nancy, and John Nellis. 2003. Winners and losers: Assessing the distributional impact of privatization. *World Development* 31 (1): 1617–33.

Brainerd, Elizabeth. 2002. Five years after: The impact of mass privatization on wages in Russia, 1993–1998. *Journal of Comparative Economics* 30 (1): 160–90.

Brown, J. David, John S. Earle, and Álmos Telegdy. 2005. Does privatization hurt workers? Evidence from comprehensive manufacturing firm panel data in Hungary, Romania, Russia, and Ukraine. Upjohn Institute, Working Paper.

———. 2006. The productivity effects of privatization: Longitudinal estimates from Hungary, Romania, Russia, and Ukraine. *Journal of Political Economy* 114 (1): 61–99.

Commander, Simon, and Fabrizio Coricelli, eds. 1995. *Unemployment, restructuring, and the labor market in Eastern Europe and Russia.* Washington, DC: World Bank.

Conyon, Martin J., Sourafel Girma, Steve Thompson, and Peter W. Wright. 2002. The productivity and wage effects of foreign acquisitions in the United Kingdom. *Journal of Industrial Economics* 50 (1): 85–102.

DiNardo, John, and David Lee. 2004. Economic impacts of new unionization on U.S. private sector employers: 1984–2001. *Quarterly Journal of Economics* 119 (4): 1383–1442.

Djankov, Simeon, and Peter Murrell. 2002. Enterprise restructuring in transition: A quantitative survey. *Journal of Economic Literature* 40 (3): 739–92.

Earle, John S., Csaba Kucsera, and Álmos Telegdy. 2005. Ownership concentration and corporate performance on the Budapest stock exchange: Do too many cooks spoil the goulash? *Corporate Governance* 13 (2): 254–64.

Feliciano, Zadia, and Robert E. Lipsey. 1999. Foreign ownership and wages in the United States. NBER Working Paper no. 6923. Cambridge, MA: National Bureau of Economic Research, February.

Frydman, Roman, Andrzej Rapaczynski, and John S. Earle, eds. 1993. *The privatization process in Central Europe.* Budapest: Central European University Press.

Gokhale, Jagadeesh, Erica L. Groshen, and David Neumark. 1995. Do hostile takeovers reduce extramarginal wage payments? *Review of Economics and Statistics* 77 (3): 470–85.

Gregory, Robert G., and Jeff Borland. 1999. Recent developments in public sector labor markets. In *Handbook of labor economics.* Vol. 3C, ed. Orley Ashenfelter and David Card, 3573–3630. Amsterdam: North-Holland.

Hanley, Eric, Lawrence King, and Istvan Janos Toth. 2002. The state, international agencies and property transformation in post-communist Hungary. *American Journal of Sociology* 108 (1): 129–67.

Haskel, Jonathan, and Stefan Szymanski. 1993. Privatization, liberalization, wages and employment: Theory and evidence for the UK. *Economica* 60 (238): 161–82.

Heckman, James J., and V. Joseph Hotz. 1989. Choosing among alternative nonexperimental methods for estimating the impact of social programs: The case of manpower training. *Journal of the American Statistical Association* 84 (408): 862–74.

Jacobson, Louis, Robert LaLonde, and Daniel G. Sullivan. 1993. Earnings losses of displaced workers. *American Economic Review* 83 (4): 685–709.

————. 2005. Estimating the returns to community college schooling for displaced workers. *Journal of Econometrics* 125 (1–2): 271–304.

Kézdi, Gabor. 2003. Robust standard error estimation in fixed-effects panel models. Central European University. Mimeograph.

Kikeri, Sunita. 1998. Privatization and labor: What happens to workers when governments divest. World Bank Technical Paper no. 396. Washington, DC: World Bank.

Kornai, Janos. 1992. *The socialist system: The political economy of communism.* Princeton, NJ: Princeton University Press.

Krueger, Alan B., and Lawrence Summers. 1988. Efficiency wages and the inter-industry wage structure. *Econometrica* 56 (2): 259–93.

La Porta, Rafael, and Florencio Lopez-de-Silanes. 1999. The benefits of privatization: Evidence from Mexico. *Quarterly Journal of Economics* 114 (4): 1193–1242.

Lichtenberg, Frank R., and Donald Siegel. 1990. The effect of ownership changes on the employment and wages of central office and other personnel. *Journal of Law and Economics* 33 (2): 383–408.

Lipsey, Robert E., and Fredrik Sjöholm. 2004. Foreign direct investment, education and wages in Indonesian manufacturing. *Journal of Development Economics* 73 (1): 415–22.

Martin, Stephen, and David Parker. 1997. *The impact of privatization. Ownership and the corporate performance in the UK.* London: Routledge.

Martins, Pedro. 2004. Do foreign firms really pay higher wages? Evidence from different estimators. IZA Discussion Paper no. 1388. Bonn, Germany: Institute for the Study of Labor.

McGuckin, Robert H., and Sang V. Nguyen. 2001. The impact of ownership changes: A view from labor markets. *International Journal of Industrial Organization* 19 (5): 739–62.

Megginson, William L., and Jeffry M. Netter. 2001. From state to market: A survey of empirical studies on privatization. *Journal of Economic Literature* 39 (2): 321–89.

Pencavel, John. 1991. *Labor markets under trade unionism: Employment, wages, and hours.* Cambridge, MA: Basil Blackwell.

Peoples, James, and Hekmat, Ali. 1998. The effect of foreign acquisition activity on U.S. union wage premiums. *International Journal of Manpower* 19 (8): 603–18.

Szakadat, Laszlo. 1993. Property rights in a socialist economy: The case of Hungary. In *Privatization in the transition to a market economy: Studies of preconditions and policies in Eastern Europe,* ed. John S. Earle, Roman Frydman, and Andrzej Rapaczynski, 17–45. London: Pinter.

Voszka, Eva. 1993. Spontaneous privatization in Hungary. In *Privatization in the transition to a market economy: Studies of preconditions and policies in Eastern Europe,* ed. John S. Earle, Roman Frydman, and Andrzej Rapaczynski, 89–107. London: Pinter.

World Bank. 2005. *Enhancing job opportunities in Eastern Europe and the former Soviet Union.* Washington, DC: World Bank.

Insider Privatization and Careers
A Study of a Russian Firm in Transition

Guido Friebel and Elena Panova

8.1 Introduction

How do firms adjust their personnel policies and internal structure to changes in their economic and institutional environment? Chandler (1977) has investigated how firms in the last century reacted to challenges posed by new technologies and by market demands by developing professional management, the line/staff, and later the multidivisional organization. Doeringer and Piore (1971) have documented how and why firms created internal labor markets to protect their workers from market shocks and to provide them with incentives to invest in firm-specific human capital. Following Carter and Carter (1985), Lazear (1992), and Baker, Gibbs, and Holmström (1994), a literature has emerged that investigates the personnel files of single firms over a long period of time to learn more about their internal labor markets.[1] One main finding is that a firm's organizational structure and career paths remain remarkably stable, even in turbulent times.

Guido Friebel is a researcher at the Institute of Industrial Economics (IDEI) and a lecturer at EHESS, the French School for Advanced Studies in Social Sciences, both at the University of Toulouse, and is affiliated with the Centre for Economic Policy Research (CEPR). Elena Panova is an assistant professor of economics at the University of Quebec at Montreal.

We would like to thank the editor, Julia Lane, and two referees. We are also grateful to Erik Berglöf, Anders Björklund, Peter Gottschalk, Joep Konings, Margaret Meyer, Marc-Andreas Muendler, Åsa Rosén, Kathy Terrell, and seminar participants at the CAFE conference in Nuremberg, Boston College, LICOS Leuven, London Business School, SITE (Stockholm School of Economics), SOFI (Stockholm University), University of Michigan, and the University of Toulouse. We are grateful for the support of SITE. All errors are ours.

1. A non-exhaustive list includes Ariga, Ohkusa, and Brunello (1999), Dohmen (2004) and Dohmen, Kriechel, and Pfann (2004), Ichino and Maggi (1999), Seltzer and Merret (2000), and Treble et al. (2001).

In this chapter, we investigate how Russian transition from a centrally planned to a market economy has affected human resource policies of a heavy-industry firm. We use a personnel data set that covers a total of 1,538 white-collar workers over up to seventeen years: from 1984 to 2000. We find that from 1984 to 1991 (hereafter, in Soviet times), the firm featured stable patterns of upward mobility that look quite similar to the career paths in Western firms. From the year 1992, when Gaidar's reforms began, to 2000 (hereafter, during the transition), these career paths seem blocked. We identify the reason for this observation: in all tiers of the firm's hierarchy except for the lowest one, both (a) more managers are hired from the outside market, and (b) fewer managers leave the firm. As a result, the firm becomes toploaded, and promotions are blocked.

What is more difficult is to identify the rationale behind such a firm strategy. We hypothesize that this strategy may be constrained optimal in the Russian environment. Here, outsiders receive notoriously weak protection for their property rights (see, for instance, Woodruff 2004). The privatization law provided insiders with favors through the so-called option 2 of the Russian voucher privatization. Hence, in 1993, incumbent managers effectively became the owners. The inside owners had the opportunity to hire managers with higher human capital than themselves,[2] most probably because skilled employees were leaving less successful enterprises.[3] The manager-owners decided both (a) to take advantage of this opportunity, and (b) to stay in the firm (in order to enforce their property rights).[4] Consequently, career paths are blocked and the firm forgoes the benefit of using careers as a device for providing effort incentives and screening workers.[5]

The remainder of the chapter is organized as follows. Section 8.2 describes the ownership structure, output performance, and employment policies from the firm-level perspective. Section 8.3 uses the personnel data to compare human resource policies in Soviet times and during the transition. The last Section summarizes and discusses the main insights.

8.2 The Firm and Its Environment

The firm we investigate is one of the largest enterprises in the machinery industry in Russia. It was established in 1949. Prior to transition, it was one

2. Managers hired after 1992 have been both more experienced and better educated than incumbents working on the same level.

3. Between 1996 and 1999, industrial employment in the region where the firm that we study is located has decreased by 9 percent. In the same period, the employment in the firm has decreased by only 6 percent.

4. Potentially, the newly hired managers could take over control of the firm. However, once again, the weak enforcement of outsider ownership rights constitutes an obstacle, as banks are not willing to provide credit for acquisition of the firm's shares.

5. Career prospects are among the most important instruments for encouraging employees to invest in firm-specific human capital (see Gibbons and Waldman 1999). Also, promotions signal the quality of employees, helping thereby to better allocate them among tasks (see Waldman 1984; Sattinger 1993).

of the leading companies in the industry and was awarded a number of distinctions. This section uses firm-level data[6] to describe how the firm was evolving in a changing institutional environment.

8.2.1   Ownership Structure

In March 1993, the firm was privatized through the so-called option 2 of the Russian voucher privatization, which provided privileges to insider workers and managers in acquiring shares. Since then, it has been a joint stock company. The annual report for 1997 indicates about 92 percent individual ownership. A total of 53.4 percent of the firm is owned by insiders. Neither municipality nor the regional government own shares, and there is no foreign capital. We have no information about the distribution of shareholdings. However, according to our interviews with managers in the firm, nonmanagerial employees delegate their votes to the manager of their department.

8.2.2   Output Performance

We do not have access to good measures of profitability. Looking at output gives, however, a good idea of the restructuring process the firm went through. In 1987 there was a first output decline when the firm had to cope with Gorbachev's perestroyka. Decentralization of decisionmaking power damaged some of the traditional supply channels and affected demand. There is thus a steep drop in output from the beginning of Gaidar's reforms in 1992 onward, which is typical for these years—in particular, for heavy industry. From 1997, there was a positive tendency, and in 1999, the enterprise won an important contract to supply equipment to India.

At different points in time, the firm experimented with new product lines—for instance, tailor-made instruments. From late 1980s until the late 90s it has also been producing consumer goods (plastic chairs and tables). However, figure 8.1 shows that there is a high correlation between the firm's output and its specialization in the core business—the production of heavy machinery items. The fact that the firm operates in a specialized market with high fixed costs and high entry barriers may explain why the firm survived transition relatively well.

8.2.3   Employment Policies, Aggregate (Firm-Level) Perspective

Between 1988 and 1997, industrial employment—that is, the number of workers employed in the core operations of the firm,[7] has steadily declined.

---

6. Unfortunately, we have no individual-level information about blue-collar workers, except for those who at some stage in their career moved into white-collar or managerial positions. However, we have firm-level information about the employment and wages by both blue-collar and white-collar employees.

7. Similar to many other large industrial firms in Russia, the firm that we study had a large number of employees in nonindustrial activities such as restaurants, hospitals, kindergartens, and housing. These individuals are out of our consideration.

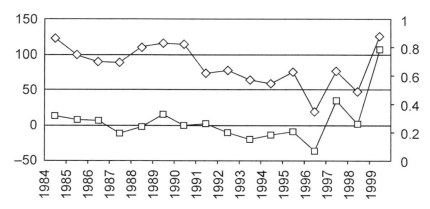

─□─ Real Output Growth (in percentage compared to previous year) - primary axis

─◇─ Share of five main items

Fig. 8.1   Output and specialization

Indeed, it fell from 4,813 in 1998 to 3,206 in 1998. Unfortunately, we cannot distinguish between an involuntary dismissal and a voluntary quit: it is a tradition in Russia to label any separation as a "quit" so as to avoid subsequent stigmatization of a worker.

During transition, employment becomes more sensitive to output changes. However, it reacts with a lag. The most important wave of separations occurred in 1997, the first year of transition in which the firm's real output has grown. Interestingly, that wave of separations followed the top manager's dismissal, initiated by the employees: an evidence of an active stance by new owners in the firm.

Furthermore, during transition, an increasing share of the total wage bill (including wage arrears and in-kind payments) was allocated to white-collar workers, and the ratio between white-collar and blue-collar workers increased. Notice that this implies that more and more blue collars leave the firm (recall that industrial employment has steadily declined).[8] Hence, the firm's defensive (cost-cutting) restructuring has mainly affected its blue-collar workers.[9]

8. By the end of nineties, however, blue collars are more and more demanded by enterprises located in the same region as the firm that we study: the ratio of white-collar to blue-collar vacancies in the region has decreased from 0.59 in 1996 to 0.2 in 2000.

9. Following Grosfeld and Roland (1997), we distinguish between defensive and strategic restructuring. For a model on defensive and strategic restructuring of insider-privatized firms, see Debande and Friebel (2004).

8.3 Personnel Policies of the Firm

8.3.1 Personnel Data

In order to better understand how transition has affected the firm's hiring and promotion policies,[10] we investigate seventeen years (1984–2000) of personnel files of 1,538 white-collar workers of the firm.

We use the raw data from the human resource department. An employee's personnel file contains the date of accession, the date of separation, dates of movements across job titles, and an occupational code for each position defined by Goskomstat, the statistical office of Russia. We also know whether, in a given moment in time, an individual works in production and engineering or in administration (sales, planning, accounting).

Moreover, we know the following personal characteristics: age, work experience, education (years of schooling), gender, party and trade union membership, ethnicity, marital status, number of children, place of birth, place of university education, and field of study. We also know some of the job history of an individual: military service, date of leaving previous job, last employer. Unfortunately, we do not have access to information about individual wages.

8.3.2 Hierarchy and Career Paths

As in other related work (for instance, Baker, Gibbs, and Holmström 1994), human resources, as measured by "persondays per title,"[11] are concentrated on few job titles.[12] In our case, twelve job titles represent about 90 percent of core white-collar staff. We thus focus on these job titles. They are located on five levels of the firm's hierarchy (see table 8.1):[13] On

---

10. Although we find more downward mobility than in other related work (there were 120 demotions in Soviet times, and 97 during the transition), we have not studied its determinants. The reason is that results could be difficult to interpret. Indeed, according to our interviews with human resource departments, demotions are typically used as an employment insurance, in cases when (a) an employee reaches a retirement age, or (b) he or she becomes unable to fulfill his or her duties for health reasons, or (c) he or she receives a primary job outside the firm—for instance, in an informal sector.

11. For any given individual, we know (a) the date of accession into the firm, and the accession job title (b), and the duration of stay on a given job title. For each job title, we can then add up the persondays over individuals. These persondays per title can be expressed as a ratio of the total human resources in the firm.

12. Of course, each job title contains a variety of specifications, as described by Goskomstat's 5-digit code. However, we have pooled down most of that variety, making a distinction between employment in production and in administration.

13. We have carried out a similar exercise as the one by Baker, Gibbs, and Holmström (1994). They looked at the flows of human resources between different job titles. They established the lowest level of the hierarchy, mostly filled by workers hired on the outside market. Afterward, they determined level 2 by looking at "where do employees mostly move from level 1." They proceeded in the same way up to the top of the hierarchy (the general manager). Carrying out this procedure, we generated a hierarchy that was identical to the one we later received from the human resource department of the firm.

Table 8.1   Allocation of human resources across jobs

Job title	Percentage of person days before 1992	Percentage of person days after 1992
Level 5		
Top management	3	4
Level 4		
Head of production department	3	5
Head of department	2	2
Level 3		
Supervisor	1	2
Head of bureau	8	9
Level 2		
Engineer	43	38
Foreman	15	17
Planning engineer	4	5
Economist	3	5
Level 1		
Technician	5	2
Accountant	2	4
Planning technician	1	2

level 1: technician, planning technician, and accountant; on level 2: economist, planning engineer, engineer working in production unit, and foreman (a managerial position in production);[14] on level 3: head of bureau, responsible for a nonproduction unit, and supervisor of a production unit; on level 4: head of production and head of nonproduction departments; on level 5: top manager.

Comparing the two columns of table 8.1, we see that during transition, the firm has shifted employees from production-oriented job titles (technician, engineer) to job titles that are related to business administration and development (accountant, economist, planning technician, and planning engineer). Moreover, it has reallocated human resources toward four managerial jobs (supervisor of production unit, head of production department, head of nonproduction department, and top manager).

To find patterns of internal mobility, we compute a transition matrix that captures accessions to and separations from the firm, and movements across job titles for the whole time interval. We find that in the Soviet era, the firm maintained career paths, some of them leading to the very top of the company (these paths are depicted by arrows;[15] see figure 8.2). The numbers represent the probability of transition of a person from one job

14. Becoming a foreman is a typical promotion for a blue-collar worker.
15. We here plot links between job titles that have a transition probability of at least 5 percent.

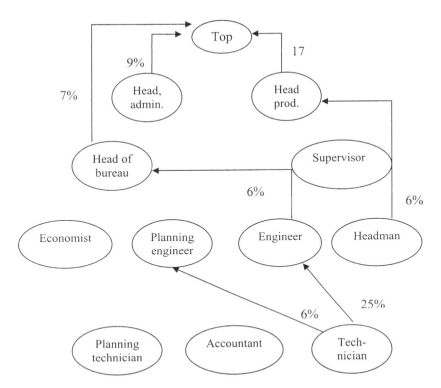

Fig. 8.2   Mobility during Soviet times

title to the job title the arrow points to. This picture is very similar to the one that Baker, Gibbs, and Holmström (1994) find. (See also figure 8.3.)

In Soviet times, employment and upward mobility were distorted by political influence. Hence, career paths may have served both efficiency and political goals. Nonetheless, there is some evidence that firms used promotions as the main instrument to incentivise, and, in particular, to retain their workers (see Kornai 1992). The main difference between Soviet and western firms is not so much the use of promotions, but rather the fact that in Soviet firms, promotions provided access to additional fringe benefits rather than substantial wage increases.

Transition changes the firm's promotion policies. Indeed, it becomes more or less impossible to move upward beyond level 2 (see table 8.2). The reason is that the previously existing career paths are blocked by increased hiring activity from the outside labor market to the upper levels of the hierarchy (see figure 8.2).[16] Managers recruited above the second level are

16. These policies may be optimal response from a constrained efficiency perspective. We thank Marc-Andreas Muendler for his discussion of this point.

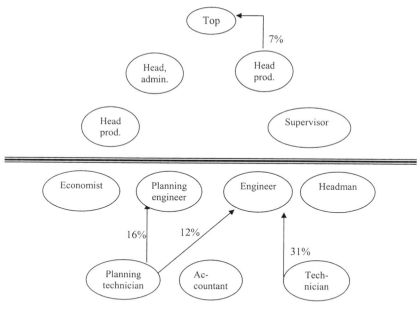

Fig. 8.3 Mobility in transition

Table 8.2   **Schooling and work experience, incumbents versus new hires**

	Level			
	2	3	4	5
Years of schooling				
1984–1991	14.24	14.40	14.33	15.66
Hired from the outside	14.73	15.08	14.70	16.00
Incumbents	13.50	14.29	14.26	15.62
1992–2000	14.26	14.32	14.53	15.79
Hired from the outside	14.62	15.47	14.93	16.00
Incumbents	13.38	13.90	14.19	15.55
Work experience				
1984–1991	11.58	19.51	18.54	20.96
Hired from the outside	8.31	21.17	15.10	22.67
Incumbents	16.56	19.24	19.18	20.76
1992–2000	14.00	21.77	18.77	21.67
Hired from the outside	12.48	22.26	20.63	23.46
Incumbents	17.67	21.59	17.21	19.55

Table 8.3   **Staffing from outside and from within (numbers in parentheses are promotions)**

	Level			
	2	3	4	5
Accession to a level	1 (895)	1 (155)	1 (118)	1 (53)
1984–1991	0.55	0.55	0.52	0.55
1992–2000	0.45	0.45	0.48	0.46
Hired from outside	0.74	0.20	0.31	0.30
1984–1991	0.37	0.08	0.08	0.06
1992–2000	0.37	0.12	0.23	0.25
Promoted	0.26	0.80	0.69	0.70
1984–1991	0.14	0.48	0.43	0.49
1992–2000	0.11	0.32	0.25	0.21

better educated and more experienced as compared both to the incumbents, and to those managers who were recruited on the same level in Soviet times (see table 8.2).

8.3.3   Hazard Rates of Promotions and Exits

In order to better understand how transition has affected labor mobility inside the firm, we consider separately two time intervals: 1984–1992 and 1992–2000. For each of them, we carry out a duration analysis on two events: (1) a promotion, that is, a move from a lower to a higher level of the hierarchy, and (2) a separation from the firm.[17] (See table 8.3.)

We first consider promotions. The data are translated into the survival time form. We observe an individual at the beginning of a time interval (controlling for the exact date of the recruitment). To adjust time-varying variables (such as age), we make at least one record in three years. We document the time spans (the "survival time") until a promotion.[18] After each promotion, the survival time is reset to 0.[19]

We use an accelerated failure-time model, in which the natural logarithm of the survival time is assumed to be linearly dependent on covariates:[20]

$$\ln(t_j) = x_j\beta + \varepsilon$$

where x_j is a covariate vector, β is a vector of regression coefficients, and ε is an error term with density $f(\cdot)$. As covariates, we pick three basic indi-

17. We use the terms of duration analysis from labor economics (Van den Berg 2001).

18. Because there is always a record at the exact date of a promotion, the time interval between two records can be shorter than three years.

19. Our data set contains repeated records of the same individuals. Hence, the assumption of independent observations may not be adequate. Therefore, we use a robust estimate of variance, controlling for identity.

20. A statistical test based on the distribution of Schoenfeld residuals rejected the Cox proportional-hazard model.

vidual characteristics: *age* and *education* (to measure human capital),[21] and gender.[22] We assume that the density of the error term follows a generalized Gamma model[23]:

$$
f(t) = \left\{ \frac{|\kappa|}{\Gamma(\kappa^{-2})} (\kappa^{-2})^{\kappa^{-2}} \exp\left(\kappa^{-2} \left\{ \kappa \frac{\ln(t) - x_j\beta}{\sigma} - \exp\left[\kappa \frac{\ln(t) - x\beta}{\sigma} \right] \right\} \right),
$$

$$
\text{if } \kappa \neq 0;
$$

$$
\frac{1}{\sqrt{2\pi}} \exp\left\{ -\frac{[\ln(t) - x\beta]^2}{2\sigma^2} \right\}, \text{ if } \kappa = 0,
$$

where κ and σ are ancillary parameters to be estimated from the data (see Kalbfleish and Prentice 1980).

We find that in Soviet times, being younger, male, and having a better education was helpful for a promotion. In contrast, during transition, age and education variables are no longer statistically significant (see table 8.4). More importantly, in Soviet times an employee could increase his or her probability to receive a promotion by simply staying in the firm. During the transition, however, only the first few years of waiting for a promotion increased the probability of this event: waiting longer would actually *decrease* the probability of moving up the firm's hierarchy (see figure 8.4).[24]

We proceed in a similar way for separations. We again use a generalized Gamma model with controlling variables: age, education, gender, and level in the hierarchy. The most important result is that despite worsening career perspectives during transition, workers are less likely to leave the firm (see table 8.5), especially from the upper levels of the hierarchy.[25]

21. Age is highly correlated with work experience.

22. We have added to the set of covariates the following individual characteristics: number of children, dummy for being born in the region, dummy for employment in production division of the firm at some point of the career, and party membership. It turned out that none are statistically significant, even though we were adding them to the set of three basic covariates one by one (indeed, party membership was significant at a 15 percent level in Soviet times, and became insignificant during transition). At the same time, age, education, and gender remained significant, with the same sign in all regressions. We have not tried to use labor union membership as a regressor, because there is too little variation in the data: until the year 2000, the firm remains highly (more than 80 percent) unionized.

23. We used the Akaike Information Criterion to select the generalized gamma form among Exponential, Weibull, Lognormal, Log-logistic, and generalized Gamma distributions. Moreover, the Wald likelihood ratio test has rejected the hypothesis of a Weibull distribution $\kappa = 1$. Hence, we have not imposed any restrictions on the highly flexible baseline hazard function of the generalized Gamma distribution.

24. Notice also, that the incidence of promotion during the transition is only 64, as compared to 150 in Soviet times (the number of individuals in the two periods is more or less the same).

25. There were only 316 separations during transition, as compared to 609 in Soviet times.

Table 8.4   **Promotion regressions**

	1984 to 1991		1992 to 2000	
	σ| *coefficient	Robust standard error	σ *coefficient	Robust standard error
Years of schooling	0.05**	0.01	−0.08	0.05
Dummy for sex (1 = male)	0.96**	0.012	0.92**	0.43
Age in years	−0.03**	0.01	0.02	0.01
Constant	−3.24**	0.029	−2.12*	1.19
$\ln_\sigma$	0.67**	0.10	0.549	0.16
κ|	−0.76**	0.18	−3.30	1.14
σ|	−0.51	0.05	1.73	0.28
Number of observations	3510		3148	
Number of promotions	158		64	
Number of individuals	1088		991	
Time at risk	5120.13		4959.95	
Log likelihood	−213.83		−195.44	
Wald χ^2	173.49		19.86	
Probability χ^2	0.000		0.000	

Note: *Significantly different from zero at the 10 percent level.
**Significantly different from zero at the 5 percent level.

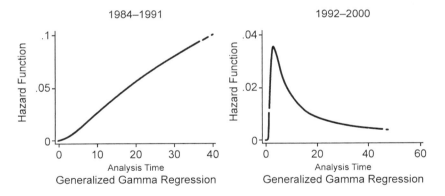

Fig. 8.4   Baseline promotion hazards, Soviet times versus transition

8.4   Concluding Discussion

We have investigated how transition, a particularly drastic process of institutional and structural change, has affected the personnel policies of a Russian firm. A sizeable literature on enterprise restructuring in transition measures the impact of privatization, the hardening of budget constraints, increasing competition, and price liberalization on enterprise performance

Table 8.5   Separation regressions

	1984 to 1991		1992 to 2000	
	σ *coefficient	Robust standard error	σ| *coefficient	Robust standard error
Years of schooling	0.06*	0.01	0.03	0.05
Dummy for sex (1 = male)	0.53*	0.012	0.97*	0.21
Age in years	0.01	0.01	−0.01	0.01
Level in the hierarchy	0.10*	0.05	−0.26**	0.11
Constant	−1.49*	0.39	−1.8**	0.79
$\ln_\sigma$	0.65*	0.01	0.59*	0.01
κ|	1.70*	0.14	−0.19	0.15
σ	1.91	0.07	1.81	0.08
Number of observations	3510		3148	
Number of separations	609		316	
Number of individuals	1088		991	
Time at risk	5120.13		4959.95	
Log likelihood	−1600.03		−712.90	
Wald χ^2	37.73		26.17	
Probability χ^2	0.000		0.000	

Note: *Significantly different from zero at the 10 percent level.
**Significantly different from zero at the 5 percent level.

(see Djankov and Murrell 2002). Insider-privatized firms usually show little signs of restructuring, while firms that are privatized to outsiders, in particular to foreigners, are more likely to improve their performance. In order to learn more about the microchannels through which transition affects enterprise performance, we open the black box of a heavy industry firm.

The main changes after the reforms are as follows:

1. Employment becomes more responsive to output changes after privatization.

2. The wage bill is reallocated from blue to white collar.

3. Separations affect blue-collar workers whereas white collars, especially those working in the upper tiers of the hierarchy, are less likely to leave the firm than before the reforms.

4. The use of white-collar human resources is shifted from production to administrative and management activities.

5. More white-collar workers are hired from the outside labor market, in particular for higher levels of its hierarchy.

6. The firm becomes toploaded, and career paths are blocked.

We cannot judge to what extent all of these changes have been introduced with an aim to increase efficiency. The fact that the inside managers are residual claimants makes us believe, though, that the firm acts in a profit-maximizing way, taking the institutional framework as given. In general, firms are frequently limited in their capacity to maintain career paths and other elements of internal labor markets when their environment changes (Bertrand 2004). The specificity of our case is the notoriously weak protection of outsider property rights in Russia, which created strong incentives for the manager-owners to stay inside the firm. At the same time, the Russian labor market became thicker, making it possible to hire new workers and managers with higher human capital. Manager-owners seem to have made use of these recruitment opportunities, even at the expense of interrupting career paths altogether.

We cannot claim any generality for Russian firms, as we only had access to one data set. The case study opens, however, a new perspective on how corporate governance institutions shape the structure and human resource policies of firms, and we hope that it may provide food for thought for theoretical analyses.

References

Ariga, Kenn, Yasushi Ohkusa, and Giorgio Brunello. 1999. Fast track: Is it in the genes? The promotion policy of a large Japanese firm. *Journal of Economic Behavior and Organization* 38:385–402.

Baker, George, Michael Gibbs, and Bengt Holmström. 1994. The internal economics of the firm: Evidence from personnel data. *Quarterly Journal of Economics* 109:881–919.

Bertrand, Marianne. 2004. From the invisible handshake to the invisible hand? How import competition changes the employment relationship. *The Journal of Labor Economics* 22(4): 723–66.

Carter, Michael, and Susan Carter. 1985. Internal labor markets in retailing: The early years. *Industrial and Labor Relations Review* 38:586–98.

Chandler, Alfred D. 1977. *The visible hand: The managerial revolution in American business.* Cambridge, MA: Harvard University Press.

Debande, Olivier, and Guido Friebel. 2004. A positive theory of "give-away" privatization. *International Journal of Industrial Organization* 22(8):1309–25.

Djankov, Simeon, and Peter Murrell. 2002. Enterprise restructuring in transition: A quantitative survey. *Journal of Economic Literature* 40:739–92.

Doeringer, Peter, and Michael Piore. 1971. *Internal labor markets and manpower adjustment.* Lexington, MA: D.C. Heath.

Dohmen, Thomas. 2004. Performance, seniority and wages: Formal salary systems and individual earnings profiles. *Labour Economics* 11:741–63.

Dohmen, Thomas, Ben Kriechel, and Gerard A. Pfann. 2004. Monkey bars and ladders: The importance of lateral and vertical job mobility in internal labor market careers. *Journal of Population Economics* 17:193–228.

Gibbons, Robert, and Michael Waldman. 1999. Careers in organizations: Theory and evidence, in *Handbook of labor economics,* ed. Orley C. Ashenfelter and David Card, vol. 3B:2373–2437. Amsterdam: Elsevier Science.

Grosfeld, Irena, and Gerard Roland. 1997. Defensive and strategic restructuring in Central and Eastern European Enterprises. *Journal of Transforming Economies and Societies* 3:21–46.

Ichino, Andrea, and Giovanni Maggi. 1999. Work environment and individual background: Explaining regional shirking differentials in a large Italian firm. *Quarterly Journal of Economics* 115:1057–90.

Kalbfleish, J. D., and R. L. Prentice. 1980. *The statistical analysis of failure time data.* New York: Wiley.

Kornai, Janos. 1992. *The socialist system—The political economy of communism.* Princeton, NJ: Princeton University Press.

Lazear, Edward. 1992. The job as a concept. In *Performance measurement, evaluation, and incentives,* ed. William J. Bruns, 183–215. Boston: Harvard Business School Press.

———. 2000. Performance pay and productivity. *American Economic Review* 90:1346–61.

Sattinger, M. 1993. Assignment models of the distributional earnings. *Journal of Economic Literature* 31:831–80.

Seltzer, Andre, and David Merrett. 2000. Personnel policies at the Union Bank of Australia: Evidence from the 1888–1900 entry cohorts. *Journal of Labor Economics* 18:573–613.

Treble, John, Tim Barmby, Sarah Bridges, and Edwin van Gameren. 2001. The internal economics of the firm: Further evidence from personnel data. *Labour Economics* 8:531–52.

Van den Berg, Gerard. 2001. Duration models: Specification, identification, and multiple durations. In J. J. Heckman and E. Leamer, eds., *Handbook of econometrics,* Vol. 5. Amsterdam: North-Holland.

Waldman, M. 1984. Worker allocation, hierarchies and the wage distribution. *Review of Economic Studies* 51:95–109.

Woodruff, Chris. 2004. Property rights in context: Privatization's legacy for corporate legality in Poland and Russia. *Studies in Comparative International Development* 38:82–108.

4

Globalization, Trade,
and Labor Markets

9

Trade and Workforce Changeover in Brazil

Marc-Andreas Muendler

9.1 Introduction

Linked employer-employee data are uniquely suited to document labor-market responses to economic reform. While the formation of multinational enterprises shapes much of the globalization debate over labor-market consequences in industrialized countries (see chapter 10), an issue of foremost importance for developing countries is the labor-market impact of trade reform. The present chapter investigates Brazil's labor demand changes following its large-scale trade liberalization in the early 1990s. Measures of labor-demand change document that the workforce in Brazil's traded-goods sector simultaneously undergoes an occupation downgrading and an education upgrading. This workforce changeover is broadly consistent with Heckscher-Ohlin-style trade theory for a low-skill abundant economy, whose low-skill intensive activities are predicted to expand and absorb larger shares of skilled workers to maintain full employment. Tracking workers across their jobs within establishments, across establishments within industries, and across firm types and industries within Brazil's formal sector, documents how employers achieve the observed workforce changeover. The reallocation pattern is not what premises of classic trade theory imply: among the displaced workers with a successful reallocation, most shift to nontraded-output industries—but almost as

Marc-Andreas Muendler is an assistant professor of economics at the University of California, San Diego, and a faculty research fellow at the NBER.

I thank conference participants at CAFE 2006 in Nuremberg, and Lars Vilhuber and Julia Lane, in particular, for helpful suggestions. I thank Jennifer Poole for dedicated research assistance. I gratefully acknowledge financial support from the NSF under grant SES-0550699 and the Alfred P. Sloan Foundation.

many displaced workers do not find formal reemployment at an annual horizon.

The linked employer-employee data source is RAIS (Relação Anual de Informações Sociais), a comprehensive register of workers formally employed in any sector in Brazil (including the public sector). The database is used to administer Brazil's federal minimum-wage supplement program and is shared across statistical agencies. RAIS offers information on worker characteristics such as age, gender, education, and job characteristics, including the wage, dates of hiring and separation, and a detailed occupational classification that permits inferences about the skill level of jobs. In this chapter, attention is limited to prime-age workers past their first entry into the active labor force and to male workers, because male workers are known to exhibit relatively low labor-supply elasticities.[1] The data are complemented with firm-level information on export status and sector-level information on economic reforms.

Much emphasis in the literature on job creation and destruction is placed on *churning:* gross job creation and destruction at shrinking or expanding employers beyond their observed net employment changes. Churning is a particular aspect of the reallocation process and, from a worker's perspective, is mostly associated with the part of job spells that are not necessarily related to ultimate reallocations across activities. By definition, churning is an employer-level phenomenon. This chapter shifts the focus from the employer to the individual worker and documents several worker-related aspects of the reallocation process. The importance of churning and excess turnover in the reallocation process notwithstanding, a paramount efficiency concern for the performance of labor markets is the ultimate reassignment of workers to new activities.

Brazil exhibits a shift toward low-skill intensive economic activities following trade reform. For the least-skilled illiterate workers and primary school dropouts, the long-term trend of dropping demand is strongly reversed during the time of trade liberalization, and results in a net labor-demand increase through 2001. For college graduates at the upper end of the skill range, demand surges before and after liberalization, especially in the nontraded sector, are so strong that the drop in their demand during trade liberalization weighs little; a net demand increase prevails through 2001. Intermediate education groups suffer a demand decline in the traded-goods industries that more than outweighs their moderate demand increase in the nontraded sector. A Katz and Murphy (1992) decomposition into between-industry and within-industry changes shows that a large part of the overall evolution is predicted by these between-industry changes. But there is also a substantial workforce changeover within industries and across occupations.

---

1. Statistics are similar in the overall nationwide sample. Statistics and estimates on the overall sample and alternative subsamples are available from URL econ.ucsd.edu/muendler.

Measuring jobholders' years of schooling by occupation, and subtracting the mean years of schooling across all occupations, shows a continuous and steady increase in net schooling intensity across *all* occupations in the traded-goods sector between 1990 and 2001. This workforce changeover is associated with employment shifts from high- to low-skill intensive occupations, while employers simultaneously fill the low-skill-intensive occupations with more and more educated jobholders. Both processes, occupation downgrading and education upgrading, are reminiscent of an interpretation of the Heckscher-Ohlin argument applied to occupational activities (instead of industries). Given Brazil's relatively low-skill abundant labor force, a Heckscher-Ohlin style argument would posit that Brazil increasingly specializes in less schooling-intensive occupations but that the traded-goods sector employs in these expanding low-skill occupations relatively more high-skilled workers while their relative wage declines by the Stolper-Samuelson theorem.

Among several economic reforms—including macroeconomic stabilization, privatization, and some capital-account liberalization—the trade liberalization program of 1990 played a dominant role for labor-market outcomes. In multivariate regressions at the establishment level, I control for employer-fixed and year effects as well as various variables related to economic reforms and find that an employer's export status, along with sectoral tariff protection levels, exhibits the most predictive power for employment changes. Trade-related interpretations of labor-demand changes are, therefore, emphasized.

Beyond conventional labor-demand analysis, the comprehensive linked employer-employee data for Brazil's economy as a whole permit the tracking of individual workers across occupations, establishments, firm types, and industries in Brazil's formal sector. There is no evidence that employers reallocate workers across tasks in-house in response to trade reform. The share of in-house job transitions is constant over time, and minor. Surprisingly, there is also little evidence that the economy reallocates workers across firms and industries. Trade theory would lead us to expect a shift of displaced workers from nonexporting firms to exporters, following trade reform. The dominant share of successful reallocations within the traded-goods sector is to nonexporters, however, and this share is dwarfed by reallocations to nontraded-output industries. An equally large share of displaced workers, around a third, finds no formal-sector reemployment at the annual horizon. Taken together, these findings imply that employers pursue the observed workforce changeover by laying off relatively less-skilled workers, especially from skill-intensive occupation categories. This form of workforce changeover following trade reform is potentially associated with important adjustment costs to the economy. It remains a task for future research to analyze the impact of economic reform on worker separations, accessions, and spell durations outside formal-sector employment.

In line with the descriptive evidence, but in contrast to what general-equilibrium trade models with full employment might lead us to expect, a firm's export status predicts significant job losses. There is no conclusive evidence, however, that exporting status is causally related to employment reductions. When firm-level export status and its interaction with product-market tariffs are instrumented with sector-year varying foreign components of the real exchange rate, export status loses its statistical significance. This addresses the possible importance of employer-level workforce heterogeneity and suggests the construction of worker-level hiring and firing samples in future research.

While there are only slight differences between metropolitan areas and the nationwide average regarding employer characteristics and the sectoral composition of the labor market, metropolitan labor markets exhibit a markedly faster reallocation success. During the sample period, almost two in three successfully reallocated workers in metropolitan areas find a new job within the month of their separation. In contrast, only one in seven reallocated workers nationwide is rehired within the same month of displacement. In metropolitan areas, 95 percent of the successfully reallocated workers start their new job within twelve months. But only 77 percent of the successfully reallocated workers nationwide find new employment within a year. These stark differences in labor-market performance could be partly due to the slightly more diverse size distribution or the more varied workforce composition of employers in metropolitan areas, or to the somewhat larger nontraded-output sector in metropolitan areas. Further investigations are called for to improve our understanding of the labor-market specific differences in the reallocation process.

In related studies to examine the effects of trade liberalization on employment, Revenga (1992, 1997) finds that import competition reduces net employment at the sector level in the United States and Mexico. Meanwhile, a large part of the literature adopts the Davis, Haltiwanger, and Schuh (1996) approach of generating gross job flow statistics by industry and year and regressing those statistics on measures of trade exposure and exchange rates. In that line of research, Roberts (1996), for instance, does not find a strong effect of trade exposure on gross employment flows in Chile and Colombia, once industry characteristics are taken into account. Neither do Davis, Haltiwanger, and Schuh (1996) identify a clear effect of trade on factor reallocation using U.S. data. However, studies that consider exchange rate effects beyond trade exposure, such as Gourinchas (1999) or Klein, Schuh, and Triest (2003), do find systematic effects on employment flows. Klein, Scott, and Schuh (2003) find for the United States that job destruction, churning, and net employment growth respond to exchange rate movements, while job creation is unresponsive. In the Brazilian case, Ribeiro et al. (2004) compute industry-level rates of job creation and destruction and find that greater openness reduces employment through increased job destruction, with no effects on job creation, and that exchange rate depreciation increases job creation with no effect on job destruction. Haltiwanger et al. (2004) use a panel of industries in six Latin American countries and report that a reduction in tariffs and exchange rate appreciations increase job reallocation within sectors and that net employment growth tends to decline as trade exposure rises. In contrast to the lacking evidence on an association between trade exposure and labor-market outcomes in much of the earlier literature, a firm-level indicator of exporting status in the employer regressions of this chapter shows a highly significant relationship between exporting status and employment reductions during a period of trade reform, and a more pronounced association in less tariff-protected sectors. Beyond the prior literature, the linked employer-employee data of this paper permit the tracking of workers across activities, employers, and industries, and document these novel aspects of the labor-market response to trade reform.

The remainder of this chapter is organized in six more sections. Section 9.2 describes the main linked employer-employee data source as well as complementary firm and sector data, while details are relegated to the Appendix. Section 9.3 presents labor demand changes over the sample period 1986–2001, discerns between-sector and within-sector changes using a Katz and Murphy (1992) labor demand decomposition, and documents the workforce changeover within sectors along educational and occupational dimensions. Section 9.4 investigates how much of the documented workforce changeover is brought about by task reassignments within firms, worker reallocations across firms and industries, and by worker separations without formal-sector reallocations. Multivariate regressions in section 9.5 document the predictive power of exports and trade-related regressors compared to competing employer and sector variables. Section 9.6 looks into labor-market performance as measured by time to successful reallocation. Section 9.7 concludes.

9.2   Linked Employer-Employee Data

Workers of particular concern for the labor-market restructuring process are prime-age male workers, who typically show a low labor-supply elasticity. Most of the evidence of this chapter nevertheless applies to workers across gender and age groups. My restriction to prime age (25 to 64 years) serves to capture workers past their first entry into the active labor force. Beyond a 1 percent nationwide random sample of prime-age male workers, a five-percent metropolitan random sample of prime-age male workers is used to assess regional differences in labor-market outcomes.

The linked employer-employee data derive from Brazil's labor force records, RAIS (Relação Anual de Informações Sociais, of the Brazilian labor ministry MTE). RAIS is a nationwide, comprehensive annual record of workers formally employed in any sector (including the public sector).

RAIS covers, by law, all formally employed workers, captures formal-sector migrants,[2] and tracks the workers over time. By design, however, workers with no current formal-sector employment are not in RAIS.

RAIS primarily provides information to a federal wage supplement program (Abono Salarial), by which every worker with formal employment during the calendar year receives the equivalent of a monthly minimum wage. RAIS records are then shared across government agencies and statistical offices. An employer's failure to report complete workforce information can, in principle, result in fines proportional to the workforce size, but fines are rarely issued. In practice, workers and employers have strong incentives to ascertain complete RAIS records, because payment of the annual public wage supplement is based exclusively on RAIS. The ministry of labor estimates that well above 90 percent of all formally employed workers in Brazil were covered in RAIS throughout the 1990s.

The full data include 71.1 million workers (with 556.3 million job spells) at 5.52 million establishments in 3.75 million firms over the sixteen-year period 1986–2001. Every observation is identified by the worker ID (PIS), the establishment ID (of which the firm ID is a systematic part), the month of accession, and the month of separation. Relevant worker information includes tenure at the establishment, age, gender, and educational attainment. Job information includes occupation and the monthly average wage; establishment information includes sector and municipality classifications. To facilitate tracking, RAIS reports formal retirements and deaths on the job. RAIS identifies the establishment and its firm, which in turn can be linked to firm information from outside sources such as export data.

This chapter's sample derives from a list of all proper worker IDs (11-digit PIS) that ever appear in RAIS at the national level, from which a 1 percent nationwide random sample of the IDs and a 5 percent metropolitan random sample was drawn, and tracks the selected workers through all their formal jobs. Industry information is based on the subsector IBGE classification (roughly comparable to the NAICS three-digit level), which is available by establishment over the full period (see table 9.10 for sector classifications). For the calculation of separation and reallocation statistics, a worker's separation is defined as the layoff or quit from the highest-paying job.[3]

---

2. Migration among metropolitan workers is substantial. Among the prime-age male workers in RAIS with a metropolitan job in 1990, for instance, 15 percent have a formal job outside the 1990 city of employment by 1991 and 25 percent by 1993. Similarly, among the metropolitan workers in 1994, 17 percent have a formal job elsewhere by 1995 and 27 percent by 1997.

3. Among the male prime-age workers nationwide, 3 percent of the job observations are simultaneous secondary jobs. Tables 9.3, 9.4, 9.5, and 9.9 are based on the so-restricted sample, whereas all aggregate statistics, Katz-Murphy decompositions, and regressions are based on the full sample. The restriction to a single job at any moment in time permits a precise definition of job separation as a layoff or quit from the highest-paying job (randomly dropping sec-

Table 9.1   Employment by employer's sector and export status

	Traded goods		Nontraded output			
	Primary (1)	Manuf. (2)	Comm. (3)	Services (4)	Other (5)	Overall[a] (6)
Allocation of workers, nationwide						
1990	.021	.238	.128	.280	.333	22,844
1997	.044	.195	.152	.320	.289	24,068
Allocation of prime-age male workers, nationwide						
1990	.029	.263	.111	.284	.314	10,763
1997	.063	.221	.131	.308	.278	11,483
Nonexporter	.882	.494	.935	.937	.930	.830
Exporter	.118	.506	.065	.063	.070	.170
Allocation of prime-age male workers, metropolitan areas						
1990	.015	.270	.104	.309	.302	5,965
1997	.024	.213	.125	.363	.275	6,060
Nonexporter	.760	.390	.887	.913	.898	.778
Exporter	.240	.610	.113	.087	.102	.222

Note: [a]Total employment (thousands of workers), scaled to population equivalent.
Sources: RAIS 1990–2001, employment on December 31, and SECEX 1990–2001. Nationwide information based on 1% random sample, metropolitan information on 5% random sample. Period mean of exporter and nonexporter workforces, 1990–2001.

Table 9.1 shows the allocation of workers across industries in 1990 and 1997 (a detailed employment-share breakdown for the RAIS universe can be found in table 9.10). The nationwide RAIS records represent almost 23 million formally employed workers of any gender and age in 1990, and more than 24 million formal workers in 1997. The bulk of Brazil's formal employment is in manufacturing, services, and other industries (which include construction, utilities, and the public sector), with roughly similar formal employment shares between a quarter and a third of the overall formal labor force. Commerce (wholesale and retail) employs around one in eight workers, and the primary sector (agriculture and mining) at most one in twenty-five formal workers.

Prime-age male workers nationwide make up slightly less than half of the total workforce in 1990 and 1997. In both years, prime-age male workers are slightly more frequently employed in the primary and manufacturing sector than the average worker of any gender and age, but less frequently in commerce, services, and other sectors. More than half of the RAIS-reported formal employment of prime-age males occurs in the six metro-

---

ondary jobs if there is a pay tie). Removing simultaneously held jobs does not significantly affect estimates of skill, occupation, and gender premia in Mincer (1974) regressions (Menezes-Filho, Muendler, and Ramey, 2008).

politan areas of Brazil: São Paulo city, Rio de Janeiro city, Belo Horizonte, Porto Alegre, Salvador, and Recife. Compared to the nationwide average across gender and age, prime-age males in metropolitan areas are slightly less frequently employed in the primary sector, commerce, and other sectors, and somewhat more frequently employed in manufacturing and services. Overall, however, the labor allocation across sectors is broadly similar across regions and gender and age groups, whereas changes over time between 1990 and 1997 are more pronounced. Between 1990 and 1997, there is a marked drop in formal manufacturing employment, which is accompanied by an increase of employment in primary sectors, commerce, and especially services. Overall, between roughly a quarter and a third of the nationwide and metropolitan prime-age male workforces are employed in traded-goods sectors, and two thirds to three quarters in nontraded-output sectors.

9.2.1 Complementary Firm-Level Export Data

At the firm level, annual customs office records from SECEX (Secretaria de Comércio Exterior) for 1990 through 1998 are used to infer an indicator variable for a firm's exporting status, which is set to 1 when SECEX reports exports of any product of any value from the firm in a given year. The export-status indicator is linked to RAIS at the firm level. SECEX includes merchandize shipments, but not services exports. National accounting data suggest that, during the 1990s, Brazilian services exports were of minor importance.

Table 9.1 shows the allocation of prime-age male employment by exporting status of the employer, and by sector, for the period from 1990 to 2001. Whereas nationwide only 17 percent of prime-age males work at exporters, that share is 22 percent in metropolitan areas. Not surprisingly, the largest share of prime-age male employment at exporters occurs in the manufacturing sector, with more than 50 percent of the sector's workforce nationwide and over 60 percent in metropolitan areas. Primary-goods producers in agriculture and mining employ only 12 percent (nationwide) and 24 percent (metropolitan) of the sector's workforce—possibly because some of their exports, especially in agriculture, are channelled through commercial intermediaries. My focus, therefore, lies on the manufacturing industries in the traded-goods sector. Occasional merchandize shipments also occur among the commercial, services, and other-sector firms (construction, utilities, and the public sector).[4] These firms have employment

---

4. Recall that the export indicator is set to 1 when SECEX reports an export shipment of any product of any value at the firm. Among the retailers and wholesalers in commerce are some specialized import-export intermediaries who employ around 7 percent of the nationwide workforce. Shipments of accessory equipment in services and construction are considered merchandize exports by law, but the SECEX data show the sales value of these exports to be expectedly minor. The main business of services and utilities firms is not merchandize sale, so that the recorded employment shares at those firms do not imply that their employees typically handle export merchandize.

shares of between 6 percent (nationwide) and 11 percent (metropolitan). Their employment shares are small, however, compared to those in the primary and manufacturing sectors, and the SECEX data show that those firms' exporting status mostly reflects occasional merchandize shipments.

9.2.2 Complementary Sector Data

Data on ad valorem tariffs by sector and year from Kume, Piani, and Souza (2003) serve as measures of output-market tariffs and, after combining them with economy-wide input-output matrices (from IBGE), provide intermediate-input tariff measures by sector and year. Those tariff series from the Nível 80 level are transformed to the subsector IBGE classification available in RAIS by taking unweighted subsector means over the original Nível 80 data.

Ramos and Zonenschain (2000) report national accounting data to calculate the *effective rate of market penetration* with foreign imports. The effective rate of market penetration is defined as imports per absorption. Absorption includes consumption, investment, and government spending, and is calculated as output less net exports. The assumption is that domestic firms find the absorption market the relevant domestic environment in which they compete. Foreign direct investment (FDI) inflow data from the Brazilian central bank (Banco Central do Brasil) are available for 1986 through 1998.

Sector-specific real exchange rates are constructed from the nominal exchange rate to the U.S. dollar E, Brazilian wholesale price indices P_j (from FGV Rio de Janeiro), and average foreign price series for groups of Brazil's main trading partners P_j^* by sector j. The real exchange rate is defined as $q_j \equiv EP_j^*/P_j$, so that a low value means an appreciated real-sector exchange rate. The underlying price series are re-based to a value of 1 in 1995. Brazil's import shares from its major twenty-five trading partners in 1995 are used as weights for P_j^*. Sector-specific annual series are obtained from producer price indexes for the twelve OECD countries among Brazil's main twenty-five trading partners (sector-specific producer price index [PPI] series from *SourceOECD;* U.S. PPI series from Bureau of Labor Statistics). These sector-specific price indexes are combined with the thirteen annual aggregate producer (wholesale if producer unavailable) price index series for Brazil's remaining major trading partners (from Global Financial Data), for whom sector-specific PPI indexes are not available.

9.3 Economic Reform and Employment Changeovers

Since the late 1980s, Brazil's federal government initiated a series of economic reforms that, by around 1997, resulted in a considerably more open economy to foreign goods and investments, a stable macroeconomy, and a somewhat smaller role of the state in the economy. In 1988, after decades of import substitution and industry protection, the Brazilian federal government under president Sarney initiated an internal planning process for trade reform and started to reduce ad valorem tariffs but, lacking public support, took little legislative initiative to remove binding nontariff barriers, so that nominal tariff reductions had little effect (Kume, Piani, and Souza 2003). In 1990, the Collor administration launched a large-scale trade reform that involved both the removal of nontariff barriers and the adoption of a new tariff structure with lower levels and smaller cross-sectoral dispersion. Implementation of these policies was largely completed by 1993.

Figure 9.1 depicts Brazil's product-market and intermediate-input tariff schedules in 1990 and 1997 for the twelve manufacturing industries at the subsector IBGE level. Intermediate-input tariff levels are calculated as reweighted product tariffs using the economywide input-output matrix. Both the level and the dispersion of tariffs drop remarkably between 1990 and 1997. While ad valorem product tariffs range from 21 (metallic products) to 63 percent (apparel and textiles) in 1990, they drop to a range from 9 percent (chemicals) to 34 percent (transport equipment) in 1997. Except for paper and publishing in 1990, sectors at the subsector IBGE level receive effective protection in both years, with mean product tariffs exceeding mean intermediate-input tariffs. By 1997, however, the relatively homogeneous tariff structure results in a small rate of effective protections for most industries—with the notable exception of transport equipment.

Brazil underwent additional reforms over the sample period. In 1994, during the Franco administration and under the watch of then-finance minister Cardoso, drastic anti-inflation measures succeeded for the first time in decades. A privatization program for public utilities was started in 1991 and accelerated in the mid-1990s, while Brazil simultaneously liberalized capital-account restrictions. These measures were accompanied by a surge in foreign direct investment inflows in the mid-1990s. The procompetitive reforms during the 1990s, mostly targeted at product markets, had been preceded by changes to Brazil's labor-market institutions in 1988. Brazil's 1988 constitution introduced a series of labor-market reforms that aimed to increase workers' benefits and the right to organize, thus raising labor costs.[5] Given their constitutional status, these labor-market institutions remained unaltered throughout the sample period.

Among the reforms, trade liberalization played a dominant role for labor-market outcomes. Multivariate regressions in section 9.5 will control

---

5. The 1988 reforms reduced the maximum working hours per week from 48 to 44, increased the minimum overtime premium from 20 percent to 50 percent, reduced the maximum number of hours in a continuous shift from 8 to 6 hours, increased maternity leave from three to four months, increased the value of paid vacations from 1 to 4/3 of the normal monthly wage, and increased the fine for an unjustified dismissal from 10 percent to 40 percent of the employer-funded severance pay account (FGTS). See Heckman and Pagés (2004) and Gonzaga (2003) for further details.

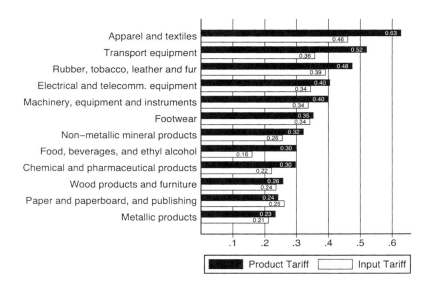

In 1990

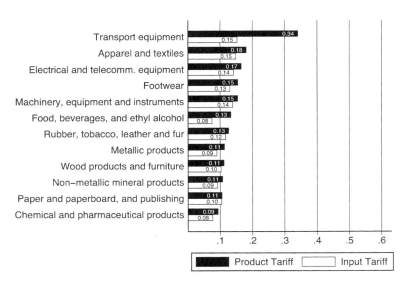

In 1997

Fig. 9.1   Tariff Rates

Sources: Ad valorem product tariffs at Nível 80 from Kume et al. (2003). Intermediate input tariffs are re-weighted product-market tariffs using national input-output matrices at Nível 80 (from IBGE). Product-market and intermediate-input tariffs are averages at the subsector IBGE level using unweighted means over the Nível 80 classifications.

for sector and year effects as well as variables related to simultaneous reforms, and confirm the overwhelming predictive power of trade liberalization and employers' export status for employment changes. In light of these findings, trade-related interpretations of the labor-demand changes in this and subsequent sections are emphasized.

9.3.1 Between and within Industry Demand Shifts

Katz and Murphy (1992) derive a framework to decompose labor-demand changes into shifts between industries, associated with variations in sector sizes given sectoral occupation profiles, and within industries through changing occupation intensities. The former shifts between industries relate to the changing allocation of employment across sectors, whereas the latter shifts within industries reflect the change in relative skill intensities of occupations or alterations to the sectoral production process. Applying the Katz and Murphy (1992) framework to employment in the Brazilian formal sector over the years 1986 to 2001 reveals main patterns of labor-market adjustment. The decomposition into between and within sector variation indicates how two important sources of change contribute to workforce changeover. Between-industry shifts are arguably driven by changes in final-goods demands, sectoral differences in factor-nonneutral technical change, and changes in the sector-level penetration with foreign imports. Within-industry shifts can be related to factor-nonneutral technical change, factor-price changes for substitutes or complements to labor, and international trade in tasks that allocates activities along the value chain across countries.

The Katz and Murphy (1992) decomposition relates back to Freeman's (1980) manpower requirement index and is designed to measure the degree of between-industry labor-demand change under fixed relative wages. The decomposition tends to understate the true between-industry demand shift in absolute terms when relative wages change. Though possibly overstating the within-industry effects, the Brazilian evidence suggests that within-industry demand changes are an important source of employment changeover in Brazil, especially since 1990. Beyond the Katz and Murphy (1992) framework, statistics are offered that document time variation in the occupation profile within industries and the skill changeover within occupations.

Under the assumption that the aggregate production function is concave (so that the matrix of cross-wage elasticities of factor demands is negative semidefinite), Katz and Murphy (1992) show that an appropriate between-industry demand shift measure ΔD_k for skill group k is

$$(1) \qquad \Delta D_k = \sum_j X_{jk} \frac{w' dX_j}{w' X_j},$$

where X_{jk} is the employment of skill group k in industry j, w is a $k \times 1$ vector of constant wages, and dX_j and X_j are the $k \times 1$ vectors of employment changes and levels in industry j, respectively. Measure (1) is simply the vector of weighted sums of industry employments for each skill group k, with the weights given by the percentage changes in the overall employments in every industry j. The measure is similar to standard labor-requirement indexes (Freeman 1980), only that changes are measured in efficiency units at constant wages rather than in head counts (or hours). Intuitively, skill groups that are intensely employed in expanding sectors experience a demand increase, whereas skill groups intensely employed in contracting sectors face falling demand. Under constant wages, the measure indicates whether the data are consistent with stable labor demands within sectors. Wages change, however, so that there is a bias in the measure. Katz and Murphy (1992) show that the bias is inversely related to wage changes if substitution effects dominate the employment decisions, so that measure (1) understates the demand increase for groups with rising relative wages.

In the Brazilian context, the formal-sector economy is divided into twenty-six two-digit industries (using the subsector IBGE classification) and five occupations (professional and managerial occupations, technical and supervisory occupations, other white-collar occupations, skill-intensive blue-collar occupations, and other blue-collar occupations). The classification of activities into both sectors and occupations is motivated by the idea that international trade of intermediate and final goods can be understood as trade in tasks along the steps of the production chain. Using the resulting 130 industry-occupation cells, an empirically attractive version of the between-industry demand shift measure (1) is

$$(2) \qquad \Delta X_k^{di} = \frac{\Delta D_k}{E_k} = \sum_i \left(\frac{E_{ik}}{E_k} \right) \left(\frac{\Delta E_i}{E_i} \right) = \frac{\Sigma_i \alpha_{ik} \Delta E_i}{E_k},$$

where E_i is total labor input in sector-occupation cell i measured in efficiency units, and $\alpha_{ik} \equiv E_{ik}/E_i$ is skill group k's share of total employment in efficiency units in sector i in the base period. Measure (2) expresses the percentage change in demand for each skill group as a weighted average of the percentage changes in sectoral employments, the weights being the group-specific efficiency-unit allocations. Following Katz and Murphy (1992), I turn index (2) into a measure of relative demand changes by normalizing all efficiency-unit employments in each year to sum to unity. The base period is the average of the sample period from 1986 to 2001 so that α_{ik} is the share of total employment of group k in sector i over the 1986–2001 period and E_k is the average share of skill group k in total employment between 1986 and 2001.

The overall (industry-occupation) measure of demand shifts for skill group k is defined as ΔX_k^{di} from equation (2), where i indexes the 130 industry-occupation cells. The between-industry component of this demand-shift measure is defined as the group-k index ΔX_k^{dj} from equation (2), where $i = j$ now indexes only twenty-six industries. Accordingly, the within-industry component of demand shifts is $\Delta X_k^{dw} \equiv \Delta X_k^{di} - \Delta X_k^{dj}$.

Table 9.2 presents the nationwide demand decomposition and the overall demand shifts by group of educational attainment for the economy as a whole, and separately for the traded-goods and the nontraded-output sectors. As in Katz and Murphy (1992), the percentage changes are transformed into log changes with the formula $\hat{\Delta} X_k^d = \log (1 + \Delta X_k^d)$. By construction, in the (vertical) sectoral dimension the economy-wide demand shift indexes for each skill group are a weighted sum of the traded and nontraded sector indexes (except for occasional rounding errors because of the log transformation), where the weights are the skill groups' shares in the sectors. In the (horizontal) time dimension, the indexes are the sum of the time periods for each skill group.

The entries for overall shifts across all sectors summarize Brazil's labor-demand evolution (five first rows of column [12]). Over the full period from 1986 to 2001, the least and the most skilled prime-age male workers experience a positive relative demand shift of 1 and 8 percent, respectively, whereas the three intermediate skill groups suffer a labor-demand drop. This overall pattern, with demand surges at the extreme ends of the skill spectrum and drops for the middle groups, can be traced back to two overlying developments. First, before and after the main economic liberalization episode—that is, in the periods 1986–1990 and 1997–2001, demand for college graduates rises by around 5 percent, while demand drops for all other skill groups in 1997–2001 and for all other skill groups but high school graduates in 1986–1990. Second, however, during the period of economic liberalization between 1990 and 1997, the reverse labor-demand change occurs, with demand for the least-educated males increasing by roughly 5 percent and dropping for college graduates by –2 percent. The demand rise for the least-educated during liberalization more than outweighs the demand drops before and after, so that a net demand increase remains by 2001. For college graduates, demand surges before and after liberalization are so strong that the drop during liberalization is of little importance and a strong net demand remains by 2001. This pattern is consistent with a Heckscher-Ohlin interpretation of the specialization pattern following trade liberalization. Brazil, whose labor force is relatively low-skill abundant, experiences a shift toward low-skill intensive economic activities between 1990 and 1997—against the longer-term trend manifested before (1986–1990) and after (1997–2001), by which demand for highly skilled workers increases but drops for lower-skilled workers.

Between and within decompositions, as well as a distinction of traded and nontraded sectors, lend additional support to a Heckscher-Ohlin

Table 9.2   Industry- and occupation-based log demand shifts, 1986–2001 (%)

	Between industry				Within industry				Overall industry-occupation			
	86–90 (1)	90–97 (2)	97–01 (3)	86–01 (4)	86–90 (5)	90–97 (6)	97–01 (7)	86–01 (8)	86–90 (9)	90–97 (10)	97–01 (11)	86–01 (12)
Economy-wide												
Illiterate or primary dropout	-0.1	4.7	-0.1	4.5	-2.2	-0.2	-1.0	-3.3	-2.3	4.5	-1.1	1.1
Primary school graduate	-2.1	-0.1	-1.7	-3.9	-1.4	0.5	-1.5	-2.4	-3.6	0.4	-3.2	-6.4
Middle school graduate	-1.9	-0.9	-0.5	-3.3	-0.1	1.5	-1.2	0.1	-2.0	0.6	-1.8	-3.1
High school graduate	0.3	-1.7	-0.8	-2.3	1.1	0.9	0.2	2.2	1.4	-0.9	-0.6	-0.1
College graduate	3.3	0.4	2.9	6.6	1.3	-2.4	2.5	1.4	4.6	-2.0	5.4	8.1
Traded-goods sectors												
Illiterate or primary dropout	-3.0	3.7	-1.7	-0.9	-0.7	-0.2	-0.2	-1.1	-3.7	3.6	-1.9	-2.0
Primary school graduate	-3.8	-2.0	-2.4	-8.2	-0.4	0.2	-0.6	-0.7	-4.2	-1.8	-3.0	-9.0
Middle school graduate	-3.9	-4.0	-2.6	-10.6	0.0	0.3	-0.5	-0.2	-3.9	-3.8	-3.1	-10.7
High school graduate	-3.7	-4.4	-2.4	-10.5	0.5	-0.1	0.2	0.7	-3.2	-4.5	-2.1	-9.8
College graduate	-3.6	-4.6	-2.1	-10.4	0.5	-0.5	1.4	1.4	-3.1	-5.1	-0.7	-8.9
Nontraded-output sectors												
Illiterate or primary dropout	3.6	0.4	1.9	5.9	-1.5	0.1	-0.7	-2.2	2.1	0.4	1.2	3.7
Primary school graduate	2.8	2.7	1.5	7.0	-1.0	0.3	-0.9	-1.6	1.9	2.9	0.6	5.4
Middle school graduate	2.3	3.3	2.3	7.9	-0.2	1.2	-0.7	0.3	2.1	4.6	1.6	8.3
High school graduate	3.2	1.9	1.2	6.3	0.6	0.9	0.0	1.5	3.9	2.8	1.2	7.8
College graduate	5.2	3.3	3.9	12.4	0.8	-1.8	1.4	0.4	6.0	1.5	5.3	12.8

Source: RAIS 1986–2001 (1% random sample), male workers, twenty-five years or older. Overall and between-industry demand shift measures for skill group k are of the form $\Delta D_k = \Sigma_j \alpha_{jk} (\Delta E_j/E_k)$, where α_{jk} is the average share for group k of employment in cell j over the period 1986–2001, E_j is the share of aggregate employment in cell j; and E_k is the average share of total employment of group k over the period 1986–2001 (Katz and Murphy 1992). Reported numbers are of the form $\log(1 + \Delta D_k)$. In the overall measure, j indexes 130 industry-occupation cells; in the between-industry measure, $i = j$ indexes twenty-six industries (fourteen traded-goods and twelve nontraded-output sectors). The within-industry index for group k is the difference of the overall and between-industry measures. Employment is measured in efficiency units.

interpretation of labor-demand changes. The decomposition for all sectors (five first rows) into between-industry and within-industry changes indicates that the overall evolution is mostly driven by between-industry changes, with demand surges at the extreme ends of the skill spectrum and drops for the middle groups (column [4]). In contrast, the within-industry labor-demand changes favor the least skilled the least, with a demand drop of –3 percent, and the most skilled the most, with a demand increase of 1 to 2 percent for high school educated workers and college graduates. The within-industry demand changes are almost monotonically increasing as we move up the educational attainment ranks (column [8]) in the 1986–2001 period, and would indeed monotonically increase if it were not for a within-industry drop in demand for college graduates during the liberalization period. In the following discussion I will return to the within-industry demand changes, with additional evidence. In fact, the within-industry workforce changeover will be found to reinforce a broad Heckscher-Ohlin interpretation of Brazil's experience.

A distinction by sector relates the between-industry demand evolution to differences across traded-goods industries (middle five rows) and non-traded-output industries (last five rows). In the traded-goods sectors, where trade liberalization is expected to exert its impact, Brazil experiences a salient labor-demand drop—beyond –10 percent for the three more educated skill groups between 1986 and 2001. Expectedly for a low-skill abundant country, the demand drop is the strongest for the highly skilled and the weakest for the low-skilled workers (column [4]). Most notably, during the liberalization episode illiterate workers and primary school dropouts experience a rise in demand due to between-industry shifts, whereas more skilled workers experience demand drops of monotonically larger magnitudes as we move up the skill ladder (column [2]). The nontraded-output sectors exhibit a relatively homogeneous demand increase of between 6 and 8 percent for workers with no college degree and a strong 12 percent increase for college graduates (column [4]). The demand increase for the least skilled in nontraded-output sectors, combined with only a slight demand drop for them in the traded-goods sectors, results in an overall positive demand for the skill group from the between-industry component (column [4]). Similarly, the strong demand for college graduates in nontraded-output sectors more than outweighs their demand drop in traded-goods sectors. For intermediate skill groups between these two extremes, the demand drop in the traded-goods sectors outweighs their demand increase in nontraded-output sectors and results in overall negative demand changes.

Within industries there is a clear and pronounced pattern of falling demand for the least skilled, and increasing demand for the more skilled, with monotonically stronger demand changes as we move up the skill ranks, except only for college graduates (column [8]). This pattern is similar across both traded and nontraded sectors and most time periods. The reason for the break in monotonicity at the college-graduate level (column [8]) is a demand drop for this skill group during the liberalization period (column [6]). A Stolper-Samuelson explanation is consistent with the outlier behavior of collage graduates during this period. Note that the Stolper-Samuelson theorem predicts wage drops for more educated workers in a low-skill abundant economy after trade reform, and Gonzaga, Menezes-Filho, and Terra (2006) document that skilled earnings differentials indeed narrow over the course of the trade liberalization period. Because labor is measured in current-period efficiency units, a relative drop in wages for college-educated workers tends to turn their within-industry demand index negative. With this explanation for the outlier behavior of collage graduates in view, there is a striking monotonicity in the increase in within-industry labor demand change as we move up the skill ranks.

9.3.2 Within-industry Employment Changeovers

The previous demand decompositions show a noteworthy within-industry labor demand reduction for low-skilled workers and a demand increase for high-skilled workers both in traded-goods and nontraded-output sectors. The sources of this change deserve more scrutiny. Abandoning the efficiency-unit perspective on employment in favor of counts of workers to keep wage effects separate, I turn to an assessment of labor allocation to activities by period.[6]

Figure 9.2 shows the evolution of the skill assignment by occupation over time. In both traded-goods and nontraded-output sectors, there is a marked increase across all five occupation categories in the educational attainment of the job holders. From 1986 to 2001, the mean number of years of schooling in unskilled blue-collar occupations rises from below four years to more than five years in both traded and nontraded sectors (in traded sectors schooling in unskilled blue-collar occupations even slightly exceeds the schooling in skilled blue-collar jobs by 2001). The average number of school years increases from around four to more than five years for skilled blue-collar jobs in traded sectors and to more than six years in nontraded sectors by 2001. For unskilled white-collar occupations, the average jobholder's schooling goes from around six to more than eight years, both in traded and nontraded goods sectors. The shift also extends to technical and supervisory positions, where the average jobholder's schooling goes from less than ten to more than ten years of schooling both in traded and nontraded sectors, and to managerial positions, where mean schooling rises from eleven to almost twelve years over the period 1986 to 2001. These largely steady within-industry changeovers in workers' occupational

---

6. An efficiency unit-based analysis shows broadly the same patterns of workforce changeovers in terms of wage bills as the head-count-based analysis that follows.

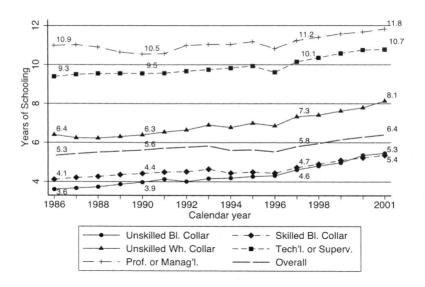

Traded-goods Sectors

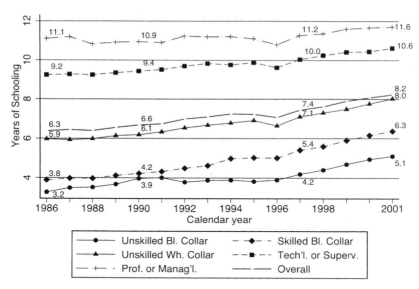

Nontraded-output Sectors

Fig. 9.2   Schooling intensity of occupations

Source: RAIS 1986–2001 (1% random sample), male workers nationwide, twenty-five to sixty-four years old, with employment on December 31. Traded-goods sectors are agriculture, mining, and manufacturing (subsectors IBGE 1–13 and 25), nontraded-output industries are all other sectors. Mean years of schooling weighted by worker numbers within occupations.

assignments between 1986–2001 overlay the shorter-lived between-industry changes with much time variation across the three subperiods 1986–1990, 1990–1997, and 1997–2001.

One might suspect that the considerable surge in schooling levels is partly due to labor-supply changes, such as the entry of increasingly educated cohorts of male workers into the labor force, or relatively more frequent shifts of skilled male workers from informal to formal work status over the sample period. In fact, the sector-wide average schooling level rises from less than six to more than six years in the traded-goods sector, and in the nontraded-output sector from more than six to more than eight years (as the respective overall curves in figure 9.2 show). To control for overall skill labor supply by sector, the Katz and Murphy (1992) idea is extended to the present context and the annual mean of years of schooling in a sector is subtracted from the occupation-specific mean in the sector. For this purpose, all traded-goods industries are considered as one sector, and all nontraded-output industries as another sector. Subtracting the annual mean years of schooling, instead of dividing by the annual total as in table 9.2 before, preserves the cardinal skill measure of years of schooling and expresses occupation-specific skill demands as deviations from the sector-wide employment evolution in terms of years of schooling.

Figure 9.3 presents average years of schooling by occupation, less the sectorwide mean schooling across all occupations. By this measure, skill demand within every occupation category increases in the traded-goods sector since 1990: from a difference of –1.6 to –0.9 years in unskilled blue-collar occupations, from –1.2 to –1.1 years in skilled blue-collar occupations, from 0.8 to 1.7 in unskilled white-collar jobs, from 3.9 to 4.4 in technical jobs, and from 4.9 to 5.4 in professional and managerial positions. For all three white-collar occupation categories, the schooling-intensity surge beyond the sector average since 1990 is a reversal of the opposite trend prior to 1990, while schooling intensity continually increases for blue-collar occupations in the traded sector since 1986. By construction, the persistent occupation-level increases in worker schooling since 1990 go beyond the change in the sectorwide workforce schooling. The puzzling pattern—that changes beyond the sector mean are uniformly directed toward higher schooling in every single occupation since 1990—implies that there must be an employment expansion in less skill-intensive occupations. Otherwise it would be impossible for every single occupation category to exhibit a faster skill-intensity increase than the average overall occupations. In contrast to the traded sector, nontraded-output industries do not exhibit the uniform pattern of schooling increases across all occupations but a drop in schooling intensity in the technical and managerial occupations, and a rise in schooling intensity in skilled blue-collar occupations.

The evolution of schooling intensity in Brazil's traded-goods sector is reminiscent of a Heckscher-Ohlin interpretation as well—though not for

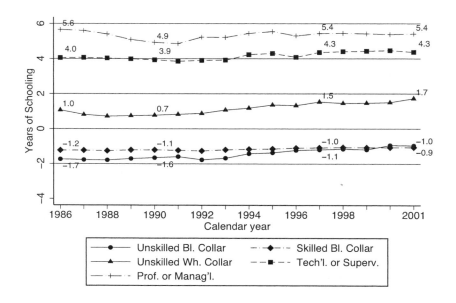

Traded-goods Sectors

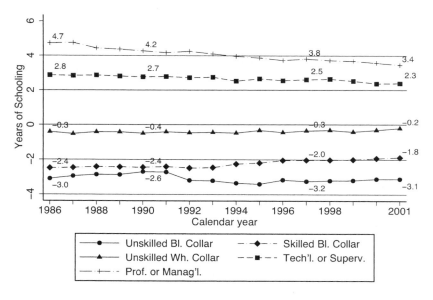

Nontraded-output Sectors

Fig. 9.3   Difference between schooling intensity of occupations and annual mean schooling level

Source: RAIS 1986–2001 (1% random sample), male workers nationwide, twenty-five to sixty-four years old, with employment on December 31. Traded-goods sectors are agriculture, mining, and manufacturing (subsectors IBGE 1–13 and 25), nontraded-output industries are all other sectors. Mean years of schooling weighted by worker numbers within occupations, less mean years of schooling weighted by worker numbers across all occupations.

industries but for tasks. Think of production activities in the Heckscher-Ohlin framework not as sectors but as occupations and suppose that Brazil has a relatively less-schooled labor force than its main trading partners. Brazil's top five trading partners in total trade volume during the 1990s are, in descending order, the United States, Argentina, Germany, Italy, and Japan. As Brazil's integration into the world economy advances, reinterpreted Heckscher-Ohlin trade theory predicts that Brazil increasingly specializes in less schooling-intensive occupations but that Brazil employs in these expanding occupations relatively more high-skilled workers, because their relative wage declines. Gonzaga, Menezes-Filho, and Terra (2006) document that Brazil's skilled earnings differential narrows over the 1990s. Of course, more research is required to discern this reinterpretation of classic trade theory from alternative explanations. The simultaneous schooling-intensity increase in every single occupation, above and beyond the sector mean, could also be related to factor-nonneutral technical change or factor-price changes for substitutes to labor, not only to international trade in tasks. Yet, the prediction of reinterpreted classic trade theory that foreign trade expands less schooling-intensive occupations in Brazil's traded-goods sector is fully consistent with the data.

Figure 9.4 depicts the nationwide occupation profile within traded-goods sectors and nontraded-output sectors for the years 1986 to 2001. In traded-goods industries, skilled blue-collar jobs expand markedly with the conclusion of the first wave of trade reforms between 1991 and 1993. The share of skilled blue-collar occupations increases from below 60 percent in 1990 to 68 percent in 1994 and to 71 percent by 2001. Recall from the evidence in figure 9.2 that the average worker's schooling in both skilled and unskilled blue-collar jobs in the traded-goods sector is roughly the same. The growing importance of skilled blue-collar occupations comes at the expense of all other occupations in the traded-goods industries. At the low-skill intensity end, the share of unskilled blue-collar occupations drops from more than 13 percent in 1990 to 8 percent in 1994 (but recovers slightly to close to 9 percent by 2001). More importantly, the expansion of skilled blue-collar occupations in traded-goods sectors comes at the expense of white-collar occupations, whose total employment share drops from 27 percent in 1990 to 24 percent in 1994 and 20 percent in 2001. In the nontraded-output sectors, in contrast, it is the unskilled blue-collar occupation category that expands the fastest, from 13 percent in 1990 to close to 16 percent by 2001, whereas skilled blue-collar jobs are cut back from a share of 34 percent in 1990 to around 29 percent by 1997. Similarly, within white-collar occupations, it is again the less skill-intensive occupations that exhibit a relative gain: the share of unskilled white-collar workers rises from 16 to 18 percent between 1990 and 1995 (with a crawling scaleback to 17 percent until 2001), and the share of technical occupations increases from 20 percent in 1990 to 21 percent in 1995. But the share of professional

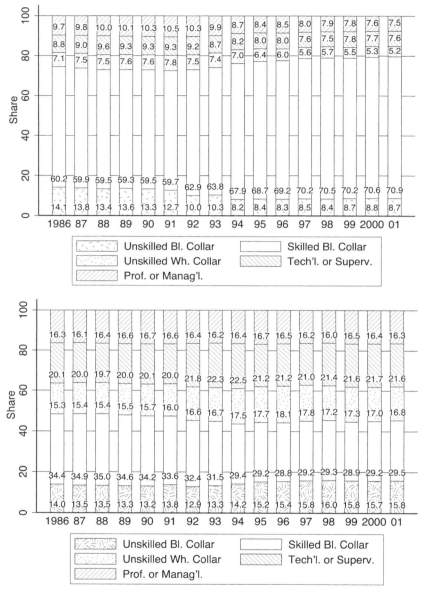

Fig. 9.4 Occupational workforce composition

Source: RAIS 1986–2001 (1% random sample), male workers nationwide, twenty-five to sixty-four years old, with employment on December 31. Traded-goods sectors are agriculture, mining, and manufacturing (subsectors IBGE 1–13 and 25), nontraded-output industries are all other sectors. Shares based on worker numbers.

and managerial positions remains roughly constant, between 16 and 17 percent, thus losing in relative importance to less skill-intensive white-collar occupations.

This shift across the occupation profile toward less skill-intensive occupations permits a skill-upgrading workforce changeover, by which less skill-intensive jobs are being filled with more educated workers, especially in the traded-goods sector. In practice, employers can achieve this workforce changeover in many ways. Employers can either reallocate workers across tasks in-house, or the economy can reallocate workers across firms and sectors, or there may be no reallocation for extended periods of time if employers pursue the workforce changeover by laying off less skilled workers from every occupation category in the absence of compensatory rehiring within the formal sector. The latter form of workforce changeover would be associated with arguably considerable adjustment costs to the economy.

9.4   Worker Reallocations across Activities

Labor-demand decompositions so far have shown that there are two main components to the observed workforce changeover in Brazil over the sample period. First, there is a labor demand shift toward the least and the most skilled male workers, which can be traced back to relatively weaker declines of traded-goods industries that use low-skilled labor intensively and to relatively stronger expansions of nontraded-output industries that intensely use higher-skilled labor. Second, there is a within-industry shift toward more educated workers, associated with a skill upgrading of all occupations in traded-goods industries. To track how employers achieve the observed workforce changeover during the sample period, the comprehensive linked employer-employee data for Brazil's economy is used to trace individual workers across their jobs within establishments, across establishments within sectors, and across firm types and sectors in Brazil's formal sector.

9.4.1   Reallocations across Tasks

Employers may choose to reallocate workers across in-house tasks. For this purpose, an in-house job change is defined as a change in employment between an occupation at the CBO base-group level to another base-group occupation. The 354 CBO base groups roughly correspond to the four-digit ISCO-88 occupations at the unit-group level.[7] Table 9.3 shows both continuing and displaced workers and tracks the workers through jobs at the annual horizon between 1986 and 1997. The task assignment pattern is

---

7. For a description of the Brazilian occupation classification system CBO and a mapping to ISCO-88, see Muendler, Poole, Ramey, and Wajnberg (2004).

remarkably stable, both before and after trade liberalization. Between 86 and 87 percent of formal-sector prime-age male workers remain in their job with the same employer. Only between 1 and 2 percent of the workers are assigned to new occupations within the same establishment. Less than 1 percent of workers switch establishments within the same firm. Between 7 and 9 percent of the workers change employing firm at the annual horizon. So, the bulk of successful reallocations does not take place on internal labor markets but across firms. The reallocations between exporters and nonexporters and across sectors are traced in the following. The remaining 3 to 4 percent of workers (not reported in table 9.3) are unaccounted. I will also turn to those failed reallocations shortly. Overall, the stable and minor percentages of occupation and establishment reassignments within employers suggest that the observed workforce changeovers, documented in the preceding section, are not achieved through job reassignments in internal labor markets.

9.4.2 Reallocations across Firms and Sectors

Between 1990 and 1998, around 6 percent of the formal-sector workforce nationwide is employed at primary-sector nonexporters—1 percent at primary-sector exporters, 11 percent at manufacturing nonexporters, and 12 percent at manufacturing exporters. The remaining 70 percent of the workforce are employed in the nontraded sector. I now look beyond internal labor markets and investigate whether and how the relative expansion of certain traded-goods industries, in the wake of an overall decline of the traded-goods sector, is associated with reallocations of individual workers across firms and sectors. To capture differences in the labor de-

Table 9.3   Annual occupation continuations and transitions 1986–1997

| | Year t | | | | | |
| | 1986 (1) | 1988 (2) | 1990 (3) | 1992 (4) | 1994 (5) | 1996 (6) |
Year $t+1$						
Employed						
In same occupation	0.867	0.859	0.864	0.859	0.850	0.856
At same establishment in new occupation	0.018	0.018	0.019	0.020	0.020	0.013
At same firm but new establishment	0.007	0.006	0.006	0.007	0.006	0.005
At new firm	0.079	0.084	0.074	0.078	0.087	0.083

Source: RAIS 1986–1997 (1% random sample), male workers, twenty-five years or older. Frequencies based on last employment of year (highest-paying job, if many); continuations at same firm exclude continuations at same establishment. Occupations are defined at the CBO three-digit base-group level with 354 categories, which roughly correspond to the four-digit ISCO-88 unit-group level.

mand responses across subsectors and firms within the traded-goods sector, individual workers are tracked across exporting and nonexporting employers in the primary and manufacturing industries.

Table 9.4 shows worker transitions between firms and sectors over the first year after trade reform, between their last observed formal-sector employment in 1990 and their last observed formal-sector employment in 1991. Only workers who experience a separation from their last employment of the year are included in the transition statistics. Trade theory might lead us to expect a shift of displaced workers from nonexporting firms to exporters following trade reform. The dominant share of successful reallocations of former nonexporter workers within the traded-goods industries, however, is again to nonexporters. Among the former nonexporter workers displaced from primary-sector employment, close to 11 percent are rehired at primary nonexporters and 10 percent at manufacturing nonexporters, but less than 2 percent shift to exporters. Among the former nonexporter workers in manufacturing, 19 percent move to manufacturing nonexporters and 7 percent no manufacturing exporters, and a very small share to primary-sector firms. Former exporter workers, in contrast, mostly transition to new formal-sector jobs within the sector of displacement and are roughly equally likely to find reemployment at an exporter or a nonexporter. These patterns suggest that reallocations within the traded-goods sectors are mostly intrasector reallocations from exporter to exporter and from nonexporter to nonexporter—contrary to what classic trade theory with full employment and only traded goods might lead us to expect.

In the initial year after trade reform, between one third and two fifths of

Table 9.4   Year-over-year firm and sector transitions, 1990–1991 (%)

| From | To primary | | To manufacturing | | | | |
	Nonexp. (1)	Exp. (2)	Nonexp. (3)	Exp. (4)	Nontraded (5)	Failure (6)	Total (7)
Primary nonexporter	10.7	.7	10.3	1.2	40.3	36.8	100.0
Primary exporter	6.7	6.7	3.3	3.3	45.0	35.0	100.0
Manufacturing nonexporter	1.4	.1	19.3	7.2	34.9	37.1	100.0
Manufacturing exporter	1.2	.1	14.5	15.5	33.5	35.2	100.0
Nontraded	1.3	.0	5.4	2.4	54.8	36.0	100.0
Failure	2.9	.3	13.2	5.6	78.0	.	100.0
Total	2.1	.2	10.1	4.8	59.7	23.2	100.0

Source: RAIS 1990–1991 (1% random sample), male workers nationwide, twenty-five to sixty-four years old. SECEX 1990–1991 for exporting status. Frequencies are job accessions in Brazil within one year after separation, based on last employment of year (highest-paying job, if many). Failed accessions are separations followed by no formal-sector accessions anywhere in Brazil within a year, excluding workers with prior retirement or death, or age sixty-five or above in earlier job.

displaced traded-sector workers with a successful reallocation end up in nontraded-sector jobs. An equally large fraction, however, fails to experience a successful reallocation to any formal-sector job within the following calendar year (retirements, deaths, and workers at or past retirement age are excluded from the displaced-worker sample).[8] Of the workers with a failed reallocation before year-end 1990, by far the largest fraction (78 percent) with a successful reallocation by year-end 1991 finds employment in the nontraded-sector. In summary, at the time of the largest impact of trade liberalization in 1990–1991, traded-goods industries exhibit little absorptive capacity for displaced workers compared to nontraded-output industries and compared to the prevalence of failed transitions out of the formal sector. Among those failed reallocations can be transitions to informal work, unemployment, or withdrawals from the active labor force, which are not directly observed in the RAIS records.

In comparison, table 9.5 tracks annual transitions six years after the beginning of trade liberalization and three years after its conclusion. By 1996–1997, more firm and sector reallocations from the primary sector are directed to jobs within the traded-goods sector. In the manufacturing sector, however, the dominant destination sector of displaced workers remains the nontraded sector in 1996–1997, both for workers from exporters and for workers from nonexporters. As in the initial period 1990–1991, in 1996–1997 former nonexporter workers most frequently find reemployment at nonexporter firms, and former exporter workers are roughly equally likely to find reemployment at exporter and nonexporter firms in manufacturing but less likely to transition to an exporter in the primary sector. By 1996–1997, an even larger fraction of displaced primary-sector workers than in 1990–1991 fails to experience a successful formal-sector reallocation and a roughly equally large share of former manufacturing workers as in 1990–1991 fails to find a formal-sector job within the following calendar year.

Together with the evidence on infrequent task reassignments in-house, these labor-market transitions suggest that the observed workforce changeovers from the preceding section are neither achieved through worker reallocations within employers nor are they brought about by labor reallocations across employers and sectors. By exclusion, the remaining explanation is that formal-sector employers in the traded-goods industries shrink their workforces by dismissing less-schooled workers more frequently than more-schooled workers, while the thus displaced workers fail to find reemployment, at least at the annual horizon. In the aggregate, the

---

8. The slightly smaller unaccounted percentage in table 9.3, compared to the reallocation failure rates in tables 9.4 and 9.5, is largely due to a restriction of the initial sample to workers with comprehensive occupation information in table 9.3.

Table 9.5   **Year-over-year firm and sector transitions, 1996–1997 (%)**

	To primary		To manufacturing				
From	Nonexp. (1)	Exp. (2)	Nonexp. (3)	Exp. (4)	Nontraded (5)	Failure (6)	Total (7)
Primary Nonexporter	32.1	2.5	6.0	2.9	15.4	41.1	100.0
Primary Exporter	17.1	13.0	6.5	3.3	18.7	41.5	100.0
Manufact. Nonexporter	5.6	.4	18.9	6.5	32.1	36.5	100.0
Manufact. Exporter	7.2	.7	12.1	13.9	27.3	38.8	100.0
Nontraded	1.3	.2	3.8	2.0	55.8	36.9	100.0
Failure	8.9	.7	12.2	6.1	72.1		100.0
Total	6.5	.6	8.8	4.7	56.9	22.5	100.0

Source: RAIS 1996–1997 (1% random sample), male workers nationwide, 25 to 64 years old. SECEX 1996–1997 for exporting status. Frequencies are job accessions in Brazil within one year after separation, based on last employment of year (highest paying job if many). Failed accessions are separations followed by no formal-sector accessions anywhere in Brazil within a year, excluding workers with prior retirement or death, or age sixty-five or above in earlier job.

lacking traded-sector reallocations result in a considerable decline of formal manufacturing employment, from 26 to 22 percent (table 9.1). The simultaneous expansion of nontraded-output industries can partly be driven by a long-term shift from primary to manufacturing to services activities in the economy, or by Brazil's overvalued real exchange rate during the sample period, or by foreign direct investment (FDI) flows in the wake of Brazil's concomitant capital-account liberalization and privatization program, by trade liberalization, or by a combination of these changes. The next section discusses the predictive power of these competing explanations and their associated variables. In the final section, the issue of reallocation durations beyond the annual horizon is discussed.

9.5   Establishment Workforce Changes

While the timing of labor-demand changes, workforce changeovers, and variations in the reallocation pattern is suggestive of the role that trade reform may play for the labor market, it remains to investigate the predictive power of competing policy variables. For this purpose, the universe of employment records on December 31 is aggregated to the establishment level and the discussion turns to an employer-level version of the linked employer-employee data by retaining all establishments that employ at least one worker from the nationwide and metropolitan random worker samples in the preceding sections. Employer-level regressions are most closely comparable to prior evidence (Davis, Haltiwanger, and Schuh 1996; Ribeiro et al. 2004). The interest lies on employment change at the establishment level and its covariation with various policy variables during the 1990–1997 period. Attention is restricted to manufacturing industries, where the bulk of Brazil's traded-goods sector employment occurs.

9.5.1   Statistical Model

Consider the regression model

$$(3) \qquad \ell_{k,t+1} - \ell_{kt} = \mathbf{1}(exp_{kt}) \, \beta + \mathbf{z}_{jt}\gamma + \mathbf{x}_{kt}\delta + \alpha_k + \alpha_t + \varepsilon_{kt}$$

for employment change $\ell_{k,t+1} - \ell_{kt}$ at establishment k conditional on an indicator $\mathbf{1}(exp_{kt})$ whether establishment k belongs to an exporting firm at time t, sector-level control variables z_{jt} for establishment k's sector j, and establishment-level variables x_{kt}, where α_k are time-invariant establishment-fixed effects, α_t are establishment-invariant time effects, and ε_{kt} is a well-behaved error term. The sector-level variables z_{jt} include predictors related to Brazil's time-varying trade regime. In the regression sample, t spans 1990 to 1997.

A concern is whether predictors can be causally related to employment changes. Establishment-fixed effects subsume sector-fixed effects and thus remove potentially confounding sector differences in labor-market consequences from the constitutional changes to labor-market institutions prior to trade reform. Recall that Brazil's abrupt trade policy shift in 1990, though surprisingly implemented by the executive and largely designed in the absence of private-sector consultations, hits previously highly protected industries with the strongest tariff reductions, so that the tariff dispersion drops—thus turning trade policy into an endogenous instrument, potentially correlated with sectoral labor-market differences. Similarly, differences in establishment-level employment growth rates may be related to export status, not only through an employer's export status itself. Drawing on prior work in Muendler (2004), instrumental variables (IVs) are used as foreign components of the real exchange rate. These components are: the U.S. PPI by industry, the PPI of select Western European countries by industry, the OECD-wide PPI by industry, and a worldwide mix of wholesale price index (WPI) and PPI for Brazil's twenty-five major trading partners for all OECD countries. These foreign prices are plausibly exogenous to Brazil's price and cost evolution. These four sector- and time-varying instrumental variables are used to predict the export indicator $\mathbf{1}(exp._{kt})$ and its interaction with product tariffs as well as the product tariff and intermediate-input tariff (in z_{jt}). Brazil's nominal exchange rate is not an instrument for model (3) because time variation is already controlled for with year indicators. Four instrumental variables for these four potentially endogenous predictors make the model just identified. The sector real exchange rate itself is retained among the predictors in z_{jt} because its variation depends on Brazil's sectoral (wholesale) price index beyond the four instrumental variables.

9.5.2   Data and Estimates

As table 9.6 shows, the nationwide mean manufacturing establishment between 1990 and 1997 reduces employment by 2.5 workers over the course of the subsequent year (1991–1998), and the mean metropolitan establishment cuts employment by a net number of 2.6 workers. Though slightly higher in levels, there is less dispersion in net employment changes across metropolitan establishments. Sixteen percent of the establishments belong to an exporting firm both nationwide and in metropolitan areas (but average employment at metropolitan exporters is larger; recall table 9.1). Not conditioning on exports status, the average size of metropolitan establishments is below the nationwide average with 16.3 workers (2.792 in logs) compared to 17.7 (2.876 in logs), while the size dispersion is wider in metropolitan areas than nationwide. Metropolitan establishments retain their workers slightly longer than the nationwide average, resulting in a higher mean tenure at the establishment, and show both more-educated workforces and a more skill-intensive occupation profile. Metropolitan manufacturing establishments produce in slightly less tariff-protected sectors and in sectors with slightly higher levels of foreign penetration. In summary, metropolitan manufacturing establishments face somewhat tougher

Table 9.6   **Employer samples nationwide and in metropolitan areas**

	Nationwide		Metropolitan	
	Mean (1)	Std. Dev. (2)	Mean (3)	Std. Dev. (4)
Employment change over next year	−2.501	132.239	−2.580	131.860
Exporter status	.156	.363	.158	.365
Establishment-level variables				
Log employment	2.876	1.519	2.792	1.533
Mean: Tenure at plant (in years)	.647	.533	.671	.554
Share: Prof. or manag'l. occ.	.061	.123	.067	.134
Share: Tech'l. or superv. occ.	.120	.193	.127	.197
Share: Unskilled white collar occ.	.083	.157	.090	.164
Share: Skilled blue collar occ.	.584	.347	.558	.350
Share: Middle school or less	.771	.271	.763	.277
Share: Some high school	.173	.222	.174	.221
Sector-level variables				
Product market tariff	.190	.110	.186	.106
Intm. input tariff	.149	.084	.147	.082
Import penetration	.055	.045	.059	.047

Sources: RAIS 1990–1998 (employers of male workers, twenty-five to sixty-four years old, with manufacturing job in 1% random sample nationwide and in 5% random sample for metropolitan areas) and SECEX 1990–1998. Sector information at subsector IBGE level.

foreign competition and are slightly smaller and more skilled, but metropolitan establishments are more diverse along several dimensions.

Table 9.7 presents regression results for the nationwide sample from five alternative specifications. All specifications condition on establishment and year-fixed effects. Sector-level tariff variables have no statistically significant predictive power when included by themselves in the first specification. Establishment-level variables are statistically significant predictors. Large establishments, in terms of log employment, grow significantly less in the subsequent year; establishments with high-tenure workers (and thus high worker-retention rates) grow significantly more. Establishments that have a larger share of professional occupations or a larger share of unskilled white-collar occupations add to their workforces during the 1990–1997 period, whereas establishments with a larger share of skilled blue-collar occupations add fewer workers to the workforce (unskilled blue-collar occupations are the omitted category). Taken together with the prior evidence that the share of blue-collar occupations expands in the traded-goods sector, these findings suggest that workforce changeovers are largely driven by more than proportional worker layoffs from high-skill occupations at low-skill intensive employers. The overall goodness-of-fit of merely .6 percent indicates that the bulk of the variation in establishment-level employment changes remains unexplained. These findings continue unaltered as the specifications become richer.

Including additional sector variables related to Brazil's international economic integration and industrial structure does not result in better predictive power of tariffs in specification 2. Import penetration partly captures unobserved nontariff barriers, the sectoral real exchange rate controls for sector variation in Brazil's relative prices beyond the time variation of the year fixed effects, FDI flows into the sample manufacturing sectors partly measure the effect of capital-account liberalization and privatization on employment changes, and Herfindahl concentration indexes approximate domestic competitive conditions. No single-sector variable is a statistically significant predictor of establishment-level employment changes itself, and neither are tariff variables good predictors. The lacking statistical significance stands in surprising contrast to the salient correlation of these regressors with firm-level productivity in Brazil's manufacturing sector (Muendler 2004).

The establishment's parent-firm export status, however, is a significant predictor of employment change once included in specification 3. Being an exporter predicts a net employment loss of more than two workers, a substantial number given the mean establishment size of sixteen workers. Contrary to what classic trade theory might lead us to anticipate, exporter establishments significantly reduce their workforces over the 1990–1997 period. The predicted employment loss at exporters between 1990 and 1997 needs to be qualified, however, as the interaction of tariff protection with exporting status is a significant control variable (specification 4). The

Table 9.7   **Manufacturing employment changes nationwide**

	FE specifications				FE-IV
	(1)	(2)	(3)	(4)	(5)
Firm-level trade variables					
Exporter status			−2.51	−8.81	−137.24
			(1.28)**	(1.85)***	(717.76)
Exporter × product tariff				35.33	−16.35
				(7.50)***	(855.35)
Sector-level variables					
Product market tariff	4.92	1.02	1.53	−1.96	48.55
	(13.65)	(14.15)	(14.15)	(14.17)	(40.85)
Intm. input tariff	−4.61	−0.78	−1.41	−0.51	−59.72
	(20.36)	(20.94)	(20.94)	(20.94)	(122.34)
Import penetration		5.75	6.00	7.56	19.52
		(13.95)	(13.95)	(13.95)	(49.01)
Sector real exch. rate (EP^* / P)		24.46	24.44	21.73	21.37
		(19.08)	(19.08)	(19.09)	(103.85)
FDI flow (USD billion)		−0.78	−0.78	−0.87	−0.90
		(.74)	(.74)	(.74)	(2.05)
Herfindahl Index (sales)		−3.45	−3.20	−2.86	7.47
		(12.40)	(12.40)	(12.40)	(118.37)
Establishment-level variables					
Log employment	−22.33	−22.34	−22.28	−22.36	−19.27
	(.45)***	(.45)***	(.45)***	(.45)***	(20.62)
Mean: tenure at plant (in years)	4.21	4.22	4.24	4.30	5.00
	(.98)***	(.98)***	(.98)***	(.98)***	(3.44)
Share: prof. or manag'l. occ.	25.62	25.62	25.64	25.66	26.57
	(3.26)***	(3.26)***	(3.26)***	(3.26)***	(5.58)***
Share: tech'l. or superv. occ.	1.10	1.10	1.12	1.08	2.38
	(2.43)	(2.43)	(2.43)	(2.43)	(9.08)
Share: unskilled white collar occ.	10.22	10.21	10.22	10.11	10.83
	(2.87)***	(2.87)***	(2.87)***	(2.87)***	(6.60)
Share: skilled blue collar occ.	−3.51	−3.52	−3.52	−3.55	−3.39
	(1.50)**	(1.50)**	(1.50)**	(1.50)**	(2.26)
Obs.	500,659	500,659	500,659	500,659	500,659
R^2 (overall)	.006	.006	.006	.005	.003

Sources: RAIS 1990–1998 (employers of 1% random sample of male workers nationwide, twenty-five to sixty-four years old, with manufacturing job) and SECEX 1990–1998. Sector information at subsector IBGE level. Controlling for establishment-fixed and year effects. Establishment-clustered standard errors in parentheses.

***Significant at the 1 percent level.
**Significant at the 5 percent level.
*Significant at the 10 percent level.

typical exporter cuts almost nine jobs in an unprotected sector with zero tariffs, but tariff protection mitigates the effect. Given a .11 standard deviation of product-market tariffs in the nationwide sample, the point estimate on the interaction term implies that raising tariffs by a standard deviation reduces the predicted job loss at exporters by four jobs, from almost nine to under five jobs lost. At the sample mean product-market tariff level of .19, the mean exporter has a predicted job loss of 2.1 jobs. There is no conclusive evidence, however, that exporting status is causally related to employment reductions. When firm-level export status and its interaction with product-market tariffs (as well as product and intermediate-input tariffs) are instrumented for with sector-year varying foreign components of the real exchange rate (specification 5), export status loses its statistical significance.[9] Yet, there is no evidence against the causal impact of exporting status on employment changes either in that the sign remains negative and the point estimate increases in absolute value. Establishment heterogeneity in unobserved workforce composition, or other unobserved sources of heterogeneity, may be associated with both exporting status and employment change and could hamper identification in the IV approach.

I estimate model (3) also for the metropolitan sample. Table 9.8 presents the results. Sign patterns and point estimates are remarkably similar between the nationwide and the metropolitan samples. The predicted number of lost jobs at exporters in unprotected sectors (with zero tariffs) is now eight—with a standard deviation increase in tariffs predicting three lost jobs less or around five lost jobs after a 1-standard deviation increase. At the sample mean product-market tariff, exporting status predicts a net job loss of 2.2 jobs, slightly above the nationwide average, arguably because of a lower tariff-protection effect. Similar to the nationwide results, an IV approach raises point estimates but shows no statistically significant effect of exporting status on net employment change.

In principle, linked employer-employee data also permit the construction of estimation samples that trace changes to establishment-level employment through accessions and separations at the job level. The construction of according estimation samples is a promising path for future research in that such samples make it possible to control for establishments' workforce heterogeneity at the individual worker and job level. A remaining concern of this chapter is what consequences the documented trade regime changes may have for labor-market outcomes.

9.6 Labor Market Performance

Most evidence so far suggests that the metropolitan areas of Brazil are strikingly similar to the national average. If anything, the lower levels of tariff protection in the sectors of the typical metropolitan exporters and the higher levels of import penetration (table 9.6) would suggest a stronger impact of trade reform on labor-market performance. Accordingly, establishment-level regressions in the preceding section predict that, at the

9. F-test statistics for the predictive power of the four instrumental variables are above values of 1,000 for the two endogenous sector-level regressors (product-market and intermediate-input tariffs) and above 100 for the two endogenous firm-level regressors (export status and its interaction with product-market tariffs).

Table 9.8   **Manufacturing employment changes in metropolitan areas**

	FE specifications				FE-IV
	(1)	(2)	(3)	(4)	(5)
Firm-level trade variables					
Exporter status			−2.39	−8.21	−356.09
			(1.28)*	(1.86)***	(714.07)
Exporter × product tariff				32.26	−568.96
				(7.51)***	(770.82)
Sector-level variables					
Product market tariff	9.54	5.65	5.90	1.14	59.15
	(13.60)	(14.02)	(14.02)	(14.06)	(120.18)
Intm. input tariff	−8.18	−4.99	−5.35	−3.87	4.68
	(20.19)	(20.74)	(20.74)	(20.74)	(234.58)
Import penetration		−0.28	−0.004	1.92	17.48
		(13.13)	(13.13)	(13.14)	(54.99)
Sector real exch. rate (EP^*/P)		30.05	29.98	27.91	62.31
		(18.70)	(18.70)	(18.70)	(61.50)
FDI flow (USD billion)		−0.72	−0.73	−0.79	−0.33
		(.75)	(.75)	(.75)	(1.42)
Herfindahl Index (sales)		1.58	1.79	1.92	51.84
		(11.98)	(11.98)	(11.98)	(118.14)
Establishment-level variables					
Log employment	−23.24	−23.25	−23.20	−23.26	−11.85
	(.46)***	(.46)***	(.46)***	(.46)***	(20.30)
Mean: tenure at plant (in years)	3.54	3.56	3.57	3.62	5.67
	(.96)***	(.96)***	(.96)***	(.96)***	(4.47)
Share: prof. or manag'l. occ.	23.52	23.53	23.56	23.59	27.95
	(3.11)***	(3.11)***	(3.11)***	(3.11)***	(8.87)***
Share: tech'l. or superv. occ.	1.81	1.83	1.84	1.80	4.83
	(2.33)	(2.33)	(2.33)	(2.33)	(5.76)
Share: unskilled white-collar occ.	8.60	8.58	8.60	8.50	13.53
	(2.69)***	(2.69)***	(2.69)***	(2.69)***	(8.65)
Share: skilled blue-collar occ.	−3.29	−3.29	−3.30	−3.34	−2.70
	(1.46)**	(1.46)**	(1.46)**	(1.46)**	(1.90)
Obs.	502,523	502,523	502,523	502,523	502,523
R^2 (overall)	.005	.005	.005	.005	.002

Sources: RAIS 1990–98 (employers of 5% random sample of male workers in metropolitan areas, twenty-five to sixty-four years old, with manufacturing job) and SECEX 1990–98. Sector information at subsector IBGE level. Controlling for establishment-fixed and year effects. Establishment-clustered standard errors in parentheses.

***Significant at the 1 percent level.
**Significant at the 5 percent level.
*Significant at the 10 percent level.

sample mean, exporters reduce employment by 2.2 jobs in metropolitan areas but only by 2.1 jobs nationwide. On the other hand, metropolitan areas have a somewhat larger services sector in employment terms (table 9.1), and a majority of displaced manufacturing workers with successful formal-sector reallocations shifts to services. Metropolitan establishments also exhibit more diversity (as measured by standard deviations) in terms of employment size and the skill composition of their workforces (table 9.6). Inasmuch as the presence of a larger services sector or the diversity of manufacturing establishments are conducive to faster reabsorptions, it is an open question whether the stronger exposure of the metropolitan areas in Brazil to the international economy would result in a better or worse labor-market performance following trade liberalization.

The empirical answer is unambiguous. In order to measure times to successful reallocation, a sample of workers with a separation at any time between 1990 and 1997 is taken and tracked as to whether the workers are successfully rehired into a formal-sector job within the forty-eight months following their separation. Table 9.9 shows that almost two in three successfully reallocated workers in metropolitan areas find a new job within the month of their separation. In contrast, only one in seven workers nationwide is successfully rehired within the same month of displacement. In metropolitan areas, 95 percent of successfully reallocated workers start their new job within twelve months. But only 77 percent of the successfully reallocated workers nationwide find new employment nationwide within a year, 13 percent need up to two years, 6 percent need up to three years, and 4 percent need up to four years. There is a slight worsening in the time-to-reallocation in both metropolitan and nationwide labor markets between 1990 and 1997, but this time variation is small compared to the substantial regional differences. In short, metropolitan labor markets perform considerably faster in the reallocation process, even though evidence in the earlier sections shows only small differences between the metropolitan employer and employee characteristics and the nationwide characteristics.

Two candidate explanations for the substantial difference between metropolitan and national labor markets, consistent with the documented

Table 9.9   **Formal-sector reallocation time spans 1990–1997**

	Mean 1990–1997		1990		1997	
Reallocation	Nation (1)	Metro (2)	Nation (3)	Metro (4)	Nation (5)	Metro (6)
Same month	.146	.597	.163	.615	.138	.576
1 year	.627	.353	.663	.351	.614	.361
1 to 2 years	.134	.031	.101	.021	.135	.037
2 to 3 years	.058	.012	.045	.008	.065	.015
3 to 4 years	.035	.007	.027	.005	.048	.011

Source: RAIS 1990–2001. Male workers nationwide (1% random sample) or in metropolitan areas only (5% random sample), twenty-five to sixty-four years old (in highest-paying job, if many), displaced from a formal-sector job between 1990 and 1997 and rehired into a formal-sector job within forty-eight months. Columns sum to 100 percent.

Table 9.10   Employment allocation by subsector

Sector and subsectore IBGE	Employment share		
	1986 (1)	1990 (2)	1997 (3)
Primary			
1 Mining and quarrying	.007	.006	.004
25 Agriculture, farming, hunting, forestry, and fishing	.015	.016	.041
Manufacturing			
2 Manufacture of nonmetallic mineral products	.016	.013	.011
3 Manufacture of metallic products	.030	.024	.021
4 Manufacture of machinery, equipment, and instruments	.020	.016	.011
5 Manufacture of electrical and telecommunications equipment	.016	.014	.008
6 Manufacture of transport equipment	.019	.016	.013
7 Manufacture of wood products and furniture	.019	.015	.015
8 Manufacture of paper, paperboard, and publishing	.014	.014	.013
9 Manufacture of rubber, tobacco, leather, and products n.e.c.	.019	.016	.009
10 Manufacture of chemical and pharmaceutical products	.024	.022	.020
11 Manufacture of apparel and textiles	.042	.035	.026
12 Manufacture of footwear	.012	.010	.008
13 Manufacture of food, beverages, and ethyl alcohol	.040	.039	.041
Commerce			
16 Retail trade	.106	.103	.127
17 Wholesale trade	.024	.025	.027
Services			
18 Financial intermediation and insurance	.038	.034	.025
19 Real estate and business services	.074	.073	.079
20 Transport, storage, and telecommunications	.050	.044	.057
21 Hotels and restaurants, repair and maintenance services	.101	.101	.084
22 Medical, dental, and veterinary services	.014	.017	.039
23 Education	.008	.009	.036
Other			
14 Electricity, gas, and water supply	.013	.014	.014
15 Construction	.045	.041	.049
24 Public administration and social services	.209	.206	.224
26 Activities n.e.c.	.025	.077	.001
Total employment (thousands of workers)	22,164	23,174	24,104

Source: RAIS 1986, 1990, and 1997, universe of workers. Employment as of December 31. Slight differences to table 9.7 are due to random sampling errors.

evidence in this chapter, are the presence of a larger services sector and the diversity of the manufacturing establishments in metropolitan areas (see table 9.10). The differences along these two dimensions seem small, however, to give rise to the considerable differences in labor-market performance across regions, and more research into the functioning of labor-market adjustment seems warranted for an understanding of the economic performance after procompetitive reforms.

9.7   Conclusions

This chapter documents the changes to labor demand and workforce composition that accompanied Brazil's largescale trade reform in the early 1990s. Several aspects of the labor-market adjustment and workforce changeover in traded-goods industries are broadly consistent with the insights of Heckscher-Ohlin trade theory. Being a low-skill-abundant country relative to its main trading partners, Brazil exhibits a shift toward sectors that intensively use low-skilled labor. Within sectors, Brazil shifts toward low-skill intensive occupations and fills those occupations with relatively better-schooled workers—just as a Stolper-Samuelson argument applied to occupational activities instead of sectors would suggest. The setting of classic trade theory in a context of full employment within traded-goods industries is a less useful guide to Brazil's further evidence, however. Among the displaced traded-goods sector workers with a successful reallocation, most shift to nontraded-output industries and almost as many displaced workers do not find formal reemployment at an annual horizon. Unexpectedly, regressions show that exporter establishments exhibit a significant employment downsizing over the period following trade liberalization, controlling for a large set of other establishment-level and sector-level predictors as well as establishment and year effects.

The reduced demand for highly skilled workers following trade liberalization implies that the returns to skill drop. This raises the question whether pro-competitive reform has the side effect to lastingly weaken incentives for educational attainment. In Menezes-Filho et al. (2008), we document (with Mincer [1974]) regressions, including employer-fixed effects, that the returns to skill fall between 1990 and 1997. But the drop is slight. Especially in comparison to industrialized countries, returns to human capital remain elevated in Brazil throughout the 1990s: a typical male manufacturing worker in Brazil with a college degree in 1990, for instance, receives wages that are 150 percent higher than a comparable worker with a high school education, and 140 percent higher in 1997 (whereas this premium stands at 70 percent in the United States, and it is only 40 percent in France in the early 1990s). The small reduction in education premia between 1990 and 1997 suggests that Brazil's trade reform has not significantly diminished incentives for educational attainment.

Though a firm's exporting status is a significant predictor of employment downsizing, an instrumental-variable approach provides neither evidence in favor nor against a causal interpretation of this prediction. Substantial workforce heterogeneity may affect the prediction. To control for the heterogeneity in workforce characteristics, linked employer-employee data can be used to construct worker-level samples and assess separations from and accessions to employers at the individual job level in future research. Although Brazil's metropolitan labor markets only slightly differ from the national average in sectoral composition and establishment-level

diversity, workers experience much shorter times to successful reallocation. The striking but unexplained difference points to the limits in our current understanding of labor-market adjustment following large-scale pro-
competitive reform.

Appendix

Brazilian law requires all Brazilian establishments to submit detailed annual reports with individual information on their workers and employees
to the ministry of labor (Ministério de Trabalho, MTE). Data collection is
typically concluded at the parent firm by March following the year of observation.

Screening

In RAIS, workers are identified by individual-specific PIS (Programa de
Integração Social) IDs that are similar to social security numbers in the
United States (but PIS IDs are not used for identification purposes other
than the administration of the wage supplement program Abono Salarial).
A given establishment may report the same PIS ID multiple times within a
single year in order to help the worker withdraw deposits from his or her
severance pay savings account (Fundo de Garantia do Tempo de Serviço
[FGTS]) through spurious layoffs and rehires. Moreover, bad compliance
causes certain PIS IDs to be recorded incorrectly or repeatedly. To handle
these issues, the census records are screened as follows. (1) Observations
with PIS IDs having fewer than eleven digits are removed. These correspond to either informal (undocumented) workers or recording error from
faulty bookkeeping. (2) Multiple employments with the same accession
and separation date at the same employer are removed. For a worker with
such multiple employments, the observation with the highest average
monthly wage level is kept (in cases of wage level ties, duplicate random observations are dropped).

Age, Education, and Occupation

The following tables present age and education classifications from
RAIS. The age range information in RAIS is used to infer the typical age
of a worker in the age range, as follows (table 9A.1).

For much of the analysis, the number of education categories for pres-
entation is reduced, and the nine education categories included in RAIS
are regrouped to correspond to five categories, as shown in the following.
Some statistical applications require a continuous years-of-schooling variable, which is defined as follows (table 9A.2).

The occupation indicator variables are obtained from the CBO classification codes in RAIS and are reclassified to conform to the ISCO-88 cate-

gories. For a description of the Brazilian occupation classification system CBO and a mapping to ISCO-88, see Muendler et al., 2004. In the available RAIS version for the nation as a whole, CBO classes are only reported at the three-digit level. The mapping from CBO to ISCO-88 is adjusted accordingly. For most of the aggregate analysis, the ISCO-88 categories are mapped to occupation levels as follows (table 9A.3).

Table 9A.1   Typical age of worker

RAIS age category	Imputed age
1 Child (10–14)	Excluded
2 Youth (15–17)	Excluded
3 Adolescent (18–24)	Excluded
4 Nascent career (25–29)	27
5 Early career (30–39)	34.5
6 Peak career (40–49)	44.5
7 Late career (50–64)	57
8 Post Retirement (65–)	Excluded

Table 9A.2   Education categories and years of schooling

Education level	RAIS education	Years of schooling
1 Illiterate or primary school dropout		
Illiterate	1	0
Primary school dropout	2	1
2 Primary school graduate or middle school dropout		
Primary school graduate	3	4
Middle school dropout	4	5
3 Middle school graduate or high school dropout		
Middle school graduate	5	8
High school dropout	6	9
4 High school graduate or college dropout		
High school graduate	7	12
College dropout	8	13
5 College graduate	9	16

Table 9A.3   mapping between ISCO-88 categories and occupation levels

ISCO-88 category	Occupation level
1 Legislators, senior officials, and managers	Professional and managerial
2 Professionals	Professional and managerial
3 Technicians and associate professionals	Technical and supervisory
4 Clerks	Other white collar
5 Service workers and shop and market sales workers	Other white collar
6 Skilled agricultural and fishery workers	Skill-intensive blue collar
7 Craft and related workers	Skill-intensive blue collar
8 Establishment and machine operators and assemblers	Skill-intensive blue collar
9 Elementary occupations	Other blue collar

References

Davis, Steven J., John C. Haltiwanger, and Scott Schuh, 1996. *Job creation and destruction.* Cambridge and London: MIT Press.

Freeman, Richard B. 1980. An empirical analysis of the fixed coefficient 'manpower requirements' model, 1960–1970. *Journal of Human Resources* 15 (2): 176–99.

Gonzaga, Gustavo. 2003. Labor turnover and labor legislation in Brazil. *Economia: Journal of the Latin American and Caribbean Economic Association* 4 (1): 165–207.

Gonzaga, Gustavo, Naércio Aquino Menezes-Filho, and Maria Cristina Terra. Trade liberalization and the evolution of skill earnings differentials in Brazil. 2006. *Journal of International Economics* 68 (2): 345–67.

Gourinchas, Pierre Olivier. 1999. Exchange rates do matter: French job reallocation and exchange rate turbulence, 1984–1992. *European Economic Review* 43 (7): 1279–1316.

Haltiwanger, John C., Adriana Kugler, Maurice Kugler, Alejandro Micco, and Carmen Pagés. 2004. Effects of tariffs and real exchange rates on job reallocation: Evidence from Latin America. *Journal of Policy Reform.* Special issue. 7 (4): 191–208.

Heckman, James J., and Carmen Pagés. 2004. Law and employment: Introduction. In *Law and employment: Lessons from Latin America and the Caribbean,* ed. James J. Heckman and Carmen Pagés, 1–107. NBER conference report series. Chicago and London: University of Chicago Press.

Katz, Lawrence F., and Kevin M. Murphy. 1992. Changes in relative wages, 1963–1987: Supply and demand factors. *Quarterly Journal of Economics* 107 (1): 35–78.

Klein, Michael W., Scott Schuh, and Robert K. Triest. 2003. Job creation, job destruction, and the real exchange rate. *Journal of International Economics* 59 (2): 239–65.

Kume, Honório, Guida Piani, and Carlos Frederico Bráz de Souza. 2003. A política Brasileira de importação no período 1987–98: Descrição e avaliação. In *A abertura comercial Brasileira nos anos 1990: Impactos sobre emprego e salários,* eds. Carlos Henrique Corseuil and Honório Kume, 9–37. Rio de Janeiro: IPEA (Instituto de Pesquisa Econômica Aplicada).

Menezes-Filho, Naércio Aquino, Marc-Andreas Muendler, and Garey Ramey. 2008. The structure of worker compensation in Brazil, with a comparison to France and the United States, *Review of Economics and Statistics.*

Mincer, Jacob. 1974. *Schooling, experience, and earnings.* New York: Columbia University Press.

Muendler, Marc-Andreas. 2004. Trade, technology, and productivity: A study of Brazilian manufacturers, 1986–1998. CESifo working paper no. 1148. Munich: Center for Economic Studies.

Muendler, Marc-Andreas, Jennifer Poole, Garey Ramey, and Tamara Wajnberg. 2004. Job concordances for Brazil: Mapping the Classificação Brasileira de Ocupações (CBO) to the International Standard Classification of Occupations (ISCO-88). Unpublished manuscript. University of California, San Diego.

Ramos, Roberto Luís Olinto, and Claudia Nessi Zonenschain. 2000. The performance of the Brazilian imports and exports based on the system of national accounts: 1980–1998. Rio de Janeiro: Instituto Brasileiro de Geografia e Estatística (IBGE).

Revenga, Ana L. 1992. Exporting jobs? The impact of import competition on employment and wages in U.S. manufacturing. *Quarterly Journal of Economics* 107 (1): 255–84.

————. 1997. Employment and wage effects of trade liberalization: The case of Mexican manufacturing. *Journal of Labor Economics* Part 2. 15 (3): S20–43.

Ribeiro, Eduardo Pontual, Carlos Henrique Corseuil, Daniel Santos, Paulo Furtado, Brunu Amorim, Luciana Servo, and André Souza. 2004. Trade liberalization, the exchange rate and job flows in Brazil. *Journal of Policy Reform.* Special issue. 7 (4): 209–23.

Roberts, Mark J. 1996. Employment flows and producer turnover. In *Industrial evolution in developing countries: Micro patterns of turnover, productivity, and market structure,* ed. Mark J. Roberts and James R. Tybout, 18–42. Oxford and New York: Oxford University Press.

Job Creation Abroad and Worker Retention at Home

Sascha O. Becker and Marc-Andreas Muendler

10.1 Introduction

The employment consequences of multinational enterprises' global expansions receive substantial public interest. Surprisingly, however, data at the job or worker level are rarely available to investigate this issue more closely. This chapter presents such novel data for Germany and provides evidence on worker separations across industries and firm types—with a particular focus on the distinction between firms that are expanding abroad through ownership of foreign affiliates and those that are not. Contrary to a wide-held perception, both among researchers and in the general public, multinational enterprises offer more stable jobs at home and exhibit lower worker separation rates than their competitors without foreign expansions do. We explore this difference in separation rates by relating it to foreign direct investment (FDI) expansions in Central and Eastern Europe, and worldwide, and by controlling for a rich set of worker, job, home-firm, foreign-affiliate, and sector characteristics.

Sascha O. Becker is Reader in Economics at the University of Stirling, UK. Marc-Andreas Muendler is an assistant professor of economics at the University of California, San Diego, and a faculty research fellow at the NBER.

We thank Till von Wachter, Dieter Urban, and participants at the Conference on the Analysis of Firms and Employees in Nuremberg for useful comments and discussions. We thank Heinz Herrmann, Alexander Lipponer, and Fred Ramb for support with BuBa firm data, and Stefan Bender, Iris Koch, and Stephan Heuke for assistance with BA employment records. Karin Herbst and Thomas Wenger at BuBa kindly shared their string-matching expertise. Regis Barnichon, Nadine Gröpl, Robert Jäckle, Daniel Klein, and Stefan Schraufstetter provided excellent research assistance at various stages of the project. We gratefully acknowledge financial support from the VolkswagenStiftung under its grant initiative Global Structures and Their Governance, and administrative and financial support from the Ifo Institute. Becker gratefully acknowledges financial support from the Fritz-Thyssen-Stiftung.

Theory predicts that trade affects labor demand and thus employment stability. Empirical evidence suggests that multinational enterprises (MNEs) channel a large fraction of cross-border trade through their global in-house activities. Multinational enterprises with headquarters in the United States, for instance, transact more than two in five exports and around half of U.S. imports through their affiliates (Zeile 1997). The UN Conference on Trade and Development reports that the world's ten largest MNEs in 2000 produce almost 1 percent of world gross domestic product (GDP), and that the one hundred largest MNEs are responsible for more than 4 percent of world GDP (up from 31/2 percent in 1990).[1]

This chapter documents that manufacturing MNEs exhibit 4 percent lower domestic worker separation rates than non-MNEs in manufacturing. Neither worker characteristics nor the MNE's workforce composition and other observable MNE characteristics, nor sector variables alone can explain the fact that worker retention rates are higher at MNEs: conditional on sector, employer, and worker characteristics, an indicator of an FDI expansion in Central and Eastern Europe (CEE) still predicts 1.6 percentage points lower worker separation rates at MNEs with expansions into CEE, and 1.8 percentage points lower separation rates for expansions anywhere worldwide. To rule out a temporary coincidence of foreign expansions and increased home worker retention rates, or transitory firm-level shocks that might drive both foreign employment expansions and home worker retentions, we instrument for current foreign expansions with an MNE's past employment, capital stock, and turnover expansions. The instrumental-variables estimate for past employment changes raises the predicted reduction in home separation rates to 2.6 percentage points for CEE. This increase in the point estimate is consistent with the ideas that either the foreign expansion itself raises the home-worker retention rate or that an MNE's permanent gain in competitive advantage raises both foreign expansions and home-worker retentions. Irrespective of the ultimate causal mechanism, which we leave for future research to settle, there is no evidence to blame MNEs for worker separations in the wake of global competition. To the contrary, our estimates are consistent with the prediction that preventing firms from a foreign workforce buildup could be associated with accelerated worker separations from domestic establishments.

Several interpretations are consistent with the finding that workers at MNEs retain their jobs more frequently than workers at non-MNEs. First, vertical foreign expansions that fragment the production process can lead to cost savings, increased world-wide market shares, and domestic employment growth. Second, horizontal expansions that duplicate production at foreign locations can lead to improved market access with potentially beneficial consequences for headquarters employment. Third, complementari-

---

1. UNCTAD press release TAD/INF/PR/47 (12/08/02).

ties between foreign and home operations can favor higher worker retention rates at MNEs (Harrison, McMillan, and Null 2007). The former three mechanisms emphasize multinational production and sales activities and their potential beneficial impact on home employment. Fourth, the stability afforded by in-house relationships across borders, compared to arm's-length trade, can result in more stable business prospects, so that the choice of contracting mode can reduce worker turnover. Fifth, foreign expansions can signal attractive career paths to domestic workers and reduce worker quits (Prendergast 1999), because an MNE's foreign investment commits a firm to expansion and thus becomes a device for worker retentions. All five prior mechanisms posit a causal link from foreign expansions to home employment stability. Sixth, a firm's inherent competitive advantage in product quality or production efficiency can cause foreign expansions and foster home-job retentions. Under this last mechanism, the foreign expansion is not causal to home worker retentions but a consequence of the firm's competitive success, as are home worker retentions. Irrespective of the causal interpretation under any of the six mechanisms, there is no evidence to suggest that MNEs should be prevented from overseas expansions to save jobs at home. To the contrary, the findings are consistent with the notion that hindering MNEs in their foreign expansion could result in even more domestic job losses to globalization and even stronger downward wage pressure on import-competing jobs.

There are largely three branches of the empirical literature that investigate impacts of global economic integration on domestic labor-market outcomes. A first group of studies analyzes the labor-demand effects of foreign trade, irrespective of the type of employing firm. Feenstra and Hanson (1999), for instance, analyze sector data for the United States and attribute about a third of U.S. relative wage changes to foreign trade and cross-border outsourcing (between or within firms). In related recent work, Geishecker (2006) uses individual household survey data for Germany to study the effect of industry-wide intermediate-goods imports on German workers and finds cross-border outsourcing to significantly reduce individual employment security.[2]

A second line of research investigates how foreign presence affects labor demands within MNEs. In this literature, Slaughter (2000) does not find foreign wages in MNEs' foreign locations to significantly affect labor demand at U.S. MNEs' home operations, and Konings (2004) reports a similarly insignificant relationship between foreign wages and home labor demands for European MNEs. Considering the preponderant role of MNEs in the conduct of foreign trade, these findings stand in surprising contrast to Feenstra and Hanson (1999) or Geishecker (2006). Taken together, they

---

2. A literature on worker separation is concerned with consequences of worker layoffs (e.g., Jacobson, LaLonde, and Sullivan 1993; Kletzer 2001).

seem to suggest that the labor-market consequences of foreign trade are largely due to between-firm trade rather than within-MNE trade. Other studies find modest substitution between workers in domestic establishments and foreign affiliates (Konings and Murphy 2006; Marin 2006). Hanson, Mataloni, and Slaughter (2005), however, shift the focus from factor demands to intermediate input uses and, as an exception to most prior firm-level evidence, report that affiliates of U.S. MNEs process significantly more intrafirm imports the lower are low-skilled wages abroad. The result challenges the view that foreign locations with a relative abundance in labor fail to attract MNE activity. Harrison, McMillan, and Null (2007) recently report that there is a positive correlation between home employment and foreign-affiliate employment in high-income countries but a negative correlation between home employment and foreign-affiliate employment in developing countries. Integrating foreign location choice (Devereux and Griffith 1998; Head and Mayer 2004) into labor demand estimation, we (Muendler and Becker 2006) discern MNEs' labor demand responses to foreign wages at the extensive margin, when an MNE establishes its presence at foreign locations, and at the intensive margin, when an MNE operates existing affiliates across locations. This approach shows salient employment adjustments to international wage differences: With a 1 percent increase in German wages, for instance, German MNEs add 2,000 manufacturing jobs in CEE at the extensive margin and 4,000 jobs overall.

A third group of studies, to which the present chapter belongs, too, contrasts MNEs with non-MNEs. Egger and Pfaffermayr (2003) compare domestic capital investments of pure exporters to those of MNEs and do not find a significant difference. Barba Navaretti and Castellani (2004) and Jäckle (2006) assess the effect of first-time FDI on firm performance regarding size and productivity and do not find significant effects of outward FDI on MNE home performance for their respective samples of Italian and German MNEs.

To our knowledge, there is to date no job-level research into the effects of MNE activities using linked employer-employee data. Linked employer-employee data allow us to investigate whether MNEs that expand abroad retain workers more or less frequently than competitors, while controlling for a comprehensive set of worker, job, and employer characteristics. We document a statistically and economically significant positive association between FDI expansions and domestic worker retention rates, for MNEs with no prior foreign presence and for expanding MNEs in CEE and worldwide. Together, the results from prior research on import competition (Feenstra and Hanson 1999; Geishecker 2006), labor substitution within MNEs (Harrison, McMillan, and Null 2007; Muendler and Becker 2006), and the evidence in the present chapter suggest that both intrafirm and cross-firm trade are associated with employment substitution but that MNEs with foreign employment expansions can offer more stable employment in the wake of global competition than non-MNEs. Put differently: global competition likely elevates home-worker separation rates, depending on an employer's industry to as much as 21 percent, but within industries MNEs manage to reduce these separation rates by four percentage points on average, compared to non-MNEs.

This chapter has five more sections. Section 10.2 describes the construction of our linked employer-employee data (details are relegated to the Appendices.). Section 10.3 presents descriptive evidence on foreign job growth and domestic worker separation along with a nonparametric univariate regression. We present parametric multivariate regression results and robustness checks in section 10.4. Section 10.5 concludes.

10.2   Data

We construct the linked employer-employee dataset from three confidential microdata sources, assembled at Deutsche Bundesbank in Frankfurt, and complement them with sector-level information on German foreign trade. We define enterprises as groups of affiliated domestic and foreign firms and consider all firms within a group as potential FDI firms if at least one firm in the group reports outward FDI activity. We weight the FDI exposure measures by the domestic ownership shares that connect the firms in the group. Firms outside any group with FDI exposure are classified as purely domestic firms.

The first component of our linked employer-employee dataset, worker, and job information, comes from quarterly social security records of the German Federal Labor Agency (Bundesagentur für Arbeit BA).[3] The observations are the universe of workers registered by the social insurance system over the years 1999 to 2001, representing around 80 percent of the formally employed German workforce.[4] The records show separations (but do not permit a distinction between voluntary quits by the worker and layoffs by the employer). The records contain worker and job characteristics such as age, education level, occupation, and wages. Wages in the German social security data are censored above but not below. The upper bound is the contribution ceiling for old age insurance, which is annually adjusted for nominal wage changes. In 2000, the upper bound was at an annual wage income of EUR 52,765, and it was EUR 53,379 in 2001—except for min-

---

3. These individual worker data were made available under article 75, Volume 10, of the German Social Security Code.

4. Coverage includes full- and part-time workers of private enterprises, apprentices, and other trainees, as well as temporarily suspended employment relationships. Civil servants, student workers, and self-employed individuals are excluded and make up the remaining 20 percent of the formal-sector labor force. Establishments within the same municipality may report under one single establishment identifier. Though our data directly derive from the BA source, the description by Bender, Haas, and Klose (2000) for the scientific-use version of the BA data also applies to our records.

ers (Knappschaftliche Rentenversicherung) with a ceiling of EUR 65,036 in 2000 and EUR 65,650 in 2001. Workers with an annual income below 3,865 EUR (in 2001) are not subject to social security contributions, but are part of our data and estimation sample, and we control for their inclusion (minor employment). We construct establishment-level information by aggregation from the individual-level information.

Second, information on outward FDI comes from the MIDI database (MIcro database Direct Investment, formerly DIREK), collected by Deutsche Bundesbank (BuBa); see Lipponer (2003) for documentation. The MIDI data on outward FDI cover the foreign affiliates of German MNEs above ownership shares of 10 percent.[5] For the purposes of the present analysis, we extract information on affiliate employment, affiliate turnover, and affiliate capital stocks as well as the FDI-reporting parent firm's ownership share in the foreign affiliate.

Third, in order to link the two data sources on domestic and foreign activities, we use the commercial corporate structure database MARKUS (from Verband der Vereine Creditreform) which allows us to identify all domestic parents and affiliates of FDI-reporting firms. Multinational enterprises are also multifirm enterprises in the home economy, so that outward FDI potentially affects workers beyond the FDI-reporting firm's workforce. Moreover, many German enterprises bundle the domestic management of their foreign affiliates into legally separate firms (mostly limited-liability GmbHs) for tax and liability reasons. Those bundling firms then report FDI to MIDI as required by German law. The economic impact of the reporting firm's FDI, however, goes beyond the firm's formal legal boundary in that jobs throughout the corporate group can be affected. We consider all firms within a corporate group (an enterprise) as *potential* FDI firms if at least one firm in the group reports outward FDI activities.

The three data sources do not share common firm identifiers. We use a string-matching procedure to identify clearly identical firms and their establishments (see Appendix A for a detailed description). We take the year $t = 2000$ as our base period because it is the earliest year for which we have firm structure information and can adequately attribute outward FDI exposure to domestic jobs. Our linked sample data provide a cross-section of establishments around year $t = 2000$, including a total of 39,681 establishments whose German parent-firms conduct FDI abroad and 1,133,920 control establishments—out of 3.8 million establishments in the full worker sample (1998 to 2002). We use a 5 percent random sample of workers (93,147 job observations) to reduce estimation runtime to acceptable

---

5. In 1999 and 2000, reporting is mandatory for all foreign affiliates with an asset total of at least EUR 10 million and at least a 10 percent ownership share of the German parent, or an asset total of at least EUR 1 million and at least a 50 percent ownership.

length. A random subsample of workers also reduces potential problems of error correlations between workers in the same establishment.

We observe worker characteristics, jobs, and domestic establishments at $t - 1 = 1999$, prior to the foreign expansion (from BA files in June 1999, June files being the most reliable during the year). The foreign expansion period (for changes to a job's FDI exposure) runs from $t - 1 = 1999$ (foreign-affiliate balance sheet closing dates in 1999) to t (closing dates in 2000). Most characteristics vary little between $t - 1$ (before the foreign expansion) and t (after the foreign expansion), so we simplify the timing in some specifications by considering t to still be preexpansion. A worker's retention or separation is observed between t and $t + 1 = 2001$.

We complement these microdata with annual information on imports by source country and exports by destination country from the German Federal Statistical Office, and on aggregate intermediate-goods imports, final-goods imports, and exports to world regions by German sector at the NACE 2-digit level.[6]

10.2.1   Domestic Worker Separations

Our dependent variable is an indicator of a domestic worker's separation from job i. We denote the occurrence of worker separation with y_i. The indicator takes a value of 1 if the holder of the job is displaced from the employing establishment between years t and $t + 1$ (note the one-year lead between foreign expansion and worker separation), and is zero otherwise. Worker separation includes both quits and layoffs. The German social security records do not distinguish quits from layoffs. A change of occupation within the employing establishment is not considered a separation.

10.2.2   Foreign Employment Expansions

We compute measures of changing FDI exposure both for FDI in Central and Eastern Europe (CEE), the region where German FDI expanded most markedly since the fall of the Iron Curtain, as well as worldwide (WW) FDI. Consistent with our employment perspective on domestic firm operations, we also consider foreign activities in terms of employment and construct two measures of the parent firm's change in FDI.[7] First, we use a binary foreign-expansion dummy that indicates an employment expansion at foreign affiliates in CEE, or anywhere worldwide. The indicator takes a value of 1 for a domestic job i if the employing enterprise expands

6. We calculate intermediate-goods imports by foreign location using the import share in sector inputs as reported by the German Federal Statistical Office, under the assumption that source-country frequencies are similar for intermediate-goods imports and final-goods imports.

7. Domestic worker separations measure changes in gross labor demand at home. So, a natural counterpart to the dependent variable is a predictor that measures the change in a domestic job i's FDI exposure.

its FDI exposure between years $t - 1$ and t, and zero otherwise. This measure is unweighted in the sense that we set the predictor to 1 irrespective of the enterprise's ownership share in the domestic FDI-reporting firm and irrespective of that FDI-reporting firm's ownership share in the foreign affiliates. Second, we use a continuous predictor: employment changes at foreign affiliates. This continuous variable is defined as the MNE's change in foreign-affiliate employment, weighted by both the ownership share of the enterprise in the domestic FDI-reporting firm and that FDI-reporting firm's ownership share in the foreign affiliates.

Using domestic ownership shares as weights, we attribute FDI (foreign employment) to related domestic firms and their jobs within the corporate group (see Appendix B for details of the procedure). We compute *cumulated* and *consolidated* ownership shares for all German firms that are in the same corporate group with at least one FDI-reporting firm. Cumulating means adding all direct and indirect ownership shares of a parent firm in a given affiliate. Consolidation removes the degree of self-ownership (α) from affiliates, or intermediate firms between parents and affiliates, and rescales the ultimate ownership share of the parent to account for the increased control in partly self-owning affiliates or intermediate firms (with a factor of $1/[1 - \alpha]$).

In 2000, 68 percent of German MNEs' foreign affiliates are fully owned (with 100 percent ownership share), and 86 percent of these foreign affiliates are strictly majority-owned (with strictly larger than 50 percent ownership share). So, foreign-ownership weighting has little impact on our continuous measure of foreign employment. We choose foreign ownership weighting for consistency because our domestic-job exposure measure to FDI expansions is weighted by the ownership share of the job's corporate group in the FDI-reporting German firm, and we extend this principle to foreign affiliates.

10.2.3   Additional Covariates

In multivariate regressions, we use a comprehensive set of covariates that can predict worker separation. Among the worker characteristics are the worker's age in years, indicators of the worker's gender and education, and the worker's (log) monthly wage in the current job. We transform education information into an indicator for more than upper-secondary schooling.[8] Among the job characteristics are the worker's occupation in a blue- or white-collar job, and indicators whether the worker's current work status is that of an apprentice, whether the employment is part time, whether the

---

8. This includes college graduates and college-qualified professionals; that is, professionals with a university-qualifying secondary schooling degree (Abitur), who completed professional training or an apprenticeship program instead of college education. By law, professional training and apprenticeship programs for upper-secondary schooling graduates can be no shorter than two years.

worker's earnings qualify the job as a minor employment exempt from social security contributions, or whether the job is temporary.[9] Among the domestic establishment characteristics that we observe or infer are workforce size, workforce composition by worker and job characteristics, and an East-West Germany location indicator. As discussed in detail previously, we observe parent-firm foreign activity as affiliate employment in CEE and worldwide. We use current employment expansions as predictors in multivariate regression, and past employment, turnover, and capital-stock expansions as instrumental variables to remove potentially confounding transitory firm-level shocks from the multivariate regression. Sector-level measures of German foreign trade complete the specifications.

To obtain a control variable for establishment-level differences in productivity, we estimate the establishment-fixed component in German wages from a Mincer (1974) regression for June 2000 workers with a full set of observable characteristics and include the establishment-specific measure among the preexpansion covariates. To the extent that FDI exposure is the result of enterprise characteristics such as productivity or capital intensity, we use the enterprise's past FDI exposure to control for those characteristics' FDI-relevant aspects.

10.3   Descriptive and Nonparametric Statistics

Worldwide employment at German-owned foreign affiliates doubles between 1991 and 2001, increasing from 1.9 million employees in 1991 to 3.8 million in 2001. Table 10.1 presents the evolution of foreign affiliate employment at German MNEs by world region. While Western Europe continues to be the region with most foreign employment in absolute terms, Central and Eastern Europe (CEE) strikes out as the region that exhibits the most rapid rise in affiliate employment. In 1991 employment at German affiliates in CEE was a mere 46 thousand, but it increased by a factor of 14 to nearly 670 thousand employees in 2001, almost reaching an employment level comparable to total employment in all remaining developing countries (DEV). One might expect this substantial increase in foreign employment within close reach to German headquarters to be associated with employment changes in Germany. We therefore focus our analysis on CEE countries and contrast the predicted employment changes from CEE expansions with predictions from worldwide (WW) foreign activities.

There is considerable diversity in the foreign employment evolution across sectors of foreign affiliates and German parents. Table 10.2 shows that manufacturing sectors are by far the most important industries in

---

9. In contrast to part-time work, temporary work status includes working family members in agriculture, employees past retirement age with temporary contracts, working retirees, and sporadically employed workers. Sailors, who formally belong to this group by German work status classifications, are excluded from our sample.

Table 10.1   **Affiliate employment by world region**

World region	1991 (1)	1994 (2)	1997 (3)	2000 (4)	2001 (5)
CEE	45.6	172.9	374.2	634.5	666.3
DEV	452.0	481.0	556.1	718.1	723.8
OIN	464.9	487.3	568.5	804.5	827.8
WEU	919.1	1,001.8	1,202.7	1,508.0	1,539.4
WW (worldwide)	1,881.7	2,143.0	2,701.5	3,665.2	3,757.3

Source: MIDI 1991–2001. Employment in thousands. World regions (see table 10B.2): CEE (Central and Eastern European countries), DEV (developing countries), OIN (Overseas Industrialized countries), WEU (Western European countries), and WW (World-Wide abroad).

Table 10.2   **Affiliate employment by affiliate and parent sector in 2000**

	Affiliate sector		Parent sector	
	CEE (1)	WW (2)	CEE (3)	WW (4)
Agriculture and mining	3.3	24.8	1.7	12.3
Food and textiles	62.3	161.1	30.3	91.4
Machinery and equipment	189.7	1,233.0	150.0	981.2
Other manufacturing	135.2	800.8	81.0	489.6
Commerce	119.6	778.0	48.6	224.9
Financial and business services	50.8	338.2	269.3	1,658.5
Other services	73.7	329.3	40.4	154.4
Household and government			13.2	53.0
Total	634.5	3,665.2	634.5	3,665.2

Source: MIDI 2000. Employment in thousands. Locations: CEE (Central and Eastern European countries) and WW (World-Wide abroad).

terms of foreign-affiliate employment (columns 1 and 2). The three broad manufacturing industries—food and textiles, machinery and equipment, and other manufacturing—constitute around 55 percent of worldwide affiliate employment and 61 percent in CEE in 2000. The sectoral distribution looks different, however, when considering the German parent sector to classify foreign employment (columns 3 and 4). Now, the financial and business services sector apparently dominates. As noted previously, however, many German enterprises bundle the domestic management of their foreign affiliates into legally separate firms (mostly limited liability GmbHs) for tax and liability reasons. In MIDI at Deutsche Bundesbank, these holding companies are classified into the financial and business services sector. The economic impact of the reporting firm's FDI, however, goes beyond the firm's formal legal boundary in that jobs throughout the corporate group can be affected. We consider all firms within a corporate group (an enterprise) as potential FDI firms if at least one firm in the group reports outward FDI activities, regardless of its own sector affiliation. Instead, we use the BA sector codes for individual domestic establishments in our later job-level analysis to make sure establishments and workers are classified according to their own activity and not according to a potentially misleading sector code from the FDI-reporting firm in MIDI. For classification of foreign activities, we use definitions from columns 1 and 2 in table 10.2.

Because the majority of workers at affiliates abroad are employed in the manufacturing sector (three in five workers by table 10.2), and because those sectors are less prone to misclassifications, we restrict our subsequent analysis to German manufacturing parents and their foreign manufacturing affiliates—as most of the prior literature does. We investigate the widely held assertion that MNEs shed more labor than non-MNEs as a consequence of the globalization process, and look at worker separation rates at the German manufacturing parent establishments in comparison to separation rates at German non-MNEs.

A concern for our measures of foreign employment expansions is that foreign employment changes might be associated with forms of foreign restructuring beyond employment buildups. To investigate the patterns of foreign expansions more closely for our manufacturing sample, we consider the four-year horizon between 1996 and 2000 and track changes to affiliate counts and country counts for MNEs with an initial presence in a foreign location in 1996. We focus on majority-owned foreign affiliates because foreign employment weighting by ownership share in our estimation sample emphasizes this group of affiliates. Table 10.3 shows that a large majority of MNEs with an initial foreign presence retains the same number of affiliates and stays present in the same number of countries. In CEE (WW), 186 (859) out of 242 (1,259) manufacturing MNEs with an initial manufacturing presence abroad exhibit the same number of affiliates over the four-year period, and 202 (946) show the same number of countries within foreign region. Naturally, in the shorter two-year time span of our linked employer-employee data, changes to the affiliate or country counts are even less frequent. Lacking changes in the counts could possibly conceal simultaneous divestments and acquisitions of affiliates, or simultaneous exits from one country within CEE and entry into another country. However, the data show that at most, 8.5 percent of the MIDI manufacturing MNEs with no change in affiliate number counts simultaneously divest and acquire another affiliate,[10] and that only 4.5 percent of them

---

10. Name changes, changes in legal form, or other reclassifications of foreign affiliates could also result in an apparently different foreign affiliate ID, so that the actual percentage may be even smaller.

Table 10.3   Affiliate and country changes at MNEs

	Affiliate changes		Country changes	
#2000 – #1996	CEE (1)	Worldwide (2)	CEE (3)	Worldwide (4)
≤–3	2	22	1	8
–2	3	31	1	15
–1	6	98	4	91
0	186	859	202	947
+1	25	149	25	134
+2	11	42	6	40
+3	2	22	0	10
≥+4	7	36	3	14
Total	242	1,259	242	1,259

Source: MIDI 1996 and 2000, manufacturing MNEs and their majority-owned foreign manufacturing affiliates. MNEs with presence of at least one affiliate in 1996 in CEE (columns [1]
and [3]) or anywhere worldwide (columns [2] and [4]). World regions for the worldwide statistics (columns [2] and [4]) are (see table 10B.2): CEE (Central and Eastern European countries), DEV (developing countries), OIN (Overseas industrialized countries), WEU (Western
European countries). Mean (median) number of affiliates by MNE in CEE in 2000: 1.49 (1),
mean (median) number of countries by MNE in CEE in 2000: 1.25 (1).

switch countries within foreign region. The median number of foreign
affiliates (and thus foreign countries) by region is 1, with a mean of 1.49
(1.25). These patterns indicate that changes to foreign employment within
a foreign region are largely driven by adjustments at two margins: entry
into the foreign region with a first affiliate, and expansions of the workforce
at existing affiliates.

10.3.1   Domestic Worker Separations

On average, across manufacturing industries, worker separation rates
are 14 percent, both at manufacturing MNEs with a presence in CEE and
WW, and 18 percent at non-MNEs. So, worker separation rates are higher
by about four percentage points across all manufacturing sectors. Regarding domestic worker separation rates, MNEs active in CEE countries do
not differ much from the MNE average. Figure 10.1 shows that this pattern
is largely preserved across main manufacturing industries. We single out
the German food and textiles sectors, which are commonly perceived to be
declining industries with a comparative disadvantage relative to Germany's trading partners, and the German machinery and equipment sector, which is generally considered to manufacture at a comparative advantage. Quite expectedly for a comparative disadvantage sector, domestic
worker separation rates in absolute terms are considerably higher in the
food and textiles sector than in other manufacturing industries. But the
difference in worker separation rates between MNEs and non-MNEs in

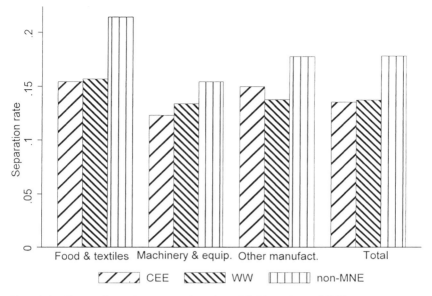

Fig. 10.1   Domestic worker separations from MNEs and non-MNEs

Source: MIDI, MARKUS, and BA 1999–2001. German manufacturing MNEs with presence in Central and Eastern Europe (CEE) and worldwide (WW), and non-MNEs. On average, across manufacturing sectors, worker separation rates are 14%, both at MNEs with presence in CEE and worldwide, and 18% at non-MNEs.

that sector stands at a striking 7 percent and is considerably larger than in the other manufacturing industries. In contrast to public perception, separation rates are lower at MNE establishments than at non-MNE establishments.

One hypothesis, consistent with these stylized facts, is that globalization in broad terms—including import competition and cross-firm cross-border trade in intermediate goods—tends to displace more workers in Germany's disadvantaged sectors such as food and textiles, but that MNEs who successfully expand abroad manage to secure considerably lower worker separation rates, close to those in manufacturing sectors with a comparative advantage. An alternative hypothesis is that a subset of highly competitive German enterprises, in the food and textiles sector as well as in other industries, tend to expand abroad while simultaneously retaining more workers at home.

10.3.2   Foreign Employment Expansions and Domestic Worker Separations

An instructive nonparametric tool to relate domestic worker separation rates to foreign employment changes is local polynomial regression—a natural extension of local mean smoothing in the spirit of the Nadaraya-Watson estimator. Consider the model

$$(1) \qquad\qquad y_i = \theta(x_i),$$

where y_i is worker separation, taking a value of 1 if and only if (iff) the holder of job i is displaced through a layoff or quit between t and $t + 1$. We omit time subscripts to save on notation. We use θ as an unknown function of the predictor variable x_i. For this nonparametric regression, we use as predictor x_i the exposure of job i to changes in its parent MNE's foreign-affiliate employment between $t - 1$ and t (note the one-year lag between foreign-expansion and worker separation).

In our case, local polynomial regression involves fitting the dependent variable (domestic worker separation rates) to a univariate polynomial form of the regressor (foreign employment changes) using locally weighted least squares. Compared to the Nadaraya-Watson estimator (which is a special case of local polynomial smoothing with a polynomial of degree zero), local polynomials of higher order exhibit preferable bias properties. For a comprehensive overview of local polynomial smoothing see Fan and Gijbels (1996).

In our local polynomial estimation, we drop the first and last job growth deciles to exclude outliers from our estimation sample. We vary the bandwidths, experiment with alternative kernels, and consider polynomials of varying degrees, including the Nadaraya-Watson estimator itself. The basic shape of the domestic worker separation curve, with a negative slope in the range of the highest foreign expansion densities and a positive slope at large but infrequent rates of foreign employment expansions, is strikingly similar across specifications.

Figure 10.2 depicts local polynomial regression estimates for CEE and WW. The estimates are based on a third-order polynomial with an Epanechnikov kernel and bandwidth .1. Domestic worker separation rates are falling at MNEs with FDI (foreign employment) expansions of up to 50 percent in CEE and of up to 20 percent WW, but worker separation rates exhibit a marked increase at MNEs with FDI expansions beyond 50 and 20 percent, respectively.

We present according density estimates for the frequency of foreign employment expansions below the local polynomial regression estimates in figure 10.2. The bulk of foreign employment expansions lies roughly between –10 and 25 percent in CEE and WW. In these ranges, where the prediction of domestic worker separation rates is more precisely estimated, domestic worker separation rates are falling with FDI, both in CEE and WW. In CEE, domestic worker separation rates exhibit a local maximum (at close to 16 percent) for small foreign workforce contractions (in the neighborhood of no foreign employment change) and a minimum (at 6 percent) for 50 percent foreign workforce expansions. Note, however, that

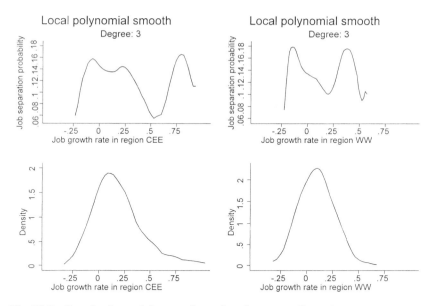

Fig. 10.2   Local polynomial regressions of worker separation rates on FDI expansions

Source: MIDI, MARKUS, and BA 1999–2001, manufacturing sectors. Upper panel: Results from local polynomial regressions of domestic worker separation rates between 2000 and 2001 on foreign employment changes between 1999 and 2000 using third-order polynomials, an Epanechnikov kernel, and bandwidth .1. Lower panel: Density estimates of foreign employment changes between 1999 and 2000 using an Epanechnikov kernel and bandwidth 0.1.

large rates of foreign employment change seldom occur at MNEs between 1999 and 2000. Over the range of foreign employment growth rates that are most dominant (between –10 percent and 25 percent, for example), domestic separation rates decrease with increases in foreign job growth rates. A similar pattern arises for expansions worldwide, but the average level of domestic worker separation rates is somewhat higher, and the minimum occurs at foreign employment expansions of around 20 percent.

A negative slope in the range of the highest foreign expansion densities is consistent with the idea that the bulk of FDI expansions is associated with lower worker separation rates, and more frequent worker retentions, at the expanding MNEs. A positive (but imprecisely estimated) slope at large rates of foreign employment expansions might suggest that domestic jobs become less secure at firms with substantial foreign workforce buildups. The illustrative results from the univariate nonparametric local-polynomial regressions deserve more scrutiny, however, for they do not condition on worker, firm, or sector characteristics.

Multinational enterprises differ from non-MNEs regarding their establishment and workforce characteristics. Table 10.4 displays summary sta-

Table 10.4   Descriptive statistics: MNE and non-MNE subsamples

	MNE		Non-MNE	
	Mean	S.dev.	Mean	S.dev.
Worker-level variables				
Indic.: Worker separation	.14	.34	.18	.38
Age	41.01	10.44	40.69	11.77
Female	.23	.42	.33	.47
More than upper-secondary schooling	.16	.37	.08	.28
Annual wage in EUR	35,317.8	11,611.6	26,847.8	13,872.2
Job-level variables				
White-collar job	.44	.50	.38	.49
Current apprentice	.02	.15	.04	.19
Part-time employed	.05	.21	.12	.33
Establishment-level variables				
Employment at domestic establishment	2,683.8	7,935.3	926.9	3,153.3
Indic.: Establishment in East Germany	.09	.29	.10	.30
Number of observations	38,046		55,101	

Sources: Linked MIDI and BA data, $t = 2000$. 5% random sample of workers in FDI exposed and non-FDI exposed manufacturing establishments.

tistics for our main sample of workers in the manufacturing sector, separately for MNE and non-MNE establishments. Workers in MNE establishments earn more, are more highly educated, are more likely to be white-collar workers, and are less likely to be part-time employed than workers in non-MNE establishments. Multinational enterprise establishments are bigger, on average, than non-MNE establishments. Median employment is 644 and 103 for MNE and non-MNE establishments, respectively.

In summary, descriptive evidence suggests that, first, German MNEs with a presence in CEE or anywhere worldwide exhibit a four percentage point lower rate of worker separations than German non-MNEs in manufacturing industries. Second, while absolute worker separation rates are higher in comparative disadvantage sectors, such as food and textiles, the drop in domestic worker separation rates is also larger (around 7 percent) for MNEs in those sectors as compared to non-MNEs. Considering, third, the varying degree of foreign employment expansions at MNEs, univariate nonparametric regressions suggest that foreign employment expansions are associated with drops in domestic worker separation rates for the bulk of FDI expansions. Fourth, however, the workforce composition of MNEs and non-MNEs is quite different, and so are other establishment characteristics. To further explore the relationship between foreign job growth and domestic worker separation, we proceed to parametric multivariate regression.

10.4   Parametric Regressions

In parametric multivariate regression analysis, we investigate the linear effect of FDI expansions abroad on an individual worker's separation chance from an MNE's home establishment, conditional on worker, job, establishment, and sector characteristics, including past levels of MNE activity. Foreign direct investment expansions (positive changes to FDI exposure) are the natural counterpart to separation as a job-level measure of changes in labor demand. We choose to contrast changes in worker separation rates with changes in foreign presence, rather than levels with levels, mostly because the descriptive evidence suggests that MNEs and domestic firms differ markedly ex ante.

For parametric multivariate regression, we specify a linear relationship

$$(2) \qquad\qquad y_i = \alpha + x_i\beta + \mathbf{z}_i'\gamma + \varepsilon_i,$$

where y_i is worker separation, taking a value of one iff the holder of job i is displaced through a layoff or quit between t and $t + 1$, x_i is a measure of job i's exposure to FDI changes between $t - 1$ and t, and $\mathbf{z}_i$ is a comprehensive vector of worker, job, establishment, and sector characteristics prior to the foreign employment change in year $t - 1$, and ε_i is a disturbance. Note the one-year lag between the foreign expansion predictor and other covariates on the one hand, and the dependent worker separation variable on the other hand. We omit time subscripts to save on notation.

We consider two alternative measures of changes to a job's FDI exposure x_i. We begin with the binary foreign-expansion indicator of an employment expansion at job i's parent MNE's foreign affiliates. This variable has two advantages: its construction does not require any weighting by ownership, and its coefficient in a linear regression provides an estimate of the mean difference in separation rates between expanding and nonexpanding firms, comparable to the 4-percent mean difference in separation rates between MNEs and non-MNEs. Then we turn to the same continuous predictor as in our nonparametric regression in the preceding section: the exposure of job i to changes in its parent MNE's foreign-affiliate employment. This variable reflects growth in head counts of foreign employment, but also changes in the enterprise's ownership share of the domestic FDI-reporting firm as well as in that FDI-reporting firm's ownership of the foreign affiliates.

An obvious concern with our specification is that the assumption of an independently distributed disturbance ε_i might be violated, despite our conditioning on a comprehensive set of preexpansion characteristics and despite the time lag between foreign employment expansions and the dependent variable. This can obstruct interpretation of the β coefficient. We therefore estimate the linear probability model (2) both with ordinary least squares (OLS) and with a two-stage instrumental-variable (IV) approach based on lagged regressors.[11] In predicting an MNE's foreign employment expansion $\hat{x}_i$ at $t - 1$ with its past expansion at $t - 2$, we can limit otherwise potentially confounding effects. The instrumentation strategy renders it implausible that a temporary coincidence of foreign expansions and increased home-worker retention rates affect the results, or that transitory firm-level shocks that drive both foreign employment expansions and home worker retentions explain our estimates. An MNE's permanent gain in competitive advantage, however, may positively affect both past and current employment expansions at foreign affiliates as well as domestic workers retentions, and cannot be ruled out with this firm-level instrumentation strategy. Host-country characteristics such as sector-level capital utilization rates or GDP are sometimes considered for instrumentation (Desai, Foley, and Hines 2005), but they can suffer from similar drawbacks as firm-level instruments. If the MNE's expansion into a low-utilization sector abroad, or into a high-GDP host location, is more likely for an MNE with an inherent competitive advantage, then capital utilization or GDP cannot serve as instruments to remove the correlation with simultaneous home-worker retentions.

Based on the descriptive statistics in section 10.3, we expect β to have a negative sign. As stressed before, at least two alternative hypotheses are consistent with this prior. Foreign direct investment expansions may contribute to an MNE's worldwide performance and help secure domestic jobs. Alternatively, MNEs that are more competitive for FDI-unrelated reasons may expand employment, both abroad and at home. If the IV estimate of β is larger in absolute value (more negative) than the plain OLS estimate, then the plausibility of the latter alternative hypothesis is arguably more compromised than the former main hypothesis. The reason is that an MNE's persistent competitive advantage over two periods should typically result in stronger employment expansions both abroad and at home in earlier periods than in later periods because they would be associated with permanent increase in workforce size. So, the IV estimate should reduce and not reinforce the employment effect and result in a smaller absolute value of β under the alternative hypothesis. We expect the opposite under the former main hypothesis, that an MNE's FDI expansion itself helps secure domestic jobs. Persistent foreign expansions under this main hypoth-

11. Nonlinear limited-dependent variable estimators, such as logit or probit, for instance, do not permit instrumental-variable corrections for the potential simultaneity of predictors. When compared to our uncorrected OLS estimates, however, logit and probit estimates are similar to the linear probability model. We discuss additional candidate instruments in the following discussion. In general, exogenous firm-level instruments that are not related to MNE performance and thus not to worker separation disturbances but do covary with FDI expansions are hard to construe.

esis should have a cumulative positive effect on domestic worker retentions and thus augment β in absolute value.

10.4.1   Ordinary Least Squares (OLS) Estimation with Foreign-expansion Indicators for CEE

Table 10.5 presents OLS estimates of equation (2), with gradually enriched specifications for FDI expansions in Central and Eastern Europe. The indicator of a job's exposure to a foreign employment expansion at the MNE is significantly negatively correlated with a domestic worker separation. So, in line with the prediction from univariate nonparametric regressions in the preceding section 10.3, MNEs that expand abroad displace domestic workers less frequently.

We start with worker characteristics as control variables. Column (1) shows results from a regression including only the worker characteristics. Older workers suffer fewer separations, but their separation risk drops at a less-than-proportional rate as they age. High-wage workers experience significantly fewer displacements, but workers with more than secondary schooling experience more frequent separations—controlling for the characteristics of the jobs they fill. There is no statistically detectable difference between female and male workers in displacement risks once their remaining individual characteristics and job covariates are taken into account. Similar to more than secondary-schooled workers, workers in white-collar jobs exhibit more frequent separations. Recall that some separations may be voluntary quits. Workers in part-time jobs, or apprenticeship positions, face lower separation rates, as do workers in minor employments, whereas workers in temporary work suffer higher separation rates. These worker-level coefficients remain remarkably similar across specifications even as we add employer and sector-level controls, and a worker's lagged log wage.

Specification 2 adds establishment characteristics, including the establishment-fixed component in German wages from a Mincer (1974) regression to proxy for establishment-level differences in productivity. Specification 3 adds sector-level measures of German foreign trade: exports, imports of final goods, and imports of intermediate inputs. Finally, specification 4 adds lagged values of wages and establishment size. Note that in all specifications, we also control for lagged levels of MNE employment in all world regions.

The negative coefficient on the foreign employment expansion indicator gradually drops in absolute value as we proceed to richer specifications by adding establishment and sector covariates, from a coefficient of –.023 to – .016 between specifications 1 and 4. So, an FDI expansion predicts between 1.6 and 2.3 percentage points lower separation rates at the expanding MNE, compared to non-expanding MNEs or domestic enterprises. The pattern of coefficient drops in absolute value suggests that a part of the

Table 10.5   **OLS Worker-separation estimates for FDI expansions in CEE**

	Specification			
	(1)	(2)	(3)	(4)
Indic.: Employment growth in CEE	−.023	−.018	−.016	−.016
	(.003)***	(.003)***	(.003)***	(.003)***
Worker-level variables				
Age	−.026	−.026	−.026	−.026
	(.0008)***	(.0008)***	(.0008)***	(.0008)***
Age squared	.029	.029	.029	.030
	(.0009)***	(.0009)***	(.0009)***	(.0009)***
log Wage	−.086	−.086	−.086	−.104
	(.003)***	(.005)***	(.005)***	(.007)***
Indic.: Female	.0001	−.004	−.003	−.002
	(.003)	(.003)	(.003)	(.003)
Indic.: More than upper-sec. schooling	.042	.037	.037	.036
	(.004)***	(.004)***	(.004)***	(.004)***
Job-level variables				
Indic.: White collar job	.028	.020	.020	.019
	(.003)***	(.003)***	(.003)***	(.003)***
Indic.: Minor employment	−.085	−.078	−.078	−.078
	(.009)***	(.011)***	(.011)***	(.011)***
Indic.: Temporary job	.038	.045	.046	.044
	(.013)***	(.013)***	(.013)***	(.013)***
Indic.: Apprentice	−.121	−.135	−.136	−.132
	(.015)***	(.015)***	(.015)***	(.015)***
Indic.: Part-time job	−.047	−.047	−.047	−.046
	(.006)***	(.006)***	(.006)***	(.006)***
Establishment-level variables				
Employment		−1.93e−06	−2.31e−06	6.97e−07
		(2.25e−07)***	(2.41e−07)***	(4.99e−07)
Average workforce age		−.0008	−.0003	−.0005
		(.0004)**	(.0004)	(.0004)
FE from Mincer log wage regression		−.043	−.050	−.051
		(.014)***	(.014)***	(.014)***
Annual average wage in EUR		.00002	.00003	.00003
		(6.97e−06)***	(7.24e−06)***	(7.27e−06)***
Share: Females		.027	.020	.019
		(.009)***	(.010)**	(.010)*
Share: More than upper-sec. schooling		.033	.011	.019
		(.016)**	(.016)	(.016)
Share: Minor employments		−.005	.013	.015
		(.018)	(.019)	(.019)
Share: Temporary job		−.077	−.098	−.084
		(.049)	(.050)*	(.050)*
Share: White collar jobs		.018	.022	.020
		(.009)**	(.009)**	(.009)**
Share: Apprentices		.163	.202	.191
		(.051)***	(.052)***	(.052)***
Share: Part-time jobs		.014	.013	.020
		(.016)	(.016)	(.016)

Table 10.5   (continued)

	Specification			
	(1)	(2)	(3)	(4)
Indic.: Loc. in East Germany		−.012	−.009	−.008
		(.005)**	(.005)*	(.005)*
Sector-level trade variables	no	no	yes	yes
Lagged log Wage				.020
				(.005)***
Lagged Employment				−6.44e–06
				(9.35e–07)***
Obs.	93,147	93,142	93,142	93,142

Sources: Linked MIDI and BA data, t = 2000. 5% random sample of workers in FDI exposed and non-FDI exposed manufacturing plants. Controlling for lagged levels of MNE employment in all world regions. Standard errors in parentheses.
*Significant at 10 percent confidence level.
**Significant at 5 percent confidence level.
***Significant at 1 percent confidence level.

lower domestic worker separation rates at MNEs may be related to employer heterogeneity, such as superior MNE performance that can lead to workforce expansions across all MNE locations, and not only to FDI expansions themselves. The negative coefficient on the FDI expansion indicator remains highly significant across all specifications, however. So, the hypothesis that FDI expansions themselves contribute to MNEs' lower domestic worker separations in the wake of globalization cannot be rejected in any specification. In fact, the small changes in the coefficient estimate between specifications 2 and 4, together with the overwhelming significance of the coefficient, make this hypothesis appear plausible.

The coefficients on establishment covariates are similar across specifications but, in the presence of worker and job-level controls, only some are statistically significant at conventional levels. Establishment employment is negatively related to worker separations: workers at larger establishments experience fewer separations. Similarly, workers at high-wage establishments (read high-productivity establishments) experience fewer separations. To identify high-wage establishments, we measure the establishment component in log wages (Mincer 1974) controlling for all observable worker and job characteristics. Average annual wages exhibit the opposite, statistically significant positive, coefficient. So, separation rates are higher at establishments with high-wage workers. Similarly, separation rates are higher at establishments with a larger fraction of white-collar jobs. The latter two estimates are in line with similar worker- and job-level coefficients on higher education and white-collar occupations. Workers at establishments with higher shares of apprentices suffer more separations.

Inclusion of lagged variables in specification 4 hardly alters any of the prior coefficients. A worker's lagged wage is significantly positively associated with the worker's separation risk, contrary to the negative association of the concurrent wage. Including the lagged log wage increases the coefficient of the concurrent log wage in absolute value from –.08 to –.10, that is, by the size of the lagged log wage coefficient itself. Lagged establishment employment takes over as the significantly negative establishment size predictor when included, whereas in specifications 2 and 3, exclusion of lagged employment resulted in a negative and significant coefficient on current establishment size.

10.4.2   IV Estimation with Foreign-expansion Indicators for CEE

Despite our comprehensive list of worker, job, employer, and sector covariates, OLS estimates do not necessarily control temporary and unobserved firm-level shocks that simultaneously affect foreign employment expansions and domestic worker separation rates. We consider past employment expansions as firm-level instruments to remove confounding effects of transient firm-level shocks. On the first stage of our two-stage IV regression, past realizations of the FDI expansion indicator turn out to be highly significant predictors of the current FDI expansion indicator.

Table 10.6 presents the results from IV estimation under the same four specifications as OLS estimation (table 10.5). While coefficients on worker, job, employer, and sector covariates hardly differ, there is a remarkable increase in the absolute value of the foreign-expansion coefficient. In specification 1, the coefficient moves from –.023 with OLS to –.035 with IV, and in specification 4 from –.016 to –.026. The consistency of this pattern across specifications is suggestive of the plausibility of our main hypothesis—that FDI expansions themselves facilitate worker retentions at MNE establishments in Germany.

As argued previously, we would typically expect the opposite finding under the main alternative hypothesis—that unobserved MNE shocks drive both foreign and home employment expansions. Under that alternative hypothesis, a positive MNE performance shock should result in strong expansions, both in foreign and home employment at impact, so that we would expect a smaller foreign-expansion coefficient in absolute value under IV than under OLS. The opposite is the case. By design, the IV estimator cannot conclusively reject the hypothesis that permanent firm-level shocks drive both foreign expansions and home-worker retentions. But at the very least, our main hypothesis is fully consistent with the IV estimates. Multinational enterprises with persistent foreign employment expansions exhibit systematically stronger covariation between FDI expansions and reduced domestic worker separation rates than MNEs whose FDI expansions are not as well predicted by past FDI expansions.

Table 10.6   IV Worker-separation estimates for FDI expansions in CEE

	Specification			
	(1)	(2)	(3)	(4)
Indic.: Employment growth in CEE	−.035	−.028	−.025	−.026
	(.005)***	(.005)***	(.005)***	(.005)***
Worker-level variables				
Age	−.026	−.026	−.026	−.026
	(.0008)***	(.0008)***	(.0008)***	(.0008)***
Age squared	.029	.029	.029	.030
	(.0009)***	(.0009)***	(.0009)***	(.0009)***
log Wage	−.084	−.086	−.086	−.104
	(.003)***	(.005)***	(.005)***	(.007)***
Indic.: Female	.0002	−.004	−.003	−.002
	(.003)	(.003)	(.003)	(.003)
Indic.: More than upper-sec. schooling	.043	.037	.037	.036
	(.004)***	(.004)***	(.004)***	(.004)***
Job-level variables				
Indic.: White-collar job	.028	.020	.020	.019
	(.003)***	(.003)***	(.003)***	(.003)***
Indic.: Minor employment	−.082	−.078	−.078	−.078
	(.009)***	(.011)***	(.011)***	(.011)***
Indic.: Temporary job	.039	.045	.046	.044
	(.013)***	(.013)***	(.013)***	(.013)***
Indic.: Apprentice	−.120	−.135	−.136	−.132
	(0.15)***	(.015)***	(.015)***	(.015)***
Indic.: Part-time job	−.046	−.047	−.047	−.046
	(.006)***	(.006)***	(.006)***	(.006)***
Establishment-level variables				
Employment		−1.80e–06	−2.23e–06	8.06e–07
		(2.29e–07)***	(2.43e–07)***	(5.01e–07)
Average workforce age		−.0008	−.0004	−.0005
		(.0004)**	(.0004)	(.0004)
FE from Mincer log wage regression		−.044	−.050	−.052
		(.014)***	(.014)***	(.014)***
Annual average wage in EUR		.00002	.00003	.00003
		(7.01e–06)***	(7.28e–06)***	(7.30e–06)***
Share: Females		.028	.021	.020
		(.009)***	(.010)**	(.010)*
Share: More than upper-sec. schooling		.033	.012	.020
		(.016)**	(.016)	(.016)
Share: Minor employments		−.003	.014	.016
		(.018)	(.019)	(.019)
Share: Temporary job		−.082	−.101	−.087
		(.049)*	(.050)**	(.050)*
Share: White-collar jobs		.017	.022	.019
		(.009)*	(.009)**	(.009)**
Share: Apprentices		.167	.204	.194
		(.051)***	(.052)***	(.052)***

(*continued*)

Table 10.6   (continued)

	Specification			
	(1)	(2)	(3)	(4)
Share: Part-time jobs		.015	.014	.020
		(.016)	(.016)	(.016)
Indic.: Loc. in East Germany		−.011	−.008	−.007
		(.005)**	(.005)	(.005)
Sector-level trade variables	no	no	yes	yes
Lagged log Wage				.020
				(.005)***
Lagged Employment				−6.50e–06
				(9.35e–07)***
Obs.	93,147	93,142	93,142	93,142

Sources: Linked MIDI and BA data, $t = 2000$. 5% random sample of workers in FDI exposed and non-FDI exposed manufacturing plants. Controlling for lagged levels of MNE employment in all world regions. Standard errors in parentheses.
*Significant at 10 percent confidence level.
**Significant at 5 percent confidence level.
***Significant at 1 percent confidence level.

10.4.3   Ordinary Least Squares and IV Estimation with Indicators for Worldwide FDI Expansions

Looking beyond CEE to FDI expansions worldwide yields even more striking results, as table 10.7 shows. Coefficients on worker, job, employer, and sector variables exhibit patterns similar to the regressions for expansions in CEE. To reduce duplication, we therefore only report worker and job coefficients. The OLS estimates—for specification 1 with only worker and job variables (column [1]), and for specification 4 with worker, job, employer, and sector variables (column [2])—are about the same worldwide as in CEE, even for the foreign employment growth indicator. Most strikingly, however, the IV estimates now almost double the OLS coefficients on the FDI expansion indicator in absolute value (columns [3] and [4]). Under the most comprehensive specification (column [4]), a foreign expansion anywhere worldwide predicts a 3.7 percent lower domestic worker separation rate—this prediction is almost equal to the unconditional mean difference of 4 percent in separation rates between MNEs and non-MNEs (table 10.4).

10.4.4   Additional IV Results

We explore additional instrumental variables to assess the robustness of results. Table 10.8 reports the OLS and IV estimates from before (in columns [1] and [2]) and assembles alongside results from specifications with additional instrumental variables (in columns [3] through [6]). Including the past foreign capital-stock growth as an additional firm-level instru-

Table 10.7   Worker-separation estimates for FDI expansions worldwide

	OLS		IV	
	(1)	(2)	(3)	(4)
Indic.: Employment growth worldwide	−.022	−.018	−.041	−.037
	(.003)***	(.003)***	(.005)***	(.006)***
Worker-level variables				
Age	−.026	−.026	−.026	−.026
	(.0008)***	(.0008)***	(.0008)***	(.0008)***
Age squared	.029	.030	.029	.030
	(.0009)***	(.0009)***	(.0009)***	(.0009)***
log Wage	−.086	−.104	−.082	−.103
	(.003)***	(.007)***	(.004)***	(.007)***
Indic.: Female	.0002	−.002	.0005	−.002
	(.003)	(.003)	(.003)	(.003)
Indic.: More than upper-sec. schooling	.042	.036	.043	.036
	(.004)***	(.004)***	(.004)***	(.004)***
Job-level variables				
Indic.: White-collar job	.028	.019	.028	.019
	(.003)***	(.003)***	(.003)***	(.003)***
Indic.: Minor employment	−.084	−.078	−.079	−.077
	(.009)***	(.011)***	(.010)***	(.011)***
Indic.: Temporary job	.039	.044	.041	.044
	(.013)***	(.013)***	(.013)***	(.013)***
Indic.: Apprentice	−.121	−.132	−.120	−.132
	(.015)***	(.015)***	(.015)***	(.015)***
Indic.: Part-time job	−.047	−.046	−.046	−.046
	(.006)***	(.006)***	(.006)***	(.006)***
Establishment-level variables	no	yes	no	yes
Sector-level trade variables	no	yes	no	yes
Lagged log Wage		.020		.020
		(.005)***		(.005)***
Obs.	93,147	93,142	93,147	93,142

Sources: Linked MIDI and BA data, t = 2000. 5% random sample of workers in FDI exposed and non-FDI exposed manufacturing establishments. Controlling for lagged levels of MNE employment in all world regions in columns (1) through (4), additionally controlling for employer and sector covariates in columns (2) and (4). Standard errors in parentheses.
*Significant at 10 percent confidence level.
**Significant at 5 percent confidence level.
***Significant at 1 percent confidence level.

ment for recent employment growth (column [3]) neither significantly alters the point estimates nor does the specification improve efficiency. Similarly, we notice no significant change in point estimates or efficiency when we use turnover, an output proxy, instead of input-related instrumental variables (column [4]).

A firm's proximity to CEE can reduce the cost of managing foreign affiliates in CEE and be associated with more frequent expansions in CEE.

Table 10.8   **Additional IV estimates for FDI expansions**

	OLS	IV				
	(1)	(2)	(3)	(4)	(5)	(6)
Indic.: Employment growth	−.023	−.026	−.021	−.020	−.029	−.287
in CEE	(.003)***	(.005)***	(.005)***	(.006)***	(.005)***	(.060)***
Indic.: Employment growth	−.041	−.037	−.034	−.030	−.042	−.276
worldwide	(.003)***	(.006)***	(.005)***	(.006)***	(.006)***	(.057)***
Instruments (for CEE or WW)						
Past employment growth		yes	yes		yes	
Past capital-stock growth			yes			
Past turnover growth				yes		
Headquarters in Land with						
CEE border					yes	yes
Obs.	93,147	93,142	93,140	93,140	93,140	93,140

Sources: Linked MIDI and BA data, $t = 2000$. 5% random sample of workers in FDI exposed and non-FDI exposed manufacturing establishments. lagged levels of MNE employment in all world regions, employer, and sector covariates. Standard errors in parentheses.
*Significant at 10 percent confidence level.
**Significant at 5 percent confidence level.
***Significant at 1 percent confidence level.

This reasoning suggests that a dummy for a firm's headquarters in a CEE-bordering *Land* (German federal state) can serve as an instrumental variable.[12] Use of the CEE-proximity dummy alongside the past foreign employment expansion for instrumentation does not significantly alter the point estimates or improve efficiency. Using the CEE-proximity dummy as the sole instrument, however, raises the point estimates to implausible absolute magnitudes, while preserving the negative sign. In summary, alternative instrumental-variable specifications never overturn and typically reinforce our prior findings.

10.4.5   Continuous Foreign-expansion Predictors

We finally turn to estimates of domestic worker separations using continuous foreign-expansion predictors: employment changes at foreign affiliates in CEE or anywhere worldwide. This type of parametric regression is most closely related to our illustrative nonparametric, but univariate, regression in section 10.3. Just as before, worker, job, employer, and sector variables exhibit results similar to the regressions using an FDI expansion indicator as main predictor. We therefore only report worker and job coefficients.

Table 10.9 shows the coefficient estimates. For FDI expansions in CEE,

---

12. We thank an anonymous referee for this suggestion.

the continuous foreign-expansion predictor still exhibits its negative sign but the estimate is not significant at conventional levels. A possible reason is that there is a reversal from a negative relationship between domestic worker separations and foreign FDI expansions to a positive one for substantial foreign employment buildups—as observed under nonparametric univariate regression in figure 10.2. A linear prediction reduces the relationship between foreign expansions and domestic worker separations to

Table 10.9   Worker-separation estimates for continuous foreign employment changes

	CEE		WW	
	OLS (1)	IV (2)	OLS (3)	IV (4)
Employment change in CEE/WW	−.0003	−.081	.006	−.216
	(.0003)	(.047)*	(.001)***	(.051)***
Worker-level variables				
Age	−.026	−.025	−.026	−.026
	(.0008)***	(.001)***	(.0008)***	(.0009)***
Age squared	.030	.029	.030	.030
	(.0009)***	(.001)***	(.0009)***	(.001)***
log Wage	−.104	−.098	−.104	−.100
	(.007)***	(.009)***	(.007)***	(.008)***
Indic.: Female	−.002	−.004	−.002	−.001
	(.004)	(.005)	(.004)	(.004)
Indic.: More than upper-sec. schooling	.037	.039	.037	.039
	(.004)***	(.006)***	(.004)***	(.005)***
Job-level variables				
Indic.: White-collar job	.019	.022	.019	.019
	(.003)***	(.005)***	(.003)***	(.004)***
Indic.: Minor employment	−.077	−.070	−.077	−.074
	(.011)***	(.015)***	(.011)***	(.013)***
Indic.: Temporary job	.043	.046	.041	.032
	(.013)***	(.017)***	(.014)***	(.016)**
Indic.: Apprentice	−.131	−.118	−.129	−.112
	(.015)***	(.021)***	(.016)***	(.019)***
Indic.: Part-time job	−.047	−.042	−.045	−.044
	(.007)***	(.009)***	(.007)***	(.008)***
Establishment-level variables	yes	yes	yes	yes
Sector-level trade variables	yes	yes	yes	yes
Lagged log Wage	.020	.019	.020	.020
	(.005)***	(.007)***	(.005)***	(.006)***
Obs.	92,090	90,623	91,943	90,899

Sources: Linked MIDI and BA data, $t = 2000$. 5% random sample of workers in FDI exposed and non-FDI exposed manufacturing establishments. Controlling for lagged levels of MNE employment in all world regions and for employer and sector covariates. Standard errors in parentheses.

*Significant at 10 percent confidence level.

**Significant at 5 percent confidence level.

***Significant at 1 percent confidence level.

the sample mean relationship so that the negative and positive effects can cancel at the sample mean. The difference in the point estimates between OLS and IV still exhibits the same pattern as in the preceding CEE regressions with a binary FDI expansion predictor. The negative correlation between employment changes at foreign affiliates in CEE and domestic worker separations becomes stronger.

For worldwide FDI expansions, OLS estimation with the continuous foreign-expansion predictor results in a statistically significant reverse (positive) sign, contrary to any prior finding and our expectations. Once we turn to IV, however, the negative sign on the foreign-expansion predictor returns. In light of our preceding findings, this sign reversal between OLS and IV is striking, and suggests that the mean MNE's current unobserved characteristics tend to be associated with both higher domestic separation rates and stronger foreign-employment expansions but that these current unobserved characteristics do not covary with past foreign-employment expansions in the same systematic way.

10.4.6   Discussion

Across regression approaches, specifications, and sample regions, we find a statistically significant negative relationship between FDI expansions and domestic worker separations. The predicted negative association corroborates the unconditional difference in mean worker separation rates between MNEs (with a 14 percent mean separation rate) and non-MNEs (18 percent separation rate). Instrumental variable estimates, from predicting FDI expansions with past FDI expansions of the same MNE, confirm the significantly negative relationship between FDI expansions and domestic worker separations with considerably larger point estimates in absolute value.

An indicator variable for FDI expansions in CEE, or anywhere worldwide, predicts a statistically significant mean difference in displacement rates between FDI-expanding and non-FDI expanding firms ranging from 1.6 (OLS) to 2.6 (IV) percentage points for CEE expansions, and from 1.8 to 3.7 percentage points for expansions anywhere worldwide. So, FDI expansions are associated with a significant portion of the difference in worker separation rates—conditional on a comprehensive set of worker, job, employer, and sector covariates.

As mentioned at the outset of this chapter, several explanations are consistent with our findings. Vertical foreign expansions that fragment the production process can lead to cost savings, increased worldwide market shares, and domestic employment growth. Similarly, horizontal expansions that duplicate production at foreign locations can lead to improved market access with potentially beneficial consequences for home employment. Complementarities between foreign and home employment can give rise to our findings. Moreover, foreign expansions may signal attractive career paths to domestic workers, reduce worker quits, and increase retention rates. The stability of trade relationships within MNEs may stabilize home employment. Further research is needed, however, to discern with confidence this set of explanations from the competing hypothesis that FDI-unrelated firm-level shocks drive the results. In subsequent research, we apply propensity-score matching to compare differences in worker separation rates between FDI-expanding and non-expanding firms (Becker and Muendler 2008). Linked employer-employee data are particularly well-suited for treatment estimators of this kind because the decisionmaking unit, the FDI-reporting firm, is empirically distinct from the unit under treatment, the individual job. The propensity-score estimates provide strong evidence that the foreign employment buildup itself is a dominant explanatory factor for reduced worker separation rates at MNEs with foreign expansion compared to firms without foreign expansion.

10.5 Conclusion

This chapter documents a novel linked employer-employee data set for German multinational enterprises (MNEs) and compares MNEs that expand their employment at foreign affiliates to both MNEs with no foreign workforce expansion and domestic firms. Between 1991 and 2001, the fastest buildup in foreign employment at German MNEs occurred in Central and Eastern Europe, where total employment rose from 46,000 employees in 1991 to around 670,000 in 2001—an employment level in 2001 almost as large as that of all developing-country workforces at German MNEs, combined. The large majority of foreign-affiliate employees work in manufacturing industries, on which we focus this analysis.

The global integration of economies has marked labor-market consequences, changing relative skill demands in developing countries (see chapter 9 in this volume) and the employment allocation within multinational enterprises (Muendler and Becker 2006). But, contrary to wideheld perceptions, multinational enterprises offer more stable jobs at their industrial-country home locations and exhibit lower worker separation rates than their competitors without foreign expansions do: the unconditional worker separation rate at German MNEs is 4 percent lower than at non-MNEs in Germany. Nonparametric regressions illustrate that foreign-employment expansions are associated with lower worker separation rates in the range of the most frequent foreign-employment changes. Multivariate linear regressions show that an indicator of foreign employment expansions in CEE significantly predicts 1.6 to 2.6 percentage-point lower domestic worker separation rates, depending on the regression specification. The indicator of worldwide workforce expansions is an even stronger predictor.

Linked employer-employee data allow us to condition on a comprehensive set of worker, job, employer, and sector covariates. Using lagged foreign expansions to predict current expansions in an instrumental-variable approach raises the point estimates in absolute value. It nevertheless remains a task for future research to conclusively discern whether the results are best explained by competitive MNEs, who simultaneously expand their foreign workforce and retain more domestic workers, or by the foreign expansion itself, which may help the MNE secure domestic jobs through cost savings or foreign market access. Irrespective of the causal explanation, however, there is no empirical evidence on domestic job security that would justify interventions to hinder the foreign expansion of MNEs. To the contrary, our findings are consistent with the idea that preventing domestic MNEs from exploiting international factor-cost differentials in-house, or hampering MNEs' access to foreign product markets through FDI, would increase domestic worker separations at MNEs.

Appendix A
Linked Employer-employee Data

We link jobs to their FDI exposure throughout German corporate groups. This requires a two-step procedure. First, we identify all MIDI firms that are in the commercial company structure database MARKUS. Departing from the MIDI firms in MARKUS, we move both down and up in the corporate hierarchy of MARKUS to select the affiliates and ultimate parents of the MIDI firms. Second, we string-match all domestic establishments in the BA worker database to the so-selected MARKUS firms for identification of all establishments related to FDI firms. We also string-match the domestic establishments to MIDI itself for identification of all those FDI reporting firms that are not part of a corporate group (but stand-alone firms).

We link the data based on names and addresses. By law, German establishment names must include the firm name (but may by augmented with qualifiers). Before we start the string-matching routine, we remove clearly unrelated qualifiers (such as manager names or municipalities) from establishment names, and non-significance bearing components from establishments and firm names (such as the legal form) in order to compute a link-quality index on the basis of highly identifying name components. Our string-matching is implemented as a Perl script and computes link-quality indices as the percentage of words that coincide between any pair of names. We take a conservative approach to avoid erroneous links. We keep two clearly separate subsets of the original data: First, establishments that are perfect links to MARKUS or MIDI, i.e., establishment names that agree with firm names in every single letter. Second, establishments that are perfect non-links, i.e., establishment names that have no single word in com-

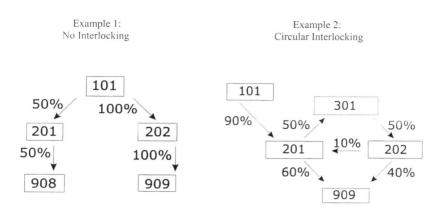

Fig. 10A.1 Examples of corporate groups

mon with any FDI-related MARKUS or MIDI firm. We drop all establishments with a link-quality index between zero and one from our sample, i.e., establishments whose name partially corresponds to an FDI firm name but not perfectly so. Those establishments cannot be told to be either foreign-expansion or control establishments without risk of misclassification.[13] The procedure leaves us with a distinct foreign-expansion group of FDI establishments and a control group of non-FDI establishments.

The BA establishment name file is from November 2002 and contains names of establishments that are no longer active so that we include exiting and entering establishments. To capture exits after 1999 is particularly important for us, because one margin of separation is establishment closure. Firm names in the MARKUS database are from three vintages of data, November 2000, November 2001 and November 2002. This is to make sure that in case of name changes in one of the years 2000 through 2002, we do not miss string-matches.

Our procedure is designed to remove laterally related firms (sisters, aunts, or nieces) from the sample so that they neither enter the foreign-expansion nor the control group. Take Example 1 of figure 10A.1 and consider firm 201 to be the FDI-conducting (and FDI-reporting) firm in the depicted corporate group. The first step of our procedure identifies firm 201 in MARKUS and its affiliate and parent 908 and 101 but does not identify firms 202 (a sister to 201) and 909 (a niece to 201). If any name component of establishments in firms 202 or 909 coincides with those of 101, 201 or 908 (but the establishment name is not an identical match to 101, 201, or 908), the establishments in firms 202 and 909 are discarded and

13. The string-matching routine runs for several weeks, checking 3.8 million establishments against 65,000 FDI firms. It is infeasible to manually treat possible links with imperfect link-quality rates.

neither enter the foreign-expansion nor the control group. If no single name component of establishments in firms 202 or 909 is the same as that of 101, 201, or 908, the establishment may enter our control group. If one considers sisters, aunts, and nieces with no single identical name component to be equally affected by FDI of firm 201 as those with common names or direct relations, their inclusion in the control group would make the control group more similar to the foreign-expansion group than it should be. If anything, however, the reduced difference would work against our worker separation estimates. Moreover, interlocking (of which Example 2 of figure 10A.1 is a special case) limits the number of only laterally related firms.

Appendix B
Corporate Ownership and FDI Exposure

We infer the economically relevant ownership share of a domestic firm in any other domestic firm. The relevant ownership share can differ from the recorded share in a firm's equity for two reasons. First, a firm may hold indirect shares in an affiliate via investments in third firms who in turn control a share of the affiliate. We call ownership shares that sum all direct and indirect shares *cumulated* ownership shares. Second, corporate structures may exhibit cross ownership of a firm in itself via affiliates who in turn are parents of the firm itself. We call ownership shares that remove such circular ownership relations *consolidated* ownership shares. This appendix describes the procedure in intuitive terms; graph-theoretic proofs are available from the authors upon request.

Consolidation removes the degree of self-ownership (α) from affiliates, or intermediate firms between parents and affiliates, and rescales the ultimate ownership share of the parent to account for the increased control in partly self-owning affiliates or intermediate firms (with a factor of $1/[1-\alpha]$). Investors know that their share in a firm, which partly owns itself through cross-ownership, in fact controls a larger part of the firm's assets and its affiliates' assets than the recorded share would indicate. In this regard, cross ownership is like self-ownership. Just as stock buy-backs increase the value of the stocks because investors' de facto equity share rises, so do cross-ownership relations raise the de facto level of control of the parents outside the cross-ownership circle.

We are interested in *ultimate* parents that are not owned by other domestic firms, and want to infer their *cumulated and consolidated* ownership in all affiliates. Consider the following example of interlocking (Example 2 in figure 10A.1). The ultimate parent with firm ID 101 holds 90 percent in firm 201, which is also owned by firm 202 for the remaining 10 percent.

Table 10B.1   **Ownership inference**

	Iteration (length of walk)					
Affiliate-parent pair	1	2	3	5	9	100
201–101	.9	.90	.900	.92250	.92306	.92308
201–202	.1					.00000
201–301		.05		.00125		
202–101			.225	.22500	.23077	.23077
202–201		.25		.00625		
202–301	.5					.00000
301–101		.45	.450	.46125	.46153	.46154
301–201	.5					.00000
301–202		.05		.00125		
909–101		.54	.540	.64350	.64609	.64615
909–201	.6		.100		.00006	.00000
909–202	.4	.06		.00150		.00000
909–301		.20	.030	.00500	.00001	

However, firm 201 itself holds a 25 percent stake in firm 202—via its holdings of 50 percent of 301, which has a 50 percent stake in 201. Firms 201 and 202 hold 60 percent and 40 percent of firm 909. Our cumulation and consolidation procedure infers the ultimate ownership of 101 in all other firms.

We assemble the corporate ownership data in a three-column matrix:[14] the first column takes the affiliate ID, the second column the parent ID, and the third column the effective ownership share. Table 10B.1 shows this matrix for Example 2 in figure 10A.1 (the third column with the direct ownership share is labeled 1, representing the single iteration 1).

On the basis of this ownership matrix, our inference procedure walks through the corporate labyrinth for a prescribed number of steps (or iterations). The procedure multiplies the ownership shares along the edges of the walk, and cumulates multiple walks from a given affiliate to a given ultimate parent. Say, we prescribe that the algorithm take all walks of length two between every possible affiliate-parent pair (in business terms: two firm levels up in the group's corporate hierarchy; in mathematical terms: walks from any vertex to another vertex that is two edges away in the directed graph).

We choose the following trick to infer the cumulated and consolidated ownership for ultimate parents: we assign every ultimate parent a 100 percent ownership of itself. This causes the procedure to cumulate and consolidate the effective ownership share for all affiliates of ultimate parents, at any length of walks. There are seven distinct possibilities in the example to move in two steps through the corporate labyrinth. Table 10B.1 lists

---

14. We assemble cleared ownership data by first removing one-to-one reverse ownerships and self-ownerships in nested legal forms (such as Gmbh & Co. KG).

these possibilities as iteration 2 (all entries in or below the second row). With our trick, there is now an eighth possibility to move from affiliate 201 to parent 101 in two steps because we have added the 101–101 loop with 100-percent ownership. As a result, our procedure cumulates ownerships of ultimate parents for all walks that are of length two or shorter. The procedure starts to consolidate shares as the length of the walk increases. Iteration 3 in table 10B.1 shows the cumulated and partially consolidated ownership of ultimate parent 101 in affiliate 201, for all three-step walks, including the first cycle from 201 through 202 and 301 back to 201 and then to 101.

In 2000, the maximum length of direct (noncircular) walks from any firm to another firm is 21. So, for all ultimate parents, the cumulated and consolidated ownership shares are reported correctly from a sufficiently large number of iterations on. Table 10B.1 shows iteration 100. The ownership share of 101 in 201 has converged to the exact measure $(.9/(1 - .1 \cdot .5 \cdot .5) = .923076)$ at five-digit precision. Firm 101 controls 92.3 percent of firm 201's assets, among them firm 201's foreign affiliates.

To calculate the FDI exposure at any hierarchy level in the corporate group, we use a single-weighting scheme with ownership shares. The economic rationale behind single-weighting is that ultimate parents are more likely to be the corporate decision units (whereas FDI conducting and reporting firms in the group may be created for tax and liability purposes). We first assign FDI exposure measures (foreign affiliate employment by world region) from domestic affiliates to their ultimate domestic parents. Suppose firm 201 in Example 2 of figure 10A.1 conducts FDI in the corporate group. We assign 92.3 percent of 201's FDI exposure to firm 101, the ultimate domestic parent. We then assign the same 92.3 percent of 201's FDI exposure to all affiliates of 101 (201 itself, 202, 301, 909). So, jobs throughout the group (including those at 201 itself) are only affected to the degree that the ultimate parents can control foreign-affiliate employment (or turnover). We assign only 92.3 percent of 201's FDI exposure to 201 itself because the ultimate parent only has 92.3 percent of the control over employment at 201.[15]

---

15. An alternative assignment scheme would be double-weighting—first weighting FDI exposure by ownership and then assigning the FDI exposure to jobs throughout the corporate group, using ownership weights again. We decide against double-weighting. Any weighting scheme results in exposure measures that are weakly monotonically decreasing as one moves upward in the corporate hierarchy because ownership shares are weakly less than 1. Double-weighting aggravates this property. Revisit example 1 in table 10A.1 and suppose firm 201 conducts FDI. Single-weighting assigns 50 percent of 201's exposure to affiliate 908, double-weighting only 12.5 percent. If 908 itself conducts the FDI, single-weighting assigns 25 percent of its own FDI exposure to 908, double-weighting only 6.25 percent. In economic terms, double-weighting downplays the decision power of intermediate hierarchies in the corporate group further than single-weighting, so that we favor single-weighting. Recall that purely laterally related firms (sisters, aunts, and nieces) are excluded from our foreign-expansion group, so that firms 202 and 909 in example 1 of table 10A.1 are not relevant for the choice of weighting scheme.

Table 10B.2   **Country group definitions**

Regions	Constituting countries
WEU	Western European countries (EU 15 plus Norway and Switzerland)
OIN	Overseas industrialized countries, including Canada, Japan, USA, Australia, and New Zealand, as well as Iceland and Greenland
CEE	Central and Eastern European countries, including accession countries and candidates for EU membership
DEV	Asia-Pacific Developing countries including Hong Kong, South Korea, Singapore, Taiwan, China, Mongolia, and North Korea; Russia and Central Asian economies; other developing countries, including South Asia (India/Pakistan), Africa, Latin America, the Middle East; including dominions of Western European countries and the United States

As we choose single-weighting in the domestic branches of the MNE, we also single-weight foreign-affiliate employment by the ownership share of the domestic parent in its foreign affiliates. Mirroring the minimal ownership threshold of 10 percent in the MIDI data on foreign affiliates, we also discard the FDI exposure of domestic affiliates with ownership shares of less than 10 percent in our single-weighting assignment of FDI exposure to domestic jobs throughout the corporate group. (See table 10B.2.)

References

Barba Navaretti, Giorgio, and Davide Castellani. 2004. Investments abroad and performance at home: Evidence from Italian multinationals. CEPR Discussion Paper no. 4284. London: Centre for Economic Policy Research.

Becker, Sascha O., and Marc-Andreas Muendler. 2008. The effect of FDI on job security. *The B.E. Journal of Economic Analysis & Policy* 8:1.

Bender, Stefan, Anette Haas, and Christoph Klose. 2000. The IAB employment subsample 1975–1995. *Journal of Applied Social Science Studies* 120 (4): 649–62.

Desai, Mihir A., C. Fritz Foley, and James R. Hines, Jr. 2005. Foreign direct investment and domestic economic activity. NBER Working Paper no. 11717. Cambridge, MA: National Bureau of Economic Research.

Devereux, Michael P., and Rachel Griffith. 1998. Taxes and the location of production: evidence from a panel of U.S. multinationals. *Journal of Public Economics* 68 (3): 335–67.

Egger, Peter, and Michael Pfaffermayr. 2003. The counterfactual to investing abroad: An endogenous treatment approach of foreign affiliate activity. University of Innsbruck Working Paper no. 02.

Fan, Jianqing, and Irene Gijbels. 1996. *Local polynomial modelling and its applications.* Vol. 66 of *Monographs on Statistics and Applied Probability.* London: Chapman and Hall.

Feenstra, Robert C., and Gordon H. Hanson. 1999. The impact of outsourcing and high-technology capital on wages: Estimates for the United States, 1979–1990. *Quarterly Journal of Economics* 114 (3): 907–40.

Geishecker, Ingo. 2006. The impact of international outsourcing on individual employment security: A micro-level analysis. Diskussionsbeiträge des Fachbereichs Wirtschaftswissenschaft 17. Berlin: Freie Universität.

Hanson, Gordon H., Raymond J. Mataloni, and Matthew J. Slaughter. 2005. Vertical production networks in multinational firms. *Review of Economics and Statistics* 87 (4): 664–78.

Harrison, Ann E., Margaret S. McMillan, and Clair Null. 2007. U.S. multinational activity abroad and U.S. jobs: Substitutes or complements? *Industrial Relations* 46 (2): 347–65.

Head, Keith, and Thierry Mayer. 2004. Market potential and the location of Japanese investment in the European Union. *Review of Economics and Statistics* 86 (4): 959–72.

Jäckle, Robert. 2006. Going multinational: What are the effects on home market performance? Deutsche Bundesbank Discussion Paper no. 03. Series 1: Economic Studies. Frankfurt: Deutsche Bundesbank.

Jacobson, Louis S., Robert J. LaLonde, and Daniel G. Sullivan. 1993. Earnings losses of displaced workers. *American Economic Review* 83 (4): 685–709.

Kletzer, Lori G. 2001. *Job loss from imports: Measuring the costs.* Washington, DC: Institute for International Economics.

Konings, Jozef. 2004. The employment effects of foreign direct investment. EIB Papers, 2004, 9 (1): 86–108.

Konings, Jozef, and Alan Patrick Murphy. 2006. Do multinational enterprises relocate employment to low-wage regions? Evidence from European multinationals. *Review of World Economics* 142 (2): 267–86.

Lipponer, Alexander. 2003. A 'new' micro database for German FDI. In *Foreign direct investment in the real and financial sector of industrial countries,* ed. Heinz Herrmann and Robert Lipsey, 215–44. Berlin: Springer.

Marin, Dalia. 2006. A new international division of labor in Europe: Outsourcing and off-shoring to Eastern Europe. *Journal of the European Economic Association* 4 (2–3): 612–22.

Mincer, Jacob. 1974. *Schooling, experience, and earnings.* New York: Columbia University Press.

Muendler, Marc-Andreas, and Sascha O. Becker. 2006. Margins of multinational labor substitution. CESifo Working Paper no. 1713. Munich: Center for Economic Studies.

Prendergast, Canice. 1999. The provision of incentives in firms. *Journal of Economic Literature* 37 (1): 7–63.

Slaughter, Matthew J. 2000. Production transfer within multinational enterprises and American wages. *Journal of International Economics* 50 (2): 449–72.

Zeile, William J. 1997. U.S. intrafirm trade in goods. *Survey of Current Business* 77 (2): 23–38.

Wage and Productivity Premiums in Sub-Saharan Africa

Johannes Van Biesebroeck

11.1 Introduction

In the textbook economics world, markets are the most efficient institution to allocate scarce resources. They clear all the time, equalizing demand and supply, and profit opportunities are arbitraged away. In particular, production factors are predicted to be paid the marginal productivity of the market-clearing factor. In the real world there are frictions, unobservable characteristics, adjustment costs, erroneous expectations, and maybe discrimination, all of which can distort the market equilibrium away from efficient allocation. This should not necessarily worry us economists, as the theory is only intended to be a stylized version of reality. However, a systematic gap between costs (wages, in our case) and benefits (productivity) can provide information about crucial omissions from the theory.

A well-functioning labor market should perform at least two tasks: matching workers with firms and setting wages. The ability of the labor market to allocate workers to firms or industries with the highest productivity or the best future prospects is of particular importance for the likely effect of trade reforms, and this has been studied extensively—see Pavcnik (2002), Eslava et al. (2004), and Filhoz and Muendler (2006) for studies on

Johannes Van Biesebroeck is an associate professor of economics at the University of Toronto, and a faculty research fellow of the National Bureau of Economic Research.

This paper was presented at the Conference on Firm and Employees (CAFE) held September 29–30, 2006, in Nuremberg, Germany. We gratefully acknowledge the financial support provided by the Institute for Employment Research (IAB), the Data Access Center (FDZ-BA/IAB), The Deutsche Forschungsgemeinschaft (German Research Foundation), their Research Network "Flexibility in Heterogeneous Labour Markets," the Alfred P. Sloan Foundation, and the National Science Foundation. Seminar participants at the University of Illinois, Kellogg School of Management, Catholic University of Louvain, the NBER Productivity meetings, and the CAFE conference provided useful suggestions.

Latin American countries. Van Biesebroeck (2005) investigates the effectiveness of labor markets in several African countries, including the three countries studied here, in performing this task, and finds that the reallocation mechanism is less effective than in the United States.

A second aspect of labor market efficiency is to determine a wage rate. If labor markets function as spot markets with minimal frictions and informational asymmetries, we would expect arbitrage to set the remuneration of characteristics at their productivity contribution. Otherwise, workers are not provided with the proper incentives to invest in human capital characteristics, such as schooling or tenure. While an important issue, it has not been studied extensively, largely because of lack of suitable data. Employee surveys do not contain information on firm level output and factor inputs necessary to calculate productivity. Datasets on firms or plants generally lack information on all but a few basic characteristics of the workforce.

The contribution of this chapter is foremost to provide evidence for three sub-Saharan countries on the extent to which observed wage premiums for a number of worker characteristics are equal to the productivity premiums associated with those same characteristics. Initially, the methodology in Hellerstein, Neumark, and Troske (1999) is followed and the two premiums are compared at the firm level. Here, the nature of the comparison is implicitly between the wage bills and output levels of two firms that are identical, except that one firm has a workforce with, on average, one more year of schooling, or a higher fraction of male workers, and so on. We consider five characteristics: gender, labor market experience, eduction, tenure with the current employer, and whether a worker has followed a formal training program. As some of the human capital characteristics are influenced by the workers, such as tenure or training, providing workers with the correct investment incentives is crucial.

Labor market frictions are likely to be at least as important in developing countries as in the more developed countries where most previous studies were conducted. As stressed by Fafchamps (1997) in the introduction to a symposium on "Markets in Sub-Saharan Africa," one should be careful not to assume outright that markets are efficient, regardless of the institutions required to perform their function. The model is estimated using data for Tanzania, Kenya, and Zimbabwe. While all three countries are relatively poor, GDP per capita for Zimbabwe exceeded that for Tanzania by a factor of five (during the sample period), while Kenya was intermediately developed.

A second contribution of the chapter is to estimate the firm-level production function jointly with the individual-level wage equation. Using the additional information of individual workers leads to more precise estimates, especially of the wage premiums, and to a more accurate test. We show how to test for equality between wage and productivity premiums in this context and implement a feasible GLS estimator. While still allowing for correlation between the error terms in the wage equation and production function, we additionally introduce a random effect in the wage equation that is shared by all workers with a common employer.

The main empirical finding is that in Tanzania, the poorest country we consider, the wage premiums deviate substantially from the corresponding productivity premiums. The gaps between wage and productivity premiums are much smaller, and all are insignificant, in Zimbabwe. Results for Kenya, an intermediate country in terms of level of development, are intermediate: equal remuneration can be rejected for some characteristics (e.g., experience), but not for others (e.g., schooling). A test for equality of all wage and productivity premiums on the firm-level estimates yields a *p*-value of 1 percent in Tanzania, 18 percent in Kenya, and 64 percent in Zimbabwe. Using the individual-level estimates, the corresponding *p*-values are 0 percent, 1 percent, and 38 percent.

Moreover, the breakdown in correct remuneration in the two least developed countries follows a distinct pattern. On the one hand, wage premiums exceed productivity premiums for general human capital characteristics (experience and schooling). On the other hand, salaries hardly increase for more firm-specific human capital characteristics (tenure and training), even though these have a clear productivity effect. Equality of the returns fails most pronouncedly for the two indicators that capture how a worker's salary rises over his or her career. Even though productivity rises more with tenure than with experience,[1] salaries rise only with experience in Tanzania and much more with experience than with tenure in Kenya. In contrast, in Zimbabwe, workers are predominantly rewarded for tenure, consistent with the estimated productivity effects.

Finally, we estimate the gaps between wage and productivity premiums separately for firms that report facing international competition and those that do not. While the results are somewhat noisy, equality of the two returns is always less likely to be rejected for firms facing international competition. The difference is most pronounced for labor market experience: excessive salary increases over workers' careers, compared to productivity growth, are more moderate. It points to an additional channel through which international trade can improve resource allocation.

There are a number of important debates in development economics that would benefit from a better understanding of the relationship between wages and productivity. First, it is often argued that more education is a prerequisite for economic growth—see, for example, Knight and Sabot (1987). However, the Tanzanian firms in this sample have, on average, a more educated workforce, but the productivity effects of schooling fall far short of the wage effects. At the very least, higher education does not trans-

---

1. In some cases, productivity declines less with tenure than with experience, or productivity declines with experience, but rises with tenure. Crucial is that, in relative terms, tenure has a more positive effect on productivity than experience, in all three countries.

late automatically into higher output. Second, the measurement of productivity growth relies explicitly on the equality of relative wages and relative productivity. When labor growth is subtracted from output growth, categories of workers are weighed by their wage shares—see, for example, Jorgenson and Griliches (1967). If the equality between wages and productivity fails to hold systematically in developing countries, productivity growth measures will be biased.

The remainder of the chapter is organized as follows. The measurement framework to compare the wage and productivity premiums associated with worker characteristics is introduced first, in section 11.2, followed by a discussion of the evidence for other regions in section 11.3. The employer-employee data and the countries included in the analysis are discussed next, in section 11.4. Results at the firm and individual level are presented with some robustness checks in section 11.5, and section 11.6 concludes.

11.2   A Measurement Framework

11.2.1   Wage and Productivity Premiums

The methodology we use to compare wage and productivity premiums owes a great deal to Hellerstein, Neumark, and Troske (1999). If labor markets are efficient, operate as a spot market, and firms minimize costs, the wage premium of a worker should equal its productivity premium. Barring imperfect information, any difference will be arbitraged away. Both premiums can be identified by jointly estimating a wage equation and production function, which characterize how wages and output depend on worker characteristics.

As an example, assume that the productivity of male workers exceeds the average productivity of female workers by ϕ_M percent. The production function can be written as a function of capital and both types of labor (men and women), which are assumed to be perfect substitutes:[2]

$$Q = A f [K, L_F + (1 + \phi_M) L_M].$$

The first-order conditions for cost minimization by the firm dictate that the composition of the firm's labor force is adjusted such that the relative wage for both types of workers is equalized to the relative productivity ratio:

$$\frac{w_M}{w_F} = \frac{MP_M}{MP_F},$$

2. Given sufficiently detailed information on the labor force composition, this assumption can be relaxed. In the robustness checks at the end, we allowed for imperfect substitutability between experienced and inexperienced workers.

or equivalently,

(1)
$$\lambda_M \equiv \frac{w_M - w_F}{w_F} = \frac{MP_M - MP_F}{MP_F} \equiv \phi_M.$$

11.2.2 Firm-Level Estimation

The identification of the productivity premium (ϕ) is necessarily done at the plant or firm level. The wage premiums associated with worker characteristics (λ) can be estimated using a standard wage equation derived from the Mincer (1974) model of human capital. The most straightforward estimation strategy is to aggregate the wage equation to the firm level and estimate it jointly with the production function—see, for example, Hellerstein, Neumark, and Troske (1999).

Labor researchers have been concerned with a potential bias introduced by unobserved worker ability in the wage equation. Productivity researchers have estimated production functions controlling explicitly for unobserved productivity differences. Joint estimation should to a large extent alleviate such concerns, as the bias works in the same direction in both equations. A large component of the unobservables in both equations are expected to represent the same factors.[3] Results in Hellerstein and Neumark (2004) demonstrate that the results tend to be relatively unaffected if more sophisticated estimation strategies are employed.

Sticking with the earlier example, we now show how one can aggregate an individual wage equation to identify the left-hand side premium in equation (1). Define a wage equation for the individual as

$$W_i = w_F F_i + w_M M_i.$$

The average wage paid to women is w_F—F_i is a dummy that takes a value of 1 if individual i is a woman—and w_M to men. Summing over all workers of the firm gives

$$W = w_F L_F + w_M L_M \qquad\qquad L_F + L_M = L$$

$$= w_F \left[L + \left(\frac{w_M}{w_F} - 1 \right) L_M \right]$$

$$= w_F L \left(1 + \lambda_M \frac{L_M}{L} \right).$$

Taking logarithms and adding an additive error term, representing measurement error in the wage and unobservable worker characteristics, gives

---

3. See, for example, Frazer (2001), where this assumption is exploited to control for unobserved ability in the wage equation.

$$(2) \qquad \ln \frac{W}{L} = \ln w_F + \ln\left(1 + \lambda_M \frac{L_M}{L}\right) + \eta.$$

Nonlinear least squares estimation of the firm-level equation (2) produces an estimate of the average baseline wage (w_F) and of the gender wage premium (λ_M). The only information needed is the average wage and the proportion of male workers by firm.

Assuming the Cobb-Douglas functional form for the production function, it can be written in logarithms as[4]

$$\ln Q = \ln A + \alpha_K \ln K + \alpha_L \ln \tilde{L} + \varepsilon.$$

Male and female workers are aggregated in $\tilde{L}$, where each type of employee (L_F and L_M) is multiplied by its relative productivity level (1 or $1 + \phi_M$):

$$(3) \qquad \tilde{L} = L_F + (1 + \phi_M)L_M$$
$$= L\left(1 + \phi_M \frac{L_M}{L}\right).$$

The total labor force is $L = L_F + L_M$. Substituting (3) in the production function allows estimation of the gender productivity gap by nonlinear least squares from just the proportion of male workers in each firm and the usual output and input variables.

Generalizing this approach to construct a wage and production equation that takes more worker characteristics into account is limited by the data. For example, differentiating workers by gender (M or F), experience (Y or X—young versus high experience), and schooling (U or S—uneducated versus highly educated), creates eight categories of workers: inexperienced, educated males, and so forth. Given that we observe a maximum of ten workers in each firm, the proportion of each category in the firm's workforce would be estimated extremely inaccurately. Furthermore, it would be entirely impossible to look at any further characteristics or at characteristics that divide the workforce more finely.

Making three assumptions for each characteristic—or rather, three sets of assumptions—avoids this type of dimensional problem. For example, if we assume that the relative number of male to female workers, the relative productivity, and the relative wage by gender are all invariant to changes in other characteristics, we can use the full workforce to estimate the gender premiums. In effect, this is an independence of irrelevant alternatives assumption on the relative number of workers and the wage and productivity returns for each characteristic. In the previous example with three characteristics, this boils down to:

---

4. It is straightforward to generalize the methodology to other functional forms. Hellerstein and Neumark (2004) demonstrate that the qualitative results are very robust to alternative specifications of the production function.

(4)   Equal proportions: $\dfrac{L_{MYS}}{L_{FYS}} = \dfrac{L_{MXS}}{L_{FXS}} = \dfrac{L_{MYU}}{L_{FYU}} = \dfrac{L_{MXU}}{L_{FXU}},$

Equal productivity: $\dfrac{\phi_{MYS}}{\phi_{FYS}} = \dfrac{\phi_{MXS}}{\phi_{FXS}} = \dfrac{\phi_{MYU}}{\phi_{FYU}} = \dfrac{\phi_{MXU}}{\phi_{FXU}},$

Equal wage premium: $\dfrac{\lambda_{MYS}}{\lambda_{FYS}} = \dfrac{\lambda_{MXS}}{\lambda_{FXS}} = \dfrac{\lambda_{MYU}}{\lambda_{FYU}} = \dfrac{\lambda_{MXU}}{\lambda_{FXU}},$

and similarly for young versus experienced workers and for uneducated versus highly educated workers. This allows the simplification of the labor aggregate in the production function from eight terms, one for each worker category, to three multiplicative factors, one for each characteristic:

(5) $\tilde{L} = L_{FYS} + (1 + \phi_{FXS})L_{FXS} + (1 + \phi_{MYS})L_{MYS} + \ldots$

$+ (1 + \phi_{MXU})L_{MXU}$

$= L\left(1 + \phi_M \dfrac{L_M}{L}\right)\left(1 + \phi_X \dfrac{L_X}{L}\right)\left(1 + \phi_S \dfrac{L_S}{L}\right),$

and similarly in the wage equation. One can proceed in the same fashion to add further characteristics to (5). These assumptions cannot be tested, or they would not have been necessary. In the small sample of employees we observe at each firm, some ratios will obviously not be equal, but this can readily arise if only a few employees are sampled.

The baseline model constructed so far is

(6) $\ln \dfrac{W}{L} = \lambda 0 + \sum_{k=1}^{K} \ln\left(1 + \lambda k \dfrac{L_k}{L}\right) + \eta$

(7) $\ln Q = \alpha_0 + \alpha_K \ln K + \alpha_L\left[\ln L + \sum_{k=1}^{K} \ln\left(1 + \phi_k \dfrac{L_k}{L}\right)\right] + \varepsilon$

where λ_0 is the base salary (in the previous example, for a female, inexperienced, uneducated worker), λ_k is the wage premium and ϕ_k the productivity premium associated with characteristic k ($k \in K$). Equations (6) and (7) are estimated jointly with Zellner's seemingly unrelated regression estimator, allowing for correlation between the two error terms.[5]

---

5. As the fraction of workers with characteristics k enters equations (6) and (7) nonlinearly, the point estimates of λ_k and ϕ_k will depend on the normalization (thanks to an anonymous referee for pointing this out). However, the effect is only noticeable for fractions that are far away from 0.5, especially 'male' and to a lesser extent 'training'. Because the correlations between fraction of male or fraction of female workers and all other variables are identical in absolute value, the effect of the normalization does not spill over to the estimates for returns on other characteristics.

11.2.3   Individual-Level Estimation

While the previous approach allows identification of the wage and productivity premiums, it does not use all available information on the wage side. We do observe salaries and characteristics for a sample of individual workers at each firm. Rather than aggregating the wage equation to the firm level, we can also estimate a Mincer wage equation jointly with the production function. Estimating with a much larger number of observations—for example, for Tanzania with 520 individuals instead of 113 firms, is likely to yield more precise estimates of the wage premiums.

As productivity can only be estimated at the firm level and the productivity premiums associated with each characteristic are still restricted as in (4), we still use the same set of worker characteristics as before. The Mincer wage regression assumes additive separability of the returns to different characteristics, which is very similar to the equal wage premium assumptions in (4). We follow the usual practice and estimate the wage equation in logarithms:

$$\ln W_i = \omega_0 + \sum_{k=1}^{K} \omega_k X_i^k + \eta_i.$$

The i subscript indexes individuals and the variable X_i^k is a dummy for characteristic k ($k \in K$)—for example, the gender dummy M_i. This specification assumes that if a female worker has a salary of w_F, the salary for a male worker with otherwise equivalent characteristics would be $w_F \exp(w_M)$. Expressed differently, the baseline salary for a worker with all characteristics dummies equal to zero is $\exp(w_0)$, while a worker with characteristic X^k switched from zero to 1 has a salary equal to $\exp(w_0 + w_k)$.

The equality in percentage terms of the productivity and wage premiums associated with gender, as in equation (1), now boils down to

$$\exp(\omega_M) - 1 \equiv \frac{w_M - w_F}{w_F} = \frac{MP_M - MP_F}{MP_F} \equiv \phi_M.$$

Expressed differently, for each of the characteristics k, we want to test whether

$$\omega_k = \ln(1 + \phi_k).$$

The individual wage equation is now estimated jointly with the firm-level production function. As in the previous set-up, we still allow the errors in the two equations to be correlated. In addition, we allow for a random effect in the wage equation to take into account that errors for employees at the same firm are likely to be correlated. We implement the feasible generalized least squares (GLS) transformation as in Wooldridge (2000, 450) and jointly estimate the transformed wage equation with the production function. Because not all firms have the same number of employees sampled, we have to correct for the unbalancedness of our panel. As long as we assume that the reason for unbalancedness is random—not too unlikely for our application—the adjustments are straightforward. All variables in the wage equation are transformed according to

$$x_{ij}^* = x_{ij} - \lambda_j \overline{x}_j \quad \text{with } \lambda_j = 1 - \sqrt{\frac{s_e^2}{s_e^2 + N_j s_f^2}},$$

with i indexing individuals and j firms. The estimate of the standard error of the full residual combining individual errors and the random firm effect is s_e^2, which itself has an estimated standard error of s_f^2. The number of employees sampled at firm j is N_j.[6]

11.3   Evidence from Other Regions

Matched employer-employee data sets contain the necessary information to compare wage and productivity premiums, but their limited availability has lead to only a small number of previous studies.[7] From the observed employees, one can estimate average values of worker characteristics for each employer. Hellerstein et al. (1999) pioneered the approach, jointly estimating a plant-level wage equation with a production function using U.S. administrative record information. They test for equality of the wage and productivity premiums associated with a number of characteristics and only find a statistically significant discrepancy for the gender dummy: women are only 16 percent less productive than their male coworkers, but paid 45 percent less.

The bulk of the evidence for developed countries points toward equal wage and productivity returns for various worker characteristics. Using more recent 1990 U.S. data, Hellerstein and Neumark (2004) confirm that the wage gap between males and females exceeds the productivity gap. In contrast, the lower wages for blacks is in line with productivity estimates, and even though attaining "some college" education only attracts a 43 percent wage premium while productivity is 67 percent higher, the difference is not statistically significant. Similar work for France in Pérez-Duarte, Crepon, and Deniau (2001) and for Israel in Hellerstein and Neumark (1999) finds no gender discrimination. In a study for Norway, Haegeland and Klette (1999) also finds that wage premiums for gender and eduction are in line with productivity premiums.

The only characteristic in those studies for which the wage premium differs significantly from the productivity premium is age in France—older

6. How to estimate the different standard errors is discussed in Wooldridge (1999, 260–261).
7. A conference symposium in the *Monthly Labor Review* (July 1998) provides an overview of sources; see also Haltiwanger et al. (1999).

workers are overpaid—while engineers are underpaid in Israel. For Norwegian workers with eight to fifteen years of experience, the productivity premium exceeds the wage premium, while the opposite is true for workers with more than fifteen years of experience.

Dearden, Reed, and Van Reenen (2006) focus on the effects of training using an industry-level data set covering the U.K. manufacturing sector. They separately estimate wage equations and production functions and find that the productivity effect of training substantially exceeds the wage effect, but no formal test is presented. They conclude that the usual approach in the literature of quantifying the benefits of training by looking at wages underestimates the impact. Another finding is that aggregation to the industry magnifies the effect of training, potentially due to externalities.

The only similar study in a developing country, Jones (2001) estimates a firm-level production function jointly with an individual-level wage equation for Ghana. However, no details are given regarding the assumptions on the variance-covariance matrix when the individual- and firm-level data is combined.[8] She finds that women are 42 percent to 62 percent less productive, depending on the specification, and paid 12 percent to 15 percent less. No formal test is reported, but the standard errors are fairly large. Her focus is on the premiums associated with an extra year of schooling, which are estimated similarly in the production function and the wage equation: both are around 7 percent. When discrete levels of education attainment are used, the results are ambiguous. The differences in point estimates are large, but the education coefficients in the production function are estimated imprecisely and none of the formal tests finds a statistically significant difference.[9]

Bigsten et al. (2000) gauge the link between wages and productivity indirectly, similar to the U.K. analysis. First, they estimate the returns to education in five sub-Saharan countries using a wage equation. Then, they separately estimate the production function, including lagged levels of education as a proxy for human capital. They find that the implied rate of return to human capital is very low—in particular, it is only a fraction of the return to physical capital.

11.4   Data

11.4.1   Countries

The three countries included in the sample are middle-sized former British colonies in East Africa that obtained independence in the early

8. We contacted the author to obtain further information, but did not receive a response.
9. Many differences are large in absolute value—five of the eight estimated differentials exceed 20 percent—but the direction of the difference varies by schooling level.

1960s.[10] The World Bank classifies all three as low income, even though they differ substantially by level of development. One way to see this is from GDP per capita, which stood at $477 (in purchasing power parity [PPP]) in Tanzania, less than half of the $1,092 attained in Kenya, and only slightly more than one fifth of the GDP per capita of Zimbabwe—all figures are for 1991 and reported in table 11.1. The differences are smaller on the United Nations' human development index, which also takes education and life expectancy into account, but the order is the same. In the most recent ranking, Tanzania occupies the 151st (or 22nd last) place with 0.440, putting it in the "low development" category. Kenya and Zimbabwe rank rather closely at places 134 and 128, with a score of 0.513 and 0.551, respectively, near the bottom of the "medium development" group.[11]

The different development levels of the countries are also reflected in the share of workers employed in industry.[12] Only 4.7 percent of all employment in Tanzania is in industry, while it is almost twice as high in Zimbabwe (8.6 percent) and intermediate in Kenya (7.3 percent). In Tanzania, the transition from agriculture to other sectors had only just begun: agriculture comprised almost half the workforce at the end of the 1990s. In Kenya, the transformation was in full swing: the employment share of agriculture declined from 42 percent in 1975 to 27.5 percent by the sample period. Zimbabwe, on the other hand, has seen a stable 18.5 percent of its workforce employed in agriculture for the last twenty-five years.

Given that Zimbabwe is much more advanced in its industrial transformation, it is not surprising that it far surpasses the other two countries in GDP per capita. The difference in labor productivity in industry is even more stark. While industry workers in Kenya produce twice as much as Tanzanian workers, Zimbabwe's output per worker outstrips Tanzania by a factor of seven and Kenya by a factor of four. It underscores the importance of developing a strong manufacturing sector. World Bank (2000) statistics also show that manufacturing workers in Tanzania earn 3.5 times more, on average, than agricultural workers, while the ratio stands at 5.7 in Kenya and even 9.9 in Zimbabwe.

Infrastructure statistics confirm the different levels of development of the three countries. Zimbabwe had 22km of paved highways per 1000 km^2

---

10. Unfortunately, only three countries could be included in the analysis due to data constraints. A partial analysis was possible with data from Cameroon (almost as developed as Zimbabwe) and Burundi (even less developed than Tanzania), but the sample size is smaller, some variables (e.g. capital) are measured less accurately, and other variables (e.g. training in Burundi) are missing. Results for these countries are in between the extremes of Tanzania and Zimbabwe. The failure of the equality between wage and productivity premiums to hold is much more pronounced in Burundi than in Cameroon: the p-values for the joint test, corresponding to the first joint test in table 11.3, were, respectively, 0.03 and 0.22.

11. Norway tops the human development ranking with a score of 0.942.

12. Manufacturing employment that corresponds to manufacturing value added was not available for Tanzania in 1991.

Table 11.1   Summary statistics

	Tanzania	Kenya	Zimbabwe
Population	26.3m	24.3m	10.0m
Percent employed in industry	4.9	7.3	8.6
Manufacturing workers[a]	126312	177738	187937
GDP / capita (PPP)	477	1092	2201
VA / employee in industry (USD)[b]	983	1705	7049
Median LP in sample[c]	38	100	142
Median TFP in sample[c]	54	100	143
Monthly wage in sample (USD)	55.9 (58.6)	117.0 (322.2)	203.3 (261.3)
Exports as % of domestic prod.[d]	8.8	23.5	23.6
Imports as % of domestic cons.	76.9	73.3	50.3
Manufacturing exports as % of total	6.1	20.9	40.5
Export participation in the sample (%)	9	22	49
Share of manuf. GDP covered	0.31	0.17	0.26
Share of manuf. labor force covered	0.15	0.12	0.31
Number of firms	113	183	110
Workers per firm	97.3	89.8	269.8
Workers interviewed per firm	4.6	6.2	5.5
Male (%)	0.79 (0.40)	0.87 (0.34)	0.84 (0.36)
Age (years)	35.3 (10.5)	34.1 (9.4)	37.0 (10.4)
Experience (years)	16.4 (10.4)	16.1 (9.8)	19.9 (10.8)
Schooling (years)	12.4 (4.8)	11.5 (3.8)	11.0 (3.6)
Tenure (years)	7.8 (6.9)	7.9 (7.2)	10.3 (8.2)
Received training (%)	0.09 (0.29)	0.12 (0.32)	0.21 (0.41)

Source: World Bank (2000) and own calculations for the sample statistics.
Notes: Data is for 1991 for aggregate statistics and for first year of interviews for sample statistics. Standard errors in parentheses.
[a] UNIDO.
[b] Using exchange rates.
[c] Relative to Kenya, see Van Biesebroeck (2005).
[d] Trade statistics are for 1993. The trade share is for manufacturing only, and manufacturing sales is assumed to be double of value added.

of land, while the corresponding numbers for Kenya and Tanzania were 15km and 4km. The same ranking is preserved in kilometers of railroad by area at, respectively, eight, five, and four kilometers, or airports per million inhabitants: 1.4 in Zimbabwe, 0.6 in Kenya, and 0.3 in Tanzania. In fact, almost any conceivable statistic that one expects to be correlated with development produces the same ranking: access to clean water, telephone penetration, school enrollments, infant mortality, and so forth.[13]

The three countries also differ substantially in their exposure to interna-

---

13. Only life expectancy at birth gives a reverse ranking, but this is due to the staggering HIV infection rate, affecting one third of the adult population in Zimbabwe and almost one-sixth in Kenya.

tional trade. Manufacturing exports as a fraction of domestic production is almost three times higher in Zimbabwe than in Tanzania, 23.6 percent versus 8.8 percent, but almost as high in Kenya. On the import side, we see that only in Zimbabwe domestic production accounts for half of the total domestic consumption. In the other two countries, approximately three-quarters of all manufactures consumed are imported. This aggregate trade exposure is reflected in the export participation rate for the firms in the sample. The differences are even more pronounced, with firms in Zimbabwe more than five times as likely to export than Tanzanian firms. The importance of the manufacturing sector in the three countries is well illustrated by the share of total export earnings accounted for by the manufacturing sector. This rises from a mere 6.1 percent in Tanzania, to 20.9 percent in Kenya, and a full 40.5 percent in Zimbabwe.

11.4.2   Firms and Workers

In 1991, Tanzania and Kenya each counted approximately twenty-five million inhabitants, while Zimbabwe only had ten million. The manufacturing sector, which we focus on, is more evenly sized because of its greater importance in Zimbabwe. All countries count between 126,000 and 188,000 manufacturing workers. A stratified sample of manufacturing firms in three consecutive years provides the micro data used in the analysis.[14] Approximately 200 firms were surveyed each year in each country, covering four broadly defined manufacturing sectors: food, textile and clothing, wood and furniture, and metal and equipment. A maximum of ten employees per firm were interviewed each year. While firms could be linked over time as a panel, this was not possible for the workers. Because questions on training were not asked in the third year, we only use the first two years in the analysis.

The resulting sample is an unbalanced panel of firms with, on average, 110 to 183 observations per year in each country. In the first year, the firms employed 19,383 to 58,108 workers and 619 to 1,206 of them were interviewed. A large part of the manufacturing sector is covered by this sample. The value added produced by the sample firms makes up 31 percent of manufacturing GDP in Tanzania, 17 percent in Kenya, and 26 percent in Zimbabwe. The share of all manufacturing workers who are employed by firms included in the sample is substantially lower in the first two countries, a result of the higher productivity levels achieved by larger firms.

The differences between the countries described earlier are equally apparent when we compare the firms in the sample. The median firm in Tanzania achieves only 38 percent of the labor productivity level of the median firm in Kenya, while labor productivity in Zimbabwe is 42 percent

14. The data was collected between 1991 and 1995 by three different research teams, coordinated by the Regional Program of Enterprise Development at the World Bank. Firms were sampled to give (the firm of) each manufacturing worker equal probability to be included in the sample—an implicit stratification by employment size.

higher than in Kenya. Total factor productivity numbers, taken from Van Biesebroeck (2005), show similar differences when capital intensity is taken into account. The median firm in Kenya is twice as productive as in Tanzania, but achieves only two-thirds of the productivity level of the median firm in Zimbabwe. The salary differences between the countries match the labor productivity differences rather well. Workers in Tanzania earn 27.4 percent of the average salary in Zimbabwe, while the median labor productivity of their employers stands at 26.8 percent. Salaries in Kenya, on average $120 (in 1991 USD), are slightly lower than one would predict from the relative labor productivity, which would imply a salary of approximately $140. The statistics for the sample confirm that Zimbabwe is by far the most developed country of the three, while Tanzania is lagging far behind.

The remainder of table 11.1 provides averages and standard errors for the variables used in the analysis. Workers in Zimbabwe work, on average, in larger firms, are slightly older, stay longer with the same firm and are more likely to receive (or choose to enroll in) formal training once they are employed. The sample of workers in Kenya is even more dominated by males than in the other countries. In Tanzania, workers receive the lowest salaries, but paradoxically they have the highest years of schooling. How these characteristics are rewarded is analyzed in the next section.

11.5   Results

The discussion of the estimation results is organized in the same three subsections as the earlier discussion of the measurement framework. This is followed by a discussion of some robustness checks and an analysis of the importance of trade exposure.

11.5.1   Wage and Productivity Premiums

Information on productivity is only available at the firm level and, hence, the identification of the productivity premiums necessarily exploits between-firm variation. For wages, we have the option to exploit only between-firm variation as well, in which case individual wages have to be aggregated to the firm level. Alternatively we can incorporate the information contained in the individual wages in the estimation. We will employ both strategies, but first we look at the wage equation in isolation to verify whether the estimated wage premiums for worker characteristics differ in important ways when we limit identification to between-firm or within-firm variation.[15]

---

15. The working paper version, Van Biesebroeck (2003), shows additional results for the individual level wage equation. A full survey of the returns to education estimated from Mincer wage regressions in sub-Saharan Africa is in Appleton, Hoddinott, and Mackinnon (1996).

Individual wage regressions with least squares capture both variation within and between firms; results for the three countries are in the columns labeled "total" in table 11.2. For example, the positive salary premium for male workers can be the result of men receiving, on average, higher salaries than women within a given firm, or men can be disproportionately employed in firms that pay higher salaries, a between effect, even without differential pay by gender. In the columns labeled "within" and "between," we separate the two effects. Within estimates are obtained using the standard fixed-effects estimator (including firm-year fixed effects) and between estimates are obtain by averaging all variables by firm-year and estimating with least squares.

All five characteristics are measured as dummy variables. Experience is coded as 1 if a worker attained more labor market experience than the median (interviewed) worker for the country, and tenure is defined similarly. The schooling dummy takes on a value of 1 if the worker has at least attended secondary school, but not necessarily finished it. The training dummy is switched on for workers who completed a formal training program (excluding on-the-job training) after they finished their formal education or apprenticeship.

The main message from table 11.2 is that in all but two cases the between estimates are of the same sign as the total estimates and in most cases even the magnitudes are very similar. The only two instances where the signs do not correspond—tenure in Tanzania and gender in Zimbabwe—the between coefficient is estimated extremely imprecisely and not significantly different from zero (the t-statistics are 0.46 and 0.78). One pattern to note is that for Zimbabwe four of the five between estimates exceed the total estimates, with the reverse being true for the within estimates. At least for Zimbabwe, identifying wage premiums from between-firm variation tends to overestimate the unconditional premiums in a sample of workers.

The magnitudes of the wage premiums for different characteristics seem reasonable. Male workers earn substantially more, but a gender wage premium of 10.5 percent to 28.6 percent is not unreasonably large. In the first two countries, the pay differential by gender is larger between firms than within, while in Zimbabwe the between estimate surprisingly turns negative. Only in Zimbabwe are female workers concentrated in higher-paying, larger firms. Experience and schooling premiums are estimated surprisingly similar in the three countries, especially the wage gradient within firms. Differences are more pronounced for tenure and training: for both variables, workers in Zimbabwe are rewarded more generously than in the other two countries. The tenure premium in Zimbabwe is exclusively driven by the between effect, indicating that salaries do not really increase with tenure, but firms that pay higher salaries have lower worker attrition.

While we could have included occupation controls, we follow the convention in the literature not to do so. A substantial fraction of the return

Table 11.2   **Mincer wage regressions at the individual level with discrete characteristics**

	Tanzania			Kenya			Zimbabwe		
	Total	Within	Between	Total	Within	Between	Total	Within	Between
Male	0.286	0.302	0.328	0.105	0.089	0.294	0.109	0.108	-0.153
	(0.044)	(0.038)	(0.120)	(0.043)	(0.042)	(0.103)	(0.063)	(0.061)	(0.196)
Experience	0.212	0.202	0.309	0.245	0.247	0.196	0.224	0.242	0.206
	(0.040)	(0.034)	(0.110)	(0.033)	(0.032)	(0.084)	(0.054)	(0.051)	(0.189)
Schooling	0.412	0.417	0.583	0.405	0.390	0.317	0.450	0.389	0.879
	(0.039)	(0.035)	(0.101)	(0.030)	(0.030)	(0.070)	(0.051)	(0.048)	(0.178)
Tenure	0.082	0.102	-0.047	0.061	0.093	0.059	0.073	0.002	0.406
	(0.040)	(0.036)	(0.107)	(0.033)	(0.033)	(0.084)	(0.052)	(0.051)	(0.157)
Training	0.042	-0.007	0.047	0.095	0.099	0.096	0.173	0.175	0.270
	(0.061)	(0.056)	(0.141)	(0.044)	(0.043)	(0.095)	(0.057)	(0.060)	(0.137)
Obs.	1215	1215	266	2180	2180	375	1162	1162	213
R^2	0.210	0.206	0.274	0.272	0.099	0.467	0.246	0.062	0.441

Notes: The dependent variable is the logarithm of the individual hourly wage rate. All characteristics are dummy variables. Male and training are coded as 1 for yes and zero for no. The other variables are 1 if the value is higher than the median for the country and zero otherwise. Total: OLS regression, controls include hours worked, firm size (log-employment), and year, sector, and location dummies. Within: Fixed-effects estimator controlling for hours worked and firm-year dummies. Between: OLS regression with variables averaged by firm (by year if applicable); same controls as in "Total."

to human capital characteristics will materialize through occupation changes—for example, promotions, which are surely endogenous.[16]

11.5.2   Firm-Level Estimation

The SUR estimation results for equations (6) and (7) by country, with discretely measured worker characteristics, are in table 11.3. In this and all following specifications, hours worked and time, industry, and location dummies are added as controls in both the wage equation and production function. The production function always has to be estimated at the firm level, and here we aggregate the wage equation to the same level. Results in the following section are for the individual wage equation jointly estimated with the firm production function, which severely complicates the estimation.

Larger firms tend to pay higher salaries, in line with evidence for many African countries in Mazumdar and Mazaheri (2002), although the effect is small in Tanzania. The capital and labor elasticities in the Cobb-Douglas production function are estimated similarly in the three countries, with labor somewhat more important in Zimbabwe and the capital coefficient highest in Kenya. Returns to scale are moderately increasing in each country. The sum of the two input coefficients ranges from 1.041 to 1.141, in line with results for the manufacturing sector in other developing countries, as surveyed in Tybout (2000).

Consistent with the results for the individual wage data in table 11.2, we find the highest wage premium for males in Tanzania and the estimate in Kenya is approximately 10 percent lower. However, these salary gaps fall far short of the higher productivity realized by firms that employ a high percentage of male workers. The extremely high point estimates on the male dummy in the production function imply that raising the fraction of males by one standard deviation would raise output by 32 percent in Tanzania, by 40 percent in Kenya, but only by 2 percent in Zimbabwe. Given that wage premiums for males are below the corresponding productivity premiums, it suggests that men are underpaid, although none of the differences is statistically significant. These estimates are somewhat misleading though, because the majority of firms in the sample employ only male workers. The choice not to employ any female workers is undoubtedly related to the line of work a firm carries out. The productivity premium by gender is also estimated extremely imprecisely, and in the following we will mostly disregard the gender variable.

The wage premiums associated with experience are not estimated very precisely either, except in Tanzania, but the point estimates again correspond well to the between results in table 11.2; only the return to experi-

---

16. Results in Van Biesebroeck (2003) illustrate that 28 percent to 55 percent of the return to schooling and education is associated with occupation changes.

Table 11.3   **A market efficiency test: Production function and wage equation at the firm level**

Dependent variable:	Tanzania		Kenya		Zimbabwe	
	Wage	Output	Wage	Output	Wage	Output
Labor	0.035	0.781	0.136	0.851	0.200	0.901
	(.025)	(.082)	(.020)	(.070)	(.035)	(.068)
Capital		0.260		0.290		0.228
		(.041)		(.039)		(.040)
Male	0.537	1.386	0.422	2.186	−0.137	0.062
	(.235)	(1.32)	(.211)	(1.59)	(.182)	(.313)
Experience	0.308	−0.404	0.193	−0.205	0.119	0.349
	(.147)	(.229)	(.126)	(.233)	(.221)	(.357)
Schooling	0.717	0.162	0.467	0.077	1.289	1.764
	(.175)	(.401)	(.133)	(.270)	(.463)	(.781)
Tenure	−0.075	−0.249	0.063	0.366	0.470	0.801
	(.104)	(.271)	(.115)	(.407)	(.246)	(.410)
Received training	−0.074	0.700	0.029	0.560	0.295	0.231
	(.157)	(.810)	(.125)	(.476)	(.195)	(.254)
*Test for equality of coefficients in both equations (*p-values*)*						
Joint test (all 5 characteristics)		0.01		0.18		0.64
Joint test—without male		0.01		0.23		0.73
Joint test—general HC		0.00		0.15		0.72
Joint test—firm-specific HC		0.55		0.42		0.73
Joint test—learning		0.29		0.28		0.42
Joint test—over time		0.00		0.21		0.79
Observations		266		375		213
R^2	0.27	0.71	0.41	0.80	0.45	0.87

Note: Controls added to both the wage equation and the production function are hours worked and year, industry, and location dummies. Estimation is with SUR. Experience and schooling are grouped as general human capital (HC) characteristics, with tenure and training grouped as firm-specific human capital. "Learning" combines schooling and training and "over time" combines experience and tenure.

ence in Zimbabwe is estimated rather low. Salaries rise substantially with experience in Tanzania and Kenya, but not in Zimbabwe, where education is rewarded higher than in the other two countries. The impact of experience in the production function follows a peculiar pattern: the relative size of the productivity premiums in the three countries is exactly the opposite of the wage premiums ranking. In the country where salaries are most responsive to experience, Tanzania, the productivity of firms drops with the experience/age of the workforce. The country that rewards experience the least, Zimbabwe, is the only one where experience is associated with a positive productivity effect. The gap between the wage and productivity premium associated with experience is more than 50 percent larger in Kenya than in Zimbabwe, and the gap in Tanzania is almost three times as large as in Zimbabwe. For Tanzania, we can reject equality between the two premiums at the 1 percent significance level and for Kenya at the 10 percent level.

For schooling, the size of the productivity premiums follows the same pattern between countries as the wage premiums: highest in Zimbabwe, lowest in Kenya, and intermediate in Tanzania. Still, in the two least-developed economies, educated workers are able to secure a wage premium that far outstrips the productivity contribution of education. In Zimbabwe, on the other hand, the difference goes the other way. Similarly as for experience, the gap between the wage and productivity premium associated with schooling is by far the largest in Tanzania and Kenya.

The tenure variable, which measures whether an employee has stayed more than the median number of years with his or her current employer, is associated with particularly large salary increases in Zimbabwe (47 percent). In the other two countries, salaries do not rise with tenure, only with experience. Strikingly, in each country the productivity effect of tenure largely exceeds that of experience. The same is true for the training dummy. In the two least-developed countries, workers who receive training are not paid a higher salary, even though training has a large (but imprecisely estimated) effect on productivity. In Zimbabwe, the wage premium for workers marginally exceeds the productivity effect.

Combined with the higher wage premium for tenure than for experience, the compensation pattern in Zimbabwe is likely to help reduce worker turnover, especially of those valuable employees that received training. This is borne out by a cursory look at the correlation between training and tenure at the individual level. Controlling for experience, workers with a longer tenure are more likely to have completed a training program. On average, workers that have completed training were employed for half a year longer at their current employer. The relationship is particularly strong in Zimbabwe, but hardly noticeable in Kenya.

A joint test for the hypothesis that for the four variables that determine the level of human capital in a firm (experience, schooling, tenure, and training) wage premiums equal productivity premiums is rejected for Tanzania at the 1 percent significance level. For Kenya, it can only be rejected if we are willing to tolerate a 23 percent significance level. The hypothesis can never be rejected for Zimbabwe, as the p-value is 73 percent. The tests follow the same pattern if we include the male dummy, with the p-value somewhat lower for Kenya and even higher for Zimbabwe.

Performing separate tests for the firm-specific aspects of human capital (tenure and training) and general human capital (experience and schooling) points to the general characteristics driving the correlation between equality of returns and development level of the country. Firms in all three countries are rewarding firm-specific characteristics more closely in proportion to the productivity gains they bring. The p-values on these joint tests are always high, although it should be noted that the effects are estimated especially imprecisely for Tanzania and Kenya.

In contrast, the differences between countries are especially stark for general human capital characteristics. The p-value is 0.00 for Tanzania, 0.15 for Kenya, and 0.72 for Zimbabwe. Grouping characteristics differently—schooling and training (learning), on the one hand, and experience and tenure (over time), on the other—points again to the importance of experience. The underlying tendency is for salaries to increase over time with experience in Tanzania and Kenya and with tenure in Zimbabwe, while productivity is more closely related to tenure than to experience in each country.

Even at the firm level, coefficients on the worker characteristics are estimated more precisely in the wage equation than in the production function, although the R^2 tends to be higher in the latter. Comparing the different countries, standard errors are somewhat larger for Zimbabwe than for Kenya or Tanzania. However, the coefficient estimates also tend to be larger (in absolute value) for Zimbabwe, with the exception of the male and training dummies even uniformly so. While the average t-statistic in the wage equation is somewhat higher in Tanzania (1.93) and Kenya (1.56) than in Zimbabwe (1.48), the average t-statistic in the production function is higher in Zimbabwe (1.26) than in Tanzania (1.00) or Kenya (0.92). Only for the male dummy is the t-statistic in Zimbabwe below those in the other two countries. There is thus no evidence that the higher p-values for Zimbabwe are simply due to less-imprecisely estimated coefficients.

11.5.3   Individual-Level Estimation

While the joint tests at the bottom of table 11.3 for the results at the firm level showed a clear pattern, many of the wage and productivity premiums were estimated imprecisely. Incorporating the information on individual employees avoids aggregation of the wage equation and is likely to improve precision, especially for the wage premiums. The estimation results using the wage equation at the individual level with the methodology outlined previously are in table 11.4. The increase in precision is very large for all coefficients in the wage equation: on average, standard errors have decreased by a factor of three. The production function coefficients are estimated more precisely as well, especially in Tanzania. While all firms were treated identically in the firm level estimation, the current results implicitly weigh firms by the number of employees that are sampled, which partly explains the nonnegligible changes in the point estimates of both equations.

The labor and capital coefficients have changed the least; only the results for Tanzania are somewhat closer to those for Kenya and Zimbabwe. In the wage equation, all premiums are now estimated positively, in line with our priors. While most of the point estimates for Tanzania and Zimbabwe are slightly lower in absolute value than before, the estimates for Kenya are

Table 11.4   **A market efficiency test: Firm-level production function and individual wage equation**

	Tanzania		Kenya		Zimbabwe	
Dependent variable:	Wage	Output	Wage	Output	Wage	Output
Labor	0.057	0.864	0.074	0.701	0.208	0.850
	(.024)	(.035)	(.018)	(.029)	(.022)	(.028)
Capital		0.238		0.326		0.262
		(.047)		(.019)		(.017)
Male	0.340	0.878	0.089	0.117	0.115	0.217
	(.052)	(.431)	(.045)	(.267)	(.068)	(.178)
Experience	0.237	−0.639	0.283	−0.238	0.271	0.347
	(.047)	(.069)	(.039)	(.152)	(.064)	(.186)
Schooling	0.503	−0.289	0.470	0.268	0.567	1.109
	(.054)	(.121)	(.039)	(.194)	(.068)	(.313)
Tenure	0.080	0.099	0.104	0.067	0.203	0.592
	(.046)	(.174)	(.036)	(.214)	(.219)	(.193)
Received training	0.039	0.281	0.104	0.453	0.177	0.079
	(.069)	(.273)	(.048)	(.290)	(.069)	(.112)
Test for equality of coefficients in both equations (p-values)						
Joint test (all 5 characteristics)	—	0.00		0.01		0.67
Joint test—without male		0.00		0.01		0.59
Joint test—general HC		0.00		0.02		0.52
Joint test—firm-specific HC		0.63		0.40		0.41
Joint test—learning		0.00		0.19		0.36
Joint test—over time		0.00		0.00		0.48
Observations	1215	266	2180	375	1162	213
R^2	0.74	0.73	0.44	0.75	0.32	0.83

Note: Controls added to both the wage equation and the production function are as before: hours worked and year, industry, and location dummies. Estimation is with SUR. The production function is at the firm level, while the wage equation is at the individual level and has first been transformed to allow for a random firm effect. Groupings of characteristics for the joint tests are the same as in table 11.3.

slightly higher for most coefficients. With only a couple of exceptions, the returns to worker characteristics in the production function are estimated lower than before in absolute value. The relative position of the countries, however, is by and large unchanged.

The average size (in absolute value) of the gap between wage and productivity premiums in Tanzania went from 61.2 percent for the firm-level results to 49.3 percent for the individual results, from 67.6 percent to 22.7 percent in Kenya, and from 26.0 percent to 24.1 percent in Zimbabwe. Even though the absolute value of the differences declined, the standard errors declined even more, resulting in more of the gaps being significantly different from zero. The same joint tests as before yield almost uniformly lower *p*-values; see the results at the bottom of table 11.4.

The rejection of equality of the wage and productivity premiums for

Tanzania is as strong as before, but not solely due to experience anymore. The *t*-statistic associated with the "excess return" to experience is now 10.5, but the "excess return" to schooling now also yields a *t*-statistic of 6.1. Moreover, the direction of the differences is the same as before: experience and schooling are over-rewarded, while tenure and training are under-rewarded, although not significantly so. The same is true for Kenya, but less pronouncedly. Only one general human capital characteristics is clearly over-rewarded—experience—and only training receives a salary premium below the productivity effect, although the gap is not statistically significant.

Results for Zimbabwe are by and large similar as before, although the standard errors in the wage equation are somewhat higher than in the other two countries. The average size of the gap between wage and productivity premiums is still the lowest of the three countries, at least if we exclude gender, but the lower precision makes the tests less powerful in Zimbabwe. In contrast with the other two countries, the only two characteristics for which the gap is more than 10 percent are schooling and tenure, and both are rewarded below their contribution to productivity.

11.5.4   Robustness Checks

The working paper version of this chapter contains a number of sensitivity analyses that demonstrate the robustness of the results—see Van Biesebroeck (2003) for details. First, the findings are very similar using continuous measures (years) of experience, tenure, and schooling. In the two least-developed countries, workers are still estimated to secure substantial pay increases over their career that are not matched by any discernible productivity effect. The wage return to schooling also exceeds its effect on productivity in each country, but the extent differs widely. As before, the excess returns (the gap between the salary and productivity premiums) for experience and schooling are highest in Tanzania, at respectively, 4.8 percent per year of labor market experience and 6.0 percent per year of education. The gaps are sizeable in Kenya as well, at 2.8 percent and 3.3 percent. In Zimbabwe, the gaps are only 0.3 percent and 1.2 percent, and formal statistical tests do not reject equality of the returns (p-values are 0.81 and 0.75). In the two least-developed countries, equality of the returns to experience can be firmly rejected, even at a 1 percent significance level. The same holds for schooling in Tanzania (albeit only at a 10 percent significance level), but not in Kenya.

Second, given that the rejection of equality between wage and productivity premiums in Tanzania and Kenya is to a large extent driven by the experience premiums, we have reestimated the model, relaxing the assumption that workers with high and low experience are perfect substitutes. We introduce two separate labor aggregates ($\tilde{L}_X$ and $\tilde{L}_Y$) in the model; each is adjusted by multiplicative factors to control for the other worker characteristics—as in equation (5).[17] To be as flexible as possible on the production side, we adopted a constant elasticity of substitution (CES) specification, which allows not only the weight on each labor aggregate, but also the elasticity of substitution between the two aggregates to be determined by the data. This requires a modification in the test for equality between the two premiums, but we refer to Van Biesebroeck (2003; section 7.2) for details. The results are qualitatively similar to the results in table 11.3, where perfect substitutability is assumed. This is not surprising given that the estimates for the elasticity of substitution between young and experienced workers are relatively high: 3.0 for Kenya, 6.3 for Tanzania, and infinity for Zimbabwe. The *p*-value on the joint test for Kenya is even lower than in table 11.3.

Third, even though we did not observe the entire workforce for most firms, we could proceed with the estimation by using the sample of observed employees to estimate the fraction of male, educated (and so forth) workers at each firm. While these are estimated quantities, we have treated them as the true means. Van Biesebroeck (2003) reports results from two Monte Carlo exercises that investigate how sensitive the findings are to the noise that enters the estimation procedure in this way. A first exercise repeatedly samples for each firm a different sample of employees from the hypothetical workforce (as implied by the estimated means) and proceeds with the estimation as before. A second exercise uses Bayes' law (based on the estimated means) to assign probabilities to randomly generated values for each characteristic. These probabilities are then used as weights in the seemingly unrelated regression (SUR), where each firm is assigned randomly generated average characteristics.

For both exercises, the average *p*-values are slightly below the *p*-values for Tanzania and Kenya in table 11.3, rejecting equality strongly. In the second, exercise, the *p*-value for Zimbabwe is much reduced, although it remains more than twice as high as the one for Kenya. Given that, on average, a smaller fraction of each firm's workforce is sampled in Zimbabwe, it was expected that sampling would introduce greater variation for Zimbabwe. Still, the qualitative finding that "the likelihood of rejecting equality between wage and productivity premiums is decreasing with the level of development" still applies.

11.5.5   Trade Exposure

In addition to the differences between countries, there are bound to be differences between individual firms within each country. One crucial distinction between firms is to what extent they are exposed to competition

17. Data limitations force us to still use the entire workforce to estimate the fraction of male workers, highly educated workers, and so on. In principle, it is possible to let the ratio of male workers as well as the wage and productivity premiums associated with gender vary by experience category.

from foreign firms. Firms that operate in a highly competitive product environment might also have to compete harder on the labor market to attract good employees. To export successfully, firms need a high-quality product, possibly requiring more highly skilled workers. To survive in an industry facing a lot of import competition, producing efficiently is crucial and investments in human capital might be one way to achieve process innovations. In any case, strong competition in the output market will make it harder to offer wage premiums for worker characteristics that do not contribute to productivity.

Results in table 11.5 are for two subsamples that pool firms from all countries, but separate firms that face international competition from those that do not. Firms "exposed to trade" are those that exported, or that indicated that the main source of competition they faced was from (a) imported goods, from (b) local production by foreign or multinational firms, or from (c) foreign firms on export markets.[18]

Results using the firm-level estimator are reported in the first two columns of table 11.5. To conserve space, the excess returns—the difference between the wage and productivity premiums—are reported directly. The pattern is clearcut. Firms that face international competition reward characteristics more in line with the productivity contributions they make. The average gap between wage and productivity premiums, even excluding the male premium, is 58.2 percent for firms that do not face international competition and 45.4 percent for firms that do. Even though the standard errors are somewhat smaller for the latter firms, the tests indicate that rejection of equality is more likely for firms not facing international competition.

The comparable average gap for the results with the individual-level estimator, reported in the last two columns of table 11.5, is 39.5 percent for domestically oriented firms and 25.1 percent for firms competing with foreigners. The tests for equality are not very different for the two samples, although p-values are always lower for the domestically oriented firms. This is mostly due to the much smaller gap for experience for firms exposed to trade. Using either estimation method, firms competing with foreigners are especially likely to equate wages to productivity premiums for the firm-specific characteristics, tenure and training. Given that these are controlled by the employee and can be adjusted over one's career, incentives will be more appropriate for employees of these firms. While the results in table 11.5 are somewhat sensitive to the controls included and to the way the samples are divided, it does provide some evidence for the importance of competition.

18. Alternative answers to the question asking about the main source of competition were (iv) none, or (v) domestic firms producing locally.

Table 11.5 Estimation on separate samples by trade exposure (pooling firms from all countries)

	Firm-level estimation		Individual-level estimation	
Trade exposure?	No	Yes	No	Yes
Male	−1.377	−0.278	−0.318	−1.703
	(1.47)	(.272)	(.312)	(.544)
Experience	1.054	0.560	0.773	0.251
	(.489)	(.323)	(.113)	(.128)
Schooling	0.404	0.586	0.488	0.497
	(.251)	(.297)	(.150)	(.151)
Tenure	0.447	−0.531	0.276	−0.216
	(.234)	(.811)	(.195)	(.233)
Received training	−0.423	0.138	−0.050	0.041
	(.552)	(.297)	(.222)	(.158)
Test for equality of coefficients in both equations (p-values)				
Joint test—without male	0.00	0.20	0.00	0.01
Joint test—general HC	0.04	0.06	0.00	0.01
Joint test—firm-specific HC	0.14	0.72	0.14	0.99
Observations	395	289	1988	1279

Note: Same estimation as in table 11.3, first two columns, and table 11.4, last two columns. Firms from all three countries are pooled: additional controls now include country-specific time, location, and industry dummies. The reported coefficients and standard errors are for the difference between the wage and productivity premiums, the 'excess return' for each characteristic. Groupings of characteristics for the joint tests are the same as in table 11.3.

11.6   Conclusions

A couple of findings are worth reiterating. First, wage premiums for a number of characteristics do not always match productivity contributions, and this failure is more pronounced for some countries than for others. Second, a lot of attention in the development literature is devoted to education, and rightfully so, because the returns in higher salary and output are important and we only capture a fraction of them in this analysis. It is nevertheless of concern that the wage increases associated with more education significantly exceed the productivity gains they bring in the least-developed countries. On the other hand, it should be stressed that the returns to education—privately and to the employers—are highest in the most-developed country. Third, a crucial aspect of remuneration is the trade-off between paying workers for general experience versus firm-specific tenure. This mirrors a similar trade-off between preemployment education and subsequent training. In Tanzania, and to a lesser extent in Kenya, general skills (experience and schooling) are rewarded relatively more than firm-specific skills (tenure and training). In Zimbabwe, wage premiums match the productivity gains that are associated with them more closely, and interestingly, the returns to firm-specific investments are higher than in the other countries. Fourth, we offer some suggestive evidence that firms facing higher product market competition are more likely to reward characteristics in line with their productivity contribution.

Data quality is often a concern when working with surveys from developing countries. As mentioned earlier, data issues have limited us to look at only three countries and at a limited set of human capital characteristics. It is our hope that these findings are sufficiently interesting to spur other researchers to check their robustness with other data sources and qualify and refine the results where needed.

References

Appleton, S., J. Hoddinott, and J. Mackinnon. 1996. Education and health in sub-Saharan Africa. *Journal of International Development* 8 (3): 307–39.

Bigsten, A., P. Collier, S. Dercon, M. Fafchamps, B. Gauthier, J. W. Gunning, A. Isaksson, A., et al. 2000. Rates of return on physical and human capital in Africa's manufacturing sector. *Economic Development and Cultural Change* 48 (4): 801–27.

Dearden, L., H. Reed, and J. Van Reenen. 2006. The impact of training on productivity and wages: Evidence from British panel data. *Oxford Bulletin of Economics and Statistics* 68 (4): 397–421.

Eslava, M., J. Haltiwanger, A. Kugler, and M. Kugler. 2004. The effects of structural reforms on productivity and profitability enhancing reallocation: Evidence from Colombia. *Journal of Development Economics* 75:333–71.

Fafchamps, M. 1997. Introduction: Markets in sub-Saharan Africa. *World Development* 25 (5): 733–34.

Filhoz, N. A. M., and M.-A. Muendler. 2006. Labor reallocation in response to trade reform. CESifo Working Paper no. 1936.

Frazer, G. 2001. Linking firms and workers: Heterogeneous labor and returns to education. Unpublished manuscript. New Haven, CT: Yale University.

Haegeland, T., and T. Klette. 1999. Do higher wages reflect higher productivity? Education, gender and experience premiums in a matched plant-worker data set. In *The creation and analysis of employer—employee matched data*, ed. J. Haltiwanger, J. Lane, J. Spletzer, J. Theeuwes, and K. Troske, 231–59. Amsterdam: North Holland.

Haltiwanger, J., J. Lane, J. Spletzer, J. Theeuwes, and K. Troske (1999). *The creation and analysis of employer-employee matched data.* Amsterdam: North Holland.

Hellerstein, J. K., and D. Neumark (1999, February). Sex, wages, and productivity: An empirical analysis of Israeli firm-level data. *International Economic Review* 40 (1): 95–123.

———. 2004. Production function and wage equation estimation with heterogeneous labor: Evidence from a new matched employer-employee data set. NBER Working Paper no. 10325. Cambridge, MA: National Bureau of Economic Research.

Hellerstein, J. K., D. Neumark, and K. R. Troske. 1999. Wages, productivity, and worker characteristics: Evidence from plant-level production functions and wage equations. *Journal of Labor Economics* 17 (3): 409–46.

Jones, P. 2001. Are educated workers really more productive? *Journal of Development Economics* 64 (1): 57–79.

Jorgenson, D. W., and Z. Griliches. 1967. The explanation of productivity change. *Review of Economic Studies* 34:349–83.

Knight, J. B., and R. H. Sabot. 1987. Educational policy and labour productivity: An output accounting exercise. *Economic Journal* 97 (385): 199–214.

Mazumdar, D., and A. Mazaheri. 2002. *Wages and employment in Africa.* Hampshire, U.K.: Ashgate.

Mincer, J. 1974. *Schooling, experience, and earnings.* New York: Columbia University Press.

Pavcnik, N. 2002. Trade liberalization, exit, and productivity improvement: Evidence from Chilean plants. *Review of Economic Studies* 69 (1): 245–76.

Pérez-Duarte, S., B. Crepon, and N. Deniau. 2001. Wages, productivity, and worker characteristics: A French perspective. Paper presented at ESEM 2001, Lausanne, Switzerland.

Tybout, J. R. 2000. Manufacturing firms in developing countries: How well do they do, and why? *Journal of Economic Literature* 28 (1): 11–44.

Van Biesebroeck, J. 2003. Wages equal productivity. Fact or fiction? NBER Working Paper no. 10174. Cambridge, MA: National Bureau of Economic Research.

———. 2005. Firm size matters: Growth and productivity growth in African manufacturing. *Economic Development and Cultural Change* 53 (3): 545–84.

Wooldridge, J. M. 1999. *Econometric Analysis of Cross Section and Panel Data.* Cambridge, MA: MIT Press.

———. 2000. *Econometric Analysis of Cross Section and Panel Data.* Boston: South-Western.

World Bank. 2000. *African development indicators.* Washington DC: The World Bank.

Contributors

Fredrik Andersson
Longitudinal Employer-Household
  Dynamics (LEHD)
U.S. Census Bureau
4600 Silver Hill Road
Washington, DC 20233

Sascha O. Becker
Center for Economic Studies and Ifo
  Institute
University of Munich
Schackstraße 4
80539 Munich, Germany

Stefan Bender
Institute for Employment Research
Regensburger Straße 104
90478 Nürnberg, Germany

Clair Brown
Department of Economics
University of California, Berkeley
Evans Hall #3880
Berkeley, CA 94720-5555

Stephen V. Burks
Division of Social Science
University of Minnesota
600 E 4th Street
Morris, MN 56267

Benjamin Campbell
Department of Management and
  Human Resources
Fisher College of Business
Ohio State University
736 Fisher Hall
2100 Neil Avenue
Columbus, OH 43210

Jeffrey Carpenter
Department of Economics
Middlebury College
Middlebury, VT 05753

Hyowook Chiang
Welch Consulting
12100 Wilshire Blvd., Ste. 1650
Los Angeles, CA 90025

Marc-Arthur Diaye
Department of Economics
University of Evry
Île de France, 3rd floor
bd. François Mitterrand
91025 Évry Cedex, France

John S. Earle
Upjohn Institute for Employment
  Research
300 South Westnedge Avenue
Kalamazoo, MI 49007

Guido Friebel
IDEI, University of Toulouse 1
Manufacture des Tabacs
21 Allée de Brienne
31000 Toulouse, France

Lorenz Götte
Center for Behavioral Economics and
    Decision-Making
Federal Reserve Bank of Boston
600 Atlantic Avenue
Boston, MA 02210

Nathalie Greenan
CNRS-CEE
Centre d'Études de l'Emploi
Le Descartes I
29 Promenade Michel Simon
93166 Noisy-le-Grand, France

Judith Hellerstein
Department of Economics
Tydings Hall
University of Maryland
College Park, MD 20742

Julia Lane
National Opinion Research Center
    (NORC)
University of Chicago
1155 East 60th Street
Chicago, IL 60637

Colleen Flaherty Manchester
Industrial Relations Center
Carlson School of Management
University of Minnesota
321 19th Avenue South
Minneapolis, MN 55455-0438

Melissa McInerney
Center for Economic Studies
U.S. Census Bureau
4700 Silver Hill Road, Stop 6300
Washington, DC 20233

Kristen Monaco
Economics Department
California State Long Beach
1250 Bellflower Boulevard
Long Beach, CA 90840

Marc-Andreas Muendler
Department of Economics
University of California, San Diego
9500 Gilman Drive, MC 0508
La Jolla, CA 92093-0508

David Neumark
Department of Economics
3151 Social Science Plaza
University of California, Irvine
Irvine, CA 92697-5100

Elena Panova
Department of Economics
University of Quebec, Montreal
315 Saint Catherine Street East
QC H2X 3X2 Montreal, Canada

Yooki Park
Department of Economics
University of California
549 Evans Hall
Berkeley, CA 94720

Kay Porter
Driver Training and Safety at
    the cooperating firm (in care of
    Stephen V. Burks)

Aldo Rustichini
Department of Economics
University of Minnesota
271 19th Avenue South
Minneapolis, MN 55455

Kathryn Shaw
Graduate School of Business
Stanford University
Littlefield 339
Stanford, CA 94305-5015

Álmos Telegdy
Central European University
Nador u. 9
1051 Budapest, Hungary

Michal W. Urdanivia
CERMSEM, Panthéon-Sorbonne
University of Paris 1
106-112 Boulevard de l'Hôpital
75647 Paris Cedex, 13 France

Johannes Van Biesebroeck
Department of Economics
University of Toronto
140 St. George Street
M5S 3G7 Toronto, Ontario, Canada

Till von Wachter
Department of Economics
Columbia University
420 West 118th Street, 1022 IAB
New York, NY 10027

Author Index

Subject Index